Tourism and the Changing Face of the British Isles

Tourism and the Changing Face of the British Isles

Allan Brodie

Historic England

Published by Historic England, The Engine House, Fire Fly Avenue, Swindon SN2 2EH
www.HistoricEngland.org.uk

Historic England is a Government service championing England's heritage and giving expert, constructive advice.

First published 2019

ISBN 978-1-84802-358-1

British Library Cataloguing in Publication data
A CIP catalogue record for this book is available from the British Library.

Brought to publication by Rachel Howard, Publishing, Historic England.

Typeset in Georgia Pro Light 9.5/11.75pt

Edited by Kathryn Glendenning
Indexed by Susan Vaughan
Page layout by Pauline Hull Design
Printed in the UK by Gomer Press

Frontispiece: In this post-war photograph by John Gay (1909–99), a group of holidaymakers are paddling in the sea, Blackpool Tower can be seen in the background. [AA086149]

Back cover: A group of tourists are taking a selfie with the 18th-century Royal Crescent in Bath as a backdrop. [DP195103]

Contents

In memory of Alastair J Durie (1946–2017)

Elie, a former fishing village in Fife, has become
popular with tourists and golfers, and counted
amongst its residents Alastair Durie.
[© Author]

Acknowledgements

When this book was first conceived in 2015, I hoped to write it with the distinguished historian of tourism, Alistair J Durie. Unfortunately, Alistair died in 2017 after a long illness and was never able to make a contribution to this book. However, in his final year he did complete a masterful study of the history of Scottish tourism and left behind a very substantial body of top-quality research.

I would like to thank Susan Barton and Amanda Martin for reading the manuscript and making very useful comments on the text. I would also like to thank the archive staff of Historic England for providing most of the excellent illustrations in this book and John Vallender for the hours he spent on the cover illustration. And I would like to thank the Society of Antiquaries of London and Sue Berry for allowing me to use illustrations from their collections in this book. My thanks also go to the excellent publishing team at Historic England, particularly Rachel Howard, who took the raw manuscript through to publication.

I would also like to pay tribute to my family, Toni, Mary and William, who have endured my absence upstairs for many years, and I would like to reassure them that it is likely to continue for many years in the future.

1

Introduction

'Tourism develops the mind, promotes the awakening of a social consciousness, improves social relations, diminishes prejudices and elevates the soul.'[1]

(Annual Report of Bórd Failte, March 1960)

More than half a century ago, Bórd Failte, Ireland's tourist body, suggested that tourism contributed to transforming the human condition. People on holiday are unlikely to be pondering such lofty ideas, but they do hope to return home improved physically, mentally and spiritually. During the Middle Ages, pilgrims visiting holy wells or witnessing sacred relics were seeking to improve their physical well-being and to guarantee their future in the afterlife. After the Reformation, the emphasis shifted to physical well-being through using spa waters and bathing at the seaside. For the wealthy, the holiday in the 18th century also allowed them to be sociable, to be entertained and to make suitable matches for sons and daughters.

As holidays became more accessible to middle- and working-class families, the change of scenery became increasingly important. The Victorian factory worker not only deserved but needed a break from long working hours, poor living conditions and an unhealthy environment, and rapidly growing seaside resorts served as vital relief from their harsh lifestyle. Tourism was as much about what they were escaping from, as what they were escaping to. It might be worth pondering whether access to a seaside holiday may have helped to reduce the level of discontent among the populace, so that while Europe was revolting, Britons were heading to the beach. With the extension of the Saturday Half-day Holiday during the late 19th century, industrial workers were also free to forget the troubles of their working week at football matches and participate in sporting activities. Easier access to Britain's countryside served as a healthy alternative to urban living, but also stim-ulated people's aesthetic and spiritual interests. During the 20th century, holidays achieved a range of more or less edifying objectives. These ranged from adventure and discovery, through relaxing and improving one's well-being by sun-bathing or in a holiday romance, to bingeing by all-day eating and drinking.

The effect of tourism on people underpins the story of holidays from the Middle Ages to the 21st century, but central to this narrative is an examination of how tourism has had an impact on Britain's cities, towns and countryside. We are accustomed to considering how the Agricultural Revolution changed the countryside and the Industrial Revolution transformed Britain's towns and cities. The largely unsung, and more slowly unfolding, tourism and leisure revolution was perhaps an altogether quieter affair, but one that has been no less profound. Tourism created places, transformed the layout of others, led to the provision of new amenities and even inspired changes of name: Llanfair PG acquired its elongated appellation (Llanfairpwllgwyngyll-gogerychwyrndrobwllllantysiliogogogoch) in the 1850s in order to attract tourists, which proved successful.[2]

In Chapter 2 of this book, the origins of Britain's quiet revolution are traced back to the Middle Ages, when Britons, like their European counterparts, travelled to pilgrimage sites within the country and further afield (Fig 1.1). As well as this well-known form of proto-tourism, the travel that was necessary to rule the country and to manage the estates of religious orders prompted, as a by-product, some inquisitive tourism. A handful of manuscripts survive illus-trating that some educated people travelled

Fig 1.1
The murder of Thomas Becket in Canterbury Cathedral in the 12th century led to it becoming England's leading pilgrimage site during the Middle Ages. This photograph of c 1900 shows the town prior to suffering heavy damage during World War II. [OP00525]

across Britain, exploring its countryside, its past and contemporary religious and military monuments. Knowledge of this aspect of the Middle Ages is highly selective due to the limited survival of records, but by the 16th century, the impact of printing led to greater numbers of known accounts.

The Reformation largely ended pilgrimage, as far as Protestants and the government were concerned, though it never entirely disappeared, despite official disapproval. In its place came an interest in physical well-being through using mineral waters. Although travel remained difficult, most spas initially serving only a local constituency, a growing number of people were prepared to endure hardship to enjoy the benefits of spa waters. In the 16th century, Bath, Buxton, Knaresborough and a new spring at Harrogate were the main destinations, but, as is discussed in Chapter 3, during the 17th century, a growing interest in the medicinal benefits of spa waters and their science led to the development of new sources, the earliest of which were at Epsom, Tunbridge Wells and Scarborough. Following an inevitable interruption to tourism during the Civil Wars, spas grew in popularity

from the late 17th century onwards and by the 18th century Bath was being transformed into the spectacular Georgian city we enjoy today. Smaller settlements, such as Harrogate and Cheltenham, were also being embellished with grand terraces and crescents to house visitors to the towns' spas, assembly rooms and theatres.

The spa town served as a model for the initial development of seaside resorts. By the early 18th century, medical writers and scientists had recognised that the sea could act as Britain's bath, prompting a small but determined number of people to head to various working coastal towns. Scarborough had the infrastructure of leisure in place as it had welcomed tourists since the 17th century because of its spa. Coastal towns such as Brighton, Hastings, Margate and Weymouth had only basic facilities to serve their local population and port, though these proved sufficient initially to attract sea bathers (Fig 1.2). Nevertheless, growing numbers of wealthy people were drawn to the seaside, ostensibly due to its health benefits, but also because it was the fashionable thing to do. Where aristocrats led, royalty followed, both George III and his son becoming seasonal residents at Weymouth and

Fig 1.2
*The first holidaymakers
to Weymouth during the
mid-18th century stayed in
houses around the harbour;
the development of the
seafront took place later
in the century.*
[DP054481]

Brighton respectively by the end of the 18th century. The humble houses endured by early sea bathers were being replaced by grand terraces and crescents, as well as the first hotels. In addition to sea bathing facilities, visitors expected to be entertained and a range of increasingly large and opulent assembly rooms, theatres and circulating libraries appeared. These were manifestations of the growing numbers of visitors and a testimony to the certainty that they would return each year. The enthusiasm for the seaside soon spread from a handful of English coastal towns to throughout the British Isles.

Chapter 4 describes how the initial development of seaside resorts was prompted by the presence of wealthy holidaymakers, but by the early 19th century a limited form of mass tourism was beginning to appear. In large part this was prompted by improved access to affordable

Fig 1.3
From the mid-19th century onwards, railways contributed to transforming Britain and drove the rapid growth of tourism and the expansion of many holiday resorts. This 1948 photograph by John Gay (1909–99) shows the Flying Scotsman *outside King's Cross station.*
[AA062841]

transport, initially by travelling by steamer to resorts such as Margate and Ramsgate, as well as 'doon the watter' to resorts in the Clyde Estuary. This phenomenon was limited by geography, a large river linking a major population centre to resorts being the necessary precondition.

With the arrival of the railways in the mid-19th century, Britain came to be open eventually to almost everyone (Fig 1.3). Affordable rail travel, in combination with increasing free time and emerging paid leave, stimulated both the growth of seaside resorts and access to sports, the early development of football particularly benefiting from the new circumstances. As Chapter 5 demonstrates, technological improvements in transport went alongside new ways of marketing and packaging tourism. The modern package holiday owed its existence to pioneering ideas employed by steamship operators, as well as, most famously, Thomas Cook. Travel for holidays was not limited to individuals and families, and during the late 19th century organised trips by groups of workers and enlightened employers offered, for some, the first taste of a seaside holiday. New forms of travel also provided challenges; people wishing to enforce the Sabbath fought a losing battle against the might of railway companies and the demand for Sunday excursions. However, at some resorts accommodations between faith and fun were reached.

Due to the arrival of the motor car, the charabanc and the bus, towns faced new pressures to adapt to forms of transport that did not concentrate visitors near railway stations. Instead they spread tourists throughout a settlement, prompting suburban and seafront development towards the edges of existing towns. The popularity of the car also soon led to congestion and the need to provide purpose-built parking facilities during the interwar years. This pressure increased in the second half of the 20th century, when a fundamental shift from rail travel to road travel took place, a transformation anticipated and accelerated by Dr Richard Beeching's reports in the early 1960s.

The transport developments over the last three centuries – better roads, more comfortable stagecoaches and, in later years, faster, cheaper trains and cars – all contributed to opening up Britain to tourists. Encouraged by what they could read in print, and particularly by guidebooks, from the 18th century onwards growing numbers of people set out to discover their home country. This is looked at in Chapters 6 and 7. At one time people had travelled to admire man's agricultural achievements, but by the 18th century they increasingly went in search of romantic, wild landscapes and natural beauty, ranging from the Lake District and the Highlands of Scotland to curiosities such as the Giant's Causeway, in Northern Ireland, and Fingal's Cave, in the Hebrides. A growing number of travellers also went in search of ancient and modern man-made sites, ranging from Stonehenge and Avebury, in Wiltshire, to contemporary architectural gems, such as Blenheim Palace, in Oxfordshire, and Chatsworth House, in Derbyshire. People who might be intrigued by castles and ruined abbeys could equally be found recording visits to the latest country houses, industrial sites and even military barracks and prisons, an early manifestation of 'dark' tourism (a form of tourism focusing on places associated with death and suffering). Initially these visits were on an ad hoc basis, the site being visited through negotiation with a prison governor or the housekeeper, but by the 19th century increasingly formal arrangements were being put in place for the growing number of visitors. And by the end of the century, the National Trust had begun to collect sites to preserve them, as well as to show them off.

Although many people roamed the countryside and travelled into towns and cities, nevertheless, the vast majority of people's holiday time was spent at seaside resorts. By the second half of the 19th century, increased individual prosperity and practical, affordable transport meant that millions of people were enjoying seaside holidays. This prompted the creation of some new seaside resorts, but also led to a rapid growth in existing ones. They grew as fast as major manufacturing towns and rightly deserve to be thought of as industrial towns, whose industry was leisure rather than textiles or ceramics. Chapter 8 considers the rapid growth of seaside resorts, looking at not only the development of accommodation for the huge numbers of visitors who were flocking there by the end of the 19th century, but also the transformation of bathing practices, including the introduction of substantial facilities for swimming. The chapter will follow the shift from small-scale sociable entertainment venues to increasingly technology-based, industrial-scale entertainment complexes (Fig 1.4). By the first half of the 20th century, seaside holidays began to come within the reach of almost everybody.

Fig 1.4
Blackpool grew from a small village in 1800 to a large town, welcoming millions of visitors, a century later. This photograph of c 1900 by W&Co was probably taken with a view to publishing a postcard. [OP00470]

To cater for this demand, new forms of accommodation became necessary, leading to the provision of holiday camps. In 1938, the Holidays with Pay Act crystallised a process that had been under way for a number of decades, legally providing a substantial part of the workforce with annual paid holidays. Unfortunately, the outbreak of war in 1939 delayed its full implementation, but by the 1950s seaside holidays had become almost universal.

In 1900 seaside resorts were the leading tourist destinations, catering for millions of holidaymakers each year. Spa towns that had once served hundreds of wealthy visitors, and later thousands of patients, continued to welcome holidaymakers, though increasingly they came because these were interesting and attractive towns with good leisure facilities rather than places of cure. In Chapter 9 this shift is examined, along with the move from spa towns being places to visit to becoming attractive places to live, commute from and retire to. While the spa function of towns such as Cheltenham, Harrogate and the city of Bath may have declined, there was still an interest in the therapeutic value of water and a growing awareness of the curative properties of fresh air and sunshine. Therefore, many hydrotherapeutic hotels and hospitals were established in the countryside, where they could exploit the natural qualities of their setting. Although hydrotherapy may have had a noteworthy impact on some villages and towns, it was an activity that catered for a small, exclusive market measured in hundreds and thousands, compared to the millions flocking to the seaside each year.

The book concludes with a chapter describing the challenges facing tourism in Britain in the late 20th and early 21st centuries. It outlines how war, weather and social and economic problems have had an impact on the British holiday resort.

Fig 1.5
Messing around in boats has become a popular form of domestic tourism, and a common leisure pastime. At Sowerby Bridge Wharf, in West Yorkshire, these holiday hire boats are moored where industrial boats once worked.
[DP073898]

It also discusses a range of factors that may have had an even greater impact, such as foreign competition and the growing complexity of people's lives, in which they spend their disposable income on activities and leisure pursuits, rather than the once ubiquitous seaside holiday. Today, people can visit theme parks or heritage sites, or enjoy shopping trips, pampering treatments at spa hotels or excursions on a canal boat (Fig 1.5). They may also attend sporting events, or perhaps try a parachute jump or simply sit in front of increasingly large and clear television sets. And, as if these challenges were not sufficiently troublesome for traditional seaside resorts, they are also having to deal with climate change. A rapid rise in sea level and increased storminess is requiring a considerable reconfiguration of the seafront of seaside resorts, the shopfront and main driver of their tourist economy.[3]

Time for a holiday

For tourism to take place, whether in the 15th or 21st century, four major circumstances need to be satisfied. The first of these is sufficient disposable income to be able to afford to travel and stay away from home. To plot the changing economic circumstances of Britain is beyond the scope of this book, but the story of tourism does illustrate how as the centuries passed more people enjoyed more disposable income to allow them to indulge in tourism. By the 19th century, working people who might not be able to afford a day trip away from home could benefit from an excursion organised by their employer. Groups of workers and other associations might also fund a day trip to a nearby resort. With savings clubs, regular, small sums of money could be put aside to allow a worker and their family a change of scenery. The financial position of an average worker was not static, fluctuating with trade conditions and, more importantly, at different stages in life. They might enjoy some form of relative affluence while single, then be reduced to near poverty while their children were young, but return to limited prosperity once their offspring became earners themselves.[4]

The second requirement for tourism to thrive is for suitable means of transport to exist, and this is discussed in Chapter 5. The third factor is the requirement to have locations that are capable of receiving holidaymakers, and meeting their accommodation and entertainment needs. This is a central theme of the book, and many

chapters describe how places were organised and reorganised to cater for growing numbers of tourists. The presence of holidaymakers initially had a limited impact on towns with spas, coastal towns or rural villages, but inevitably, as John Urry recognised, the act of observing inevitably transformed the object being observed.[5]

And the transformation was not only physical, but often also involved a change of social tone and status, as is best demonstrated in genteel Victorian seaside resorts that struggled to survive influxes of day trippers.[6] Scottish traveller William Miller in 1888 recorded how local residents complained that clerks and others who got a week's holiday created 'an incessant racket of music or other din ... indeed, gaiety was the order of the day' and dances were held at hotels around the resort until 'late an hour'.[7]

The fourth requirement, but perhaps the key one, is the time to be able to enjoy tourism, whether it is a day trip or a long holiday. During the Middle Ages, holidays were 'holy days', major dates in the Christian calendar or days with significance to a local community, perhaps the feast day of the saint to whom the parish church was dedicated. After the Reformation, while most of Britain's population was still rural, the pressure for holidays was probably felt less acutely as the rhythm of life was slower. Often respite from work came when trade was slack, as well as during the frequent traditional holidays, at religious feasts and during local fairs.[8]

In some counties, fairly firmly defined customary holidays developed. In 1842 *Chambers's Edinburgh Journal* described the arrangements that existed in Lancashire and Yorkshire:

> Wakes are merry-makings which occurred annually in various parts of rural England, sometimes on Sunday, sometimes on one or several of the ordinary days of the week, and are much like fairs in Scotland, excepting that no business is transacted at them. Originally, they were religious festivals, appropriate in each case to the eve of the day of that saint to whom the parish church was dedicated; but they have long lost all trace of their pristine character, excepting the occurrence on the same day as in ancient times. The vulgar revels by which they are marked give occasion to the assembling of vast numbers of people from the country round – who may, on the morning of any particular wake, be seen pouring to its scene, on foot, and in all sorts of humble vehicles.[9]

At Bradford, the wakes in 1841 involved sports and games, races, smoking matches, wheelbarrow races, dancing, music and drinking, while at Eccles wakes horse racing and gambling were the main amusements of the day.[10]

Before the arrival of railways, local holidays were often enjoyed at home, when local fairs were held. The Glasgow Fair originally took place within the grounds of Glasgow Cathedral and by the early 19th century it was held on Glasgow Green. Like other fairs, it originally focused on selling horses, cattle and other produce, but during the 19th century it became renowned for its amusements. One author described succinctly the story of fairs: 'Their origin was religious, their development commercial, and their apotheosis an unrestrained indulgence in pleasure or license, as you may choose to regard their diversions.'[11] However, with the arrival of steamers and later railways, the time allowed off to enjoy a fair could instead be spent at a nearby resort.

With industrialisation, the pattern of traditional holidays was soon undermined, as the welfare of the working people became subordinated to the efficiency of factories and the profitability of businesses.[12] Workers tried hard to cling on to accepted holidays, but with only slight success. A mine at Levant, in Cornwall, was deemed exceptional as it granted six holidays per year, while in 1842 London journeymen fought to continue taking the eight hanging days at Tyburn as holidays.[13]

The types of holidays described in various reports about factory conditions during the early 19th century fell into three groups. Some holidays were enforced by employers when the order book or the industry dictated, regardless of the wishes of the workers. In Birmingham, larger factories closed for a week up to Christmas for stocktaking.[14] Other holidays might be agreed by both employers and employees, but the biggest challenge for industry was those taken by the workers contrary to the wishes of their employer. Saint Monday, the practice of taking a holiday on the day after the weekend when wages were paid, was so general in some industries that employers accepted it as inevitable and the number of absentees might lead to the suspension of work until the full complement might return on Wednesday or Thursday.[15]

By the mid-19th century, the demand for holidays was being recognised by employers and society in general. A need to improve the lives and conditions of Britain's working population was behind this, but it was also hoped that reforms would deal with the issue of Saint Monday and increase observance of the Sabbath. This issue became of sufficient importance that in 1832 a Select Committee on the Observance of the Sabbath Day was established.[16] Initially, adult males could expect no relief from Parliament, but they benefited indirectly from measures taken to protect children. The 1833 Factory Act modestly provided that persons under 18 years old should be entitled to eight half-day holidays each year, as well as Christmas Day and Good Friday, a provision extended further by the 1850 Act.[17] The Lord's Day Observance Society, the Early Closing Association and the Saturday Half-Holiday Committee all campaigned for workers to be paid earlier in the day on Saturday and to finish work at lunchtime. The half day on Saturday spread gradually across the country during the mid-19th century. By the 1840s, it had reached Sheffield and in 1858 the Jarrow Chemical Company in Gateshead became the first employer in the north-east to finish work early on a Saturday.[18] The Royal Commission on Labour in the 1890s reported that most working people had a weekly half-day holiday, or at least work stopped earlier than usual on Saturday.[19] A direct consequence of this was the rise of professional football as a mass spectator sport in the last decades of the 19th century.[20]

By the 1850s, there was a growing groundswell in favour of adding further full days of holiday to the calendar and as early as 1856, a committee was advocating the creation of four additional national holidays.[21] In 1824, the Bank of England had closed for 39 days' holiday, but by 1871 only Christmas Day, Good Friday, 1 May and 1 November (All Saints' Day) were still being observed.[22] The Bank Holidays Act in 1871 began to tentatively redress this through the creation of four additional bank holidays (Fig 1.6), including the first Monday in August, which stimulated a huge expansion in the provision of excursions to resorts.[23] The Act, which covered only banks but had a knock-on effect on other businesses, was largely the work of Sir John Lubbock (later Lord Avebury; 1834–1913), and the *Daily Telegraph* ironically suggested that the August Bank Holiday should be christened 'Saint Lubbock's Day'.[24] In 1875 the Holidays Extension Act extended the provision of the 1871 Act to docks, customs houses, Inland Revenue offices and bonded warehouses.[25]

By the second half of the 19th century, a number of employers and industries were begin-

Fig 1.6
Bank holidays were not always spent at seaside resorts, but could also be enjoyed at local fairs and events, such as this one in the grounds of Alexandra Palace, in north London. [CC97/01486]

ning to provide employees with paid leave. Professional people had been able to enjoy holidays even before this, presumably having come to individual arrangements with their employer. Daniel Benham (1789–1873), secretary to the City of London Gaslight Company, had time to go on lengthy holidays to Ramsgate (1826 and 1829), Weymouth (1847) and Ilfracombe and elsewhere in Devon (1849 and 1852).[26] It is uncertain whether he enjoyed paid holidays, though some examples of paid leave seem to predate the Great Exhibition of 1851 and by 1860 the Southern Metropolitan Gas Company was giving its staff a week of paid leave.[27] This practice spread slowly towards the end of the 19th century, but for many people the only opportunity for a 'holiday' was through organised activities such as militia camps, temperance and religious trips, excursions arranged by benevolent employers and working holidays such as hop or fruit picking. In 1925, 71 'hoppers' specials were run by the Southern Railway, carrying 68,000 hoppers and friends on Saturdays, with another 13,850 being brought on Sundays.[28] For people living in east London, the annual September journey out to Kent for hop picking provided a well-earned break and a chance to enjoy fresh country air, despite having to work for 11 hours each day.

In 1928, the first statutory provision allowed shop assistants in seaside resorts to have paid leave in lieu of the extra time that they worked during the summer season.[29] The Committee on Holidays with Pay (1937–8), chaired by William Warrender Mackenzie, 1st Baron Amulree (1860–1942), collected evidence about the extent of paid holidays.[30] By 21 October 1937, the Minister of Labour estimated that between 2.5 million and 2.75 million workers were covered by collective agreements providing paid holidays in at least 34 separate industries and services. The TUC estimated that around 5 million employees, excluding salaried staff, received paid holidays in one form or another, compared with 4 million in the previous June. Nevertheless, this still meant that three-quarters of the workforce was outside the scope of such provisions.[31] The Holidays with Pay Act 1938 effectively provided most people with a week of paid leave.[32] By June 1939, over 11 million people enjoyed paid holidays and by 1955, 96 per cent of manual workers were receiving two weeks' paid leave (Fig 1.7).[33]

The growth in demand for holidays was the result of paid annual leave combined with rising real incomes and living standards, increasing levels of car ownership and a cultural change in attitudes towards holidays. In 1948, 24.9 million

people went on holiday each year, 20.9 million to seaside resorts and four million elsewhere. Another 4.9 million people went on day trips. However, this meant that 14.7 million people still took no holiday.[34] In 1965, 29.5 million holidays were taken in Britain, with only 5 million being enjoyed abroad.[35] However, between 1975 and 1985 there was a dramatic drop in the number of major holidays taken in Britain, from 27 million to 20 million, while in the same period overseas holidays rose from 12 million to 22 million. In 1974, 61 per cent of spending on main holidays was domestic, with 39 per cent overseas, but by 1981 the proportions had dramatically switched to 45 per cent and 55 per cent respectively.[36]

Today's holidays may still be spent by the seaside (Fig 1.8), whether at home or abroad, but increasingly people are taking more diverse types of breaks. They are also spending their free time and disposable income on leisure pursuits rather than holidays taken away from home. However, to start this journey through the ways that tourism in Britain has evolved it is necessary to return to its very origins, when holidays were still 'holy days'.

Fig 1.7
John Gay's portfolio of photographs in c 1950 captures the essence of post-war holidaymaking at Blackpool. In an era before leisurewear, mum and her parents are wearing everyday clothes, including grandpa sporting his cap.
[AA047919]

Fig 1.8
Although many people are now drawn to warmer climes for their main beach holiday, British seaside resorts, such as Weymouth, in Dorset, still remain popular for day trips and short breaks.
[AA037412]

2

The origins of tourism in Britain

In the Middle Ages, travel was a necessity for maintaining order and carrying out secular and religious business. In the wake of such journeys came deliberate tourism in the form of pilgrimage and what might be described as accidental tourism. This often occurred as a by-product of business travel and consisted of a relatively small number of scholarly and curious individuals who sought to record what they saw. Due to the scant survival of written materials from this period, we have only a limited picture of these pioneering early 'tourists', their interests and destinations.

With the dislocation of society that occurred as a result of the Reformation and the Dissolution of the Monasteries, pilgrimage soon became a minor, even dangerous, activity pursued by a few covert adherents to the old faith. In its place, travelling to springs with apparent healing qualities began to occur. By the end of the 16th century, some settlements had begun to enjoy a significant income from wealthy visitors with the time and money to indulge in a visit to their mineral waters. At the same time, a distinct strand of antiquarianism emerged and, when combined with a new interest in classical art, architecture and learning, it inspired travel to the Continent, with Italy being the ultimate destination for inquisitive tourists. Therefore, by the time the Civil Wars rocked the country in the 1640s, two key aspects of tourism were firmly in place. An interest in spas and a strand of investigative tourism would both have a major impact on Britain from the late 17th century onwards.

Travel in the Middle Ages

Although travelling was a fundamental part of medieval society, road travel was slow, uncomfortable and dangerous. Until the 18th century the road system was still largely based on major Roman routes (Fig 2.1).[1] London was the principal hub, with major roads leading to Exeter, Bristol, St David's via Oxford, and Carlisle, along with the Great North Road with a branch off it to Norwich. There were, however, significant gaps in these major routes, due to inconsistent medieval repairs.[2] The Middle Ages also contributed some roads to link new population centres and religious sites of significance to the ancient network.[3] The main road for pilgrims heading to Little Walsingham, in Norfolk, is still called the Palmers' or Pilgrims' Way, the same name being applied later to the ancient route from Winchester, in Hampshire, to Canterbury, in Kent.[4] The most famous medieval pilgrimage route, as described by Geoffrey Chaucer (c 1343–1400)

Fig 2.1
Today the road system still uses Roman routes in places, and the names of some ancient roads, such as the Fosse Way through the Cotswolds, are still expressed on road signs. In some remote parts of Britain, such as at Wheeldale near Goathland, in Yorkshire, remains of a Roman road can be found. [K011229]

in *The Canterbury Tales*, involved his pilgrims leaving London through Southwark, Deptford and Greenwich to head towards Sittingbourne, Boughton-under-Blean and ultimately Canterbury (*see* Fig 1.1). This journey followed broadly the path of Watling Street (the modern A2), a road of Roman or older origin connecting London to Dover.[5] Roads were also developed between properties held by religious institutions, so there was a well-worn monastic track between Abbotsbury and Cerne Abbas Abbey, in Dorset.[6] These might be routes rather than formal roads and were often dependent on where suitable new bridges or causeways had been built to cross previously problematic or impassable waterways (Fig 2.2).[7]

Even the best roads had rough surfaces, meaning that vehicles might break down, but the most significant impact was that travel was slow. Some travellers managed an average of 15 to 20 miles (24 to 32km) per day, though on some days they might cover 30 or more miles (48km), presumably during long days on better roads.[8] The speed of a journey was also dependent on the season and the weather. A mid-18th-century pocket travel guide recorded that London could be reached from Bath and Bristol by stagecoach in two days during the summer months, but it took three days during the winter, when the days were shorter and the weather was more likely to

soften the road surface.[9] Travel was also slowed by having to share roads with droves of livestock and heavy, slower carts; on one particular occasion in 1294 21 carts of treasure managed only 12 miles (19km) per day.[10] Faster travel on horseback was possible; in 1603 Sir Robert Carey (1560–1639) rode from London to Edinburgh to inform James VI of Scotland of Elizabeth I's death. He accomplished this feat by riding for 60 hours over three days.[11]

Maps had been included in medieval manuscripts, such as in the *c* 1250 work of Benedictine monk and chronicler Matthew Paris (*c* 1200–59), while the so-called Gough Map of *c* 1360 shows almost 3,000 miles (4,800km) of road covering most of England.[12] By the 17th century printed maps were available, though these were not primarily intended for use on the road and so travellers relied on local information and sometimes used paid guides.[13] A person such as John Leland (*c* 1503–52), travelling around so much of England in the mid-16th century, must have relied on directions to find his way to so many monastic houses during his documentation of these sites. John Taylor, 'the Water Poet' (1578–1653), employed a guide to take him to Malmesbury: 'For one shilling I hired an old drunkard to guide me eight long miles to the towne of Malmesbury.'[14]

Fig 2.2
In the Middle Ages, most new bridges and causeways were funded by local landowners or religious institutions with an economic goal in mind. However, Maud Heath's Causeway near Chippenham, in Wiltshire, is a mid-15th-century example of a woman leaving money in her will to improve the route to market, including providing a causeway to cross the flood plain of the River Avon. [© Author]

In places there were 'signposts' that might have been helpful. Glastonbury Abbey, in Somerset, was surrounded by swamps and therefore, to guide pilgrims, posts were erected to show safe routes through the marshes.[15] Stones alongside the road denoted the route from Chester, in Cheshire, to Holywell, in north Wales, and in Wales tall stones marked some drovers' routes.[16] Today the routes of drovers' roads may be evident in place names and historic inn names that indicate the location of overnight stops.[17]

River travel was significant in some places, including part of the route between York and Lincoln due to the absence of suitable direct roads, while the Thames might also be used on part of the journey to Canterbury.[18] There was also the option of using coastal shipping, and ships were key to maintaining the links between England and the territories of the Angevin Empire on Continental Europe, through waters that could be hazardous to cross.

While travelling around their kingdom, royal households used tents or called on major landowners for accommodation. The options for most medieval travellers comprised accommodation in monastic houses, inns and private homes. Monasteries offered accommodation in hospices and inns that they owned, providing religious houses with an income.[19] For instance, the Chequers Inn at Canterbury served as an overflow for the nearby monastic hospice.[20] Inns might be used by the highest and the lowest in society (Fig 2.3). While in England during the 1440s, Aeneas Sylvius (1405–64), the future Pope Pius II, seems to have stayed at monastic sites and in inns, as did the Bursar of Merton College in 1464 while collecting rents in the north of England.[21] Even major aristocratic families such as the Berkeleys, Howards and Seymours availed themselves of the facilities of inns.[22]

Private houses of all statuses might provide travellers with accommodation. Hospitality was a significant part of the life of a major household and extended to tending for travellers' horses and accompanying domesticated animals.[23] The grand homes of major landowners or clerics might be suitable if the traveller was of a sufficiently high status, but anyone could avail themselves of accommodation in a convenient farmhouse. Aeneas Sylvius had an unpleasant night in a farmhouse in Northumberland in the 1440s, 'in a chamber strewn with straw'.[24] Making do with humble accommodation in vernacular buildings continued through to the 17th century. Unable to find accommodation, the central character in a 1693 poem about Tunbridge

Wells knocked on the door of a 'humble Cottage … poor and low' and by showing the old lady the colour of his money, his party was admitted and 'enjoyed' a hearty meal of cold mutton and ale in the rustic dwelling.[25] Travellers might also stay with family members; Cheshire antiquary Laurence Bostock seems to have regularly been able to find distant 'cousins' to stay with.[26] John Taylor often managed to insinuate himself into the best company that he could find to guarantee a night's accommodation, the host's recompense being the news he brought and his good conversation.[27] However, while sailing along the south coast, he was forced to sleep on the floor of a weaver's cottage. He wrote of the experience:

No meat, no drink, no lodging (but the floore),
No stoole to sit, no locke unto the doore,
No straw to make us litter in the night,
Nor any candlesticke to hold the light.[28]

In 15th-century Scotland, staying in private houses was threatening the livelihood of inns and therefore in 1425 James I (1394–1437) forbade travellers from staying in private homes. However, if they did stay in a house, their animals had to be lodged at an inn, though by the reign of James V (r 1513–42), not every borough could yet provide an inn.[29]

Fig 2.3
This late 19th-century photograph shows the courtyard of the Talbot Inn at Southwark. The inn has been linked with the meeting place used by the pilgrims in Chaucer's Canterbury Tales. [DD97/00055]

The business and pleasures of royal government

Although travel may have been slow and hazardous, and accommodation often uncomfortable, medieval society was far from static. Government in the Middle Ages began as itinerant after the Norman Conquest and gradually became more settled as the court and law courts became established permanently in London. Royal itineraries show the extent to which monarchs travelled. In 1204–5 King John (1167–1216) moved almost daily, making 360 moves to 145 royal manors or demesnes, 129 castles, 46 religious houses and 40 other locations.[30] He also famously lost his baggage train in the Wellstream in 1216, or as *1066 and All That* put it, he lost 'the Crown and all his clothes in the wash'.[31] Edward I (1239–1307) was also a very active traveller, particularly while undertaking military campaigns in Scotland and Wales. In January 1300 he travelled 360 miles (579km) in 25 days travelling from Bamburgh, in Northumberland, back to Windsor, in Berkshire.[32] This peripatetic life was necessary to govern royal estates and enforce and reinforce the ties of feudal society and many great households also moved around the countryside using trains of packhorses, carts, wagons and coaches.[33]

In the Middle Ages the common law courts and the Court of Chancery either followed the progress of the king around the country or were held at Westminster. However, the Crown also dispensed justice throughout England, first through the Eyre and later the Assizes.[34] By the 14th century a system of Assizes had evolved, with England being divided into six circuits.[35] Two judges travelled from Westminster around each circuit two or three times each year to hear civil cases and serious criminal ones. The arrival of the Assizes in a county town heralded a period of festivity, a tradition that continued into the 19th century, when the serious business of enforcing the law was accompanied by balls, fairs and race meetings.[36] Crowds flocked into county towns during the Assizes, but such a popular event also inevitably attracted unwelcome visitors, including beggars and thieves.[37]

Travel may have been a necessity to govern the country, but for those monarchs who enjoyed hunting, feasting and pageants, their itinerant lifestyle allowed them to pursue these interests across the country. At Kenilworth Castle, in Warwickshire, which came into the possession of Henry V (*c* 1387–1422) in 1413, Henry created a 'virandarium', or pleasure garden, probably in 1417–18.[38] In most parts of England and Wales there were royal forests, where a distinctive code of law prevailed to maintain the beauty and productivity of these estates. Itineraries show monarchs visited them regularly as they provided a rich supply of meat for their large retinue, but probably more importantly they were playgrounds for men who enjoyed hunting. As well as the Crown, major landowners might establish their own hunting grounds, or 'chases' as they were known.[39]

Royal forests probably reached their maximum extent during the reign of Henry II (r 1154–89), though they remained an important part of the royal lifestyle throughout the Middle Ages.[40] In *The Dialogue Concerning the Exchequer*, Henry II's Lord High Treasurer, Richard FitzNeal (*c* 1130–98), said the following:

> The forests, moreover, are the sanctuaries of kings and their greatest delight; thither they go for the sake of hunting, having laid aside their cares for a while, so that they may be refreshed by a short rest. There, the serious, and at the same time natural uproars of the court having ceased, they breathe in for a while the boon of pure liberty; whence it comes that they who transgress with regard to the forest are subject to the royal displeasure alone.[41]

To enjoy royal forests, kings erected hunting lodges. In the New Forest, in Hampshire, there were eight royal houses and each substantial forest would offer at least one royal residence.[42] A number of these hunting lodges grew into large houses, some of which earned the accolade of becoming 'palaces'. Clarendon Palace, in Wiltshire, was first referred to in 1072 as a lodge used by William I (*c* 1028–87) while hunting in Clarendon Forest, though the site may have been inherited from his Saxon predecessors.[43] Henry II transformed the site into a palace capable of hosting major councils at which the leading figures of the kingdom were represented.[44] During the reign of Henry III (r 1216–72), between £3,000 and £4,000 was spent on enlarging and refurbishing the palace, including improving the accommodation for the queen.[45] After 1485 the palace was largely ignored by Tudor rulers, though some of the buildings were still in use in 1574 when Elizabeth I (1533–1603) took shelter there during a journey.[46]

Religious travel

Travel was important for the maintenance of secular order, but it was also central to the business of Christianity. Senior clerics travelled to manage the spiritual life of the Church, as well as the estates that provided its wealth. The structure of the church's religious orders encouraged travel. Cistercian houses in Britain were directly, or ultimately, linked to the founding houses of the order at Cîteaux and Clairvaux in Burgundy. Initially the order had a system of annual visitation, the founding mother house having responsibility to inspect daughter houses, though this proved difficult to enforce as the order grew.[47] This type of close, regular link allowed the dissemination of religious thinking and the diffusion of artistic thinking, especially St Bernard of Clairvaux's strict aesthetic and the rigorous austerity of the Bernardine plan during the 12th century.[48] Another, perhaps more important, concept that travelled along this path from Burgundy was the pointed arch, which became a significant feature in some otherwise largely Romanesque structures in Britain (Fig 2.4).[49] A c 1400 manuscript of the Premonstratensian Abbey of Titchfield, in Hampshire, reveals regular travel to sister houses as far away as in the north of England.[50]

Fig 2.4
Buildwas Abbey, in Shropshire, originally a Savignac House that became Cistercian in 1147, has a nave with pointed main arcades. Arcades with pointed arches and pointed barrel vaults were features of Cistercian Abbeys by the 1140s, and spread with emerging French Gothic ideas before fully developed Gothic forms arrived directly from the 1170s onwards.
[K940422]

Fig 2.5
Records as far back as
the 12th century contain
claims for the healing
properties of the water
from St Winefride's Well at
Holywell, in Flintshire.
[© Author]

Churchmen were active travellers for business reasons, but through going on pilgrimage this important type of travel became the earliest form of popular tourism. Pilgrimage was an expression of faith, but also a search for spiritual well-being and physical cures through miracles that might be accomplished through being in the presence of a revered relic or by the use of the water from a holy well. Pilgrimage was also a sociable activity and something of this can still be experienced today on the Camino de Santiago de Compostela, in Spain. There are a few places where approximate numbers of pilgrims have been compiled. On one day in 1392, Munich, a town with a population of around 10,000, welcomed an estimated 40,000 pilgrims and a century later 142,000 pilgrims were counted at the gates of Aachen on a single day. At the miraculous statue of the Virgin at Altötting in Bavaria, 130,000 souvenir badges were sold in 1492.[51] Such figures may not exist for British sites, but there is no reason to believe that the islands' population was any less pious, though it is doubtful whether many Continental pilgrims came to our native shrines.

St Swithun's shrine at Winchester was the most popular religious destination in England from the 10th century until it was overtaken by that of St Thomas Becket at Canterbury Cathedral. Becket was canonised in 1173, only three years after his murder.[52] Another important destination was Walsingham, where the Shrine of Our Lady was visited by huge numbers annually, including reigning monarchs, and it features regularly in the letters of the Pastons (a gentry family from Norfolk).[53] At times the small settlement could be very crowded. In 1469 Edward IV (1442–83) visited with a huge retinue, inspiring the Duke of Norfolk to visit with 200 men.[54]

A number of mineral water springs also became associated with miracles. At Holywell, in north Wales, St Winefride's Well (see Chapter 3) became a popular place at which to take the water and an elaborate structure with a chapel and a bathing pool in front was built (Fig 2.5).[55] It was brought to greater prominence by visits from Henry V and Edward IV, who provided the shrine with a series of chaplains.[56]

Although travel to shrines and holy wells in England was commonplace, it was arduous and therefore a person may have done it only once in their life, perhaps when they felt in particular need of spiritual comfort or a miraculous cure.

In Scotland there were a number of important shrines. Scottish kings in the 15th century visited those to St Ninian at Whithorn in Dumfries and Galloway, and St Duthlac at Tain in the Highlands. To visit English shrines, or to pass through England to the Continent, Scottish pilgrims at times required safe conduct licences from the English Crown.[57] This situation eased somewhat after the 1357 Treaty of Berwick and in the mid-15th century large parties were travelling south to St Cuthbert's tomb at Durham, as well as to Canterbury and Walsingham. In 1445 a pilgrim from Aberdeen apparently experienced a miracle cure to his worm-ridden feet after visiting the shrine of St Thomas Becket.[58] Pilgrims sometimes ventured on to the Continent to visit Santiago de Compostela, Rome and occasionally St Denis, the shrine of the French patron saint outside Paris.[59]

Pilgrimage also led to the creation of a lively trade in souvenirs at some shrines. Badges were a symbol of piety, but also served as proof that a person had been to a shrine.[60] Anyone sporting the scallop shell during the Middle Ages, and today, would be proclaiming that they had made the long pilgrimage to Santiago de Compostela, while a badge of the statue of the Virgin of Walsingham proved completion of a visit to the Norfolk shrine. Badges could be made of any material, but most commonly, and most affordably, they were composed of a lead-tin alloy, the amount of the latter metal depending on the profit being sought by the vendor.[61]

Inquisitive and investigative tourism in the Middle Ages

Senior clergymen, as well as noblemen, travelled with large retinues on official business. Among these substantial parties there might be people who had their own private interests. The most famous example is Gerald of Wales (c 1146–1223), who visited and described sites in Wales and Ireland during the 1180s, many of which can still be recognised today. His visit to Ireland in 1185 was made in the retinue of Henry II's son, John; one of his trips through Wales was also made while in royal service and in 1188 he went with Archbishop Baldwin to preach the crusade in Wales. Although he was travelling on royal and church business, Gerald's curiosity led him to record visits to churches and castles, and to describe the landscape, natural wonders and the habits and behaviours of the people he observed or was told about.[62]

Most medieval antiquarians and historians compiled their works from manuscript sources, Gerald of Wales being a rare, early example of someone taking his amateur curiosity out on tour with him, but William Worcestre (1415–c 1485) took this interest further.[63] He was an antiquarian with an interest in history, topography, geography and botany. However, he was principally concerned with architecture and was able to draw and describe complicated mouldings using detailed architectural terms, suggesting a professional interest.[64] On his trip from Norwich to Cornwall in 1478, his main interest was churches and his manuscript contains some interesting details about them, including their dimensions in yards and feet or in his steps (Fig 2.6). St Mary Redcliffe in Bristol, a magnificent Decorated and early Perpendicular church, is afforded a lengthier than usual account of its dimensions and includes some information about its glass.[65] The westernmost point on his journey was St Michael's Mount. He describes its geography, including the dimensions of the church, the visions witnessed there and the story of the submersion of the land between Cornwall and the Isles of Scilly (Fig 2.7).[66] In 1479, he embarked on another journey and included a visit to Great Yarmouth, in Norfolk, where he recorded key

Fig 2.6
For Tintern Abbey, in Monmouthshire, William Worcestre's manuscript included the dates of the deaths of major donors and a detailed description of its architecture.
[DP031969]

historical events, as well as all its churches, including the most recent work at St Nicholas' Church.[67] He wrote that it was 'a town noted for its divine worship, the beauty of its buildings, neatness in dress etc'.[68] On his 1480 trip, he continued describing churches, but at Malmesbury, in Wiltshire, he also noted the presence of the mill, perhaps near where a large converted textile mill now stands on the River Avon. He also visited Wookey Hole, in Somerset, which he described in terms of the rooms and architectural features of contemporary houses.[69] In his manuscript he also included the itinerary of Thomas Clerk of Ware, who visited and recorded sites such as ruined castles, bridges and harbours.[70]

In the 16th century, the most famous antiquarian traveller was the poet John Leland.[71] In 1533, he received a commission to collect and catalogue books held in monasteries, but with the beginning of the Dissolution of the Monasteries, he broadened his interests to topography and local history. Between 1539 and 1545, he travelled through England recording the buildings and places he saw. Interestingly, he never complained about the state of roads, but this may simply be due to their poor state being the norm.[72]

William Worcestre and John Leland left their mark in writing, but one person with an interest in visiting one of the country's great churches left a drawing as proof. In the west tower of the parish church of Ashwell, in Hertfordshire, there is a graffito of medieval St Pauls Cathedral, which is a work by someone who had clearly seen the magnificent Gothic church, probably during the traumatic mid-14th century (Fig 2.8). There is also plentiful evidence of the extent to which people with an interest in art and architecture travelled around Britain and in Europe. This must have been in part facilitated by the Plantagenet Empire occupying land on both sides of the English Channel. Geography and very different national boundaries on the Continent may explain why some churches in southern England, such as Old Sarum Cathedral, near Salisbury, and Malmesbury Abbey, employed motifs that have been described as originating in France, as well as the links suggested between early 12th-century English workshops and the origins of Gothic architecture. The influence of a major workshop such as Old Sarum can be traced to churches in or near estates held by the cathedral and its Bishop, Roger of Salisbury (d 1139), as well as in some that belonged to Roger's relatives, including Lincoln Cathedral, where Roger's nephew Alexander (d 1148) was Bishop.[73] Old Sarum's influence can even be detected as far away as Roscrea and Cashel in County Tipperary in Ireland, as well as in south

Fig 2.7
St Michael's Mount, in Cornwall, with its chapel and castle, which is now a family home, can be reached at low tide by a causeway.
[DP018959]

Wales. Links between architectural and sculptural details in distant buildings could be explained by the distribution of drawings. However, technical drawings containing engineering information were probably only in their infancy in the 14th and 15th centuries and therefore cannot be used to explain the apparent links between the designs of Thomas of Witney (fl 1292–1342) and William Joy (fl 1329–47) in the West Country and the work of Peter Parler (c 1330–99) at Prague Cathedral.[74] How Parler could have ended up in the West of England is unclear, but he seems to have been firmly based in Prague from 1356 until his death, suggesting any visit may have been part of his youthful education.[75]

Travel and tourism in the 16th and 17th centuries

The Reformation and the Dissolution of the Monasteries resulted in major changes in English society. In terms of travel and tourism, this led to the loss of monastic hospices for travellers, though in some places the tradition of religious charity continued. Celia Fiennes (1662–1741), who kept notes of her travels which have thankfully survived, experienced the hospitality shown to pilgrims at St Cross in Winchester in the late 17th century (Fig 2.9).[76] From the mid-16th century, inns became more significant and more widespread, though private homes remained essential for all classes of traveller.

Although there was a prohibition against the veneration of relics and an official end to pilgrimage, shrines in remoter locations in Wales and Scotland continued despite official disapproval. The diocese of St David's, in Pembrokeshire, still had 'Welles and blinde Chapelles' active in the 1570s and orders were issued by the Council of

the Marches to prevent people from visiting Holywell.[77] Despite official disapproval, Holywell continued as a destination to visit and for worship; Celia Fiennes visited in 1698 and devout Catholic landowner Nicholas Blundell and his family went there on a number of occasions during the early 18th century to improve their physical as well as spiritual health.[78]

The growing Tudor economy undoubtedly put greater pressure on existing roads and this may be why historian and topographer William Harrison (1535–93) in 1586 reckoned that they had deteriorated markedly during the previous two decades.[79] An Act of Parliament was passed in 1555 to improve roads and this remained in force for two centuries.[80] Parishes were made responsible for maintaining highways under the Lords of the Manor and the Justices of the Peace. Two parishioners were elected each year to act as highway surveyors or waywardens to inspect bridges, roads, watercourses and pavements. If a landowner held land worth more than £50, they had to provide

Fig 2.8
This incised graffito in Ashwell Church, in Hertfordshire, shows the medieval Gothic cathedral of St Paul's in London, with its tall spire and elaborate tracery windows. This magnificent church was badly damaged by the Great Fire of London in 1666 and subsequently demolished.
[© Author]

Fig 2.9
St Cross at Winchester, photographed here in 1975 by John Gay, offered hospitality to passing pilgrims in years gone by, and continues this tradition today, as well as looking after its community of elderly men.
[AA092193]

two able-bodied men and a team of animals and tools to repair highways for four consecutive days of eight hours, which was increased to six days in 1563.[81] This Act covered only highways, byways being left in the care of individual landowners, and although its implementation was probably patchy, roads did begin to improve during the 17th century.

One of the most enthusiastic travellers during the second half of the 16th century was Elizabeth I and her frequent progresses (state tours) helped to change people's opinions about travelling.[82] The queen, her courtiers and fellow aristocrats constituted most of the small number of people with the time, wealth and inclination to indulge in leisure travel, but due to their lofty status they had an impact wherever they went. The queen travelled in a carriage in 1568 and a coach in 1572, while her court and servants were transported in dozens of carriages, carts and wagons.[83] Elizabeth I travelled to enjoy aristocratic company, and to indulge in her love of pageantry, music, poetry and theatre, but she was also interested in seeing, and being seen, by her subjects.[84] She and her successor, James I (1566–1625), also used progresses to evade potential London plagues, which were often at their worst during the late summer months.[85]

Hosting the queen was prestigious, but potentially expensive. For towns it might cost the corporation to prepare for her presence, but it might also increase the prosperity and prestige of the town.[86] In 1615 when James I visited Bath and Salisbury, inhabitants of the counties through which he was to pass petitioned 'to be spared the honour in respect of the hard winter and hitherto hot and very dry summer whereby cattle are exceeding poor and like to perish

Fig 2.10
In his efforts to woo Elizabeth I, Robert Dudley created a new garden at Kenilworth Castle in her honour. This has been reconstructed in recent years by English Heritage. [DP082993]

everywhere'.[87] The petition went unheeded. In 1574 Elizabeth I visited Bath escorted by 300 soldiers and took the opportunity to visit Longleat House, in Wiltshire, which was in the process of being transformed into one of the finest houses of the period.[88] While visiting Bristol, the queen stayed with Sir John Young and a large 'fort' was erected to serve as the centrepiece of a theatrical performance that included a mock battle and fireworks.[89] On another progress the queen visited Sir Nicholas Bacon at Gorhambury, in Hertfordshire, in 1577. He brought a dozen cooks from London who were well-rewarded for cooking 60 sheep, 8 oxen, 18 calves, 34 lambs and 10 kids, as well as a bewildering range of accompaniments. The cost of the five-day festivities was £577 6s 7½d.[90] This extravaganza, which cost just over £100 a day to stage, was eclipsed by the festivities put on by Robert Dudley, the Earl of Leicester, at Kenilworth Castle in 1575 (Fig 2.10). His 19-day-long festival of feasting, hunting and theatrical performances cost around £1,000 per day to stage.[91] It is little wonder that it has been described by one author as 'sixteenth-century England's grandest and most extravagant party'.[92]

The queen's impact was significant wherever she travelled; her presence meant a period of great festivities, and helped to attract people to towns that she was visiting. A similar, but smaller-scale, effect could also occur when senior clergymen and aristocrats visited. Among these were the Cecil family and the Earls of Warwick and Leicester, who followed her example in visiting Bath.[93] Sir Walter Raleigh (c 1554–1618) was another of the noblemen who visited Bath in the 1590s. His large retinue included entertainers who could also be enjoyed by the wider public.[94]

Fig 2.11
For over three centuries,
the Roman Baths complex
at Bath was Britain's
leading spa. Today it is
still a must-see tourist
attraction, almost 2,000
years after its creation.
[AA037965]

Bath and the origins of spa tourism

During the Middle Ages, shrines and springs had created a tradition of travelling to a particular place to improve spiritual or physical well-being. After the Reformation there was recognition that mineral waters, rather than holy waters, could be used to treat physical rather than spiritual conditions. Dr William Turner, who had taken refuge in Europe during the mid-16th century, returned to England after Mary I's death in 1558 and in 1562 he published a book in which he questioned the need to travel abroad for remedies, when England could provide similar health resorts.[95] By the 1550s Bath was welcoming patients to its springs (Fig 2.11).

Fig 2.11
For over three centuries, the Roman Baths complex at Bath was Britain's leading spa. Today it is still a must-see tourist attraction, almost 2,000 years after its creation. [AA037965]

The mythological origin of Bath is that Bladud, an ancient King of the Britons, drank the spring water and was soon cured of leprosy.[96] The Romans established *Aquae Sulis* to exploit these springs, the only naturally hot mineral waters in Britain.[97] In the mid-12th century Bath's hot springs, which were used by the monastery for cures, were mentioned in the chronicle *Gesta Stephani* (Deeds of King Stephen).[98] During the Middle Ages, Bath's economy was based on it being a religious centre and a cloth-producing town, but by the time of John Leland's visit in the early 1540s it was already beginning to show

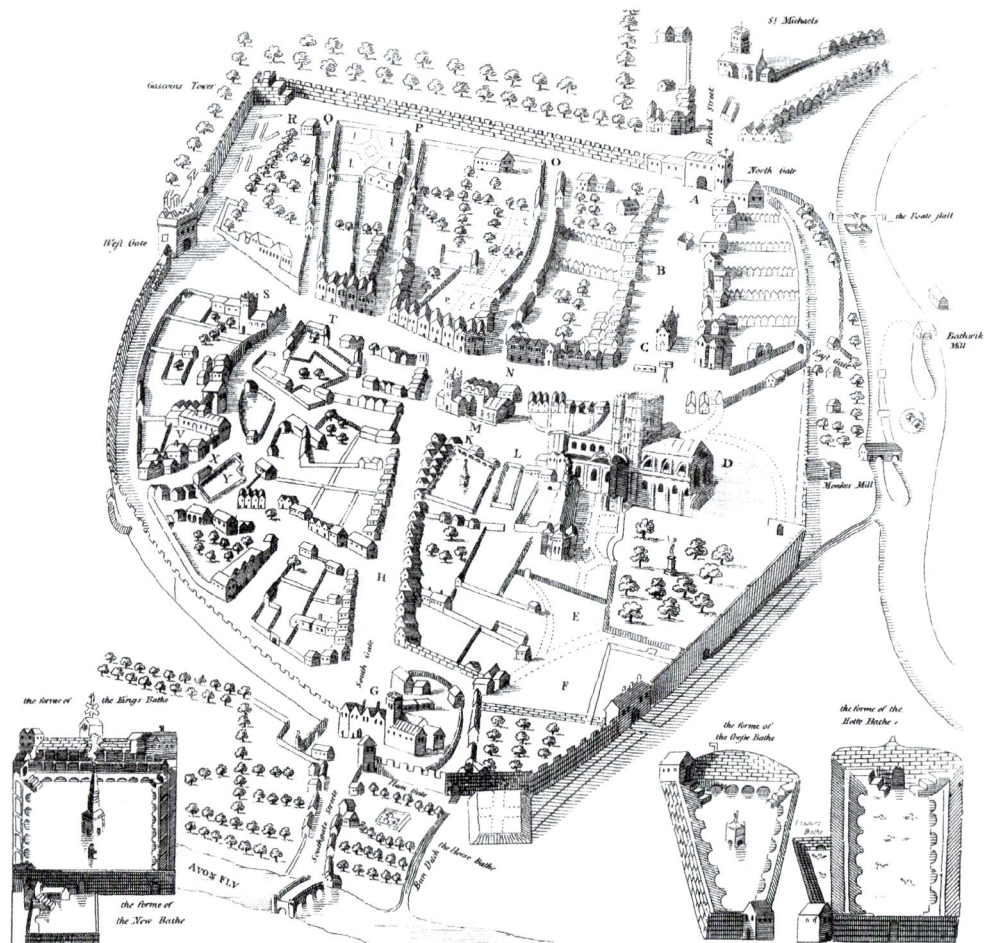

Fig 2.12
This map of medieval Bath shows the small settlement still largely confined within its walls, with the abbey at the centre. Figure 3.9 shows how much Bath expanded during the 18th century.
[From Warner 1801, facing p23]

signs of decline.[99] This seems to have been due to a contraction in the cloth industry, bad harvests and outbreaks of disease. Bath also suffered during the Civil Wars, but unlike other West Country towns, it does not seem to have enjoyed a recovery in its manufacturing economy after the Restoration.[100] Instead Bath's success would be dependent on the creation of a leisure economy based on its springs and pools.

Although Bath was Somerset's leading city, it was still a small settlement (Fig 2.12) crammed within its almost mile-long medieval walls until the 18th century.[101] Its streets were narrow and crowded and the 1,500 inhabitants in the 16th century were accommodated in 300 houses.[102] After the hiatus of the Dissolution, control of Bath was assumed by the Corporation. It invested £4,000 in new houses in 1569, rebuilt a market house in the 1550s and repaired the Guildhall during the late 16th century. A large investment was also incurred in an effort to improve the city in anticipation of Elizabeth I's visit in 1574.[103]

By the 1570s, there were already considerable influxes of wealthy visitors to Bath, as well as the sick poor, in search of cures for a wide variety of medical conditions. In the 1590s, Sir John Harington (bap 1560, d 1612) recorded that Bath was already 'resorted unto so greatly (being at two times of the year, as it were), the pilgrimage of health to all saints'.[104] In the late 16th century Bath contained five baths (Fig 2.13). The King's Bath was the large surviving Roman Bath near the Abbey, while a new, smaller bath was built in 1567, which would later be known as the Queen's Bath in honour of visits by James I's wife in 1613 and 1615.[105] There was also the Cross Bath, named after the cross located in its centre, and the Hot Bath, with the warmest water. The Leper's Bath, fed by water from the Hot Bath, was established at a safe distance from where wealthy and fashionable bathers gathered.

The first books praising the waters were published in 1562 and 1572 and by the early 17th century there were perhaps more than a dozen physicians practising in the city.[106] The 1572 Vagabonds Act contained provisions regarding sick paupers and beggars, a measure designed to relieve the financial burden on the Corporation by limiting the number of poor that were allowed to visit Bath.[107] To supplement existing hospitals, new almshouses were created, including the Leper's Hospital in 1576; in 1609 Thomas Bellot, steward to William Cecil,

Lord Burghley, founded and endowed another hospital for the poor and the visiting poor.[108]

Although bathers could have enjoyed taking the waters at more rural springs, the virtue of Bath was that in addition to its hot waters it offered visitors leisure facilities. These included two tennis courts and two bowling greens, as well as entertainment provided by companies of players, musicians and acrobats attracted to the town by the presence of wealthy visitors.[109] Underpinning the development of Bath – Britain's earliest leisure-based economy – was the provision of accommodation. In 1596 local landowner Sir John Harington praised the lodgings and inns, as did Dr Tobias Venner in 1628 and Henry Chapman in 1673, who both wrote about Bath and its waters, but this is perhaps predictable as they sought to portray the town positively.[110]

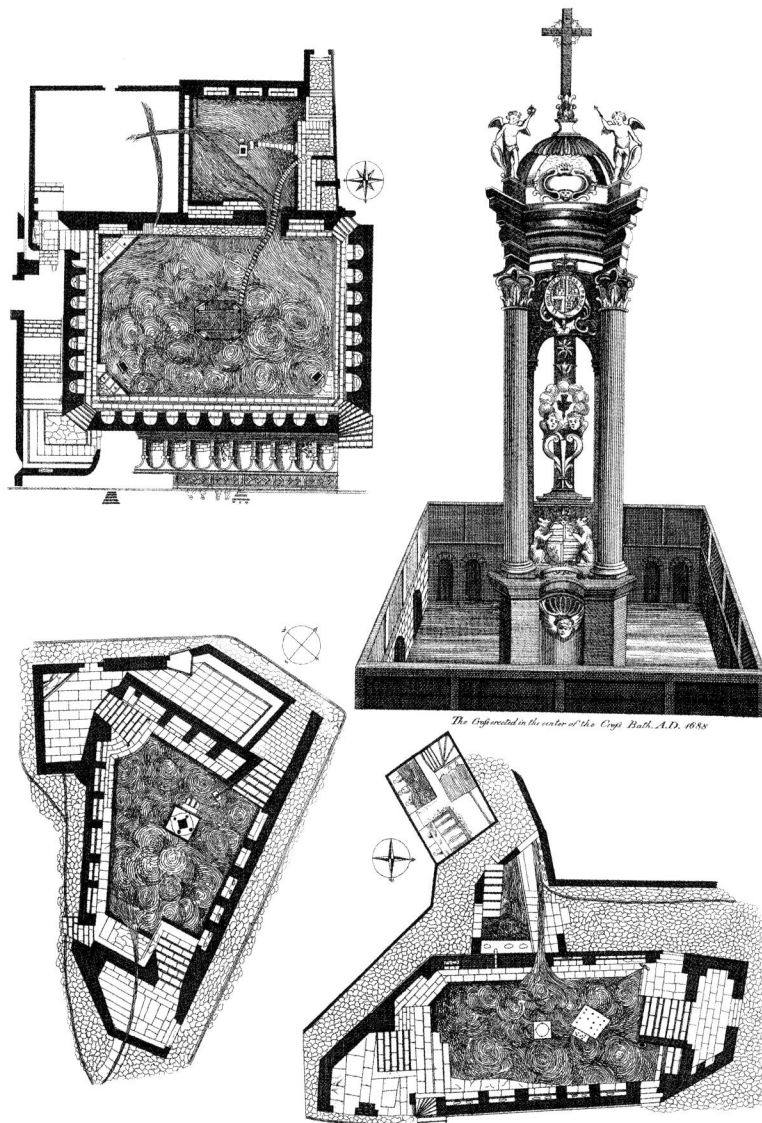

Fig 2.13
This illustration depicts the four main baths in Bath, the Leper's Bath being the one omitted. In the 16th century, the baths were little more than pools, lacking any changing facilities, though Elizabeth I's visit in 1574 seems to have marked the start of initiatives to redress this.
[From Warner 1801, facing p315]

Establishing spas

The story of Bath, or 'The Bath' as it was sometimes described, set a pattern for other spas and subsequently seaside resorts.[111] Its evolution involved a number of distinct stages. It began with discovery or rediscovery and then recognition, which led initially to local popularity. Once medical endorsement had been acquired, successful patronage could be hoped for. This would preferably be royal endorsement, or at least recognition by major local aristocrats, which would stimulate what might be described as popularity, as far as there was any recognisable mass tourism in the 16th century.

In 1572 physician John Jones (fl 1562–79) wrote treatises about the curative properties of the waters at Bath and Buxton.[112] Buxton, in Derbyshire, had been settled by the Romans, who called it *Aquae Arnemetiae*, and during the Middle Ages St Anne's Well seems to have been a popular local destination. Behind the popularity of Buxton in the 16th century was George Talbot, 6th Earl of Shrewsbury (*c* 1522–90), who was responsible for Mary, Queen of Scots' imprisonment from 1569 until 1584.[113] During this period she was allowed to enjoy the baths, as is revealed by the official petitions to the Crown to allow her to visit Buxton.[114] Although

Elizabeth I never visited the spa, her Lord High Treasurer Lord Burghley (1520/21–98) tried to visit several times during the mid-1570s, but on one occasion found that there was no accommodation available. To remedy this problem, Shrewsbury erected the four-storey Hall between the spring and the baths for use by visitors, the earliest post-medieval example of purpose-built accommodation for tourists (Fig 2.14). Built in 1572, it was thought to have been replaced during a series of building campaigns during the 17th and 18th centuries.[115] However, during work in the early 1990s the structure was discovered beneath the Georgian facade of the Old Hall Hotel.[116] Despite this addition, Buxton continued to suffer from a lack of accommodation, as well as its lingering association with Catholicism, but with the execution of Mary, Queen of Scots in 1587, interest in Buxton declined in favour of Bath.

Bath and Buxton were the leading spas during the late 16th century, but elsewhere new sources were beginning to be identified and popularised. Harrogate, in Yorkshire, consisted of two hamlets, High Harrogate and Low Harrogate, that were close to Knaresborough, which was famous for its petrifying well. It had become associated with Mother Shipton, an alleged witch and prophetess who appears to have flourished

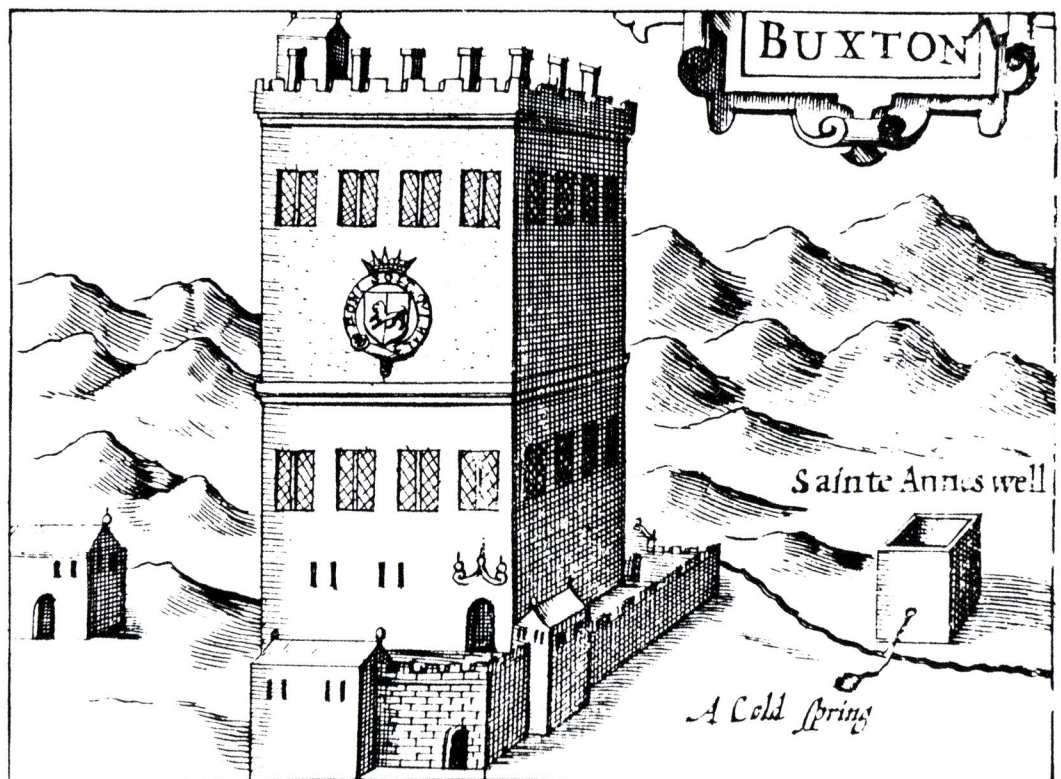

Fig 2.14
The Hall at Buxton, in Derbyshire, is known from a detail on a 1610 map by John Speed, which also shows the nearby spring used by patients.
[AA91/21028]

around 1530, though perhaps she was more mythological than real as John Leland did not mention her when he visited a few years later.[117] The first mineral spring was discovered at Harrogate in 1571 by William Slingsby (1520–1606), whose early home had been at Harrogate. He found that water from the chalybeate (iron-rich) Tewit Well in the forest possessed medicinal properties. During the early 17th century it became a popular destination.[118] As elsewhere, discovery was only the first step in the development of a spa and to secure recognition by the public required endorsement by a doctor. The spring at Harrogate only came to wide public attention with the publication in 1626 of *Spadacrene Anglica*, a book about the spring by physician and author Edmunde Deane (1572–*c* 1640).[119]

Antiquarianism, classicism and the taste for travel

Spas and the attendant tourism they created were a direct impact of the transformation of English society that took place due to the Reformation. Another strand in the history of tourism, the Grand Tour, was sometimes an unintended by-product of changes in religious worship and political upheavals. The term 'Grand Tour' was first coined in 1670, but the phenomenon was already under way a century earlier.[120] One of the earliest Grand Tourists was William Thomas (d 1554), who fled to Italy in 1545 after stealing money. He spent three years there, including a spell in prison, and on his return to England completed writing *The Historie of Italy*.[121]

In 1542 William Turner (1509/10–1568) travelled to Germany, northern Italy and Switzerland to advance his medical studies, though it also seems to have inspired his interest in natural history.[122] During the reign of Mary I (r 1553–8), Turner, as a fervent protestant, returned to the Continent, where his exposure to the curative properties of mineral waters would have a profound impact on the development of the early spas in England following his return in the late 1550s.

Sir Thomas Hoby (1530–66) first went to France in May 1551 in the train of William Parr, Marquis of Northampton, but with the accession of Queen Mary he chose to remain abroad.[123] While in Paris he translated Baldassare Castiglione's *Il Libro del Cortegiano* as *The Courtier*, a work that would have an impact on the stand-

ards of social behaviour for the cultured English society (Fig 2.15).

John Shute (d 1563) was a writer on architecture who was sent to Italy by John Dudley, Duke of Northumberland, to study and record contemporary Italian architecture. He returned to England with drawings of buildings, sculptures and paintings.[124] In 1563 he published the first architectural treatise in Britain, the first in the English language, entitled *The first and chief groundes of architecture…*, which was dedicated to Elizabeth I.

These first intrepid travellers were heading to France and Italy to immerse themselves in the vibrant culture of the Renaissance, but also to experience the heritage of ancient Rome. Turner and Hoby had been in self-imposed exile due to their religious beliefs, but Sir Philip Sidney (1554–86) travelled not only because of his up-and-down relationship with the Court, but also to experience modern Italian and ancient Roman culture.[125] From 1573 to 1575 he visited Venice, Padua, Genoa and Florence. During these visits he met leading artists, learned about the arts of war and horsemanship and enjoyed the friendship of important politicians and diplomats who attended these major Renaissance courts. Sidney's Grand Tour was effectively a blueprint for future Grand Tourists, taking in the sights, buying books, works of art and antiquities, as well as having his portrait painted by the celebrated Italian painter Paolo Veronese.

In 1593, accomplished linguist, traveller and writer Fynes Moryson (1565/6–1630) visited northern Europe before heading southwards to Italy to visit Padua, Naples and Rome.[126] Not content with seeing just Italy, by 1596 he had also

Fig 2.15
Sir Thomas Hoby also visited Italy and recorded its state-of-the-art fortifications, its ancient ruins and modern sculpture, as well as its religion and politics. This is a detail of the Hoby monument in All Saints, Bisham, in Berkshire, showing effigies of Sir Thomas Hoby and his half-brother Sir Philip Hoby. [DP137800]

managed to visit Jerusalem. In 1617 he wrote an account of his travels and the history of the countries he visited, including Scotland in 1598, where he saw James VI at Falkland Palace (Fife), and Ireland, where he served as a soldier.[127]

Peace treaties in 1598 and 1604 made travel around Europe easier, though on a still predominantly Catholic Continent, discretion about a British traveller's Protestant faith was essential.[128] Thomas Howard, Earl of Arundel, (1585–1646) visited Spa and Padua in 1612, while his trip in the following year took him to Milan, Parma, Padua and Venice.[129] During these journeys he made important contacts with European politicians, diplomats and artists, connections that would stand him in good stead in the future, as he built his formidable private art collection. His second journey was of great importance to English architectural history, as he was accompanied by Inigo Jones (1573–1652), who went on to become one of England's most significant architects. Jones had the opportunity to buy key books on Italian architecture, meet leading architects and visit a number of important Palladian villas.[130] Jones had spent several years in Italy a decade earlier and his fluency in Italian may have been why Howard wanted to have him in his substantial entourage.

During the 1640s, the Civil Wars again drove many people abroad in the wake of the flight of the royal family. Exile was effectively a badge of honour, a pledge of allegiance to the exiled Crown.[131] When the Restoration took place in 1660 the returning, well-read and well-travelled aristocrats and middle-class exiles helped to create a culture more aware of the Continent and the pleasures it held. However, all the travelling to the Continent during the early 17th century may have also contributed to a growing interest in Britain itself. Britain might not have the classical ruins of ancient Rome, but the 'discovery' of Avebury, in Wiltshire, by antiquary and biographer John Aubrey (1626–97) and Inigo Jones' study of Stonehenge, prompted by James I's curiosity, show that the antiquarianism of the late Middle Ages was being transformed by exposure to Renaissance thinking and the growing 'scientific' culture into a more detailed appreciation of the country's past.[132] Centuries later, Stonehenge is now firmly one of the main sights on any world traveller's bucket list (Fig 2.16).

Conclusion

By the 16th century, the centuries of pilgrimage and some sporadic investigative 'tourism' that had occurred in the wake of travelling during the Middle Ages had begun to coalesce into strands that would help to shape the future development of tourism. The Reformation abruptly disrupted, though never totally vanquished, pilgrimages and shrines. Instead, people set off in search of physical cures through using mineral waters. This created the spa town – the earliest example of a settlement economically dependent on leisure rather than commerce or industry – and ultimately led to the seaside resort. These distinctive settlements will be examined in the next two chapters.

Changes to society in the 16th century also contributed to travel being extended to Renaissance Europe, which had an impact on British society, science, the arts, architecture and even gardens. It also had an impact on tourism, encouraging growing numbers of people to head through Europe on grand tours. And it stimulated more interest in travelling around Britain itself, helping to establish the discovery of Britain as a central motive for tourism in the 18th and 19th centuries, which will be examined in Chapters 6 and 7.

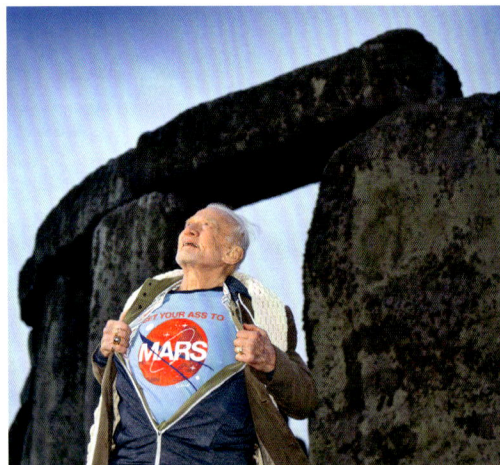

Fig 2.16
Stonehenge, in Wiltshire, is one of Britain's leading tourist attractions. In 2014 President Barack Obama made a stop at it on his visit to Britain and astronaut Buzz Aldrin posed for photographs in 2015, while promoting trips to colonise Mars.
[DP167193]

3

The spa 1500–1800

Sir Walter Scott (1771–1832) in his novel *St Ronan's Well* described the process by which a successful spa was created:

A fanciful lady of rank in the neighbourhood chanced to recover of some imaginary complaint by the use of a mineral well about a mile and a half from the village; a *fashionable doctor was found to write an analysis of the healing waters*, with a list of *sundry cures*; a speculative builder took land in feu [an archaic form of leasehold], and erected lodging houses, shops and even streets.[1]

Bath's early development echoed Scott's formula. Initially, the benefits of its waters were predominantly restricted to the wealthiest in society, attracted by a growing recognition of the spa's medicinal value and the testimony of their fellow aristocrats, the 'Company' as it came to be known. As the 17th and 18th centuries progressed, visiting spas would broaden in appeal and the Company would become an attraction in itself. Spas provided an opportunity to rub shoulders with people of status, with the prospect of betterment for eligible daughters, and Bath, and other leading spa towns, found a place at the heart of the English social calendar. Spa facilities improved, reflecting their increasing significance and the growing enthusiasm for taking the waters. Larger and more ornate entertainment facilities were established as income from tourists increased. Initially, visitors were accommodated in existing inns and houses within these towns, but as the 18th century unfolded, Bath led the way in expanding beyond its historic core, first uphill and then across the river.

The handful of mineral water sources being used as spas in the early 17th century had become dozens a century later. But perhaps more importantly, by the 18th century entire towns were developing to cater for the growing popularity of taking the waters, an activity based as much on entertaining tourists as curing them. And these settlements were different from historic market towns or the emerging industrial cities, due to their distinctive town plans, types and quality of buildings and the range of leisure facilities they offered.

Spas in the 17th century

During the early 17th century, the number of spa sites began to increase rapidly. They were located where suitable waters were discovered, but perhaps more importantly where a potential market existed or could be created. Therefore, new spas developed at Tunbridge Wells in Kent, and Epsom, convenient for London, but perhaps also surprisingly at Scarborough on the Yorkshire coast.

The first of these new spas was Tunbridge Wells. In 1605, Dudley, Lord North (1582–1666) 'fell into a lingering, consumptive disorder' and to improve his lifestyle 'it was judged expedient to separate him from the scenes of pleasure, in which he must unavoidably continue to be engaged while he remained in the vicinity of the court'.[2] The following year he spent the summer at Eridge House, south of Tunbridge Wells, and during his return journey to London he discovered chalybeate springs in the woods at Tunbridge Wells and took samples to physicians for analysis. Dudley returned to Eridge House in 1607, where he spent three months and departed apparently feeling totally cured.[3] Within a generation, Tunbridge Wells had come to the attention of the royal family. In 1630, the doctors of Queen Henrietta Maria (1609–69), the wife of Charles I (1600–49), recommended that she should visit the springs to recover following the birth of the future Charles II (1630–85). As there was no accommodation near the wells, visitors normally took rooms a few miles away at Tonbridge, but instead the queen's party set up camp at the springs.[4] Her presence prompted Lodowick Rowzee, the first doctor to celebrate the springs, to christen them *The Queenes Welles*, undoubtedly to help to market them to prospective patients.[5] With the waters now enjoying medical endorsement and royal patronage, investment began, albeit on a modest scale. In the late 1630s, the first two houses were erected near the spring and a walk was established that would eventually become the elegant parade known as the Pantiles.

At Epsom, in Surrey, during the dry summer of 1618, a spring was apparently discovered by Henry Wicker, a local farmer. By the 1660s it was being patronised by Charles II and the court, who came to enjoy its fashionable amusements as well as its water.[6] Like Tunbridge Wells, the advantage of Epsom initially was that its proximity to London made it more accessible to the capital's huge population than Bath. However, this would also subsequently lead to the town being overwhelmed by some of the masses of London, prompting the loss of wealthier patrons and the decline of its spa function. Proximity to London was not the only stimulus to the development of spas. Scarborough's spa waters were discovered in around 1626 by 'Mrs. *Farrow* a Gentlewoman of good Repute'.[7] Initially its patrons were relatively local, but by 1660 Dr Robert Wittie (bap 1613, d 1684), the spa's first champion, noted that in addition to people from Hull and York it was beginning to attract national attention.[8]

The Civil Wars of the 1640s and the Commonwealth (the republican period of government) in the subsequent decade interrupted the development of spas, though it did not entirely stop their use. During the 1640s, Bath was a Royalist garrison town and the baths were used by soldiers and prisoners for treatment.[9] Under the Commonwealth, the baths were not able to welcome significant numbers of aristocrats, but with the Restoration in 1660 Bath returned to being Britain's leading spa. Underpinning its growing success was the presence of royalty, including Charles I in 1628 and his wife Henrietta Maria, who came at the height of the Civil Wars in 1644.[10] During the following year, the future Charles II visited Bath and after the Restoration he continued to enjoy visits to spas.[11] He visited Bath along with his family in 1663, his mistresses came in 1674, while his wife, Catherine of Braganza (1638–1705), followed in 1677 and again in 1686. The queen had been encouraged to visit Bath for her health by her physician, Alexander Fraizer. James II's wife, Mary of Modena (1658–1718), visited in 1687 and became pregnant with her son, the future Old Pretender, bolstering the town's reputation for overcoming infertility.[12] James II's daughter, Princess Anne (1665–1714), visited Bath in 1692 and returned as Queen Anne in 1702 and 1703.[13] In the wake of the royal family, wealthy, aristocratic visitors came and their presence proved to be increasingly important for a town that had suffered from a decline in income from its clothing industry.[14]

Although Bath was enjoying considerable popularity with fashionable society, it remained small and densely packed, still hemmed within its medieval walls (Fig 3.1). Its populace faced problems with refuse and poor drinking water, ironic for a place famed for its waters, and between 1665 and 1690 Bath suffered from a series of outbreaks of smallpox and other infectious diseases.[15] It was often unpleasant to visit, being dusty or muddy, depending on the weather, but nevertheless the city prospered.[16] It was usually popular during spring and autumn as it was apparently too hot in the summer, when more rural Epsom or Tunbridge Wells were instead favoured.[17] Despite these issues, by the end of the 17th century Bath's popularity had forced up the cost of living and the first ribbon development had begun to appear on roads leading out from the centre.[18] In the 1640s, Bath already had more than 16 inns, the earliest of which dated back to 1503. By 1686, 324 beds were available

Fig 3.1
Although Bath would become famed for its classical Georgian architecture, its early development as a tourist destination relied on the existing houses and buildings of the town. A range of older houses can be seen in this illustration of the street beside the Guildhall. [From Shepherd and Britton 1829, facing p19]

in inns and alehouses, as well as some accommodation provided by doctors for their patients.[19] Many visitors were also lodging in existing, if refurbished, houses, but by the late 17th century, some new buildings were being erected. Among the new developments within and beyond the city were bowling greens, bookshops, a coffee house and a playhouse near the abbey.[20]

Bath was a small but busy city during its two seasons, but Tunbridge Wells enjoyed a different reputation, allowing people to enjoy pleasant company and entertainment, but also the countryside and therefore fresh air around the spring (Fig 3.2).[21] By the Restoration, Tunbridge Wells had emerged as Bath's main competitor, a rivalry that lasted for over a century. It offered visitors an assembly room, a bowling green and other amusements at Rusthall, a mile from the well, while at Southborough, two-and-a-half miles away, there was a bowling green, coffee house and some houses providing lodgings. Both were inconveniently distant from the spring and therefore facilities, including some houses, began to be established on emerging streets on the hillsides of Mount Ephraim and Mount Sion (Fig 3.3).[22] In 1663, Charles II and his queen spent two months on Mount Ephraim, establishing it as an emerging smart location for fashionable visitors.[23] The king was followed in 1670 by his brother, the Duke of York (the future James II), his wife and his two daughters Mary and Anne.[24] During the 1680s, Princess Anne, who would later become queen, returned to

Tunbridge Wells on the advice of her doctors to recover from her numerous miscarriages and problematic births.[25] The presence of royalty led to the erection of houses and shops and in 1676 a subscription was launched to erect a chapel. In 1687 a fire destroyed buildings that had been erected on the walk, though the chapel survived, and a new assembly room, coffee houses, shops and houses were erected with a colonnade in

front of them (Fig 3.4).[26] At the end of the 17th century, despite having attracted visitors for almost a century, Tunbridge Wells was still small and rural in character, its main walk being viewed almost as an urban intrusion into an otherwise rural setting:

The Upper-Walk's a rich and pleasant Street,
Gentle as any, more than any Sweet:
Where pleasures of the Town and Country
    meet.[27]

Tunbridge Wells could boast about its curative mineral waters and its fresh air suffused with herbs from the Kent countryside, but a key factor in its success was its convenience for inhabitants of the capital. Epsom was similarly convenient for London. Charles II visited in 1662, along with his wife and brother, and at other times during the decade actress Nell Gwynn (c 1651–87) and diarist Samuel Pepys (1633–1703) visited.[28] In around 1690, an avenue of trees was laid out, along with new houses, a ballroom and new inns, and by 1700 Epsom was at the peak of the its popularity. The reason for Epsom's rapid success also proved to be the reason for its swift decline. Being within easy reach of London, the growing town could be enjoyed by the growing numbers of middle-class patrons. Unfortunately vagrants, thieves and prostitutes were inevitably quick to pursue these tempting targets.[29] The town proved too crowded for the likes of Samuel Pepys and in 1712 Celia Fiennes (1662–1741) noted that 'Epsham shall be clutter'd with Company from Satturday to Tuesday'.[30] By the early 18th century, interest in taking the water was being replaced by a taste for assemblies, racing and gambling, though the 1722 account of writer and spy John Macky (d 1726) still produced a balanced description of 'its most healthful Air, and excellent Mineral Waters', along with the man-made facilities.[31] While taking the water declined in importance, enterprising Epsom found a way of marketing the salts from evaporated water, a product still on sale today.

Tunbridge Wells and Epsom were popular as they were convenient for London. They are a short train journey today from the capital, but during the 17th and 18th centuries it still involved some effort to visit them. To cater for the daily needs of Londoners, a series of wells began to be exploited immediately around the edges of the growing conurbation, wells set in gardens that developed during the 18th century into pleasure gardens. In 1684, the chalybeate spring of Islington Spa was discovered and was soon being hailed as the New Tunbridge Wells. By the early 18th century there was a coffee house, a promenade and music to entertain visitors and by the 1730s, members of the royal family were frequent visitors. Increasingly, the waters took second place to amusements, despite attempts to again promote them during the mid-18th century. By the early 19th century the gardens had closed.[32] Between 1674 and 1684, Edward Sadler discovered a spring on his north London property and by 1684 around 500 people were visiting it daily. Initially a place to drink the water, it soon became known for its entertainments, including tightrope walkers and acrobats. By the mid-18th century, buildings had been erected for theatrical performances and drinking water. In 1764, the theatre was rebuilt and soon attracted the best performers of the day.[33] Today, the original spring is forgotten, but Sadler's Wells is still renowned for its dance performances.

In the West Country, the only significant alternative to Bath before the mid-18th-century rise of Cheltenham was Hotwells at Clifton, Bristol (Fig 3.5). As early as 1677, Queen Catherine had visited the spa and by the end of the 17th

Fig 3.4
This late 19th-century photograph of the northern end of the Pantiles at Tunbridge Wells shows the bathhouse to the left, with the chapel, which survived the fire in the 1680s, in the distance. Dedicating the chapel to King Charles the Martyr was probably a device to seek the approval of royal and aristocratic patrons.
[BB85/01060]

century, local businessmen were investing in a pump room and lodging houses. In 1696, Hotwell House was built to enclose the spring, at a cost of £500, a considerable vote of confidence in the economic viability of the spa.[34]

In northern England, despite falling out of favour with the highest strata of society, Buxton, in Derbyshire, nevertheless remained an important destination for people wanting to take the waters. Sir John Floyer (1649–1734) visited the spa and recorded, 'These in the Opinion of the Northern People, cure all their Diseases, whether depending upon a hot or cold Cause.'[35] In the late 16th century, Harrogate, in Yorkshire, emerged as a rival to Buxton, with new mineral water sources being found to extend its appeal. The Sweet Spa was discovered in 1631 and in 1656 a stone basin was provided to collect the water.[36] There were also three sulphur-rich wells in the area in the 17th century, including the Starbeck between Knaresborough and Harrogate, where there was also a chalybeate spring.[37] At the end of the 17th century, Celia Fiennes visited Harrogate. She was struck by the strong smell of sulphur from the 'Sulpher or Stincking Spaw', which was actually two wells with basins. Within a quarter of a mile, she visited the 'Sweete Spaw', which she likened to Astrop, in Northamptonshire, or Tunbridge Wells, while between these two renowned sources there was also 'a fine cleare and sweete Spring of Comon water'.[38]

In the late 17th century Scarborough seems to have been the most prestigious and most popular spa in the north of England, despite travel to such a remote town being difficult. Selecting Scarborough was probably influenced

Fig 3.5
From the small village of the 17th century, during the 18th century Clifton developed into a large settlement. This Aerofilms photograph dates from 1920, by which time it had become a suburb of Bristol. [EPW001268]

by a cocktail of medical claims, fashion, the status of the Company staying in the town and the quality of the facilities (Fig 3.6).[39] In 1662, Sir John Reresby (1634–89) noted that 'many persons of quality came that Summer for their health or their diversion' and in 1667 Wittie recorded that 'people of good fashion' were coming to Scarborough.[40] While the town did attract some metropolitan visitors, it was more usually a favoured destination for the wealthy from the north of England and Scotland. Author Daniel Defoe (1660–1731), writing in the 1720s, said, 'We found a great deal of good company here drinking the waters, who came not only from all the north of England, but even from Scotland.'[41] In 1733 Edmund Withers described the Com-

pany at Scarborough, saying, 'The numbers of strangers resorting to the Spaw was never known to be so great at any time as the present, most of them from remote corners, especially crouds of Scotch gentry.'[42]

The leading mineral spring in Wales was favoured for its apparent medicinal value, but was especially popular with Roman Catholics as a religious shrine. St Winefride's Well at Holywell, in Flintshire, was a medieval shrine with a 15th-century well chamber and chapel (*see* Fig 2.5). As a shrine it was obviously affected by the Reformation, but during the late 17th century and early 18th, Holywell remained a popular destination for the Catholic and curious alike. James II and his wife Mary visited the well in

Fig 3.6
The so-called King Richard III's house at Scarborough is one of the older houses near the harbour in which people would have stayed when visiting the spa during the 17th century.
[AA45/06186]

1686 and the devout Catholic landowner Nicholas Blundell took his family there on a number of occasions.[43] On 24 June 1707, he wrote, 'We went from Chester to Holly Well & Lodged at the Starr.'[44] The Star Inn, run by Jesuit priests, was a regular meeting place for worshippers, who were still having to gather secretly at Holywell. Although apparently a secret place to congregate, it was obviously well known and more or less tolerated by the authorities. Celia Fiennes visited in 1698 and said, 'There I saw abundance of the devout papists on their knees all round the Well; poor people are deluded into an ignorant blind zeale and to be pity'd by us that have the advantage of knowing better and ought to be better.' She also said, 'They tell of many lameness's and aches and distempers which are cured by it.'[45]

Daniel Defoe also visited the shrine in the 1720s, writing:

The stories of this Well of S Winifrid are, that the pious virgin, being ravished and murthered, this healing water sprung out of her body when buried; but this smells too much of the legend, to take up any of my time; the Romanists indeed believe it, as 'tis evident, from their thronging hither to receive the healing sanative virtue of the water, which they do not hope for as it is a medicinal water, but as it is a miraculous water, and heals them by virtue of the intercession and influence of this famous virgin, St Winifrid; of which I believe as much as comes to my share.[46]

The science of mineral waters

Epsom's long-running industry of producing and selling salts and Scarborough's reputation for improving patients' health were both a product of a new-found interest in the science of mineral waters. By the beginning of the 18th century, the popularity of a spa was not only dependent on its patrons and their word-of-mouth impact but increasingly relied on the published and personal testimony of doctors and scientific writers who might influence visitors. A re-examination of classical scientific writings, increasingly sophisticated chemical analysis and the wisdom of years of observation of patients were combined to make potent arguments for the efficacy of spa waters. However, the same science would soon proclaim the medicinal value of seawater, with profound consequences for the popularity of spa towns.

The spring at Harrogate, discovered in the 1570s, only came to wide public attention with the publication by Edmunde Deane of *Spadacrene Anglica* in 1626, while Dr Lodowick Rowzee published his description of Tunbridge Wells' spa water in 1632.[47] At the Restoration, Dr Robert Wittie established himself as the authority on Scarborough's spa waters, which he claimed could cure a huge range of physical conditions, but his science and his medical claims were challenged by other writers, particularly Dr William Simpson, a rival since they had practised medicine together in York.[48] In 1669, Simpson criticised Wittie for suggesting that the spa waters treated too many conditions and in the following year, Dr George Tunstall from Newcastle upon Tyne dared to suggest that Scarborough's waters could actually be harmful.[49] After several rounds of heated exchanges, Wittie retired, leaving Simpson as the unchallenged advocate of Scarborough's spa waters.[50]

At Bath, Henry Chapman published *Thermae Redivivae* in 1673 in which he described, more anecdotally than scientifically, the use of the waters and their impact on patients, sometimes in unpleasant detail. He included the assertion that Bath's hot waters were 'one of the greatest Miracles in Nature'.[51] Bath had been predominantly a bathing spa, but drinking the water seems to have grown to be more significant from the late 17th century onwards.[52]

As well as doctors using their local medical experience and knowledge to promote their own springs, the first scientists with national perspectives were examining the medicinal impact of mineral waters. Sir John Floyer set out to examine the types of water that people in England could drink and bathe in. In *An Enquiry into the right Use and abuses of the hot, cold, and temperate Baths in England* in 1697, Floyer examined each type of water, documenting its temperature, taste and the conditions it could treat.[53] He pioneered a more scientific approach to examining mineral waters and a number of other writers followed his example. In 1699, Benjamin Allen (1663–1738) first published *The Natural History of the Mineral-Waters of Great-Britain*. He systematically categorised the various types of waters (saline, chalybeate, chalybeate purging, sulphurous and steamy) and reviewed the ways in which they could be used.[54] In 1737, the apothecary John King's *An essay on hot and cold bathing* drew on the work of contemporary scientists including Sir Isaac Newton and Robert Boyle. He also cited the work of

George Cheyne, whose *An Essay of Health and Long Life* (1724) became a key text for the informed public as well as medical men to consult.[55] King also made extensive use of classical and Renaissance sources, revealing that he was probably one of the most widely read men in his profession.

By the 18th century, scientific analysis generally classified waters as being chalybeate (meaning they were high in iron) or sulphurous or saline, but to further refine this classification some medical writers carried out chemical analysis. A focal point for this new scientific approach was Scarborough's spa waters in the 1730s. In around 1730, a former ship's surgeon, John Atkins (bap 1685, d 1757), published a study of the use of mineral water springs.[56] Although it concerned waters in general, it was his study of the spa at Scarborough that triggered another round of scientific debate similar to those of the 1660s and 1670s. During the following decade, Atkins, along with the physicians Thomas Short (*c* 1690–1772) and Peter Shaw (1694–1763), advanced different theories about how the waters worked, but all agreed that they could cure a bewildering range of medical conditions.[57] To support his ideas, Shaw used his detailed knowledge of chemistry to analyse the mineral contents of the waters, evaporating and distilling the waters to produce the solid salts they contained.

Although people were visiting spas to drink or to bathe in mineral waters, many doctors had also recognised that a change in environment, improved diet and exposure to fresh air and sunshine were therapeutic for their patients. By the early 18th century, Bath might have been the most fashionable spa centre, but it was a city, and strongly urban in character. Tunbridge Wells, smaller and less lively in character, made a virtue of its more rural setting and something of this bucolic character is still evident today (Fig 3.7). In the 1690s, one poet summed up the town's curative virtues:

> Not all new Towns for wealth, but some for
>   Fame
> Are built, or Health; some to preserve a Name.
> Let these bright Springs some brighter name
>   preserve
> Than dirty Tunbridge; better they deserve.
> For Health, the Miracles which here are done
> By Air and Water, methinks should have won
> The cur'd in Gratitude; the sick at last
> Shou'd be convinc'd by their own Interest,
> To finish these beginnings of a Town,
> Which thus unbuilt bring such a concourse
>   down.[58]

Writing in 1766, the first historian of Tunbridge Wells, Thomas Benge Burr, praised the food produced in the rich countryside around the growing town. He was clear that the clean, fresh air was an important reason for visiting Tunbridge Wells.[59] He stated that 'the soil is dry,

Fig 3.7
This postcard shows the rural setting of Mount Ephraim at Tunbridge Wells, on which new houses were built to accommodate the growing numbers of visitors to the spa.
[PC10361]

MOUNT EPHRAIM, TUN. WELLS.   H.G.Groves

the air pure and healthful', and other writers were clear that the air of the emerging town was key to curing patients.[60] Promoting the geographical virtues of a particular spa town was important in marketing a destination from the 18th century onwards. It would assume even greater significance for seaside resorts that would use the health-giving qualities of seawater as well as their climate to promote tourism at the expense of many spa towns.

Spas during the 18th century

By the early 18th century, mineral water springs for medical use were being exploited in large numbers all over the country. Cheshire had 20 springs in use in 1700 and by 1712 Northamptonshire had 38, while during the 1730s Dr Thomas Short studied more than 220 mineral water sources in central and northern England alone.[61] Although springs were being exploited all over the country, there were still only a handful of popular destinations. Foremost among these were still Bath and Tunbridge Wells, though a number of smaller spas were beginning to grow in size and popularity.

Bath

At the beginning of the 18th century, Bath could boast facilities designed to cater for a large number of visitors. New and refurbished houses provided lodgings, and there were also assembly rooms, theatres, circulating libraries and coffee houses to fill the day after taking the waters during the morning. These facilities were initially fairly rudimentary, often in adapted buildings, but during the 18th century Bath led the way in providing the grandest entertainment venues and large houses in its elaborate crescents and squares.

The visits of Queen Anne in 1702 and 1703, the last by a reigning monarch until 1917, helped to stimulate Bath's development at a time when it was at a low ebb financially.[62] Although monarchs may not have visited, many princes and dukes did, and in their wake, large numbers of gentry and middle-class visitors came. This was stimulated by improved roads, as by 1743 the route from London to Bath was entirely turnpiked. It was also prompted by the longer season, stretching from September to May, made possible by plentiful supplies of coal from Mendip.[63]

As spa towns evolved, a distinctive culture and sets of activities and manners developed. This process was under way during the 17th century, but was first codified by Bath's charismatic Master of Ceremonies, Richard 'Beau' Nash (1674–1761). The 'King of Bath' arrived in 1704 or 1705, and was soon the assistant to the Master of Ceremonies, Captain Thomas Webster.[64] Webster died in a duel in 1705 and Nash was elected as his successor by visitors to the resort. In 1725 a group of Cambridge students visited Bath during their summer holiday trip around southern and central England and saw Beau Nash in action. They wrote:

> Beau Nash a man of great Gallantry; and of uncommon assurance, though no [not] young but a batter'd old Beau turned of fifty years and not at all handsome, is the greatest promoter of the diversions at Harrison's [Assembly Room], and one of the greatest Gamesters, and the first man in the Ladys good-Graces, tis though [thought] that he shares with Harrison in the good profitts arising from these rooms.[65]

Oliver Goldsmith's biography of Nash, an early example of the celebrity biography, described how Nash's rules shaped and regulated the spa's day, beginning with bathing and drinking water at one of Bath's baths (Fig 3.8). After breakfast, entertainments such as visiting

Fig 3.8
This view of the Queen's Bath at Bath shows the heat of the water in the pool. It also illustrates the built-up character of the centre of the town and how close many people's lodgings would have been to the baths and entertainment venues. [From Nattes 1806 (plate XIX)]

the assembly rooms and circulating libraries were enjoyed, so long as visitors had paid the appropriate subscriptions. In the evenings, visitors attended the theatre or took part in balls at the assembly room. Nash's rules were posted in the Pump Room, where all visitors would pass through, as this was where the town's waters were drunk. The carrying of swords was banned, 11pm was set as the time when the evening balls should finish and antisocial behaviours, such as smoking and drinking, were regulated. Men and women were expected to dress appropriately and behave in a sociable way, avoiding gossiping and avoiding feeling snubbed if invitations were passed over.[66] This regulation of manners came at a price: Nash drew his income from gambling and from the subscriptions paid by visitors.[67] His vision of the central, regulatory role of the Master of Ceremonies became a model for other spa towns and would later contribute to formulating the shape of a Georgian day at the seaside.

At the start of the 18th century, despite its growing popularity, Bath still had limited facilities and although it was being used as a drinking spa as well as for bathing, there was nowhere official to drink the waters.[68] In 1706 the first pump room opened to the north of the King's Bath and in 1725 the Cambridge students visited it and the baths during their summer holiday, noting:

> The most remarkable places, are, the pump room, where the Company meet in a morning between seven and eight, and drink the waters pumped up from the spring which supplies the bath, the pump is of marble, and the water so hot that tis but just fit to drink, I drank a Glass of it.
>
> The Company meet in their undress and have musick every morning; this room opens with three arches next the street, hath a large window looking into the Bath and is shut up about ten every morning.[69]

An assembly room opened in 1708 and was enlarged in 1720 and 1749. A second assembly room opened in 1730 and two theatres were created at the beginning of the 18th century.[70] The

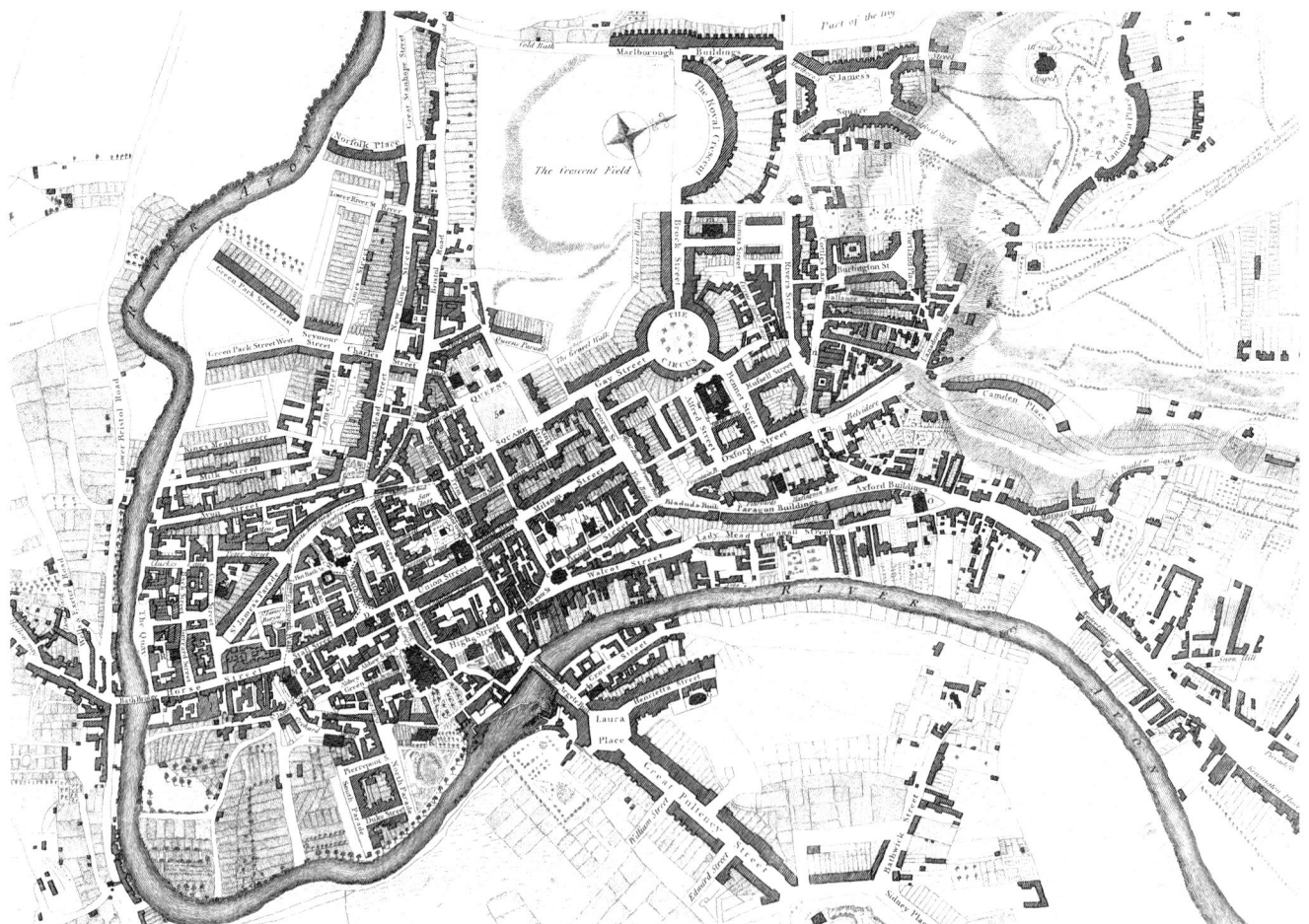

Fig 3.9
This plan of Bath from c 1801 shows that development had spread from beyond the medieval city walls up the hill to the Upper Town and across the river towards Bathwick, where William Johnstone Pulteney's developments were located.
[From Warner 1801, facing p1]

Cambridge students in 1725 visited the first assembly room, run by Mr Thomas Harrison, 'where gaming, dancing, Consorts of musick &c are to be met with', at a cost of two guineas for the season.[71] Music was such an important dimension of 18th-century Bath that the 1766 guidebook devoted an entire letter to it, including the supposed greeting each day of new arrivals by ringing the abbey's bells.[72] In 1742, Bath became the first spa centre to publish a 'guidebook', though a few years earlier a book had been published that served effectively as a guide to Scarborough.[73]

Initially, development at Bath was largely confined to within the historic town, but by the late 1720s the first substantial developments outside its walls began to appear (Fig 3.9).[74] The first step involved the creation of new sewers in the Old Town, followed by the construction of Queen Square to the north.[75] Built between 1728 and 1736, this fashionable Palladian scheme acted as the trailblazer for the classical forms that would dominate the next 100 years.[76] At the heart of this boom in Bath were three men: Beau Nash, Ralph Allen (bap 1693, d 1764), who provided the stone from his quarries, and John Wood the Elder (1704–54), the architect who helped to establish Bath's new visual identity (Fig 3.10).[77]

Further entertainment facilities were built, including a new theatre in 1750 and a new Pump Room in 1750–51 (Fig 3.11), but the most prestigious architectural endeavour of the

Fig 3.10
Ralph Allen's town house in the centre of Bath is small but very ornate. Its facade was designed by John Wood the Elder, who transformed an older building into what resembles a miniature version of a contemporary country house.
[AA037682]

Fig 3.11
The new Pump Room became central to the social life of Bath and remains one of the city's key attractions. It was built adjacent to the Roman Baths (the King's Bath).
[AA037826]

Fig 3.12
This aerial photograph
of 1949 shows the King's
Circus and Royal Crescent
in Bath, with the 23 houses
of Lansdown Crescent
(c 1789–93) in the distance.
The historic town lies
down the hill, beyond the
bottom-right corner of
the photograph.
[EAW027311]

Fig 3.13
The new Upper Assembly
Rooms at Bath, by John
Wood the Younger, became
the grandest venue in
the town, hosting card
assemblies and balls for
the town's wealthiest
residents and visitors.
[AA044608]

Fig 3.14 (facing page)
Pulteney Bridge in Bath is
a rare surviving example
of a bridge with buildings
on it, and therefore
resembles the medieval
Ponte Vecchio in Florence.
Its construction opened up
Bathwick for new develop-
ment, including Bath's new
prison of 1772–3.
[AA98/05118]

decade was the King's Circus (1754–66), a circular development of houses costing almost
£62,000 (Fig 3.12).[78] To integrate the original
historic settlement with the new developments,
the city gates and parts of the walls were demolished during the 1750s.[79] The creation of the
King's Circus, along with the Royal Crescent of
30 houses (1767–74) and the opening of the
new Upper Assembly Rooms in 1771, meant
that the city's fashionable centre was shifting up
the hillside (Fig 3.13).[80] Nevertheless, there was
still considerable development in the Old Town,
including improving its bathhouses and enlarging the Pump Room in the 1760s and 1770s; the
new Upper Town still only accounted for a third
of the 235 lodging houses that were available in
Bath in the early 1770s.[81]

By the early 1790s, around 1,000 houses
were being constructed in the Upper Town and
to the east of the Old Town, where the ambitious
Bathwick development of William Johnstone
Pulteney was taking place, a development made
possible by the construction of the Pulteney
Bridge in 1769–74 (Fig 3.14).[82] The architect,
Thomas Baldwin (c 1750–1820), proposed a
scheme to create a new town consisting of 5,000

houses, but the outbreak of war with France in 1793 coincided with, and contributed to, a financial collapse that delayed development.[83] In 1799, entertainer and author George Saville Carey (1743–1807) was unusually complimentary about Bath. He likened its grandest streets to the finest ones in London and even concluded that it was one of the most splendid cities in Europe.[84]

Although royalty may have deserted Bath in the 18th century, they had been succeeded by gentry, clergy, retired military men and professionals such as physicians, surgeons and attorneys.[85] Painters followed these potential patrons, including Thomas Gainsborough (1727–88) and Thomas Lawrence (1769–1830). Bath also featured prominently in literature, including in works by Tobias Smollett (1721–71), Richard Brinsley Sheridan (1751–1816) and Jane Austen (1775–1817).[86] Substantial service industries grew up to cater for large numbers of visitors. Alongside market stalls and shops providing necessities, there were many shops offering luxury goods, including milliners, hairdressers and perfumers, essential services for fashionable Georgian tourists.[87] There were also many circulating libraries (Fig 3.15) and coffee shops and a royal patent was granted to Bath's theatre in 1768, though it took until 1805 for a new building to be opened.[88] The number of lodging houses reflected the growing visitor numbers, rising from 235 in 1773 to 362 in 1791 and 457 in 1799.[89]

Fig 3.15
Circulating libraries were a key feature of the entertainment scene in 18th-century spa towns. Usually located in buildings that had been erected as houses, signs are often the only way to locate one in a street, such as this example on a c 1765 house in Milsom Street in Bath. [© Author]

Tunbridge Wells

Tunbridge Wells was Bath's main rival during the 18th century, though for much of the period they shared a Master of Ceremonies. Thomas Benge Burr in 1766 recorded the visits of royalty as proof of the success and salubrity of his town. Investment in buildings and entertainments on the walks prompted visits by Frederick, Prince of Wales and his wife Princess Augusta in 1739, Princess Amelia in 1762 and the dukes of York and Gloucester in 1765.[90] Benge Burr said with considerable local pride:

> This place itself is now in a very flourishing state, with a great number of good houses for lodgings, and all necessary accommodations for company; its customs are settled, its pleasures regulated, its markets and all other conveniences fixed, and the whole very properly adapted to the nature of a place, which is at once design[ed] to give health and pleasure to all its visitants.[91]

Most medical writers suggested that spa patients needed to drink the waters for several weeks, but John Macky in the 1720s was clear that even after a week, life at Tunbridge Wells would become tedious due to the repetitive shape of each day.[92] As at Bath and later at seaside resorts, there was a belief that bathing and consuming water should take place in the morning, so that the benefits could take effect before the middle of the day, leaving the remainder of the day free for leisure. Visitors seem to have been permitted to stagger out of bed in a state of half-dress to drink the waters, but they had to return home to dress properly for the rest of the day, which would begin with prayers for the pious or coffee houses for probably the majority of visitors. Dinner in the early 18th century was at around 2pm, though by the end of the century it was shifting to later in the day and therefore luncheon, initially a small snack, was introduced to fill the gap between breakfast and dinner. After dinner, bowling greens were popular and balls with dancing were provided on some days. In the 1720s, Macky does not mention an assembly room, an institution that was only beginning to emerge as a distinct entity, and there was no theatre. Instead, evenings at Tunbridge Wells were spent at play in the Pantiles, which Macky described as 'the Shops on the Walks'.[93] Later in the 18th century, public balls were held at the assembly rooms on Tuesdays

Fig 3.16
On the Pantiles at
Tunbridge Wells visitors
could enjoy drinking the
water and visiting the
assembly rooms. Shops
included silversmiths,
jewellers, milliners,
booksellers and stores
selling Tunbridge Ware,
as well as a market where
visitors could buy produce
for cooking at their lodgings.
[AA011846]

and Fridays, while private balls were held on some other days. People coming to Tunbridge Wells could also enjoy concerts and spend time in the coffee houses and the bookseller's shop. The latter was open to both sexes, but coffee houses were for the separate sexes in larger towns such as Bath, as the politically charged atmosphere of the men's one was felt to be unsuitable for women.[94]

By 1766, Tunbridge Wells consisted of four distinct areas: Mount Ephraim, Mount Pleasant and Mount Sion, where lodgings were available in a growing number of houses, and the Wells, which was 'the center of business and pleasure'.[95] The original modest walk had been transformed into the Pantiles, a name acquired from its paving (Fig 3.16). Along the length of the walk there was a loggia on 'Tuscan pillars' and a line of trees 'in the midst of which is erected a gallery for the musick' (Fig 3.17).[96] As urban Bath was too hot during the summer, Tunbridge Wells marketed itself as an alternative destination and

Fig 3.17
This building on the
Pantiles at Tunbridge Wells
was once a music gallery.
In the 18th century, visitors
subscribed to pay for
musicians and, as at Bath,
music greeted new arrivals
and entertained them at
their lodgings, as well as
when they promenaded
along the street.
[© Author]

doctors recommended that its water was best drunk between May and October. As Bath and Tunbridge Wells had seasons that did not overlap, from 1735 they shared a Master of Ceremonies. Beau Nash commuted between Bath and Tunbridge Wells in a suitably regal procession consisting of a 'post chariot and six greys, with out-riders, footmen, *French* horns, and every other appendage of expensive parade'.[97] At both towns he enforced strict rules of behaviour in the assembly rooms, at balls and more widely in the town, including expecting visitors to Tunbridge Wells to attend the chapel beside the Pantiles twice a day.[98]

By the end of the 18th century, Tunbridge Wells was popular because of its good facilities, healing waters, royal endorsement and convenient location for London. It had its elegant promenade, two assembly rooms, libraries, a playhouse and a chapel that played a key role each morning.[99] A cold bath was built in 1780 and in 1802–4 a bathhouse was constructed over the springs (Fig 3.18).[100] George Saville Carey was exceptionally complimentary about Bath in 1799, but he was rather more predictably acerbic when considering Tunbridge Wells, describing its visitors as mostly being 'peevish old maids', 'bloated old dowagers' and 'a frisky young tit or two'.[101]

Buxton and Harrogate

Bath and Tunbridge Wells were the most popular spa towns through the 18th century. Towns such as Buxton and Harrogate continued to cater for their local and regional customers and developed more slowly. The focal point of Buxton remained the site of the original well, though the century did see a growth in the size of the town. The baths had been repaired by Cornelius White in 1695 and 1696, who also added a new open-air bath for poor bathers. In 1709 the original St Anne's Well was rebuilt. Despite this investment, Buxton remained a small town or even just a village, as Defoe claimed, and large, urban development had to wait until later in the 18th century.[102] The largest single addition was the Crescent in 1780–88 by John Carr of York (1723–1807) for the Duke of Devonshire, at a cost of £120,000 (Fig 3.19).[103]

Unlike some spa towns, Harrogate had no shortage of water, 88 springs having been found within a two-mile (3km) radius of the old sulphur well, the original focal point for development.[104] Each spring that was discovered represented an opportunity for an enterprising businessman or innkeeper to develop a facility to exploit it. Therefore, both High Harrogate and Low Harrogate had a patchwork layout and,

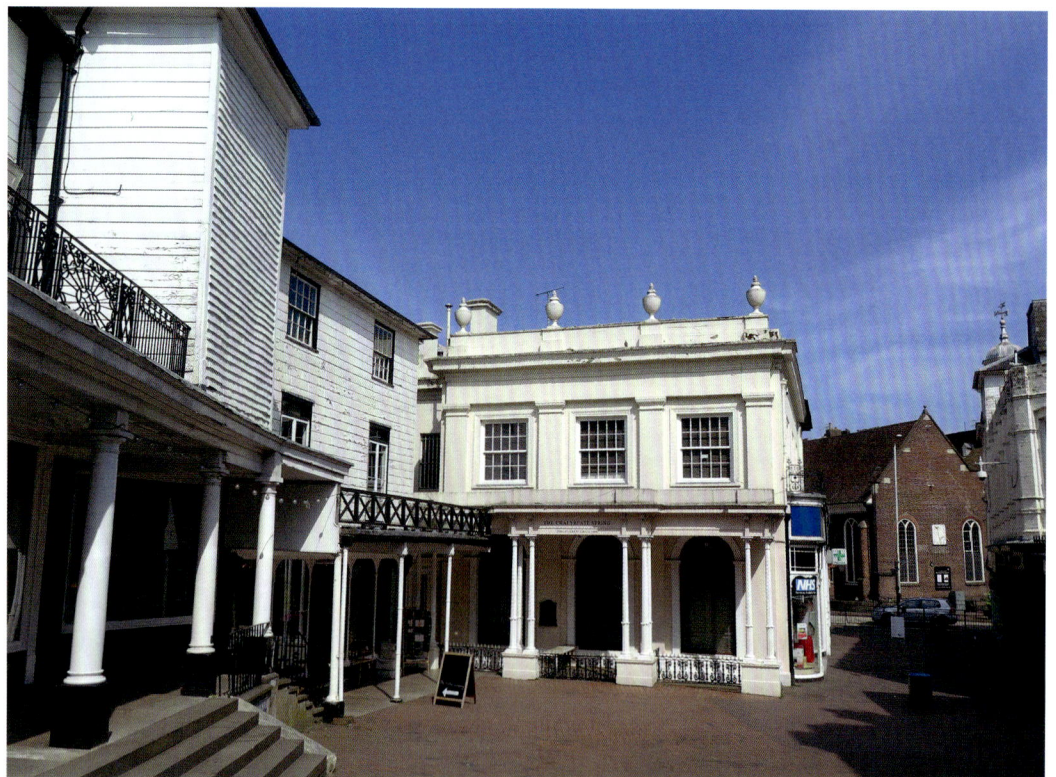

Fig 3.18
This modern view of Tunbridge Wells shows the bathhouse of 1802–4 with the chapel beyond, at the northern end of the Pantiles. A late 19th-century version of the same view can be seen in Fig 3.4.
[© Author]

Fig 3.19
Erected beside the Old Hall and St Anne's Well, Buxton's crescent contained a hotel, assembly room and lodging houses. It was an attempt to emulate, albeit on a smaller scale, the Royal Crescent in Bath. [J930069]

Fig 3.20
This photograph of 1903 by Bedford Lemere (1865–1944) shows the Crown Inn at Harrogate. A century earlier, it was Low Harrogate's largest inn and was one of the town's main places for accommodation and entertainment. [BL17932b]

interestingly, novelist Tobias Smollett had already noted in 1771 the scattered nature of development.[105] In 1781 around 1,500 visitors came to Harrogate each year, but by 1810 this had almost quadrupled, a reflection of the town's growing popularity and the increasing number of facilities.[106]

In contrast to the southern spa towns that boasted large communal facilities, the pattern in northern spas, such as at Harrogate, involved more entertainment and socialising in a small number of inns (Fig 3.20). Smollett described in 1771 how each inn formed 'a distinct society, that eat together, and there is a commodious public room, where they breakfast in disabille, at separate tables, from eight o clock till eleven, as they chance or chuse to come in'.[107] In the afternoon the same room would be used for tea and in the evening for playing cards or dancing. Each night one of the houses held a ball that anyone could attend if they purchased a ticket and Smollett stated that this meant Harrogate was emulating the 'gaiety and dissipation' of Bath, but was more 'sociable and familiar'.[108] However, some central facilities were provided: a chapel was built in the 1740s and by 1760 a barn had been fitted out as a theatre, which was replaced in 1788 by a purpose-built theatre fit to entertain the celebrated actor and theatre manager Tate Wilkinson (1739–1803).[109] By 1800, the growing town could also boast a museum, an assembly room, a circulating library

and a billiard room.[110] Despite an Enclosure Act, the Stray, a central open space, remained undeveloped, except for being used as a racecourse from 1793, and this is still essential to Harrogate's quasi-rural appeal today.[111]

London and Cheltenham

London's local wells continued to be popular and new wells soon became an attraction in emerging pleasure gardens. The pleasure gardens at Bagnigge Wells, on the site of what is now King's Cross railway station, began as a 17th-century house reputed to have been the home of Nell Gwynn.[112] While she was alive, her house may have been used as a place of public entertainment, but it was only much later, in 1757, that the then tenant Mr Hughes recognised that he could promote the waters of the well for their health-giving properties.[113] Dr John Bevis

(1695–1771) analysed the waters and declared that it was a good chalybeate well, leading to a second well being sunk, and in 1760 a booklet was published about the wells.[114] Visitors could enjoy the pleasant gardens, including a fish pond with a fountain, a little cottage and a shell grotto. A small classical structure called the Temple was created in which the waters were dispensed from pumps, as well as a Long Room for tea drinking.[115] By the end of the 18th century, Bagnigge Wells had a reputation as a place of low morals, its visitors being described as 'apprentices, shopmen, hairdressers, milliners, mantua-makers, ladies maids, and women of the town'.[116] By around 1810, the pleasure garden was suffering a series of financial problems and changes of tenant and it closed in 1840.

As well as traditional old spas, some new ones emerged and grew in popularity. Prior to the discovery of its mineral water springs, Cheltenham

Fig 3.21
By the early 19th century, Cheltenham's townscape was being transformed by the construction of monumental classical terraces and houses. This view, taken by John Gay, is of a terrace of 15 houses (built c 1837–45) on St George's Road, which includes the George Hotel.
[AA092108]

was a small market town with around 1,500 inhabitants living in 312 houses in 1666.[117] In 1716, a mineral water spring was discovered in a nearby field and two years later it was enclosed by a rail by its owner William Mason.[118] By 1720, its purging waters were being advertised locally and in London. During the following year, the waters were analysed by Dr Baird of Gloucester and Dr Grevil of Worcester.[119] When Mason died in the early 1720s, his property passed to his daughter, who married Captain Henry Skillicorne, who erected a small pump room and a brick canopy over the well.[120] Skillicorne's diary reveals that the spring attracted 414 visitors in 1740, 667 in 1742 and 644 in 1743, the type of figure that London spas enjoyed every day.[121] Despite being a small spa, it nevertheless attracted visitors such as composer George Frederick Handel (1685–1759), writer Dr Samuel Johnson (1709–84) and theologian John Wesley (1703–91).[122]

Following Skillicorne's death in 1763, his son William took over the running of what would become known as the Old Well. In 1775, he collaborated with William Miller to create the first assembly room and the town's first modest theatre was established in 1782.[123] In 1784, a second assembly room was built in a classical style, the earliest appearance of the style that would shape much of the town's architecture over the next 50 years. A third set of assembly rooms was erected in 1791 and in 1809 another opened at Montpellier, the multiplicity of these facilities reflecting the patchwork pattern of estate development around where suitable mineral water springs were being discovered and exploited. Cheltenham's first Master of Ceremonies, Simeon Moreau (d 1801), produced the town's earliest guidebook in 1781 and a treatise about the medical value of the town's waters was published in 1785.[124] In 1786, a body of Improvement Commissioners was established to improve the conditions in the growing town, including providing a new market building and paving the streets.[125] People had originally come to drink the waters, but in 1787 the town's first baths opened on the High Street, offering warm and tepid baths.[126] A shortage of lodgings initially limited the speed of the town's growth, there being only four inns in 1783, but a rapid growth in the town's housing stock in future decades remedied this.[127]

By the 1780s, Cheltenham was beginning to thrive and its medical reputation encouraged the doctors of George III (1738–1820) to recommend a stay there to improve the king's health. In July 1788, he arrived to spend five weeks drinking the waters and riding out into the countryside.[128] He stayed in the recently built house of Lord Fauconberg near the Old Well.[129] It may have been the king's brief presence that encouraged a new level of investment in buildings. Cheltenham's Colonnade, a three-storey, 26-bay block, was begun in 1791 and was soon followed by the town's first square (laid out in 1809) and the Royal Crescent (before 1812).[130] By the mid-1790s, around 1,500 people came to enjoy the waters each year and in 1801 the town's population had increased to just over 3,000, with 150 lodging houses (Fig 3.21).[131]

Scottish spas

Many spas across the country were prospering as the national economy was growing, leading to an increasing number of people with the time and wealth to enjoy leisure. This was not only being felt in England but also in Scotland. Despite periods of turbulence during the first half of the 18th century, Scotland had emerging spa sites that were likened by some writers to English counterparts due to the taste and curative powers of their waters, though none could match the size and popularity of southern English spa towns. A letter signed by 'Etonensis' in the *Gentleman's Magazine* in 1787 stated that there were only three Scottish spas of real significance: Moffat, in Dumfries and Galloway, Pannanich, in Aberdeenshire, and Peterhead, also in Aberdeenshire. It stated, 'The resort to these places has, of late years, been frequent, and that too by persons of bon ton.'[132] Pannanich, near Ballater, was only a small rural spring with limited facilities and Peterhead offered both a spring and sea bathing, drawing comparison with Scarborough, though its development was later than its English equivalent.[133]

Moffat, 'The Scottish Cheltenham', which was foremost among the Scottish spas, had been a destination for the upper classes of Edinburgh since the 17th century. By the mid-18th century, Moffat was firmly established as a health resort, patronised by the legal and landed profession during the summer vacation of the law courts at Edinburgh. To exploit this interest, local landowners, particularly the Douglas family, funded the construction of inns to provide a better class of accommodation, as well as constructing paths and walks to the newly discovered Hartfell Springs, where a pavilion was provided. The wells proved so successful medically that they attracted poor and sick people, potentially deterring more profitable customers. The Marquis of Annandale had appointed keepers at the well, but John Clerk of Penecuik complained in 1748, 'As the well is quite open night and day there is a number of diseased scrophulous, leperous people lying about it and who seem to be watching for an opportunity to wash their sores unseen by the two keepers.'[134] The solution at Moffat was to fence the springs and build a small house where the waters were served, for a reduced charge, to the poor. Separate covered apartments for ladies and gentlemen were provided, to which none of the lower order were to be admitted. Moffat spa was a reasonable success, though it would never be able to match the leading English spas. In April 1805, one visitor found no fewer than 250 invalids who had come 'to drink a mineral water' in a village of perhaps only 1,200 residents.[135]

Scarborough

Although Scotland could offer some spa facilities for its population in the 18th century, many of its leading citizens availed themselves of facilities in northern England, including Scarborough. The town's 1734 guidebook included a list of visitors to the town in 1733 compiled from the subscription books of the Spa, the Long Room (its assembly room), the bookseller's shop and the coffee house.[136] Included among the 695 names of male visitors and 360 ladies there were two dukes, the Marquis of Lothian, seven earls, three barons, five Yorkshire knights, 22 titled women apparently unrelated to any of the men, a dozen clergy, 8 doctors and 20 military men.[137] Among the famous visitors were the architect Nicholas Hawksmoor (c 1661–1736), who was working

Fig 3.22
The spa at Scarborough was located to the south of the town at the opposite end of the sands from the harbour. It was rebuilt again during the mid-19th century, as is shown in this late 19th-century photograph.
[CC76/00420]

at nearby Castle Howard, as well as the actor-manager, playwright and Poet Laureate Colley Cibber (1671–1757). However, the 1730s was also a challenging decade for the town. A landslide in December 1737 required the Corporation to rebuild the spa and erect a large sea wall around it. By 17 May 1738, 'the Room for the Reception of the Ladies' had opened, followed soon after by a room for the men.[138] This facility lasted for over a century, through alteration and amendment. It was finally replaced comprehensively in the mid-19th century by the building that is still in use today, which was based around entertainment rather than health facilities (Fig 3.22).

Although the spa's business resumed quickly, and Scarborough was already taking advantage of its coastal location to allow people to bathe in the sea, the town did not grow quickly during the 18th century. In the 1720s and 1730s it was described as a town of about 2,000 families, suggesting a population perhaps in excess of 8,000, while in 1743 it was estimated to be home to 1,500 families. This may have been a significant overestimate, as Scarborough's population numbered only 6,688 inhabitants in 1801. Nevertheless, Scarborough remained a prominent destination for visitors; Tobias Smollett featured Humphry Clinker visiting the town as well as Bath and Harrogate in his 1771 novel *The Expedition of Humphry Clinker*, though he did note that its reputation was in decline.[139] However, Scarborough was by then no longer simply a destination because of its spa. It was the seaside, sea bathing and sometimes drinking seawater that was attracting patients and tourists to a range of coastal towns.

Conclusion

From the mid-16th century onwards, spas became the main focus for tourism in Britain. In a sense they were simply replacing shrines and holy wells as popular destinations, but where these had been popular sites of devotion, potentially for all the population, spas were usually restricted to the wealthiest part of society. An evolving system of treatments involving drinking and bathing in mineral waters was being espoused in a growing body of scientific literature, which provided validation for local doctors seeking to promote their water source, as well as their town. Beginning in the mid-16th century with Bath and Buxton, gradually new sources of mineral water were discovered, predominantly within easy reach of major population centres, but by the 18th century there were popular spas throughout the country.

The process of establishing a new spa began with the discovery of a mineral water source, which was subsequently validated by scientific analysis and then actively promoted by a local doctor. The aim of this process was to encourage wealthy and influential patrons whose celebrity would encourage further visitors. While they ostensibly visited a spa for medical reasons, the treatments were over during the morning, leaving the remainder of the day free for entertainment in subscription facilities such as circulating libraries and assembly rooms, theatres and coffee houses. By the 18th century individual spa towns had a more or less fixed daily timetable of activities, often enforced by the Master of Ceremonies.

In the mid-18th century, at the height of the success of spa towns, the seaside resort began to emerge. This would lead to the decline and transformation of spa towns during the 19th century. In Chapter 4, the origins of the seaside resort will be explored and central to this story is Scarborough. In the 1660s, at least one local doctor was using seawater to treat his gout. By 1700 seawater was being considered by scientists and doctors in a similar fashion to mineral waters, leading Sir John Floyer to declare that the sea around Britain could be the nation's bath. This simple assertion would underpin the birth of the seaside resort.

4

The Georgian seaside

By the mid-18th century, a number of coastal towns had begun to welcome people wishing to bathe in the sea. As was discussed in Chapter 3, mineral waters had been seen as the cure of choice, prompting the growth of a number of spa towns. The development of seaside resorts would follow a similar pattern of discovery, recognition and the patronage of aristocrats and, more desirably, royalty. The discovery phase in the case of the sea was a realisation that seawater could have a similar medicinal impact to spa waters, while also yielding profits. It often required works by local doctors espousing the virtues of the particular location, as well as explaining how seawater should be used, for an individual resort to prosper in the 18th century. Bathing machines and bathhouses were created ostensibly to aid sea bathers, but they also allowed doctors and entrepreneurs to monetise the sea.

The healthy reputation of a town and the provision of suitable bathing facilities were the first steps to attracting visitors, but these arrivals also expected to be entertained and accommodated in some comfort. Initially this involved using adapted buildings and existing homes, but as visitor numbers increased, and tourists predictably returned each year, investors, initially local innkeepers and householders, were increasingly willing to invest in new buildings. As early as the 1760s, the first large-scale developments were beginning to appear in port towns and by the early 19th century the largest developments were the size of towns, and were being constituted as separate administrative entities. By the end of the 18th century, some resorts were also being established independently of ports, either through the provision of bathing hotels around which housing and facilities gradually clustered or through the creation of entirely new settlements.

As well as following comparable stages in their development, seaside resorts also adopted a daily timetable similar to spas, with a programme also sometimes regulated by a Master of Cere-

monies. Beginning in the morning with bathing before breakfast, the period until dinner (in the early afternoon during the 18th century) was spent socialising in circulating libraries, coffee houses and assembly rooms, if a subscription was paid. After dinner the socialising continued, sometimes at a theatre, an increasingly common feature of resorts from the late 18th century onwards. The small number of wealthy tourists in the early 18th century had grown by the early 19th century as the country's population and prosperity increased, but also as transport improved and investment in facilities became more reliably profitable. Even before railways transformed the way that people travelled around Britain, the first signs of a form of mass tourism were evident and were already helping to transform the small ports of the early 18th century into the large seaside resorts of the 19th century.

The origins of sea bathing in England

Medical writers began to advocate seawater as a treatment from the second half of the 16th century, contemporary with the earliest writings promoting the waters of Bath and Buxton. Thomas Vicary, the Sergeant Chirurgion (d 1561), recommended that a patient should stand in a cold seawater bath for 'three or fower howers or more, and he shall be perfectly holpe [healthy]', while in 1578, the French Royal Surgeon, Ambroise Paré, advised Henry III of France (1551–89) to bathe in the sea at Dieppe to cure 'tormenting' and skin diseases.[1] In 1581, writer and headmaster Richard Mulcaster (1531/2–1611) advocated swimming in the sea for medical conditions, a treatise of 1610 recommended seawater, or water combined with salt, as a treatment for impotence in horses, and a revised 1613 edition of Vicary's book prescribed sea bathing for 'the Itche', probably scabies.[2]

Physicians were also beginning to recognise the restorative qualities of the coastal environment. Henry Manship (c 1550–1625), in his history of Great Yarmouth, Norfolk, in 1619, referred to doctors in Cambridge who sent patients there 'to take the air of the sea'.[3]

Political upheavals during the mid-17th century inevitably interrupted the exploration of seawater bathing, but by the end of the century a number of medical writers were again recommending seawater. In 1660, Dr Robert Wittie (bap 1613, d 1684), while promoting the spa at Scarborough, warned that internal consumption of seawater could be detrimental to health, but in the 1667 edition of his book, he noted that seawater bathing had rid him of his gout.[4] By around 1700, Sir John Floyer (1649–1734) had emerged as the leading advocate of cold-water bathing. He was the first writer to explicitly realise that the sea could act as a huge bath, noting, 'Since we live in an Island, and have the Sea about us, we cannot want an excellent Cold Bath, which will both preserve our Healths, and cure many Diseases, as our Fountains do.'[5] Floyer recommended that sea bathing should last for only two to three minutes. It should be undertaken only before dinner or after fasting and the bathing programme should consist of nine or ten dips at least two or three times a week.[6] He also suggested that bathing between June and September would be safest.[7]

By the early 18th century, there is evidence that sea bathing was spreading to ordinary people. Sea bathing was common on the Lancashire coast at the August spring tide, when it was believed that the waters had special powers of purification and regeneration.[8] This may have been part of an established local tradition, but would not necessarily have left any mark in early published sources. However, the *Great Diurnal* of Nicholas Blundell (1669–1737), who lived at Crosby Hall, near Liverpool, recorded several visits to the seaside at this time of year (Fig 4.1), some for no specific reason, but on other occasions he was there to shoot game. His first recorded venture into the sea occurred on 5 August 1708: 'Mr Aldred & I Rode to the Sea & baithed ourselves.'[9] No ailments were mentioned and therefore he may have been there for pleasure during hot weather, but a year later, Blundell's children bathed on three consecutive days to cure 'some out breacks'.[10] That his earliest reference to sea bathing occurred in 1708, six years after his diary began, could be seen as an indication that sea bathing was not yet an approved treatment in 1702, but within a few years it had achieved some medical respectability.

In 1718, Samuel Jones, a customs officer at Whitby, praised the spa waters and the sea for curing jaundice.[11] In Lincolnshire, the earliest reference to sea bathing is in a letter dated 2 May 1725. Mrs Massingberd of Gunby described how 'Sr Hardolf Wastnage & his lady come in Whitsun week to a farmhouse in this neighbourhood to spend three months in order to bath in ye sea'.[12]

This handful of references suggests that bathing might occur wherever someone wanted to go in the sea, a convenient house being the only facility required. However, scattered references

Fig 4.1
The Blundell family appear to have visited the stretch of coast nearest their house, possibly Crosby Beach, where Antony Gormley's atmospheric Another Place *art installation has become a modern place of pilgrimage. [DP034504]*

and the absence of any mention of sea bathing in major travelogues of the early 18th century by writer and spy John Macky (d 1726) and novelist Daniel Defoe (1660–1731) suggest it was still only an occasional practice. Yet by the 1730s it is clear that sea bathing was beginning to spread nationally and would grow in popularity to transform many coastal towns.

Ports and the origin of seaside resorts

Scarborough, like Whitby, could make use of mineral waters as well as seawater to cure patients and by the 1730s there is also evidence of organised sea bathing at Margate and Brighton. Scarborough's first 'guidebook' was published in 1734; a year later an engraving depicted people bathing in the sea (Fig 4.2), while annual miscellanies of poems were being published describing the resort's lively social life.[13] The guidebook provides the first description of sea bathing at Scarborough, noting:

It is the custom for not only gentlemen, but the ladies also, to bathe in the seas; the gentlemen go out a little way to sea in boats (called here 'cobbles') and jump in naked directly ... The ladies have the conveniency of gowns and guides. There are two little houses on the shore, to retire for dressing in.[14]

In 1736, a visitor to Brighton described how his family were 'sunning ourselves on the beach' after their 'morning business' of 'bathing in the sea'.[15] Margate was sufficiently busy in 1730 to attract a theatre company to perform during the summer and in 1736 a seaside bathhouse was advertised in local papers.[16]

While modern seaside resorts may be the obvious place to look for the origins of sea bathing, in the 18th century these resorts were active ports and therefore it is perhaps not surprising that there is evidence of a short-lived sea bathing culture at Liverpool.[17] As a growing port, Liverpool could offer residents and visitors accommodation and entertainment venues as well as bathing facilities. The earliest reference to sea bathing is on 2 August 1721 when Nicholas Blundell wrote in his journal, 'I went with Pat: Acton to Leverpoole & Procured him a Place to Lodg at & a Conveniency for baithing in the Sea.'[18] The word 'Conveniency' is being used here for something that hasn't yet acquired a name – it refers to something to aid bathing, probably a bathing machine. A similar use of the word appears in 1735, when Dr Peter Shaw (1694–1763) writes about sea bathing at Scarborough: 'The Ladies have Guides, Rooms, and Conveniences for it, under the Cliff.'[19] Artist John Setterington's view of Scarborough (see Fig 4.2), published in 1735, contains a visual clue to the word 'Conveniences'.[20] It depicts a naked man emerging from a primitive bathing

Fig 4.2
This detail from John Setterington's View of the antient Town, Castle, Harbour, and Spaw of Scarborough *(1735) shows bathers entering the sea from small boats and emerging from a primitive bathing machine.* [CC80/00145]

Fig 4.3
Samuel and Nathaniel Buck's engraving of the river frontage, The South-West Prospect of Liverpoole *(1728), shows the bathhouse as a small, rectangular building standing on its own beside the river, at the far left of this engraving.*
[BB86/03830]

machine and this seems to be the only 'Convenience' to which Shaw can be referring.

As well as the bathing machine, Liverpool had a pioneering role in the provision of bathhouses. Its earliest bathhouses were in the centre of town, convenient for residents and users of the port.[21] However, by the 1720s a new bathhouse had been built to the north-west of the town and this was where bathing machines were available later in the century (Fig 4.3).[22]

By the 19th century, bathhouses were elaborate, specialised structures, but in the mid-18th century they were still essentially domestic buildings housing small, single baths. For instance, Quebec House, beside the docks at Portsmouth, appears to be a house in general form and scale, but is actually a bathhouse dating from 1754, the earliest surviving seaside example in Britain (Fig 4.4).

The original location for sea bathing at Liverpool and Portsmouth has long been swallowed up by port development, and this has also occurred at Southampton, where George II's son Frederick Prince of Wales (1707–51) bathed in the sea in 1750.[23] In 1750, Leith, beside Edinburgh, was said to be the site for 'dooking' (sea bathing) and by the beginning of the 19th century, Dover, Harwich, Plymouth and Swansea also had a significant sea bathing element to their economy, the latter against a background of dramatic skies caused by copper smelting.[24]

These large ports were also pioneering resorts, though dock expansion during the 19th century has removed most of the physical evidence. However, a number of other, smaller ports and coastal towns were beginning the reorientation of their economy towards leisure. On the Kent

coast, visitors were staying at Margate, Ramsgate, Folkestone and Deal by the end of the 18th century, while in Sussex, Brighton, Hastings, Seahouses near Eastbourne, and Worthing were hosting visitors by the 1750s.[25] Great Yarmouth, a port focused on its river since the Middle Ages, erected its first baths on the undeveloped seashore by 1759 and a theatre was built in 1778.[26] In 1750, Exmouth, in Devon, was being visited by Exeter inhabitants in search of improved health.[27] The earliest reference to sea bathing at Weymouth, in Dorset, dates from 1748: 'R Prowse and Jos Bennet had twenty-one year leases granted to them, so that they might erect

Fig 4.4
Quebec House in Portsmouth, photographed from a passing ferry, is now an isolated fragment of the Georgian town surrounded by modern housing. (Quebec House is the white building in the foreground, with a modern pool.)
[© Author]

two wooden bathing houses on the N side of the Harbour.'[28] In 1754, Reinhold Rücker Angerstein (1718–60), a Swedish metallurgist, civil servant and entrepreneur, described the scene he witnessed, including early bathing machines.[29]

England led the way in pointing patients towards the sea, but by the second half of the 18th century, a number of references suggest a similar process was under way in Scotland. Bathing was taking place at Leith, near Edinburgh, from 1750, though nearby Portobello became more popular towards the end of the 18th century.[30] At the port town of Peterhead, in Aberdeenshire, a bathhouse was built in 1762 to supplement the facilities already provided at its spa, and at Elie, in Fife, sea bathing was mentioned during the 1790s.[31] Novelist Sir Walter Scott (1771–1832) bathed in the sea at Prestonpans, in East Lothian, in 1777 or 1778 and an English visitor to Brodie Castle went to Lossiemouth, in Moray, to bathe in the sea in 1790.[32] The relative lateness of Scotland heading to the sea is illustrated by the fact that Dr William Buchan's *Domestic Medicine*, first published in 1769, did not include a chapter on sea bathing

until its ninth edition in 1786.[33] At Tenby, in Pembrokeshire, the earliest references to sea bathing are in the 1760s and 1780s, and by 1791 a guidebook suggests that the first facilities for it were in place. Wales also has other pre-1800 references to sea bathing at Aberystwyth and at Swansea, suggesting that it was widespread by then, at least in the southern half of the country.[34]

An alternative to ports

During the mid-18th century, the ports of Scarborough, Bridlington and Whitby were the main places where sea bathing was being enjoyed in the north of England, but Blackpool was beginning its slow emergence as a resort on the west coast, independent of any port or harbour (Fig 4.5). The earliest reliable reference to sea-bathing visitors at Blackpool is by Bishop Richard Pococke (1704–65) in June 1754, who recorded, 'At Blackpool, near the sea, are accommodations for people who come to bathe.'[35] In 1788 historian William Hutton (1723–1815) said that the

Fig 4.5
This view of Blackpool by Edward Finden (1840) shows the scatter of houses along the cliff top that had gradually been added since the mid-18th century. At the left end, beside a large Georgian house, can be seen the thatched roof of a vernacular building, a type once common in the Fylde. [Author's collection]

only place where visitors could have stayed in Blackpool 40 years ago was the Foxhall, the former seat of the Tyldesley family. In 1821, newspaper proprietor, politician and historian Edward Baines (1774–1848) said that Blackpool as 'a place of fashionable resort for the recovery of health is not of more than seventy years standing', again suggesting a mid-18th-century origin for the emergence of the resort.[36] Blackpool's coastline was largely uninhabited, though there were nearby hamlets and a small village at Poulton-le-Fylde. Its growth, albeit slow, demonstrates that by the mid-18th century there was sufficient interest in sea bathing to encourage people to visit stretches of coastline with limited facilities. By the 1780s various large houses were serving as hotels and as entertainment facilities for the wealthier patrons.[37]

At nearby Southport, there was also no port on which to graft a resort and therefore a bathing house was built in 1792 by William Sutton (1753–1840), followed by his hotel in 1798. A range of other facilities accrued gradually during the early 19th century.[38]

In East Anglia, Old South End, a small hamlet around a farmhouse, began to develop in the mid-18th century as a resort.[39] A large house, built before 1758, had become the Ship Inn by 1764 and in 1768 South End was first recognised as a separate administrative entity. Lincolnshire faced a similar lack of ports to colonise for leisure and came up with similar solutions. By 1673, the New Inn at Saltfleet was being visited by local gentry who wished to eat fresh fish.[40] In the mid-18th century, an L-shaped wing was added facing the sea, including a first-floor dining room with bow windows, providing views of the sea. The tiny resort at Freiston Shore, also in Lincolnshire, was described as a place where 'a number of tradesmen and farmers resorted with their wives, in hopes of receiving benefit from the use of the salt water'.[41] Visitors could stay at two sea-bathing hotels or at a few lodging houses. Plummer's Hotel, built in the early 18th century, probably as a house, was extended during the late 18th century, but the Marine Hotel was erected in the late 18th century specifically for the sea-bathing trade. It was three storeys high, providing not only a substantial amount of accommodation, but also views of the sea over the adjacent sea bank.

These Lincolnshire examples never developed into popular destinations, but some of the county's main resorts also began as the sites of sea-bathing hotels. In 1797, diarist and lead manufacturer Abigail Gawthern (1757–1822) spent much of August at Sutton-on-Sea, probably at the Jolly Bacchus Hotel.[42] The village of Mablethorpe at the beginning of the 19th century had a 'bathing house', presumably the Book in Hand Hotel, which was being visited by people from Louth, while Cleethorpes had an inn established around 1760.[43] A map of 1779 shows that Skegness was a small, inland settlement, but a short distance to the south, and closer to the sea, there was a 'Bathing House and Tavern', the Vine Hotel, which had been built in 1770.[44]

The science of seawater

These developments indicate that the seaside was more than just a fad and would become a fundamental part of Georgian life. The growing popularity of the seaside was underpinned, as spas had been, by a growing body of scientific and medical literature, as well as doctors and entrepreneurs who found ways to profit from the natural practice of bathing in the sea. The works of Floyer and other medical writers reveal the strength of the emerging science that encouraged the observation of the impact of seawater bathing on ordinary people, and prompted experiments to try to prove its curative value. Floyer cited the case of a local fisherman who claimed to be more than 140 years old, a feat achieved despite his diet being 'Coarse and Sowr' because 'he frequently swam in the Rivers after he was past the Age of One hundred Years'.[45] At Brighton, Dr Richard Russell (1687–1759) observed the women working on the seashore to prove that the sea and sea air were good for health.[46]

As well as making observations, some medical writers carried out experiments to determine why seawater had beneficial effects. In 1735, Dr Shaw at Scarborough studied seawater's salts after evaporation and the weight of seawater, as he believed seawater could exert a greater pressure on the body, forcing the water through the pores to dilute the blood and improve its circulation.[47] Dr Russell believed that the sea was enriched with particles supplied by 'Submarine Plants, Salts, Fishes, Minerals, &c' that could cure illnesses.[48] The most widely held opinion was that bathing in cold water stimulated the circulation of the blood, an effect that raised fears in some people, though Dr John Anderson (c 1730–1804) at Margate reassured his patients, pointing out the fertility of female guides who accompanied bathers into the sea.[49] At Scarborough in the mid-18th century, the improved flow of blood, particularly around the male body, was reputedly the key to improving the libido, though the presence of women bathing in the sea in thin, clinging, linen slips would have also served to sharpen male appetites.[50]

The 'scientific' opinions of medical writers filtered their way down to ordinary sea bathers. In the 1770s, author and painter George Keate (1729–97) described an amusing conversation that he apparently overheard in one of the bathing rooms in Margate. Opinions among the bathers were 'that it thinned and it thickened the blood – it strengthened – it weakened – it made people fat – it made them lean – it braced – it relaxed – it was good for every thing – and good for nothing. – *It will wash you all clean*, however, says a grave gentleman in the gallery, if it does nothing else.'[51]

Although there might be differences of opinion about why bathing improved health, there was widespread agreement that it should take place during the morning. Dr Thomas Reid recommended that it should occur before the sun had a deleterious effect on the sea and Dr John Crane warned against a 'great depression of the spirits' if bathing took place later in the day.[52] These explanations might be medical, but another reason for bathing early was to leave the remainder of the day free to socialise and enjoy the entertainments that resorts had to offer. Dr Belcombe at Scarborough in the early 19th century asserted, 'Bathing can be performed at all times of tide, and in almost all kinds of weather, with security and ease. The morning, however, in general is the most convenient time for bathing; as it leaves the rest of the day for other exercises and amusements.'[53]

Fig 4.6
James Theobald's drawing (1750s), which was inserted into a book in the Society of Antiquaries, shows a bathing machine in the harbour at Margate.
[By kind permission of the Society of Antiquaries of London]

a View of Margate Peer & Harbour.

Bathing machines and bathhouses – profiting from the sea

James Rymer (fl 1770–1842), a naval surgeon, bemoaned the fact that an infrastructure was needed for bathing in the sea, saying, 'I would prefer the "crystal pool" and salubrious sea to all cisterns and reservoirs whatever. But delicacy and the valetudinarian state are here excepted: to such we recommend bathing houses, machines, and such like.'[54] While bathing machines, bathhouses and bathing rooms (waiting rooms for bathing machines) might seem medical in nature, many were in the hands of entrepreneurs rather than doctors, and were a means to make money from the sea.

The first primitive bathing machines were simple boxes or carts; the form of the earliest depiction at Scarborough suggests a simple shed, while Zechariah Brazier, the first Margate guide, took bathers into the sea in a 'simple machine, a cart'.[55] In 1753, Benjamin Beale added a concertina, canvas hood at the rear of a vehicle at Margate, allowing a modest bather to enter the sea unseen, as well as providing some protection from wind and waves. Merchant, antiquary and amateur artist James Theobald (bap 1688, d 1759) depicted a bathing machine in the 1750s (Fig 4.6). His drawing was accompanied by a description of how the 'Bathing Waggons' operated:

The above is a View of the Machine to bath with, it contains a Room to undress and dress in with Steps to go down into the Sea [. It] will hold 5 or 6 People. There are men and Women Guides who if desired attend. The price is 4 shillings a Week or £1 1s for Six Weeks and you pay your Guide for every attendance. They drive into [the] sea till it is about breast high and then lets down the Screen which prevents being seen under which you go down the Steps into a fine sandy bottom.[56]

Richard Pococke was also among the first to describe the use of bathing machines at Margate, in September 1754:

This is a fishing town, and is of late much resorted to by company to drink the sea water, as well as to bathe; for the latter they have the conveniency of cover'd carriages, at the end of which there is a covering that lets down with hoops, so that people can go down a ladder into the water and are not seen, and those who please may jump in and swim.[57]

When Angerstein visited Scarborough in 1754, his two views of the town show four-wheeled bathing machines, much as Setterington depicted them almost 20 years before.[58] Beale's novel hood had not yet arrived at Scarborough. This innovation had reached Brighton by the 1760s as Dr John Awsiter recommended that half the bathing machines should be fitted with 'skreens ... somewhat after the manner of those at Margate'.[59] The bathing machine was such an odd way to head into the sea that guidebooks, such as Margate's earliest ones in the 1760s, provided descriptions of how to use them and novelist Tobias Smollett (1721–71) included a lengthy passage explaining this oddity in *The Expedition of Humphry Clinker* (1771).[60]

Proof of bathing machines' peculiarity is also suggested by the fact that it was recommended they should be used under the direction of guides, often referred to as 'dippers' (Fig 4.7), though guides also had a role in safeguarding the bathers in the sea and even enforcing gender segregation on the beach.[61] Some dippers came to be admired for their medical knowledge; in 1795 Dr Anderson cited the opinions of a number of guides who had witnessed the positive effects of seawater on the health of their invalid customers.[62]

As resorts grew in popularity, the number of bathing machines increased. At Sidmouth, in Devon, in 1762, the fledgling resort offered two bathing machines on the beach, but by 1817, this number had risen to 16.[63] Between the mid-1790s and the early 1830s, the number of bathing machines at Hastings, in East Sussex, rose from around a dozen to more than 30 and by the mid-1850s Weston-super-Mare, in Somerset, could boast 50 bathing machines.[64] By the late 19th century, the beach of every major resort was dominated visually and often practically by bathing machines (Fig 4.8). However, at some busy

Fig 4.7
The most famous dipper was probably Martha Gunn, who is buried in St Nicholas' churchyard, Brighton. She died on 2 May 1815, aged 88, after serving as a guide for nearly 70 years.
[From Horsfield 1835, 143]

Fig 4.8
This late 19th-century view of Scarborough shows the busy beach, with more than 60 bathing machines in and out of the sea.
[BB67/08931c]

Fig 4.9
This photograph of
Margate's High Street in
the late 19th century shows
the bathing rooms on the
left side of the street.
Although these have now
gone, they have left their
imprint on the street in a
series of single-storey shops.
[BB67/08933]

rooms into bathhouses offering a wide range of treatments (Fig 4.9).

The term 'bathing room' was used in other resorts, but in most cases it seems it simply referred to a bathhouse. However, around 1795 improvements were made at Ramsgate 'for the accommodation of the company, while waiting for their machines'.[70] An engraving published in 1782 depicts a few weatherboard huts from which bathers passed via wooden gangplanks on to the beach, where they could board bathing machines.[71] At Broadstairs, in Kent, there were waiting rooms at the bathing place beside the harbour, while at Hastings, the waiting room in 1797 was described as 'a small box, called the bathing-room, for the use of the company while waiting for the machines'.[72]

Bathing rooms appear to have been limited to a handful of the busier resorts in the south-east of England, but bathhouses were available around the coast. The earliest written description of a seaside bathhouse is in 1736 at Margate: 'This is to inform all Persons, that Thomas Barber, Carpenter, at Margate in the Isle of Thanett, hath lately made a very convenient Bath, into which the Sea Water runs through a Canal about 15 Foot long. You descend into the Bath from a private Room adjoining to it.'[73] In a 1737 advertisement for his expanded facility, the baths were described as being accompanied by 'Lodging Rooms, Dressing Rooms, and a handsome large sash'd Dining Room' and 'a Summer House ... which affords a pleasant Prospect out to Sea'.[74] A further reference in 1740 to the baths described them as 'quite enclosed, and covered by a handsome Dining Room; and that there is a neat Dressing Room, and Dresses, adjoining to the Bath; and as the House fronts the Sea, there is a most delightful Prospect'.[75] Like the bathhouse at Liverpool and Quebec House at Portsmouth, this was essentially a domestic structure, probably an adapted house containing small single baths. The larger pool would be a phenomenon that emerged later as seaside bathhouses became more sophisticated in terms of their facilities and grander architecturally.

Bathhouses were provided for people unwilling or unable to enjoy cold water, offering some measure of comfort and increased safety compared to dipping in the sea. The consensus of Georgian medical writers was that people should bathe in cold water, but Dr John Awsiter at Brighton in the 1760s suggested that a warm bath might more effectively open the pores and allow saltwater to penetrate the skin, while

locations there was a struggle to meet the demand in the mornings, when sea bathing was advised.

At Margate the number of bathing machines rose from 11 in 1763 to 30 in 1790 and 40 in 1793.[65] Nevertheless, this was never sufficient to meet demand and so bathing rooms were established, waiting rooms where bathers could socialise, read newspapers and play music while they waited for a machine. The earliest reference to one at Margate is in 1753, when a group of local men signed a 21-year lease on a plot of land 'to build and erect a waiting Room for Bathing in the sea at his and their own Expense, Cost and Charges'.[66] Two years later, a similar lease was signed for another plot and by 1763 three bathing rooms were available.[67] In 1770, five bathing rooms were served by 20 bathing machines and by 1797 there were seven such rooms, with at least one of these also providing heated saltwater baths.[68] In 1808, a storm destroyed many of the buildings on Margate's seafront, but in 1822 there were still six bathing rooms at the foot of the High Street.[69] By this date they also provided warm and cold baths, shower baths and a vapour bath; they had effectively evolved from waiting

Dr Thomas Reid in Kent observed that a warm bath heated to between 90°F and 100°F (32°C–38°C) could benefit those weakened by disease as warm water could be a sedative.[76] Awsiter's opinion may have been based on medical experience, but he was also keen to promote this form of bathing to encourage people to use his proposed bathhouse. In 1768, he published a blueprint for one and a year later erected the first bathhouse in Brighton at the southern end of the Steine, the most fashionable part of the resort (Fig 4.10).[77] A description in 1780 recorded, 'On one side of a spacious vestibule are six cold-baths; and on the other side are the hot baths, sweating bath, and showering-bath. The baths are supplied with water from the sea by means of an engine.'[78]

Early bathhouses were adaptations of an existing structure or at best a small-scale, new building, a reflection of the number of patrons and the likely financial returns for investors. However, by the early 19th century bathhouses were becoming larger, architecturally grander and more multifunctional in character. In the mid-1820s, the Pelham Baths, erected along with Pelham Crescent at Hastings, was regarded as the finest facility in the town: 'The Entrance is by a spacious stone hall, which leads into two handsome saloons, of an octagonal form and decorated with beautiful Chinese scenery ... Here are eleven warm baths – two vapour – two shower – and a fine plunging bath.'[79] By the 1830s, in nearby St Leonards, the bathhouse offered 11 baths, shower baths and a plunge bath.[80] It had a small central, elliptical projection facing seawards and at either end were pedimented pavilions, conscious echoes of small Greek temples.

Combining baths with rational, genteel entertainments such as a library was a means to improve profits by making the building work for the entire day and evening. The Clifton Baths at Margate, begun in 1824 and completed by 1831, was an exclusive and innovative bathhouse that combined health and leisure facilities with storage space for bathing machines (Fig 4.11).[81] Another way to increase income was to accommodate visitors. In July 1820, Howe's Baths in Weston-super-Mare opened on Knightstone Island, which was accessible only at low tide at this date.[82] Howe also erected a two-storey house, part of which was used as lodgings while

Fig 4.10
Dr Awsiter's bathhouse, attributed to architect Robert Golden (c 1738– 1809), was rectangular in plan and had a neo- classical facade that included a pediment with dentil cornice. This was a very grand finish to a very modest building. [Courtesy of Sue Berry]

Fig 4.11
The Clifton Baths at Margate were excavated from a chalk cliff near the harbour and were constructed in a circular form topped with a domed room that contained newspapers, an organ and a billiard table. [Author's collection]

the rest served as public tea and coffee rooms and a reading room. In September 1830 the site was purchased by Dr Edward Long Fox (1761–1835) and together with his son Dr Francis Ker Fox, he built a new bathhouse in 1832. As well as baths and shower baths, the building included a reading room, three sitting rooms, seven bedrooms and a suite of service rooms (Fig 4.12).

Bathhouses like Dr Fox's had begun to diversify into a wider range of cures that were edging towards modern pampering treatments. In the early 1820s, Deen Mahomed (1759–1851; *see* p 171) erected a bathhouse at Brighton in which he offered his 'shampooing' treatments, involving massaging with scented oils.[83] In contrast, other bathhouses sought to broaden their appeal by becoming more medical in character. Weymouth's new bathhouse of 1842 combined 10 white, marble baths with attached dressing rooms on either side of the central corridor with public rooms, the Literary and Scientific Institute, an eye infirmary and the Royal Dispensary.[84]

Fig 4.12
The plan of Dr Fox's Baths on Knightstone Island, at Weston-super-Mare, as it was arranged in 1860 reveals that men (on the left) were separated from women by the central entrance hall. [DMP/DFB001]

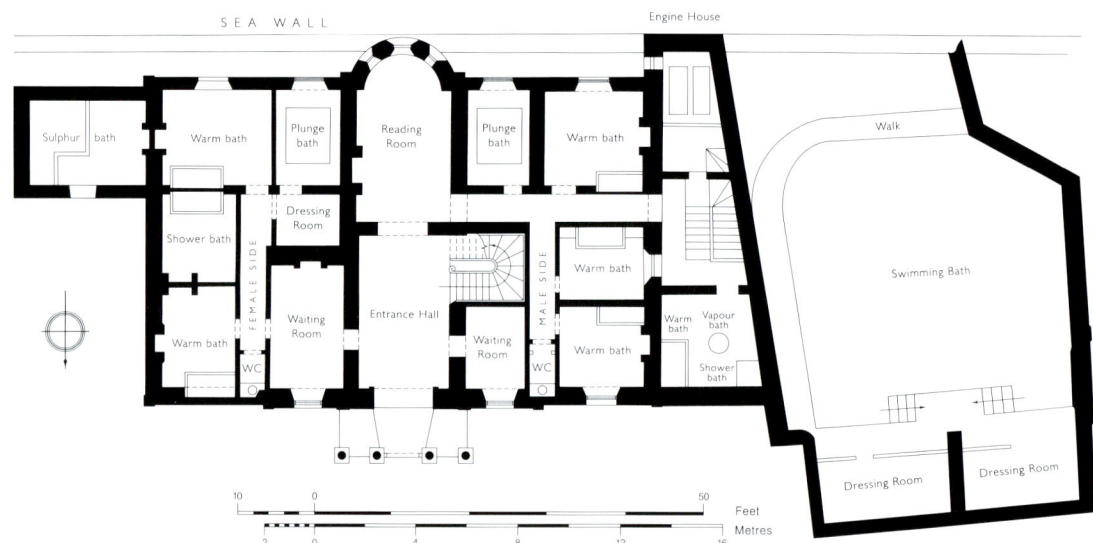

Facilities for visitors

To prosper, nascent resorts needed to provide suitable entertainment facilities and accommodation to attract tourists, and perhaps more importantly to attract them back each year. These first resorts were mostly small working towns, or 'fishing holes' as soldier and diarist John Byng (1743–1813) described them.[85] John Macky saw Margate in the early 18th century as 'a poor pitiful Place' and Revd John Lewis in 1736 recorded that it was 'irregularly built, and the Houses generally old and low'.[86] Something of the character of these original towns can still be experienced in the Lanes at Brighton (Fig 4.13), in the old town at Margate (Fig 4.14) or behind the harbour at Scarborough, where small, vernacular buildings in small plots line narrow streets.

The arrival of visitors transformed the buildings, facilities, activities and behaviours in coastal towns previously dominated by commerce and fishing. The model for this process was the spa town, with its range of facilities and the timetable of its day. Bathing in the morning left the rest of the day free for varied social encounters and more or less formal entertainments. 'Scarborough: A Poem', published in 1732, celebrated the town of 'Health and Mirth' that audaciously claimed to rival Bath.[87] As its spa had been attracting visitors since the mid-17th century, Scarborough already provided a range of facilities required by its aristocratic clientele.[88] In the 1730s, it could offer a bookshop that served as a primitive form of circulating library, a coffee house, theatrical entertainments and an assembly room, which was described as 'a noble, spacious building, sixty two Foot long, thirty wide, and sixteen high', with a 'Musick-Gallery' and attached card rooms.[89]

By paying a subscription, visitors could enjoy circulating libraries, coffee houses and assembly rooms. Circulating libraries and coffee houses could be housed in any suitable building, though by the late 18th century some leading resorts were providing elegant, purpose-built libraries. The Hawley Square library of 1786 was the grandest one built in Margate and arguably one of the finest ever built at a seaside resort.[90] Its main space was 42ft square (12.8m) and was divided transversely by a row of Corinthian columns that separated the library from the shop.[91] In the centre of the shop was a dome, 18ft (5.5m) in diameter, topped by an octagonal lantern 8ft (2.4m) high, while in the centre of the library

Fig 4.13
Meeting House Lane, in the Lanes of Brighton, shows the narrowness of the streets of the historic town, which still contain a number of timber-framed buildings.
[DP017965]

Fig 4.14
The old town at Margate retains a handful of buildings that provide a glimpse of the types of structures that were initially used as lodgings, including timber-framed houses, as well as some with knapped-flint facades such as this house in King Street.
[AA050591]

Fig 4.15
This is a rare surviving purpose-built circulating library in Regent Street in Teignmouth. Erected in 1815, it was later taken over by WHSmith, which began operating a circulating library chain in 1860. The architect was William Edward Rolfe. [AA046140]

Fig 4.16
This is the facade, designed by John Crunden, of the former Castle Tavern in Montpelier Place, Brighton. The monumental classical detailing is a strong indication of the status that the institution had achieved by 1776. [DP17962]

there was a chandelier.[92] The library had chimney pieces depicting 'the history of the Muses in the frieze'.[93] Externally the building had a colonnade around it. Unfortunately, purpose-built circulating libraries such as this have rarely survived at seaside resorts, but at Teignmouth, in Devon, one remains to provide an impression of their impact on Georgian resorts (Fig 4.15).

In the early stages of resort development, new facilities were created in adapted buildings, but as local entrepreneurs became more confident of a return on their investment, new purpose-built structures were erected. For instance, the need for an assembly room was initially recognised by enterprising innkeepers who converted outbuildings. In 1763 an assembly room was established in Margate at the New Inn on the Parade and in 1772 Thomas Hovenden held his first assembly at the Swan Inn in Hastings in 'a suitable room, with a gallery for music'.[94] Brighton was sufficiently popular to sustain two assembly rooms. The Castle Tavern was operating by 1754, though a prestigious new facade, designed by John Crunden (c 1741–1835) in around 1776 implies a substantial growth in its business (Fig 4.16).[95] In 1761, John Hicks of the Old Ship Inn opened new assembly rooms in Brighton.[96] German author Johanna Schopenhauer (1766–1838), writing later in the 18th century, described both:

> The Assembly rooms are in two taverns or inns, The Castle Tavern and The Old Ship Tavern. In the first, one may play cards and there is a coffee-house with a billiard-table and that sort of thing. The second is similar but has the advantage of accommodation for visitors although we thought the reception inferior to what we had met elsewhere in England. The rooms of both places consist, as do those in Bath, of a dance hall and several adjoining rooms for playing cards, taking tea and making conversation. All are prettily decorated and usefully furnished.[97]

Margate's new assembly rooms in Cecil Square, built around 1769, were probably the grandest of the period at a seaside resort. The main external feature was 'a large piazza', a deep colonnade, facing the square.[98] The main assembly room on the first floor measured 87ft (26.5m) long and 43ft (13.1m) wide, apparently making it one of the largest in the country, and there were adjacent rooms for taking tea, and playing cards.[99] The main rooms were described as being decorated 'with rich chimney-pieces, compartments, beautiful cornices, and expensive chandeliers and girandoles'.[100] Behind the

assembly room was a four-storey building that contained the accommodation of the tavern.

Most of the entertainment facilities were paid for by subscription, but in theatres anyone could purchase a ticket in a section of the auditorium that they could afford, bringing a carnival atmosphere to Georgian theatres. Like assembly rooms, the first theatres were in adapted buildings, often agricultural structures large enough to stage performances. In the 1760s Brighton had a makeshift theatre in a barn on the northwest corner of Castle Square and in 1788 Blackpool offered a similarly rudimentary facility. William Hutton said of it:

> Beauty displays itself in the dance, and the place is dignified with a Theatre; if that will bear the name which, during nine months in the year is only the threshing-floor of a barn … Rows of benches are placed one behind another, and honoured with the names of pit and gallery; the first two shillings, the other one. The house is said to hold six pounds; it was half filled.[101]

The earliest purpose-built theatres appeared at seaside resorts from the 1770s, once resorts were sufficiently large and popular to make investment worthwhile. The first performance at the future Theatre Royal in Weymouth was in 1771. At Brighton, a purpose-built playhouse was erected in North Street in 1773 by Samuel Paine, though it was superseded in 1789 by a larger one in Duke Street.[102] By 1778 a theatre, described as 'neat, and well adapted to its destination', had been built at Great Yarmouth.[103]

As well as entertainment venues, a supply of accommodation was crucial for resort development. When visitors first arrived they would normally stay in existing inns for short periods until they found longer-term accommodation in the homes of the resident population. To cater for new visitors at Scarborough, there were a number of 'ordinaries', taverns providing meals. In the 1734 guidebook, five ordinaries are listed, four of which can be identified on a 1725 map.[104] The first lodgings in seaside resorts were in small houses, even just cottages, but by the third quarter of the 18th century, there is evidence that some of the original vernacular houses of early resorts were being refurbished or rebuilt to cater for visitors. Dr Anthony Relhan recorded the start of this process at Brighton in the 1760s, noting, 'The town improves daily, as the inhabitants encouraged by the late great resort of

company, seem disposed to expend the whole of what they acquire in the erecting of new buildings, or making the old ones convenient.'[105] One of Weymouth's early guidebooks suggested, 'The inhabitants by such an influx of money have been encouraged to rebuild, repair, and greatly enlarge the town, which in little more than twenty years has undergone a considerable transformation.'[106] In All Saints Street in the old town of Hastings, the original pattern of medieval timber-framed houses is still clear, but some have been replaced by taller, more regular, brick Georgian houses.

The first new houses were cheap, modest in size and limited in architectural ambition, but by the 1760s a handful of wealthy people were prepared to erect more impressive buildings for their own use. East Cliff House (1760–62) was built on part of the East Fort at Hastings for Edward Capell, a Shakespearean scholar who spent his summers at the resort.[107] In 1766, Captain John Gould (1722–84), a wealthy tea-planter from India, returned to England and settled in Margate in India House, reputedly a copy of his home in Calcutta (Fig 4.17). However, the most prestigious of these early houses was probably Marlborough House on the fashionable Steine in Brighton, built between 1765 and 1769, but rebuilt in a grand style by Robert Adam in 1786–7 for the politician William Gerard Hamilton.[108]

Fig 4.17
Built at the edge of Margate's Old Town, India House has an odd plan, being single-storey at the front, with grand but small public rooms flanking a stair hall. The rear section consists of two low storeys, and contains bedrooms above service rooms. [AA050186]

Endorsement and patronage

These new houses are the first indication of the status of visitors seeking to live in resorts during the summer. By 1760, the Pelham family, which had close links to the royal family, were visiting Brighton, leading in 1765 to a visit by Prince William Henry, the Duke of Gloucester (1743–1805), a brother of George III. In 1783, the town enjoyed the first of many visits by George, Prince of Wales, the future George IV (1762–1830).[109] His presence guaranteed Brighton's position as the foremost resort in the late 18th century. Johanna Schopenhauer wrote, 'Brighton, twenty years ago a small, insignificant fishing village, is striking proof of miracles brought about by fashion ... When he [the Prince of Wales] was absent, the town was empty and desolate; only when he returned did life and pleasure reappear.'[110] In 1786 the prince leased a farmhouse on the Steine and in the following year Henry Holland (1745–1806) was employed to enlarge the building, creating a large, white-tiled, neo-classical design incorporating the original farmhouse as one of a pair of blocks separated by a central, domed structure. In 1815–22 John Nash (1752–1835) was employed to extend and transform the neo-classical house into a building combining Indian, Islamic and even Gothic detailing on the exterior, with lavish, predominantly Chinese, interiors (Fig 4.18).[111]

Weymouth also benefited from royal endorsement from an early date. The first celebrated patron to make regular visits to this small port was Ralph Allen (bap 1693, d 1764) from Bath, who had made a fortune from the postal service and later by having a near monopoly in the provision of building stone. His presence between 1750 and his death in 1764 led to growing numbers of wealthy patrons visiting Weymouth, including the Duke of Gloucester, who built a house on the seafront in the early 1780s. It was this grand, end-of-terrace house that accommodated George III during his 10-week stay in 1789.[112] From 1791 to 1802 the king returned each summer, except 1793, and in 1801 he bought Gloucester Lodge from his brother (Fig 4.19). A late 18th-century guidebook to Weymouth noted, proudly:

Fig 4.18
The Royal Pavilion at Brighton was the most elaborate oriental building of its period. The basic structure of the neo-classical house is still obvious beneath the oriental veneer.
[FF98/00167]

Fig 4.19
In 1802, Weymouth town
council decided to
commemorate the visits
of George III with a statute
on the seafront, but it took
until 1810 for this to be
completed, five years after
his last visit to the resort.
[DP058189]

middle-class visitors, including London shop-keepers.[115] Guidebooks and poems refer, usually unflatteringly, to the social range of Margate's visitors, especially after steamers were introduced in the early 19th century, though there was already evidence of Margate's social diversity even in the 1770s. George Keate wrote:

> The decent tradesman slips from town for his half crown, and strolls up and down the Parade as much at ease as he treads his own shop. – His wife, who perhaps never eloped so far from the metropolis before, stares with wonder at the many new objects which surround her ... The farmer's rosy-cheeked daughter crosses the island on her pillion, impatient to peep at the London females .... The Londoner views with a disdainful surprise, the awkward straw hat, and exposed ruddy countenance of the rustic nymph; who in turn scrutinizes the inexplicable coiffure of her criticiser.[116]

Margate was the first resort to enjoy a form of mass tourism. The substantial number of visitors meant that Margate was the first town in which significant development took place beyond the footprint of the original historic settlement. This breach of the old town's plan echoes how the construction of Queen Square qualitatively marked a new phase of development at Bath in the late 1720s.[117] In 1769, Cecil Square was laid out in Margate by 'Mr Cecil', Sir John Shaw, Sir Edward Hales and several other gentlemen, the first new square built at a seaside resort: 'The new-square, which is a large one, principally built by Mr Cecil, an eminent attorney in Norfolk-street, in the Strand, consists of some very handsome houses, intended for the reception of the nobility and gentry (Fig 4.20).'[118]

At other resorts, terraced houses began to be built along the seafront. In Weymouth, the first of a series of terraces was constructed to the north of the historic town during the 1780s and by the early 19th century, long terraces, squares and crescents, with houses intended to accommodate visitors during the summer, were being erected at resorts all around the coast of England. At Brighton, the New Steine (1790), the Royal Crescent (1795–6) and Bedford Square (1801) were built and, after peace resumed following the Napoleonic Wars, the first large-scale seafront development was Regency Square in 1818.[119]

The impetus for development being felt in established resorts was beginning to stimulate

It is indeed astonishing, that a place which a few years since consisted of very little else than a knot of fisherman's huts, should in so short a space have undergone such an amazing change, as now to be the first watering place in the kingdom, honoured by the Royal Family, and continued influx of visitors.[113]

Lesser members of the royal family were a prized capture for smaller resorts. In 1797 Princess Amelia (1783–1810) came to Worthing, in West Sussex, on the recommendation of her doctors, inspiring the arrival of other leaders of fashion and prompting a decade of rapid growth. Princess Charlotte (1796–1817) proved popular when she was taken to Southend, in Essex, as a child in 1801.[114] Richard Hotham (1722–99), a successful London businessman, built his ambitious development near Bognor in 1791 (*see* p 64) in the hope that a member of the royal family might provide it with the status to guarantee success.

The rapid growth of resorts from around 1800

Margate was also attracting some distinguished guests, though none of the leading members of the royal family were regular visitors. Its convenient location on the Thames Estuary meant that it was the first resort to be able to attract large numbers of middle-class and even lower-

Fig 4.20
*Cecil Square in Margate
contained a row of shops as
well as the purpose-built
assembly rooms and
circulating library that had
been erected in front of
Fox's Tavern. These were
on the south side of the
square and were
demolished in around 1970,
but the west and north sides
of the square (shown in this
2004 photograph) have
largely survived.
[AA049298]*

Fig 4.21
*Most of the accommodation
at Hothamton, near Bognor
Regis, was in short terraces
between three and seven
houses long, though there
were also some detached
and semi-detached houses.
All the houses were large-
scale, three-storey, brick
buildings, the most
distinguished being the
Dome House at the centre
of the Crescent.
[DP022284]*

sizeable investment in new resorts, where there was no pre-existing settlement. The earliest of these risky new developments was Hothamton, in West Sussex, near where Bognor Regis stands today. Sir Richard Hotham invested up to £160,000 in a prestigious new development aimed at wealthy visitors (Fig 4.21). It opened in 1791 and in the following years 'it was honoured with the company of several families of the first fashion in the kingdom'.[120] Hothamton was a widely dispersed settlement with some of the largest houses and terraces set inland, while the hotel and subscription room were near the seafront.[121]

During the Napoleonic Wars, expenditure continued in existing resorts, as well as some small-scale investment in new resorts such as Southport, in Merseyside, and Bournemouth, in Dorset. Southport began in the 1790s with a bathing house and hotel on an uninhabited stretch of coastline. Bournemouth's founder, Lewis Tregonwell (d 1832), initially built a house on an uninhabited stretch of coastline in 1811–12, followed by an inn and a handful of cottages for invalids in search of improved health.[122] Mrs Arbuthnott wrote in 1824 that Bournemouth was 'a collection of hills lately planted by a gentleman of the name of Tregonwell who has built four or five beautiful cottages which he lets out to persons who go sea-bathing'.[123] An 1837 guidebook stated that Sir G W Tapps Gervis was carrying out a series of improvements on the east side of the River Bourne, employing Benjamin Ferrey to prepare plans for buildings. It noted, 'Villas, crescents, streets and baths, in all varied styles of architecture are rearing their heads as if by magic.'[124]

This development was wholly separate to the activity taking place on the west side of the Bourne, where Tregonwell had constructed his 'neat marine villa', inn and several detached houses 'in the cottage style'.[125]

The emphasis on both sides of the Bourne was on detached villas rather than more formal projects with terraces, squares and crescents. Bournemouth's origin was in marked contrast to Hothamton, as its development was gradual

rather than attempting to create a town from new at the outset. With the resumption of peace in 1815, new schemes on a scale previously unimaginable began to emerge, though the earliest of these was still relatively modest, yet unsuccessful. In 1816, a large development beside the existing village of Herne Bay, in Kent, was promoted by the local landowner Sir Henry Oxenden, but in the absence of a pier, steamers from London could not land significant numbers of visitors. The initial small scheme yielded only a few houses and the later one of the 1830s, despite the construction of the pier, was similarly unproductive.

However, during the 1820s, a new scale of scheme began to emerge at several resorts, with Brighton, perhaps inevitably, leading the way. The new schemes were the size of towns and sought to provide that scale of entertainment and bathing facilities, as well as accommodation. In 1823, Thomas Read Kemp (1782–1844) embarked on the construction of a large estate on his land to the east of Brighton and most of the development was completed over the following two decades (Fig 4.22). At the west end of Brighton and in Hove, Brunswick Town was built from 1825 on land owned by the Scutt

Fig 4.22
This Aerofilms photograph of Kemp Town, at the east end of Brighton, in 1951 shows the scale of the development begun in the 1820s.
[EAW037807]

family (Fig 4.23).[126] The architects responsible for the overall design and layout of Kemp Town were Amon Henry Wilds (1784–1857) and Charles Augustin Busby (1786–1834), though little had been built or completed by the time their partnership was dissolved in June 1825.[127] In Kemp Town and Brunswick Town, long terraces were built, along with centrepieces consisting of squares open at the seaward end, with attached quadrants of crescents, a lavish form of plan designed to maximise the number of houses with sea views. In both schemes the houses were decorated with Corinthian columns and pilasters that sought to emulate the grandest examples of fashionable architecture found in central London developments such as Regent Street, Regent's Park and Eaton Square, as well as the finest houses in Bath.

The impact of Kemp Town and Brunswick Town was felt immediately. By January 1825, a prospectus had been published for a huge new development at Bognor, inspired by what was expected to be the success of the Brighton schemes.[128] According to the prospectus, the Bognor New Town Company had capital of £300,000 for the architect Samuel Beazley to erect houses and facilities for visitors, the houses being 'unconnected' except for 'light colonnades'. Unfortunately, the scheme did not prove popular with investors and was not built.

Another grandiose project inspired immediately by Brighton, and ultimately by Bath's Royal Crescent, was undertaken at Hayling Island, near Portsmouth. In 1822–4, a bridge was built to link it to the mainland and this prompted ideas for a new development.[129] The London architect Robert Abraham prepared plans for villas and the foundation stone of the crescent was laid on 3 September 1825.[130] A new hotel containing a billiard room was also built, as well as a library, a bathhouse and gardens. The library, a small temple-like building with a Grecian Doric portico, contained 'a spacious reading room, possessing an excellent collection of modern works, the newspapers, and periodicals of the day, many pleasing pictures, and the advantage of a separate room for chess players'.[131] It was located at the centre of 'a well-made esplanade three hundred yards in length' with a bathhouse at one end providing facilities for hot, tepid and cold bathing.[132] The crescent was never completed, the library closed in 1867 and became a house, and the baths, library and esplanade have now disappeared.

The developments at Kemp Town and Brunswick Town were also having an impact at Hastings. However, even before these schemes had been conceived, Hastings was already proving a fertile ground for significant new development. Pelham Place on the seafront was erected immediately after peace resumed in 1815 and Wellington Square followed in 1819–23.[133] In 1824, Thomas Pelham, Earl of Chichester (1756–1826), employed the architect Joseph

Fig 4.23
Brunswick Town, most of which is in Hove, contains some of the grandest terraced houses ever built at the seaside. This section of Brunswick Terrace (numbers 33–42) has tall Corinthian pilasters reminiscent of a grand baroque country house. [DP017943]

Fig 4.24
The Den Crescent at
Teignmouth consisted of a
large assembly room
between two quadrants of a
crescent, much as Pelham
Crescent at Hastings had a
chapel as its centrepiece.
[BB67/08928b]

Kay (1775–1847) to build a crescent of houses with a large parish church at its centre, along with a lavish bathhouse and a large bazaar.[134] Pelham's modest-sized scheme contained some of the key elements found on a larger scale in Brighton's two huge projects, but at Hastings another scheme, begun in the late 1820s, rivalled Kemp Town and Brunswick Town in ambition. James Burton (1761–1837), the leading London builder of the early 19th century, who had worked with John Nash on terraces at Regent's Park, purchased farmland in February 1828 for the construction of a new town a short distance to the west of Hastings. As erected, St Leonards consisted of grand terraces along the seafront flanking a hotel, with elegant, low buildings in front housing baths, a bank and a library.[135] Behind there was an assembly room and on the hillside a park was created surrounded by villas. Two lower-status inland streets were created to meet the needs of the new settlement's inhabitants, Mercatoria to house merchants and Lavatoria for laundry services.[136] In 1836, Theodore Hook described St Leonards as 'a thickly-peopled town'.[137] Legally it was initially a separate administrative entity, with an Improvement Act in 1832 appointing 75 commissioners, with powers to borrow £16,000 to develop the town.[138]

The pioneering schemes erected at Brighton and Hastings influenced a number of other ambitious developments around the coast. At Teignmouth on the seafront Den, the Den Crescent, with the Assembly Rooms at its heart, was built in 1825–6 (Fig 4.24).[139] In 1828, Thomas Ellis Owen (1804–62) designed Crescent Road at Alverstoke near Gosport, in Hampshire, as the centrepiece of a new settlement, Anglesey.[140] An 1841 guidebook described the newly formed 'bathing station' as having a 'noble range of mansions', with a bathing establishment, which was in front of the crescent, and a hotel that opened on 18 May 1830.[141] In 1829, Amon Henry Wilds designed Park Crescent at Worthing, in West Sussex, a scheme of 22, three-storey houses, though only 14 were built. On the seafront at Dover, Waterloo Crescent was built in 1834–8 by Philip Hardwick (1792–1870) (Fig 4.25).[142] It was built in three parts, a central block of 19 houses flanked on either side by a pair of blocks containing five houses.

Although Waterloo Crescent was a large development dominating the southern half of Dover's seafront, it was simply a grand housing scheme with no intention of being considered as

Fig 4.25
This late 19th-century view
shows bathing machines in
front of Waterloo Crescent,
Dover. As it was located on
the seafront, the crescent
was in the front line during
World War II and suffered
considerable damage.
[BB88/03995]

a self-contained town or even as a suburb. However, the situation at Herne Bay on the north Kent coast was quite different. Sir Henry Oxenden's scheme at Herne Bay in 1816 had been slow to develop due to the absence of a pier, but in 1830 a plan for the new town of St Augustine at Herne Bay was proposed. The Herne Bay Pier Company expected 'to cause commodious Hotels, Baths, and other public Resorts to be erected, in addition to those already built, for the accommodation of the Nobility and Visitors'.[143] In 1831, an Act of Parliament was obtained and the first timber pile of the pier was driven on 4 July 1831 (Fig 4.26).[144] The new town was created on two farms owned by Sir Henry, who sold the necessary land to developers.[145] The plan consisted of a regular grid made up of a series of major parallel roads, the northernmost part of the scheme comprising three squares linked by short roads. However, progress was slow as developers were hesitant to start building work until roads were constructed, sewers laid and a large church provided.[146] By the end of 1838, there had been 15 bankruptcies or failures and the new church in Brunswick Square was abandoned with its walls a few feet above the ground. In 1855, *Kelly's Directory* dryly described the problem, stating, 'The town is laid out on too large a scale, and but partially built upon.'[147]

The largest projects in the 1820s and 1830s were concentrated on a small stretch of the south coast of England, but schemes with similar ambitions were beginning to appear in other parts of England. The Crescent at Scarborough was designed in 1832, but was built over the next 25 years. Hesketh Crescent at Torquay, in Devon, is a crescent of 15 houses with three-bay-wide end pavilions and a five-bay centrepiece with Corinthian pilasters (Fig 4.27).[148] At Great Yarmouth, Britannia Terrace was built in 1848–55 as a palace-fronted terrace of 20 four-storey houses.

Conclusion

None of these more modest projects could rival the schemes at Brighton or Hastings; nevertheless they indicate that even in smaller, more remote parts of the coastline, the seaside industry

Fig 4.26
This view of Herne Bay in 1841 shows the earliest parts of the new town that had been built on the seafront near the landward end of the long pier.
[Author's collection]

Fig 4.27
Hesketh Crescent at
Torquay was built in
1845–8 by the speculative
builder Jacob Harvey
(1783–1867). The scheme
was the brainchild of
the local landowner
Sir Lawrence Palk.
[DP001355]

was sufficiently mature to sustain ambitious investments aimed at a wealthy market. They reflect the growing number of people visiting the seaside in the first half of the 19th century, but also demonstrate the wealth in the rapidly growing national and seaside economies.

The 1820s and 1830s projects were aimed at the middle- and upper-class residential and visitor market, the type of people with time and wealth to spend weeks at the seaside. However, from the 1840s onwards the rapidly growing railway network, combined with increased prosperity, led to the growth of a new market for seaside holidays among working people. This helped to bring new investment into seaside resorts, resulting in huge areas of development, often modest housing aimed at the growing residential population. Increasingly the wealthier end of the housing market was being satisfied by estates of detached and semi-detached villas, away from the heart of increasingly busy resorts. Wealthier visitors could also withdraw into Grand Hotels that formed small, self-contained communities, particularly when hydropathic facilities were added. These Grand Hotels have their roots in the new hotels appearing at resorts in the 1820s, combining the elegance of the architecture of Kemp Town and Brunswick Town with the kind of extensive and exclusive facilities being provided in prestigious domestic schemes such as St Leonards and Alverstoke.

Although these developments were aimed at an elite market, the pier, another innovation of the 1810s and 1820s, would be central to mass entertainment during the 19th century. Beginning at Margate, Ryde, Leith and Brighton, the first piers designed for middle-class visitors to promenade and for steamers to land passengers would blossom into the elaborate iron piers of the second half of the 19th century, attracting millions of visitors each year.

Technology was set to transform the entertainments available at seaside resorts, but it would have a more profound impact on the nature of holidaymaking. Beginning with steamers along the Clyde and Thames, growing numbers of working-class people would become tourists because of the train. The arrival of the railway transformed the economy of Britain, cut journey times and reduced the cost of travelling. It would open the seaside to most of the population during the second half of the 19th century, changing the shape of seaside resorts and transforming the character of seaside holidays.

Transport and tourism 1500–1939

For tourism to thrive, a set of interconnecting circumstances is required. The first of these is sufficient disposable income to be able to afford to travel and stay away from home. The second is the time to undertake leisure. Initially, these restricted tourism to a small, wealthy elite, but by the 19th century national wealth and individual income were increasing, and, as was outlined in Chapter 1, this coincided with the confirmation, establishment and reinstatement of days off and, gradually, week-long and longer holidays. By the 20th century everyone was entitled to some form of holiday and growing personal disposable income meant that this could be taken domestically and, increasingly, internationally. There was also a need for destinations that had developed an infrastructure and facilities to cope with the tastes and demands of tourists.

The final major circumstance required for tourism is the means to travel. Tourists in the 17th and 18th centuries had to endure the rigours of travelling on roads, some of which were in the process of being improved, but nevertheless were still in a poor condition. Coaches were uncomfortable, journeys were slow, and highwaymen could make any trip hazardous. If a tourist chose to travel by river or sea, they faced hazards caused by bad weather, but by the end of the 18th century destinations such as those 'doon the watter' on the Clyde or along the Thames at Margate were benefiting from influxes of visitors from Glasgow and London.

In the early 19th century, technology began to intervene to make transport faster, cheaper and safer, a process that would transform tourism from being the preserve of an elite in 1800 to an activity that was potentially within the reach of everyone a century later. This began with the introduction of steam-powered ships during the 1810s, plying the Clyde and the Thames, but the process of democratisation due to the introduction of new technology gathered pace with the creation of a national railway system from the 1830s onwards. It ended long-distance coaching routes that had developed in the previous 200 years, though shorter routes continued and sometimes prospered by connecting railway stations to smaller, nearby destinations.

During the late 19th century, other new technologies impacted on travel, tourism and leisure, beginning with the humble bicycle. The development of the internal combustion engine as a practical means to power road transport continued the process of increasing the market for tourism, but it also extended the reach of tourism, taking holidaymakers into every corner of the country, beyond where railways had previously gone. This chapter will outline the story of how transport has been a key factor in promoting tourism and how changes in technology have impacted on the experience of travelling and increased the number of people able to enjoy a holiday.

Road transport

Roads during the 17th century were a mixture of Roman roads, a few medieval roads, drover and packhorse routes and some roads that had undergone modest improvement during the 16th century. The growing amount of traffic during the 16th and 17th centuries put greater pressure on already poor road surfaces. Nevertheless, the first coach service had begun to run in 1637, serving routes from London into Hertfordshire and Cambridge, and by 1650 Bath and Bristol also had services, mostly during the summer months.[1] In 1669 the writer Edward Chamberlayne (1616–1703) spoke enthusiastically about England's roads:

> There is of late such an admirable commodiousness, both for men and women of better rank, to travel from London to almost any

great town of England and to almost all the villages near this great city, that the like hath not been known in the world, and that is by stage coaches, wherein one may be transported to any place sheltered from foul weather and foul ways, from endamaging one's health or body by hard jogging or over-violent motion, and this not only at a low price, as about a shilling for every five miles, but with velocity and speed as that the posts in some foreign countries make not more miles a day.[2]

In the 1662 Act of Parliament 'for enlarging and repairing of the common highways', surveyors could, with the sanction of the Justices of the Peace, levy a highway rate.[3] In the following year, the first toll gate was erected at Wadesmill, in Hertfordshire, after Justices of the counties of Hertford, Cambridge and Huntingdon had been given the right to levy tolls to repair sections of the Great North Road.[4] However, it was not until the 1690s that the idea of using tolls from road users for highway maintenance and improvement began to become the accepted way forward. In 1696 'justice trusts' were established to manage roads between Shenfield and Harwich, in Essex, and between Wymondham and Attleborough, in Norfolk, and eventually 13 were established before being superseded by turnpike trusts.[5] In 1706, a turnpike trust with 32 independent trustees, with powers to borrow money, appoint officers, manage the road and provide for its repair, was established to improve a section of road between Fornhill in Bedfordshire and Stony Stratford in Buckinghamshire, part of a programme to improve the road to Holyhead, in north Wales. This administrative model was used for almost all turnpike acts during the next 130 years.[6]

Turnpike trusts were an administrative and financial tool for road improvement by borrowing money against the security of the predicted tolls. They were also economic investments that might yield between 3 and 5 per cent return, and inevitably they were established where there was money to be made.[7] Therefore, the first examples were predominantly in the southeast around London, while during the mid-18th century a growing number were being developed in the counties where industrialisation was occurring.[8] By the 1730s, turnpikes were heading northwards up the Great North Road, but were also beginning to improve roads in the Midlands, as well as to serve areas around

Manchester and in Lancashire. By 1750, a network of major roads radiating from London had been established and in the next two decades, the period of the so-called 'Turnpike Mania', county networks of major roads began to be created.[9] In 1752 there was only one turnpike road in Wales, running from Shrewsbury to Wrexham, but by 1800, north Wales had around 1,000 miles (1,600km) of turnpike roads providing a comprehensive network between the larger settlements.[10] By 1763, Brecon and Monmouth had a weekly coach to London, followed in 1774 by Carmarthen and Haverfordwest.[11]

Road improvements in the north of England were in part stimulated by the experience of the 1745 Jacobite Rebellion (better-quality roads enabled the faster deployment of troops to suppress uprisings). They were also a result of the need to move more cattle into England.[12] Scotland's roads were first improved as a result of the uprisings of 1715 and 1745, and particularly when General George Wade was sent to the Highlands, creating a network of 'military roads' from the mid-1720s onwards.[13] The army not only constructed these roads, but was charged with their maintenance. Home Counties resident Elizabeth Diggle, while touring the Highlands in June 1788, saw army tents pitched near the road she took through the mountains.[14] Scotland also benefited from the creation of turnpike trusts, which by 1770 were still largely confined to counties in the borders and the Central Valley.[15]

Turnpike trusts improved roads by the introduction of new construction techniques that provided a firm, smooth surface for traffic. Another key factor in faster, smoother journeys was the removal of sharp bends and the easing of excessive gradients by using deep cuttings or embankments.[16] As well as road maintenance and improvement, turnpike surveyors also had to provide bridges for the new routes (Figs 5.1 and 5.2). The leading names in road-building innovation were the engineers John Loudon MacAdam (1756–1836) and Thomas Telford (1757–1834).[17] Both were Scotsmen and their main contributions to road-making techniques and repairs came during the second decade of the 19th century, late in their distinguished careers.

Despite these improvements, travelling by road was still often uncomfortable and even dangerous. In the novel *The Expedition of Humphry Clinker*, Matthew Bramble bemoaned the state of turnpikes:

Fig 5.1
Tolls were also charged to travel across some bridges. At toll gates the cost of tolls had to be displayed and often a toll house was provided for the keeper responsible for collecting the payments, as at Clopton Bridge, Stratford-upon-Avon, Warwickshire. [DP154510]

Fig 5.2
Another requirement was to provide milestones along roads and many of these still grace the sides of Britain's roads today. This milestone may date from around 1743, when the road between Cherhill and Marlborough, in Wiltshire, completed the improved road between Bath and its main market in London. [© Author]

Considering the tax we pay for turnpikes, the roads of this county constitute a most intolerable grievance. Between Newark and Weatherby, I have suffered more from jolting and swinging than ever I felt in the whole course of my life, although the carriage is remarkably commodious and well hung, and the postilions were very careful in driving.[18]

Later in the exchange of letters there are accounts of incidents where the coach was washed away by a flash flood and another where the springs broke but were heroically mended by Clinker in a blacksmith's forge.[19] Breakdowns due to defective, worn carriage parts were common, as were problems with horses, poor weather and accidents due to the state of the roads.[20] The opening scene of Jane Austen's Sanditon involves an accident en route to the seaside on a 'very rough lane' where the surface was 'half rock, half sand'.[21]

Not everyone was enthusiastic about the improved communications. Some farmers, drovers and carriers opposed changes to their traditional ways and conservative traders believed that the new roads would harm their economic interests by changing market patterns, as well as raising costs through the imposition of tolls.[22] Soldier and diarist John Byng (1743–1813) was an outspoken opponent of turnpike roads. He looked back nostalgically to the roads and inns of his youth and disliked new turnpikes, considering them flat, straight and ugly.[23] In 1782, he complained, 'The country is only improv'd in vice and insolence, by the establishment of turnpikes.'[24] Byng disliked them for spreading ideas from the capital into the English countryside: 'I wish with all my heart that half the turnpike roads of the kingdom were plough'd up, which have imported London manners, and depopulated the country. I meet milkmaids on the road, with the dress and looks of strand misses.'[25]

Travelling by coach

With better roads came improvements in road transport. In 1734, relays of horses were introduced to rehorse the Newcastle-to-London 'flying coach'.[26] In around 1760 steel springs were first employed in stagecoaches to improve comfort, but also to allow safer travel at speed.[27] In 1763, the first one-day 'flying coaches' began to run, avoiding overnight stays by leaving during the evening and travelling through the night.[28] The French writer and historian Pierre Jean Grosley (1718–85) published a description of coach travel in England in 1772:

I myself set out on a Sunday with seven more passengers in two carriages called flying machines. These vehicles which are drawn by six horses, go twenty-eight leagues in a day from Dover to London for a single guinea. Servants are entitled to a place for half that money, either behind the coach, or upon the coach box, which has three places. A vast repository under this seat, which is very lofty, holds the passengers luggage, which is paid for separately.[29]

In 1776, the enterprising landlord of the White Lion in Chester started a daily 'flying post chaise' service to Holyhead and three years later another innkeeper in Shrewsbury established a link between Holyhead and London. The success of these services prompted the creation of a national mail coach service with carefully scheduled horse changes and well-planned routes with well-appointed inns. In 1784, the first mail coach was introduced on the London-to-Bristol route, offering quicker, more comfortable and (as there was an armed guard protecting the mail) safer journeys.[30] By law, the number of passengers on a stagecoach was limited to six inside, six outside and two on the box, though as roads improved the number on top rose at times to eleven. In rural areas restrictions could be flouted and one country coach involved in an accident was found to have had 34 passengers.[31]

Running a stagecoach business involved major and regular investments. Each year a stagecoach provider would have to buy large numbers of horses, as well as paying wages for coachmen and stable boys, and the cost of tolls and duties to the government.[32] A coachman's average day involved covering around 50 miles (80km), and while his life was undoubtedly hard, writer Catherine Hutton (1756–1846) noted in 1799, 'The life of a post-horse is everywhere miserable.' She reported how the landlady of an inn at Llangollen, Denbighshire, complained that 'no horse lasts me above a year and a half'.[33] The normal working life of horses was around three years for mail coaches, four years for stagecoaches and up to seven years for slower coaches.[34]

In 1658, the first stagecoach from London to Exeter took four days. A century later this had been reduced to two days; it was further reduced to 32 hours by 1784 and to 17½ hours in 1832, an average speed of 10mph.[35] The summer journey from London to Edinburgh took 10 days in 1754. By 1776, it had been reduced to 4 days and on the mail coach in 1837 it regularly took 45½ hours to cover the 373 miles (600km).[36] In 1750, the estimated average speed of coaches was 4.7mph and by 1770 it had risen to 6.4mph.[37] No further, significant improvement took place until around 1820 when, with road improvements, the average speed rose to 8mph, reaching 9.4mph by 1830.

In this period, fares did not rise significantly, resulting in a growth in demand and therefore an increase in the numbers of coaches needed.[38] Between 1773 and 1796, services from London to all parts of the country increased fourfold, while between 1781 and 1809 the number of weekly coaches from London to Scarborough rose from 12 to 60 and the number from London to Weymouth increased from 12 to 73.[39] By 1829, 23 coaches ran each day between Brighton and London.[40]

Many travellers and tourists covered long distances on horseback. A horse could move quite quickly over short distances, but for longer distances it moved at a more sedate trot.[41] John Byng travelled by horse with a small portmanteau, while a servant usually rode ahead with most of the luggage to secure appropriate accommodation at an inn where they would spend the night.[42] People unable to afford a horse, or travel by stagecoach, could use the slower, more uncomfortable wagons that provided the carrier system for goods and parcels.[43] In 1800, Weymouth was served by wagons from London, but the arrival of the railway ended these long-distance carrier routes.[44]

Inns were central to travelling during the 18th century (Fig 5.3). They provided food and drink for passengers, but were also where horses were changed during a journey. German author

Fig 5.3
The early 17th-century King's Arms, in the High Street in Malmesbury, in Wiltshire, was once a coaching inn and has now been converted into a hotel. [OP06575]

Johanna Schopenhauer (1766–1838), who visited Britain in 1787–8 and 1803–5, was particularly struck by the hospitality and courtesy of the innkeepers, finding that the further one travelled northwards, the greater the warmth of the welcome.[45] Richard Fowke, a tenant farmer, travelled to Freiston Shore, in Lincolnshire, in 1805, and his diary describes the journey there from his home in Elmesthorpe, in Leicestershire. He began by walking 11 miles (18km) to Leicester, where he picked up the coach to Stamford, in Lincolnshire, paying 13 shillings for the 32-mile (51km) journey. At Stamford he changed to a chaise to Market Deeping, a journey on which he was accompanied by a group of Lincolnshire farmers. Fowke spent the night at the Bull Inn at Market Deeping before taking another chaise to Spalding on a road that he described as 'very level and good', where he caught another chaise to Boston and a final one to Freiston Shore.[46] All the staging posts on this two-day journey were at local inns, providing him with opportunities for refreshments and meals, as well as a bed for the night. In the same year, Welsh woman Mrs Parry Price described a journey from Plymouth to Exeter. It involved changes of horses, as well as meals and refreshments, at a series of inns on the route, culminating in 'a tolerable night' at the New London Inn.[47]

Highwaymen were a genuine menace to travellers during the 18th and early 19th centuries, but Celia Fiennes (1662–1741) on all her travels only once recounted meeting two men whom she suspected were highwaymen.[48] However, these robbers often became the stuff of legend, featuring in popular publications and chapbooks published during the 18th century.

Road travel and tourism

Although trade and industry were the main reasons to establish a turnpike, a secondary driver was tourism and England's two leading leisure destinations in the mid-18th century, Bath and Tunbridge Wells, both began to be served by improved roads. The route from London to Bath was the subject of a series of turnpikes during the first half of the 18th century, the last piece of the puzzle being put in place in 1743 when the improved road between Cherhill and Marlborough, in Wiltshire, completed the route between Bath and its main market in London.[49] In the 1690s, Celia Fiennes noted that there was a range of coach services available from London to Tunbridge Wells.[50] During the course of the 18th century, Tunbridge Wells became part of an elaborate network of improved roads, in part due to being a popular destination, but also because it was en route to the Sussex seaside resorts and a stopping-off point on the way to Kent.[51]

Seaside resorts were also the object of improved roads and transport services. In 1752, the case for improving the road between York and Scarborough was being discussed as it had long been used 'by persons resorting to Scarborough ... from most parts of England'.[52] This meant that passengers would soon be able to travel from most major inland towns to the resort on roads that had been rebuilt during the previous 20 years.[53] In Sussex, Hastings had a turnpike from Ticehurst by 1753, but it took until 1765 before it was possible to enjoy easier journeys to Tunbridge Wells, and therefore gain access to the wider network of improved roads in the south-east.[54] Brighton was not connected by turnpikes until 1770, though it was already beginning to prosper.[55] Lewes, as the county town, rather than the upstart resort, was at the heart of the transport network in the south of the county.[56] However, the generally improved travel conditions in the south-east of England may have helped to stimulate Brighton's rapid development as a resort, as well as attracting more aristocratic and royal visitors.

Although there was a huge increase in road travel during the 18th and early 19th centuries, which coincided with the growth of spas and seaside resorts, it is difficult to prove direct correlations between the two. However, there is one example of a speculative scheme linked to the creation of a new road. A turnpike was created in 1814 from Herne to Sturry to improve access to the road between Thanet and Canterbury, in Kent. By 1835, coaches ran several times a day from Herne Bay to Canterbury and there were direct coaches to and from London.[57] The new road connection may have prompted local landowner Sir Henry Oxenden to build the Terrace in Herne Bay in 1816, part of an unsuccessful scheme he promoted for the foundation of a large resort at Herne Bay (see p 64). A plan in the early 1830s shows that most of the new buildings were concentrated in a small area at the east end of the resort, where the turnpike terminated.[58] Although the road seems to have stimulated some immediate development, it took the creation of a pier in the early 1830s, and therefore the possibility of landing seaborne visitors, for a larger scheme to be undertaken.

The last days of coach travel

By the accession of Queen Victoria in 1837, coaching was enjoying a golden age, with fast, reliable, frequent services from London and between provincial towns and cities (Fig 5.4).[59] By 1830, mail coaches nightly covered more than 12,000 miles (19,000km).[60] More than 18,000 miles (29,000km) of English roads had been turnpiked, along with 2,000 miles (3,200km) in Wales, and there were 3,783 turnpike trusts in existence.[61] Transport was a huge industry, with 20,000 toll collectors gathering annual revenues of £1.5 million in 1837. More than 3,000 coaches were operating on England's roads, requiring 150,000 horses and 30,000 workers, ranging from coachmen and guards on mail coaches to people at inns who tended the horses.[62] By 1835, the most important inn of any market town might have 50 or 60 horses on call in its yard.[63]

While coaching was at its peak by the 1830s, profound changes were already under way. During the late 18th century, canals took much of the long-distance bulk traffic market and even some passengers away from roads. This was a prelude to what the railways would do a few decades later, dealing a death blow to the turnpikes and leading to the disappearance of long-distance carriers and famous stagecoach routes.[64] The railway line between London and Brighton opened on 21 September 1841. Within a month, the Day Mail had stopped running, the Night Mail lasted five months and in the summer of 1845 only one coach was still running compared to 23 six years earlier.[65] Although railways soon replaced most coaching services, some continued to prosper through the 19th century where railways had not reached, completing the final legs of many journeys predominantly undertaken by train. In 1845, 18,000 people still used coaches between Edinburgh, Dundee and Aberdeen, while 22,000 travellers took the route between Edinburgh and Perth.[66] On the Isle of Thanet there were still active coach services between Ramsgate, Broadstairs and Margate during the 1880s, although the resorts were linked by a railway.[67] From 1860, 'dis-turnpiking' was actively pursued. By 1881, only 184 trusts remained and in 1895 the last one vanished. The trunk roads of Britain would have to wait for the internal combustion engine to give them a new lease of life.[68]

Railways may have ended long-distance coaching services, but there was nevertheless a large increase in the number of horse-drawn vehicles on roads in towns and cities. In 1840, there were 30,000 four-wheeled, horse-drawn

Fig 5.4
This late 19th-century photograph by Henry William Taunt shows an elegant coach-and-four, with some of its passengers, outside the Queen's Hotel in Abingdon, in Oxfordshire.
[CC72/02160]

Fig 5.5
This image, one of a pair
of stereo photographs,
shows a busy traffic scene
at King's Cross, London,
with a variety of horse-
drawn vehicles.
[CC97/01085]

vehicles on the roads, rising to 120,000 in 1870.
The number of two-wheeled coaches rose from
40,000 in 1840 to 250,000 in 1870 and 320,000
in 1902.[69] Photographs of major cities in the late
19th century illustrate how congested they had
become (Fig 5.5).

Sailing boats, steamers and early tourism

The application of steam power would cause a
revolution in transport and tourism when
applied first to powering boats and later to create
railways. However, before steam became a practical means of powering boats, sailing ships were
already having an impact on holidaymaking.
Margate, in Kent, could be reached by boat as

well as by land. By the 1770s, this relatively
cheap, and sometimes quick, alternative to road
travel led to the extension of the holiday habit
from the highest in society to the growing middle
classes and even the derided London shop-
keeper.[70] Hoys were single-masted ships of 60 to
100 tons that sailed along the Thames, transporting grain from Kent to London, and
importing other goods such as coal and timber.
Gradually passengers and their luggage displaced the cargo and dedicated sailing packets
developed.[71] Hoys were cheaper than travelling
by coach; in the 1790s, a single coach trip to
Margate cost between 21s and 26s, while the
cheapest hoy fare was only 5s.[72] However, they
were often unpleasantly crowded, drawing com-
parisons with life in prison, and passengers often
had to endure the consequences of rough seas.[73]
Because of the geography of the west coast of

Scotland, travellers from Glasgow also used sailing boats and later steamers to reach the various islands. The diary of Adam Bald (b 1770), a dealer in chemicals, provides colourful insights into his trip along the Clyde to Rothesay and Campbeltown in July 1794.[74] Elsewhere, there is some evidence of people using river travel for leisure. Packet boats sailed from Liverpool and Manchester to Runcorn, allowing people to enjoy some of the sights of the Cheshire countryside.[75]

As well as rivers, passengers could also make use of coastal shipping and sometimes boats on canals.[76] Between 1716 and 1790, around 1,000 miles (1,600km) of navigable canal were established, changing the pattern of transport in the Midlands and north-west England and reducing the cost of transporting bulk goods to less than a third of road transport.[77] Canals had an impact on passenger travel. Boats began to run on the Bridgewater Canal, in north-west England, as early as 1767. In 1774, two new, purpose-built passenger boats were running on the Altrincham–Manchester route. Included in the facilities were a 'Coffee room at the head' and three classes of cabin, ranging in price from 2s 6d to 1s.[78] Southport's rapid growth after 1820 was partly due to the provision of a through passenger service from Manchester on the Leeds and Liverpool Canal.[79] In 1805, John Phillips (fl 1778–c 1817), a writer on inland navigation, had suggested that its proprietors would profit from running a passenger service using boats similar to those of the Bridgewater Canal.[80] In 1836, Scotland's Forth and Clyde Canal carried nearly 200,000 passengers on new boats modelled on those of the Paisley Canal.[81]

The creation of steamers revolutionised waterborne travel, allowing the faster transport of industrial goods, passengers and tourists. In 1816, James Cleland (1770–1840), a Glaswegian statistician and civic administrator, proudly explained how steam had come to be applied to powering boats on the Clyde. He recognised that it was largely perfected by 'Mr. Henry Bell, an ingenious, untutored engineer, and Citizen of Glasgow' in January 1812 with the *Comet* 'propelled on the Clyde by an engine of three horse power, which was subsequently increased to six' (Fig 5.6).[82] Twenty steamers had already been built on the Clyde by 1816, with one being exported to Liverpool and four sent to London to operate on the Thames.[83] Technological progress had been rapid in the four years since the *Comet* was launched. The *Comet* was 38ft (11.6m) long, latterly powered with a 6hp engine, but by 1816 the new boats were twice as long, with some powered by motors over 30hp.

Steamers made the Clyde Estuary more accessible, creating the famous 'doon the watter' holidays, as well as promoting, to a lesser extent, tourism along the east coast of Scotland. The first passenger steamer service in Britain was run in 1812 between Glasgow and Greenock, using Bell's *Comet*. When it went to Bo'ness, near Falkirk, for a refit Bell grasped the opportunity to put on an excursion to Leith, decades before Thomas Cook would pioneeringly employ the train for a similar venture.[84] By 1814, there were steamer services to Rothesay, on the Isle of Bute, and a year later to Tarbert, Campbeltown and Inverary, in Argyll and Bute. In 1816, Loch Lomond was served by the steamer *Marion*, which provided day-long excursions.

Steamers also had a profound impact on tourism along the Thames. In 1763, hoys were able to carry 60 to 70 passengers, while a guidebook in 1797 estimated that more than 100 people could be transported.[85] Steamers were considerably larger than hoys. On the Clyde, landscape painter and engraver William Daniell (1769–1837) claimed that one running between Glasgow and Greenock carried 247 passengers in 1813, while in 1820, the *London Engineer* steam yacht transported 270 people along the Thames.[86] By the end of the 19th century, the steamers that plied the route to Margate were huge compared with their predecessors: the steamer *La Marguerite* measured 341ft 6in (104m) long, 73ft (22.3m) wide, 21ft 6in (6.6m)

Fig 5.6
This is a replica of the PS Comet *in Port Glasgow, Henry Bell's pioneering steamship that provided passenger services as well as excursions.*
[© HES (Historic Environment Scotland). Reproduced courtesy of J R Hume]

high and weighed 2,204 tons.[87] The size of boats contributed to driving down fares, as did growing competition between companies. In 1827 there were 10 steamboats running from London to Margate and between 1829 and 1846 12 different companies operated on the route.[88] In 1815, the lowest fare on a steamer was 12s, but 20 years later it had fallen to 6s, reduced fares prompting a significant growth in visitor numbers.[89] At the beginning of the 19th century, around 20,000 visitors arrived at Margate by sea, but by 1821, six years after the introduction of steamers, this had risen to 44,347 and in 1835–6 the number peaked at 108,625.[90] In 1834, half a million passengers are believed to have used steamers on the Clyde and a similar number were probably using ships running between London and Greenwich, Woolwich and Gravesend. In 1845, 30,000 people used coastal steamers linking Edinburgh, Dundee and Aberdeen.[91]

Although steamers continued into the 20th century on the Thames, they became very much secondary to railways. However, many seaside destinations within easy reach of Glasgow were on islands, such as Bute and Arran, or were difficult to reach easily by land, so the steamer remained a primary means of visiting them. Glaswegians went 'doon the watter' in huge numbers, some getting the boat at the Broomielaw, in Glasgow, and going all the way by water to Rothesay. As early as 1833 half of Rothesay's 600 houses were providing holiday accommodation.[92] In 1891, during the Glasgow Fair, the 9,000 residents of Rothesay, who had already been joined by another 700 families staying for the summer, were inundated by a further 30–40,000 weekend visitors.[93] Some holidaymakers went to the coast by train, and then embarked at pier head stations. Wemyss Bay station, in Renfrewshire, which opened in 1865, is the most spectacular of the remaining Victorian rail–sea hubs. Loch Lomond's steamers benefited from the rail link between Glasgow and Balloch Pier, which provided a year-round service for passengers, mail, cargo and livestock.[94] This pattern of travel survived the disruption of wars, and only faded during the 1960s, with only one paddle steamer left in service today, PS *Waverley*.[95] It was the arrival of a reliable steam packet service in the 1830s that led to the Isle of Man becoming a tourist destination and steamers also had a role in promoting tourism in the Severn Estuary, opening resorts on the north Devon and Somerset coast to tourists from south Wales.

During the 19th century, the journey by steamer was already being considered part of the holiday. On the *Comet* there were two classes of accommodation. James Cleland explained, 'The cabin and steerage are fitted up with every suitable convenience; the former is provided with interesting books, and the various periodical publications. Breakfasts, dinners, &c. are provided for those who may require them. The cabin fare is four shillings, and the steerage two shillings and sixpence.'[96] William Daniell described the games available to play in the better class of accommodation on Clyde steamers and a similar range of entertainment was also available on the Thames steamboats, depending of course on the fare paid.[97] William Fry (1763–1849) on his return journey from Margate to London in 1826 chose the *Royal Sovereign* steamer, a journey lasting seven hours, during which entertainment was provided: 'To amuse us on our passage we had music, viz a Harp, Clarinet, & French Horn, they played a vast number of tunes, & among the rest, did not forget to play Rule Britannia & Cherry Ripe.'[98] An 1820 guidebook to the Thames recorded that 'backgammon tables, draught and chess boards' were provided on board some ships and 'a band of music constantly accompanies each vessel, to give hilarity to the scene'.[99]

Guidebooks were published to aid travellers on steamboats. In 1823, *A Companion for Canal Travellers between Edinburgh and Glasgow* listed the sights on either side of the canal, and in 1825, the first edition of the *Scottish Tourist and Itinerary* included descriptions of six main routes.[100] Travellers could purchase pocket-sized guidebooks with illustrations to allow the identification of features on the banks of the Thames. Among the small guidebooks with far from pocket-size titles were William Kidd's *The Picturesque Pocket Companion to Margate, Ramsgate, Broadstairs & the parts adjacent*, published in 1831, and William Camden's *The Steam-Boat Pocket Book: A descriptive guide from London Bridge to Gravesend, Southend, the Nore, Herne Bay, Margate, and Ramsgate, etc*, which appeared four years later.

The advent of the pier

The emergence of larger steamers during the 19th century led to the provision of piers, as the increased draught prevented these ships from mooring in shallow water (Fig 5.7). The pier usually awarded the accolade of being the earli-

Fig 5.7
This oblique aerial view of c 1920 shows the paddle steamer Eagle III, moored alongside Dunoon Pier, in Argyll and Bute. Eagle III took part in the Dunkirk evacuations in May 1940 and ran aground twice on the French beach to assist with the embarkation of other ships. Although refloated without damage, she never returned to active passenger duty.
[© HES]

est seaside pier was at Ryde on the Isle of Wight, although there were various stone piers forming harbours at Scarborough, Lyme Regis and Weymouth, as well as the timber jetty at Great Yarmouth where commerce and promenading had been combined.[101] The pier at Ryde opened on 26 July 1814, although landing passengers was difficult at low tide until the pier was subsequently lengthened.[102] It consisted of a simple wooden deck carried on brick arches at the shore end and driven wooden piles further out to sea. The new pier at Margate, the stone arm of the harbour, was completed in time for steamers to ply the Thames in 1815. Visitors could walk along its raised promenade if they paid a 1d toll, its introduction sparking a near riot in 1812 (Fig 5.8).[103]

At the other end of the country, the need to handle steamers serving Edinburgh led to the creation of the ambitious Leith Trinity Chain Pier in 1821 by the civil engineer and naval officer Captain Samuel Brown (1776–1852).[104] Constructed at a cost of £4,000, it consisted of

three spans, 209ft (63.7m) long, but its timber deck, suspended from chains carried by timber towers, was only 4ft (1.2m) wide. In 1823, Brown constructed another chain pier at Brighton and this remained a central feature of the resort until its destruction in 1896 (Fig 5.9).[105] In the 1834 book *Holidays at Brighton*, a fictional youthful visitor to the resort wondered why 'that strange-looking bridge' ran into the sea before he and his father strolled along it to watch passengers embarking onto the steam packet to Dieppe.[106] Brighton's pier is proof that confidence was growing in the reliability and safety of steamers, with services expanding from estuaries to around the coast and across the Channel.[107]

The apparent sophistication of the superstructure of the Chain Pier at Brighton should not disguise the fact that it was constructed using driven wooden piles, the mainstay of pier construction until the 1850s. The timber structure known as Jarvis' Jetty at Margate, constructed in 1824 at a cost of £8,000, was

Fig 5.8
The harbour arm at
Margate is roughly half-
octagonal in plan, with a
raised promenade along
its seaward side. It is
approximately 900ft
(270m) long, but still could
not cope with steamers at
low tide, necessitating the
construction beside it of a
timber and later a cast-iron
jetty (seen behind it in this
1920 photograph).
[EPW000162]

Fig 5.9
Brighton's Chain Pier, seen
in this late 19th-century
photograph, was 1,154ft
(351.8m) long and cost
£30,000 to erect. Although
the chains and the upright
elements of the super-
structure were made of
iron, the pier was still
constructed on timber piles.
[BB85/01743b]

designed to improve access to the resort for increasingly large steamers that were no longer able to land passengers at the stone pier at low tide. It was over 1,000ft long (305m), yet still proved too short at low tide and sometimes people had to land, as before, by rowing boat.[108]

Timber remained the key structural element of new piers in the 1830s, such as the first pier at Southend-on-Sea, in Essex, which opened in June 1830, and the pier at Herne Bay, in Kent, the first timber pile of which was driven into the seabed in July 1831.[109] These piers had been constructed to grab some of the lucrative passenger traffic along the Thames that had hitherto largely been monopolised by Margate. Both these new piers required significant repairs within a few years due to being constructed of wood, and so pier designers were beginning to look to the use of iron piles. The Town Pier at Gravesend, in Kent, designed by the engineer William Tierney Clark (1783–1852), was completed in July 1834 and consisted of three graceful arches carried on 26 iron columns. In 1835, an iron pier opened at Sheerness, in Kent, and the other pier at Gravesend, the Royal Terrace Pier, was replaced in iron in 1842.[110]

Despite these early examples, a definitive shift to using iron piles took place only during the 1850s with the construction of the new jetty at Margate. The timber Jarvis' Jetty had been breached twice in 1851, and therefore the decision was taken to employ the civil engineer Eugenius Birch (1818–84) to build a new jetty, the first of his 14 piers.[111] His most important contribution to pier construction was to employ the screw pile. It was patented in 1833 by Alexander Mitchell (1780–1868) and used a screw on the end of an iron rod to fix the pile into the seabed.[112] Mitchell had already used this system in lighthouses, before creating his first jetty at Courtown harbour in County Wexford, in Ireland, in 1847.[113] The first pile of Margate's new jetty was driven in May 1853 and it opened in April 1855, although the structure, 1,240ft (378m) long, was not completed until July 1856 (Fig 5.10).[114]

The railway era

Railways would have both a direct and an indirect impact on the growth, and in some cases the creation, of seaside resorts during the 19th century. This could be through the leadership of railway companies or more usually in more or less formal partnerships with local landowners and entrepreneurs. Railways also helped to shape the plan of seaside resorts, as well as the activities taking place in them, as the character of holidaymakers changed. The rapid growth of the railway network from the 1830s also had an indirect impact on seaside tourism, creating by the end of the 19th century the circumstances in which tourism could flourish.[115]

Railways using horse-drawn carriages were a key part of some heavy industries and as early as 1807 the Swansea-to-Oystermouth Railway provided a passenger service. The Kilmarnock and Troon line opened in 1817 to meet the demand for Ayrshire coal in Belfast, but also carried passengers on one of the first services to employ George Stephenson's locomotives.[116] Numerous small railways sprang up to meet local industrial demands, but it was not until the opening of the Stockton and Darlington Railway in 1825, followed in 1830 by the Canterbury and Whitstable Railway (C&WR) and the Liverpool and Manchester Railway, that passenger services were more than peripheral to the new businesses. In 1834, the C&WR issued the world's first season

ticket to take passengers to Whitstable's beaches during the summer.[117] However, even as late as 1842, some railway companies still thought passengers were a fringe benefit to their core business.[118] The prospectus of the Preston and Wyre Railway in 1834 suggested that visitors to Blackpool would represent only 3 per cent of the expected receipts.[119] However, in 1845, passenger fares actually accounted for 64 per cent of the gross receipts, falling to 57 per cent in 1848, and this revenue stream was never lower than 40 per cent during the 19th century.[120]

Railways and seaside resorts

Seaside resorts were one of the main beneficiaries of the emerging railway system. During the 1840s, many existing resorts began to be connected to the rapidly growing railway network. Brighton led the way, followed by more than a dozen existing resorts including Great Yarmouth, Scarborough, Margate, Hastings, Teignmouth, Whitby and Torquay.[121] Six rival schemes were proposed in 1834–5 for a route from Brighton to London, with the most direct line being chosen in 1836 and opening in 1841.[122] In 1840, the Preston and Wyre Railway opened, running to the new port and resort of Fleetwood, in Lancashire, and in 1846, a branch line was established into the heart of Blackpool.[123] As the 19th century progressed, railways spread to smaller, more remote resorts and areas of the country. Perhaps the most surprising latecomer to the railway era

Fig 5.10

Eugenius Birch's Margate Jetty (photographed here in c 1870) was originally a very simple promenade pier capable of landing passengers from steamers. The construction of a polygonal extension at its seaward end in 1875–7 increased the number of landing stages and provided space for a bandstand, kiosks and shelters. See also Figure 8.2. [BB88/04260]

was Bournemouth, in Dorset, which only acquired its first two stations during the 1870s. In Wales, the railway arrived at Conwy in 1849, coincidentally when a building plan for Llandudno was being drawn up. A Board of Commissioners was appointed in 1854 and four years later the town secured a direct railway link.[124] The north Wales coast could be reached from London in five hours, but perhaps more importantly it was only two hours from Manchester and an hour and a half from Liverpool.[125] Tenby, in Pembrokeshire, had a station in 1863, but it was not until 1897 that it was connected to the national network.[126]

Railways had a major impact on the growth of seaside resorts, responding to an upsurge in demand, especially from a new wave of working-class holidaymakers.[127] Between 1851 and 1901, the population of Britain grew by 51 per cent, from 27.5 million to 41.6 million, but many resorts grew much faster. Blackpool most spectacularly increased by almost 1,400 per cent, as much a result of its low population in 1851 as its huge popularity in 1901. Similar reasons explain Southport's growth by 588 per cent. In Kent, a heartland of early resort development, Folkestone grew by 310 per cent, a reflection of its cross-Channel link as much as its growing resort function. The population of the parish of Herne with Herne Bay increased by 173 per cent and Margate, after a mid-century dip, grew again ultimately by 165 per cent over 50 years. In Sussex, Brighton grew at just around the national average (56 per cent) as it was so well developed by 1851, but adjacent Hove grew by 624 per cent, Eastbourne by 1,144 per cent, Hastings by 272 per cent and Bognor 143 per cent. Scarborough, which had not grown much between the mid-18th century and the mid-19th century, almost trebled in size in the decades after the railway arrived. During the second half of the 19th century, seaside resorts grew as quickly as major industrial manufacturing towns and cities, the new industry of leisure being as economically potent in some places as cotton spinning or steel making.

The emergence of the railway system created new resorts, often as a by-product of the establishment of a line for other commercial reasons. The Morecambe Harbour and Railway Company was established to build a link to a harbour on Morecambe Bay, in Lancashire, close to the fishing village of Poulton-le-Sands, the creation of a resort being an incidental benefit.[128] Bexhill-on-Sea, in East Sussex, was established on the route of a line passing by its location while connecting other places on the coast.[129] North Wales was largely undeveloped for tourism until the arrival of the railway promoted by Samuel Morton Peto, the chairman of Chester and Holyhead Railway. The motivation for the line was to meet the ferry from Ireland, but incidentally it also stimulated the growth of Rhyl, Colwyn Bay (Fig 5.11) and Llandudno.[130] It was this easier access that saw a shift at Colwyn Bay from a settlement in the hands of landed aristocracy, who opposed development, to involvement by Manchester businessmen seeking to profit from the new connections.[131]

At some resorts a more or less formal cooperation existed between landowners and railway companies. At Hunstanton, in Norfolk, the local landowner Henry Le Strange (1815–62), an architect himself, was determined to have a town designed to high standards and therefore well-known London architects were employed. He also provided land for public gardens and for the Lynn and Hunstanton Railway that opened in 1862, the year of his untimely early death. The railway company built its own hotel, the Sandringham Hotel, and paid an average annual dividend of 7.5 per cent in 1866–74, despite the fact that (or perhaps because) it was 100 miles (160km) from the nearest large industrial town.[132]

At Saltburn, in Yorkshire, local landowner Lord Zetland (1795–1873), Quaker railway company promoter Henry Pease (1807–81) and the Stockton and Darlington Railway Company undertook the development.[133] The town was centred on the station, which opened in 1861, and in 1863 William Peachey (1826–1912), the architect of the station, completed the 50-bedroom Zetland Hotel.[134] Uniquely, the hotel had a railway line almost up to its back door. At Cleethorpes, in Lincolnshire, the Manchester, Sheffield and Lincolnshire Railway invested more than £100,000 to build an exhibition hall, a museum, aquarium, amusement park and baths, as well as the promenade and gardens.[135] The main landowners in the town, Sidney College Cambridge and the Earl of Yarborough, took advantage of this investment by laying out large numbers of building plots for speculative development.[136]

Although the activities of railway companies might prompt investment by landowners and businessmen, there are only a handful of examples of them leading the development of new resorts. In 1854, the Hull and Holderness Railway opened a line to Withernsea, in Yorkshire,

Fig 5.11
This aerial photograph of
Colwyn Bay in 1936 shows
the railway line running
along the coast, almost
cutting the resort off from
its pier and beach.
[WPW051604 © Crown
Copyright: Royal
Commission on the Ancient
and Historical Monuments
of Wales: Aerofilms
Collection]

and established an Improvement Company, but the new settlement never prospered as a resort, instead serving as a dormitory for Hull.[137] In 1879, a group of directors from the Furness Railway planned a promenade, the Grange Hotel and semi-detached houses at Seascale, in Cumbria, but a decade later only around a dozen houses had been built (Fig 5.12).[138] Silloth, also in Cumbria, was created to plug a hole in the Carlisle and Silloth Bay Railway Company's cash flow while its new dock was being built.[139] An architect was commissioned to lay out this proposed large resort during the 1850s. A terrace was built in Criffel Street, costing over £5,000, along with a £7,000 hotel, baths, pleasure gardens, the sewers and gasworks, an investment in total of more than £34,000.[140] However, by the mid-1880s, with little else built, responsibility for the town passed to a Local Board and a Town Improvement Society.[141]

Railway companies were also keen to exploit the growing popularity of their services by estab-lishing hotels. The first hotel for rail travellers was built by Lord Crewe (1812–94) at Crewe in 1837, while the earliest erected by a railway company were twin hotels at Euston, London, in 1839.[142] During the course of the 19th century, hotels were established in major cities, perhaps the most celebrated being the revived hotel at St Pancras Station, London, but some were also established in more rural locations where there was a new market to exploit. The Great North of Scotland Railway Company commissioned a new golf course at the small seaside resort of Cruden Bay on the Aberdeenshire coast, which opened in 1899. In the same year, a tramway was built to link the company's main line to the new course, and a pink granite hotel, 'The Palace in the Sandhills', was built.[143] Railway companies also established hotels at a number of seaside resorts, the most famous probably being the Midland Hotel at Morecambe.[144] The North Western Hotel opened in 1848 and was renamed the Midland Hotel in 1871.[145] In the early 1930s,

Fig 5.12
This aerial photograph of Seascale in 1929 shows some of the large houses that had been built as part of the railway company's development.
[EPW029167]

Oliver Hill (1887–1968) was commissioned by the London Midland and Scottish Railway to design a replacement and the resulting gem of Art Deco was described by Irish aristocrat and politician Lord Clonmore (1877–1946) as meaning that Morecambe would be 'well emancipated from Victorian gloom'.[146]

Railways were a vital new facility for Victorian Britain, but not all towns, or more accurately, not all of their citizens, were in favour of having a railway station. In the 1830s, Weston-super-Mare, in Somerset, was bypassed because of local opposition, but the town relented and a short branch line was soon built to link it to the main line.[147] In 1846, some townspeople at Bridlington, in Yorkshire, objected to a station near the quay, the more fashionable part of town, and therefore it was built further inland, while it took Cromer, in Norfolk, until 1877 to have a rail link.[148] The inland spa at Strathpeffer, in the Scottish Highlands, initially resisted the Skye Railway, but the succession of the new laird led to a branch line opening in 1885.[149] Frinton-on-Sea, in Essex, owes its existence to the Great Eastern Railway, which opened a station in 1888 – the town prides itself still as being the most sedate resort in the country, as anyone wanting to watch football in a pub will know![150]

Although some towns and landowners tried to resist what was seen as progress, others were quick to embrace it. The Duke of Devonshire (1790–1858) actively campaigned to get a line to Eastbourne and invested in the resort. On 15 June 1849, he wrote in his diary, 'The railway has certainly improved the prospects of the place considerably.'[151] At Ilfracombe, in Devon, developers had to struggle to get the London and South Western Railway to extend its line beyond Barnstaple and it was only in 1874 that they succeeded.[152]

Railways and the growth of mass tourism

Railways contributed to changing the shape and size of tourism in Britain. Initially, major lines linked London and large conurbations, but as the 19th century progressed, the reach of railways stretched into less populated areas of England, such as Cornwall, as well as into north Wales and fairly remote parts of Scotland.[153] It also helped to take people out of Britain. As early as the 18th century, some British people were spending winters on France's Côte d'Azur. In 1876, *The Popular Encyclopedia* stated, 'Nice is much resorted to in winter by foreigners, particularly English, whose numbers have been estimated at 5000 to 6000, besides French, Germans, Russians, and Poles, and for whom ample accommodation is provided.'[154]

Within Britain, the growth of railways contributed to the shift from visiting spas. Railways were ideal for transporting large numbers of people cheaply, particularly if they did not mind discomfort (Fig 5.13). The seaside was a relatively cheap place to pass a day or two for a poor family, as 18th- and early 19th-century visitors to Blackpool demonstrated, walking from Lancashire towns or arriving in carts to bathe in the sea.[155] However, at spas everything had to be paid for, including access to the health-giving water and all the entertainments, and therefore they were less likely to be a major destination for the passengers of the first railway companies.

The tale of the impact of railways can also be told through ticket sales. Between 1850 and 1870, first-class ticket sales rose by 280 per cent, second-class by 193 per cent, but most significantly third-class sales grew by 584 per cent.[156] During 1837, stagecoaches had brought around 50,000 travellers to Brighton, but in a single week in 1850, 73,000 people arrived by train.[157]

On 3 August 1863, more than 30,000 people travelled to the newly opened station at Cleethorpes, with a further 4,000 arriving on horse-drawn vehicles.[158] Blackpool was a large village in the early 1850s, when it welcomed up to 12,000 visitors by train during a busy summer weekend (Fig 5.14). During 1861, 135,000 passengers arrived annually and by 1879 this had risen to almost one million. By 1914, around four million passengers were travelling to Blackpool each year and in July 1945, 102,889 people arrived in one 24-hour period.[159] On 15 July 1933, the *Glasgow Herald* reported that 150,000 people left Glasgow on the Friday of the Glasgow Fair in 355 special trains. Around 200 of these were heading to long-distance destinations such as London and Manchester, as well as Whitley Bay, Blackpool and Scarborough.

Advertising was key to stimulating demand for rail travel, destinations and excursions, and by the 20th century railway companies led in the development of advertising and the art of the

Fig 5.13
This photograph of Liverpool Street Station in London shows expectant travellers waiting to board the train to Felixstowe for a Monday morning excursion to the seaside (c 1930).
[AA78/02492]

poster. One of the most famous is the Great Northern Railway poster produced in 1908. 'Skegness is so bracing' shows a cheerful, rosy-cheeked fisherman skipping along the beach. 'Bright, breezy, bracing, Bridlington – Boating Bathing' was produced by the North Eastern Railway. In these posters the sun always shone, though to the alert the word 'bracing' was a warning of cold winds. In 1924, the Great Western Railway (GWR) created a new publicity department, which coined the phrase 'Go Great Western' and produced its own *Holiday Haunts* guidebook, 200,000 copies being printed in 1928. The GWR was also responsible for coining the phrase 'Cornish Riviera' before World War I, and this has remained central to marketing strategies ever since. Resorts followed the example of railway

companies and invested in marketing and posters. In 1925, Torquay spent £3,000 on promoting the resort.[160] The 1930s was the heyday of the art of the railway poster, a decade beset with economic problems that impacted on passenger numbers. Therefore, advertising was a key tool employed by railway companies to stimulate travel. Between 1932 and 1934, the GWR doubled its production of posters to 100,000.[161]

A key way in which railways changed the face of tourism was through the provision of excursions. Although modern train travel can range from unpleasantly crowded to quiet luxury, many early excursionists were hardy people prepared to endure travelling in open carriages sometimes in foul weather. Thomas Hardy's 1890s short story *The Fiddler of the Reels* describes the novelty of the excursion train that left its passengers 'in a pitiable condition: blue-faced, stiff-necked, sneezing, rain-beaten, chilled to the marrow (resembling) people who had been out all night on a rough sea rather than inland excursionists for pleasure'.[162]

Some of the earliest excursions were staged by railway companies offering introductions to the experience of train travel and in 1830, the first year of its operation, the Liverpool and Manchester Railway ran introductory excursions.[163] One of the earliest railway companies to take an active interest in tourist excursions in the early 1830s was the Garnkirk and Glasgow Railway, which offered evening, afternoon and day trips from Glasgow to the then rather unattractive town of Airdrie, in North Lanarkshire.[164] But the trips sold, which suggests that it was the experience of travelling and the views en route rather than the destination that was the attraction, as only one hour was spent there. By 1849, the North British Railway was offering day excursions from Edinburgh to Berwick-upon-Tweed and Newcastle, not just to experience life 'abroad', but perhaps more importantly 'because the district of country through which the Party will pass is famed for its varied and picturesque scenery'.[165] During the course of the 19th century, reduced-price excursion tickets were key factors in increasing access to the network. By 1860, the London, Brighton and South Coast Railway was running 36 excursion trains from London on a Sunday, providing customers with up to 12 hours by the sea.[166]

Special train services were also provided for events, such as the performance of an opera in 1831, while a train was put on every morning from Manchester for a fortnight from 1 August

Fig 5.14
The 29 platforms of the two rebuilt 1890s stations at Blackpool could handle up to 80 excursion trains per day, as well as regular services. This aerial photograph of the Central Railway Station, taken in the mid-20th century, shows its seafront location, making it very convenient for day trippers.
[Afl03/aeropictorial/ r20518]

1842 so that people could attend the Liverpool Assizes.[167] However, the major event in terms of interest in rail travel was the Great Exhibition in 1851, which brought millions of visitors to London and established Thomas Cook (1808–92) as a leading figure in providing organised trips.[168] One railway company alone, the London North Western Railway, carried 774,910 passengers to London for the Great Exhibition by excursion trains between June and October 1851.[169] Excursions were good for the income of railway companies (Fig 5.15). In 1865, the Midland Railway carried nearly 400,000 excursionists and in the decade 1900–9 the London, Brighton and South Coast Railway issued nearly 19 million excursion tickets, a revenue stream accounting for about one-eighth of the company's income.[170]

In addition to trains laid on by railway companies, enlightened, philanthropic employers were also important providers of trips. In 1848, Sir Titus Salt, the founder of Saltaire Village and a number of mills, took 2,000 employees into the countryside and in 1865, Bass Brewery provided its first family day trip to the seaside, an event that became an annual occurrence from 1889.[171] The 1914 Bass trip took the staff to Scarborough on Friday 24 July in 14 trains, consisting of 225 carriages. The company thoughtfully provided its staff with a timetable and a guidebook to the resort, and had also arranged preferential rates for entry to many of the leading attractions.[172] The annual trip of the GWR workshop employees involved transporting 21,000 people in 500 carriages from Swindon to Weymouth by the 1890s, and in July 1914, 26,000 were taken on the trip, amounting to more than half of the town's population.[173]

As well as employers, groups of workers and charitable bodies provided trips for their members. Mechanics institutes arranged trips that were both pleasurable and educational and organisations of working people, including the Oddfellows and the Foresters, also ran their own excursions.[174] On 7 September 1841, a party of 1,200 travelled up from Birmingham to Liverpool for a Mechanics Institute function, a trip involving coordination between the Liverpool and Manchester Railway and the Grand Junction Railway.[175] Employees at Portsmouth dockyard formed their own excursion committee in 1883 and ran their first trip to the Fisheries Exhibition in London.[176] Political organisations also arranged large excursions. In June 1929, the National Union of Railwaymen organised a day excursion to Blackpool. A special deluxe train conveyed 500 passengers from Stirling at 7am, arriving in Blackpool at midday and returning at 6pm. Breakfast, lunch and tea were served on the train and as the weather was ideal throughout, the day was voted one of the most enjoyable yet held.[177]

A by-product of the availability of trains and an appetite for excursions was the appearance of the first travel agents. Although Thomas Cook was not the first or only private individual to arrange trips, his name has become synonymous with organised excursions. This Baptist wood-turner's career as a travel agent was launched as a result of his involvement with the temperance movement. On 5 July 1841 he arranged a railway excursion from Leicester to Loughborough for 500 temperance supporters and during the mid-1840s organising railway excursions became his main business.[178] The 1850s were a time of success, the decade starting with the Great Exhibition, when Cook became the Midland Railway's agent for excursion traffic. His trips delivered 165,000 excursionists to Euston, while

Fig 5.15
This poster, produced by the Great Western Railway, rather dryly offers an educational excursion to Stonehenge, in Wiltshire, a half-day trip from Paddington. Motor vehicles would meet the trippers at Lavington Station and take them to see the stones.
[DP166521]

the London and North Western company apparently conveyed a further 90,000 people.[179] However, he faced potential ruin in 1862 when the Scottish railway companies refused to issue any more group tickets for his tours and so, in 1865, he opened an office in London and began to look to Europe. His first ventures abroad were tours to France and Switzerland, but later he organised a trip to the Holy Land and Egypt. In 1878, Thomas Cook retired, leaving his son John to run the business (Fig 5.16).

Although most excursionists were well behaved, there was a fear, sometimes backed up by fact, that new influxes of day trippers would lower the standards of behaviour in well-established holiday resorts. Concerns about excursionists often focused on their drinking and their impropriety in bathing in the nude.[180] In 1872, a newspaper reporter at Cleethorpes wrote, 'This tremendous worship of Bacchus on Good Friday proclaimed the nearest approach to an earthly pandemonium I have ever been able to discover. There were back room and passage scenes of which delicacy forbids a description,' while in August 1872 respectable locals were offended by nude bathing.[181] In 1859, French

novelist Jules Verne (1828–1905) enjoyed a day bathing in the sea at Portobello, on the outskirts of Edinburgh. Verne and his companion were surprised that they could hire a bathing machine, but were unable to procure a costume, meaning that they bathed naked and then waded back to the beach 'quite oblivious of the misses, mistresses and ladies on shore'.[182] Revd Francis Kilvert had exactly the opposite problem while staying on the Isle of Wight in June 1874. Accustomed to bathing in the nude, as men had done in Georgian times, he found that he was scandalising respectable Shanklin and therefore had to 'adopt the detestable custom of bathing in drawers'.[183] A resident of Scarborough said that the railway 'brought a new host of invaders who were the pale, emaciated inhabitants of murky and densely populated cities seeking to restore their sickly frames to health and vigour by frequent immersion in the sea'.[184] The solution to this problem was realised by the railway company in 1908 when a separate excursion station was erected a short distance from the town. It had its own route down to the beach, allowing the segregation of the unwashed hordes from the genteel residents.

The greatest issue in the conflict between genteel inhabitants and determined trippers was the observance of the Sabbath. Residents of Blackpool, Lytham, Southport and Morecambe successfully petitioned local railway companies to suspend Sunday excursions, albeit only temporarily as idle rolling stock generated no profits.[185] However, for the majority of workers for most of the 19th century, the only day of rest or leisure was Sunday and railway companies were keen to realise the potential of this market. The Lancashire and Yorkshire Railway offered 'sea bathing for the working classes' on Sundays and promised that 'parties availing themselves of these trains will be enabled to bathe and refresh themselves in ample time to attend a Place of Worship'.[186] Religious groups, such as Sunday Schools, had used the railways for excursions from the outset. In 1843, the Stanley Lads of Alderley welcomed almost 3,000 children out from Manchester to enjoy 'seeing such scenery and breathing such pure air'.[187] However, some religious campaigners and groups opposed the way that excursions undermined the observance of the Sabbath. An article in the *Dunfermline Sunday Press* in September 1867 entitled 'Aberdour versus the Sunday Steamers' reported how the author had seen that while some people visiting Blackpool were enjoying the beach and the

Fig 5.16
This photograph by Bedford Lemere was commissioned to record the new offices of Thomas Cook and Son in Gallowtree Gate in Leicester in 1894. At first-floor level is a frieze of four panels illustrating important milestones in Cook's career as a travel agent.
[BL13497]

countryside, 'for the most part the excursionists take a short course from the railway station to the neighbouring beer-houses, which on Sundays are crowded to excess, and the "day out" means drinking in Blackpool instead of drinking in Preston'.[188]

Excursions were an important part of the income of railway companies. The one drawback was seasonality. There was too much demand for their rolling stock in the summer, particularly during Wakes weeks, but too little in the winter. This was something that was true of not just the day and weekend flows to the resorts, but also seasonal, longer-distance movement, notably the sporting traffic to Scotland, which reached a crescendo in early August.

The arrival of railways increased the number of working-class visitors, but it also sometimes drove middle-class visitors out into their own estates and Grand Hotels, as well as to resorts that still lay beyond the reach of railways. The 1820s and 1830s had witnessed a series of grand architectural projects in the south of England aimed at the small, but economically significant, middle- and upper-class residential and visitor market, the type of people with time and wealth to spend weeks at the seaside. However, from the 1840s onwards the railway network, combined with increased prosperity, saw the beginning of the growth of a new market for seaside holidays among working people. This helped to bring new investment into seaside resorts where previously much of it had been drawn from local landowners and businessmen. It also led to huge areas of development, often modest housing aimed at the growing residential population, while the wealthier end of the housing market would be satisfied by developments of detached and semi-detached villas, away from the heart of increasingly busy resorts. For wealthier visitors to withdraw from the busy centres of resorts, Grand Hotels began to be built, forming small, self-contained, exclusive resorts in their own right (Fig 5.17).

In larger resorts, and those with twin settlements – like Brighton and Hove, Hastings and St Leonards or Margate and Cliftonville – it was possible to have some level of separation between excursionists and polite residents. Hove and West Brighton began to be considered as 'Belgravia-sur-Mer'.[189] However, in other towns more or less formal attempts at social zoning

Fig 5.17
The Grand Hotel at Scarborough, designed by Cuthbert Broderick (1821–1905), contained 300 bedrooms. When it opened in 1867 it was the largest hotel in Europe. [DP006187]

developed by directing arrivals away from polite residential areas or sometimes more overtly through measures such as enclosing and policing estates. At Scarborough, the separate excursion station subtly allowed trippers to be directed to the seafront without having to go through the respectable centre of town. In many resorts, large areas of new housing were established, with wealthier estates on the seafront and in areas away from the town centres, while more affordable homes were created in less desirable areas often in and around stations and along the railway lines. At Whitby, in Yorkshire, West Cliff began to be developed with new housing and at Lowestoft, in Suffolk, the arrival of the railway opened up the area to the south of the town to develop as a fashionable resort.[190] At Blackpool the visitors with the least money might find lodgings in Bonny's Estate near the Central Station, while wealthier visitors and residents enjoyed the solace of life behind the gates of the Claremont Park Estate on North Shore.

Railway stations concentrated dense development in the heart of resorts, where trains disgorged their cargo of trippers. Often railway stations were created at the edge of the centre of the settlement as it existed when the line arrived, and this created a new focus and new axes of development. For instance, at Blackpool the first station led to a shift in the town's main axis from Church Street to Talbot Road. The town's first pier was subsequently established in 1863 at the seaward end of this new direct route from the station.

Bicycles and the countryside

Railways transformed the character and size of tourism during the second half of the 19th century. The handful of simple locomotives of the 1830s had become thousands of sophisticated engines transporting millions of people to work every day and on leisure trips at weekends and during summer holidays. During the 20th century, the internal combustion engine – first through the bus and charabanc, and later the car – would be fundamental to creating a new level of personal mobility. It would also have a huge impact on leisure and tourism, opening more of Britain to more people. However, an earlier, quiet revolution in personal mobility and the extension of tourism was under way in the late 19th century through the humble bicycle.

In 1869, James Starley (1831–81), a foreman at the European Sewing Machine Company in Coventry, devised the Ariel, which was known as the penny-farthing or 'ordinary'.[191] The first safety bicycle was designed by Harry Lawson (1852–1925) in 1876 and improved by the addition of a chain drive in 1879. However, it was only in 1885 that John Kemp Starley (1855–1901), a nephew of James Starley, produced the first commercially successful model, called the Rover, and within a few years the 'ordinary' was obsolete.[192] Cycling was further transformed by the introduction of the pneumatic tyre. It was devised by John Boyd Dunlop (1840–1921), who first fixed air tubes or hoses covered in rubber to his son's tricycle in 1887.[193]

Bicycles and tricycles were relatively cheap and, as the years went past, could be acquired second-hand in growing numbers. While a horse was expensive to buy and look after, a bicycle once purchased required little further outlay and a cyclist could travel twice as far in a day as a person on horseback.[194] This meant that people could travel to and from work more quickly, potentially leaving more free time during the working week, as well as allowing leisure trips on days off (Fig 5.18). A plethora of guidebooks began to be published aimed at the growing market for cycling day-trip destinations. Among these were a guide by Richard Greene to *Northampton as a Cycling Centre* and another about Northamptonshire written by the architect John Alfred Gotch.[195] Both these guides were published in 1889, in time for the cycling boom of the 1890s.

Although cycling was an individual activity, some cyclists joined clubs, such as the Cyclists' Touring Club, which was formed as the Bicyclists' Touring Club in 1878 with 142 members. Between 1885 and 1890, the club boasted around 20,000 members and it peaked at 60,449 in 1899 before tailing off.[196] There was also a political dimension to the humble bicycle. The Clarion Cycling Club, originally called the Socialist Cycling Club but renamed after the socialist newspaper *The Clarion,* was created in Birmingham in February 1894.

Cycling had an impact on the lives of women, after some initial concerns that it was unladylike, unhealthy and indecorous (Fig 5.19).[197] Women could now travel further from home without chaperones, although a Chaperone Cyclists' Association was established to accompany female cyclists.[198] The suffrage movement used cycling to spread the word and convert people in villages to support votes for women.[199] In 1893, an article in the *Northern Wheeler*

Fig 5.18
This c 1900 photograph shows male and female cyclists in Hyde Park in London, with interested onlookers lining the route. Was this a pleasant Sunday afternoon outing perhaps? [CC97/01240]

proclaimed, 'Woman has taken her stand, and her seat in the saddle, unlike the author of the historic phrase, we men can only say – this is not a revolt, it is a revolution.'[200]

The bicycle also became a means to travel on holiday. The earliest cycling tourists may have been two members of the Liverpool Velocipede Club who set off for Chester and London in 1869.[201] The Cyclists' Touring Club arranged its first Continental tour in 1879 and in 1887 published a Continental road book.[202] Bicycle maker

and pioneer motorist William Henry Ireland and a friend undertook a cycling tour of England in 1888, including Ireland's first visit to London. After spending two days there, they cycled on to Newhaven, in Sussex, where they caught a cross-Channel packet to Dieppe, from where they rode on to Paris.[203] In July 1893, John and George McGregor, two brothers from Motherwell, in North Lanarkshire, went on a week-long cycle trip to the north of Scotland, covering 695 miles (1,118km), which was recorded in their journal, called 'Wheel wanderings'.[204] The McGregors were touring Scotland for pleasure, but other cyclists were more concerned with distance records, the route from Land's End, in Cornwall, to John o'Groats, at the north-east tip of Scotland, being the ultimate challenge. They looked through the Visitors Book at the hotel at John o'Groats and 'read the accounts of the great rides against time done by road scorchers from Land's End'.[205]

Charabancs, cars and caravans

The bicycle was not the only mechanical means of transport running on Victorian roads. Steam-powered carriages were experimented with by Richard Trevithick (1771–1833) in 1801 and gradually became more practical, though their heavy iron wheels damaged roads, leading turnpike trusts to impose prohibitively heavy tolls

Fig 5.19
Riding a bicycle required less-restrictive clothing, something encouraged by the 'Rational Dress Society', leading to a change of attitude about what was acceptable female attire. This photograph, taken at some point between 1896 and 1920, shows a young woman riding along a street in Culworth, in Northamptonshire. [BB98/06038]

(Fig 5.20).[206] The Locomotive or Red Flag Act of 1865 compelled road locomotives to be preceded by a man carrying a red flag and imposed a speed limit of 4mph on country roads and 2mph in towns.[207] Although there was some amendment of this restrictive Act in 1878, there were still significant restrictions on road transport in place when the first cars began to appear.[208]

The earliest instance of mounting an internal combustion engine on a vehicle was 1860, but the significant breakthrough came in 1885, when Karl Benz (1844–1929) produced the first petrol-driven car, followed in 1886 by the independent innovation from Gottlieb Daimler (1834–1900).[209] In 1895, the first British-made car was manufactured by John Henry Knight (1847–1917) of Farnham, in Surrey. During the following year, the Daimler Motor Company was established in Coventry by Henry (Harry) John Lawson (1852–1925), after Lawson bought the rights to the Daimler name. Meanwhile the Lanchester brothers, based in Birmingham, built their first car in 1896.[210]

Harry Lawson established the Motor Car Club in 1895. By the following year, he had successfully campaigned for the Locomotives on Highways Act, which abolished the need for motor vehicles to be preceded by a flag-bearing pedestrian and raised the speed limit to a dizzy 12–14mph.[211] To mark this event, he staged an Emancipation Day Run from London to Brighton on 14 November 1896, probably the maximum distance achievable comfortably by cars of the period, and this became an annual event from 1927.[212] Similar events were held elsewhere, including annual runs in Scotland (Fig 5.21). The British motor car industry in 1914 was still tiny, with fewer than 34,000 vehicles a year being manufactured. In 1914 there were only 132,000 private cars registered to run on Britain's roads, along with 259,000 public and commercial vehicles.[213] Nevertheless, the growing number of motor vehicles on the road was outpacing reforms to the speed limit and in 1903, another Act raised the general speed limit to 20mph.[214]

Although it would be the motor car that would have the most profound effect on tourism habits, initially the greatest impact came from the charabanc, the omnibus and the coach. These forms of transport can trace their ancestry back to horse-drawn precursors during the 19th century. During the summer at Great Yarmouth in the 1880s, 'cross-benched cars' were available every morning to take visitors to Lowestoft, as well as to other places. Scottish traveller William Miller wrote, 'In fine weather this method of conveyance is to the generality of people the most pleasant method of seeing the country.'[215]

When motorised charabancs and coaches began to appear in the early 20th century (the first London-to-Brighton motorised omnibus set out on 30 August 1905), they were not usually replacing the railways.[216] Instead, the charabanc and coach extended the reach of visitors from towns and resorts to smaller destinations without railway stations and out into the countryside. Since the 18th century, resort guidebooks had included walks and rides into the countryside, but increasingly they featured more ambitious excursions made possible by these new forms of transport. For instance, there were excursions to the Lake District from both Blackpool and Morecambe during the interwar years.[217] By the late 1920s, travel writer and journalist Henry Canova Vollam Morton (1892–1979) could proclaim, 'The remarkable system of motor-coach services which now penetrate every part of the country has thrown open to ordinary people regions which even after the coming of the railway were remote and inaccessible.'[218] Coach tours began to be organised by enterprising companies. In 1910, Chapman's of Eastbourne arranged a coach trip to north Wales and, impressed by its popularity, the firm went on to arrange a three-week tour to John o'Groats.[219]

Fig 5.20
This toll bridge sign at the Barbican in Sandwich, in Kent, described the charges being levied in June 1905, including the hefty fees for heavy coaches and large locomotives.
[DP032054]

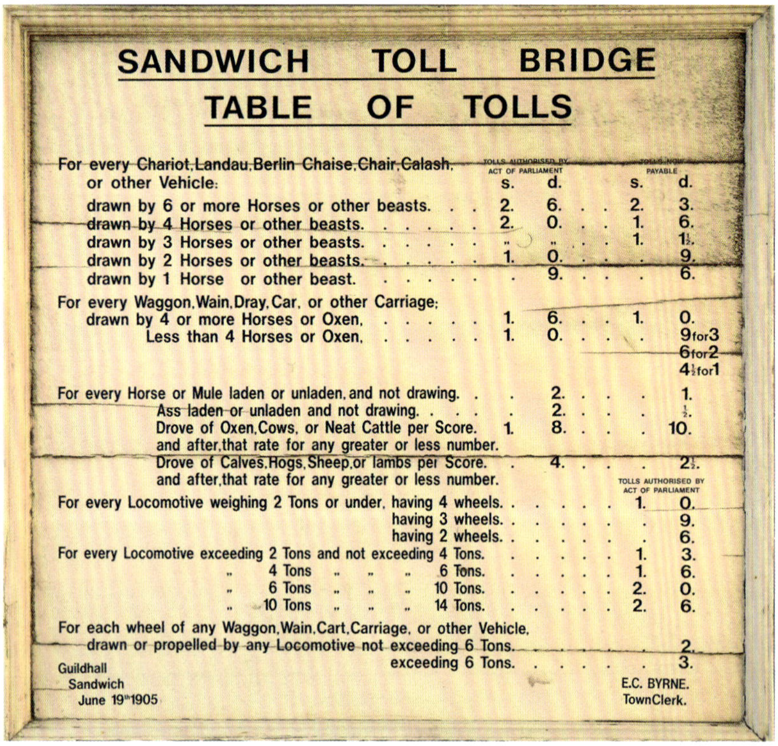

SANDWICH TOLL BRIDGE
TABLE OF TOLLS

	TOLLS AUTHORISED BY ACT OF PARLIAMENT		TOLLS NOW PAYABLE	
	s.	d.	s.	d.
For every Chariot, Landau, Berlin Chaise, Chair, Galash, or other Vehicle:				
drawn by 6 or more Horses or other beasts	2.	6.	2.	3.
drawn by 4 Horses or other beasts	2.	0.	1.	6.
drawn by 3 Horses or other beasts	"	"	1.	1½.
drawn by 2 Horses or other beasts	1.	0.		9.
drawn by 1 Horse or other beast		9.		6.
For every Waggon, Wain, Dray, Car, or other Carriage:				
drawn by 4 or more Horses or Oxen	1.	6.	1.	0.
Less than 4 Horses or Oxen	1.	0.		9 for 3 / 6 for 2 / 4½ for 1
For every Horse or Mule laden or unladen, and not drawing		2.		1.
Ass laden or unladen and not drawing		2.		½.
Drove of Oxen, Cows, or Neat Cattle per Score	1.	8.		10.
and after that rate for any greater or less number.				
Drove of Calves, Hogs, Sheep, or lambs per Score		4.		2½.
and after that rate for any greater or less number.				
For every Locomotive weighing 2 Tons or under, having 4 wheels			1.	0.
having 3 wheels				9.
having 2 wheels				6.
For every Locomotive exceeding 2 Tons and not exceeding 4 Tons			1.	3.
" 4 Tons " " 6 Tons			1.	6.
" 6 Tons " " 10 Tons			2.	0.
" 10 Tons " " 14 Tons			2.	6.
For each wheel of any Waggon, Wain, Cart, Carriage, or other Vehicle, drawn or propelled by any Locomotive not exceeding 6 Tons				2.
exceeding 6 Tons				3.

Guildhall
Sandwich
June 19th 1905

E.C. BYRNE
Town Clerk.

Fig 5.21
This photograph taken
during the Scottish
Reliability Run in c 1905
shows the car enthusiast
John Cunninghame
Montgomery at the wheel
of an 18hp Arrol Johnston
motor car.
[© HES]

Previously quiet, middle-class resorts that had survived the impact of railways during the 19th century were affected by the arrival of coach parties during the 20th century. English teacher and writer Robert Roberts (1905–74) described how his family and friends went on trips after World War I:

> Wealthier members of the proletariat, in their week's unpaid annual holidays, took en masse to motor char-à-banc tours round Britain. Middle- and upper-class people, resident in posh hotels and spas and along the south coast, were startled, then amazed to see horny-handed sons of toil and their spouses sitting, diffidently it is true, but sitting in the lounges and dining-rooms of places they had previously considered their own preserve.[220]

The new forms of road transport also changed patterns of travel within towns, allowing towns to spread outwards, creating huge areas of inter-war suburbia. Cars also created serious congestion problems on roads to popular holiday destinations and within resorts. The road between Preston and Blackpool, the busiest holiday route in Britain, suffered a sevenfold increase in traffic between 1914 and 1924.[221]

Initially, cars were parked on roads, while larger charabancs and buses found refuge at the undeveloped ends of resorts or were catered for in empty spaces set away from the beauty spot or seafront. The rapid growth in car ownership meant that new purpose-built facilities would soon be required. In 1920, there were 591,000 licensed vehicles in Britain, but a decade later this figure had almost quadrupled to 2.25 million.[222] In 1950, 2.5 million people held driving licences in Britain for 4.4 million vehicles, and by 2010 there were 24 million people with driving licences for 34 million vehicles.[223] While the number of cars remained small, little specific provision needed to be made for parking, though new parking areas on the seafront of seaside resorts were creating 'an annoying barricade between the visitor and the sea'.[224] However, increasingly seaside local authorities had to spend large sums to deal with traffic control and parking (Fig 5.22). Blackpool created an underground car park at Little Bispham close to a new tram station, effectively a proto park-and-ride scheme.[225] In 1936,

Fig 5.22
At Hastings, in East Sussex,
a major transformation of
the seafront took place in
the early 1930s and the
earliest underground car
parks in Britain were
included in the scheme,
masterminded by the
borough engineer Sidney
Little. Underground
parking is still in use in
Hastings today, as is shown
in this photograph, taken
in 2011.
[DP139356]

the Annual Report of the British Association for the Advancement of Science observed that Blackpool still did not have enough car parks, prompting the creation of a car park on Talbot Road near Blackpool North railway station (Fig 5.23).[226] However, the earliest example of a seaside multistorey car park had been erected in 1906, when the Caffyn brothers opened a three-storey garage on Marine Parade at Eastbourne for around 100 cars. At Bournemouth a multistorey car park in the modern sense was built in 1932.[227]

As well as having an impact on towns, the car also allowed more people to travel into more of the countryside. Gradually, the infrastructure for tourism was put in place, including petrol stations, picturesque tea rooms and signposts to beauty spots.[228] In the post-war years, the car would prompt the creation of motels, rural bed-and-breakfasts and roadside cafes and diners. Cars, charabancs and coaches also increased the number of people who could travel to major events, such as key race meetings at Cheltenham and Epsom.[229] A sea change in road travel came with the opening of motorways, providing fast travel between major cities, from where access to resorts and the countryside became possible. For instance, the opening of the M5 during the mid-1970s brought an extra 18 million people within a 3½ hour drive of Devon's seaside resorts.[230]

By 1934, the London and North Eastern Railway (LNER) was carrying more than 500 cars annually on open trucks to Scotland from London. In 1955, the introduction of the Car-Sleeper between London and Perth, which was rebranded as Motorail in 1966, eventually provided a much wider network of services, linking London to many places, including Penzance, Fishguard, Carlisle, Edinburgh, Inverness and Fort William.[231] At its peak the service carried 100,000 vehicles a year, but it came to an end at the close of summer 2005, due to its high charges and improvements in trunk roads and motorways.

Robert Roberts said that the 'horny-handed sons of toil' troubled the 'resident in posh hotels and spas', but this new market also had a more profound impact on tourist destinations.[232] New plot-land settlements (land subdivided into small, affordable plots on which people could build whatever they wished) were intended to be idyllic rural or coastal escapes from the intensity of urban life. However, by the end of the 1930s they were already being recognised as a significant sanitation and architectural issue.[233] An article published in 1938 in *The Architectural Review*, entitled 'Leisure as an architectural problem', outlined the planning challenges facing the coastline: 'Bungalow colonies, camps, city refuse dumps and general ribbon development along coastal roads all contribute to the general decomposing process which will soon leave very little of England's 1,800 miles of coastline that is not irreparably damaged.'[234] Peacehaven, in East Sussex, was the most famous of these new types of 'bungalow colonies'. Intended to be a commemoration of the horrors of World War I, it was described by philosopher Cyril Edwin Mitchinson Joad (1891–1953) as 'a pigsty of hideously coloured bungalows, shacks and even tents, set down, without rhyme or reason, in a fair, green land'.[235] Peacehaven still exists today, and while it retains some of its original informality, its 'shacks' have been replaced with modern bungalows. However, something of the original informality can still be appreciated in the structures built from old boats at Bungalow Town at Shoreham-by-Sea, in West Sussex, and at Sutton-on-Sea, in Lincolnshire, where a number of the houses have been constructed from old railway carriages.[236] On some stretches of the coastline caravan sites and chalet settlements have merged into vast, seemingly uncontrolled settlements, something that is particularly obvious in Lincolnshire. The number of static caravans between Cleethorpes and Skegness rose from 4,200 in 1950 to around 21,000 in 1974, representing 8 per cent of the UK total (Fig 5.24).[237]

Horse-drawn caravans had been in use since the 17th century and they reached their peak

Fig 5.23
At Blackpool, the Talbot Road car park, photographed here in 2010, was constructed above a ground-floor bus station in 1937–9. In recent years it has been entirely refurbished as part of a regeneration scheme for the centre of Blackpool. [DP119494]

Fig 5.24
By the 1980s, the coast from
Skegness to Mablethorpe, in
Lincolnshire, had 120,000
holiday bed spaces available,
of which 90 per cent were
in caravans and chalets.
At the top of this aerial
photograph, taken in the
early 2000s, the Butlin's
holiday camp at Skegness
can be seen.
[NMR 17471/15]

around 1900 (Fig 5.25), though with the advent of the car they were quickly superseded. By the outbreak of World War I, the first motorhomes, resembling a caravan on a lorry chassis, and small, towed caravans had been produced, their size being restricted by the limited power of car engines at the time.[238] Caravans became larger, more sophisticated and more comfortable during the 1920s and 1930s. By the mid-1930s, there were about 3,500 caravans in use in Britain and the industry acquired its first magazine.[239] The first caravan rallies took place in the 1930s, but, at a time when there were no caravan sites, people had to negotiate with a friendly farmer for the use of a corner of a quiet field (Fig 5.26).[240]

The caravan holiday, whether by the sea or in the countryside, was, before World War II, confined to people able to afford a car, but after the war it became an activity that came within the reach of most of the populace. Towed caravans were still an expensive luxury, but by the mid-1950s, static caravans to rent were being established at many resorts. These were often privately owned and rented out for an income, as well as providing the owner with a place for their own holiday. By the late 1960s, residential chalets had also been established at many caravan sites and at holiday camps offering affordable second homes. Though similar to static caravans, they were more expensively finished to suit their longer-term occupation.[241] An alternative to caravan holidays was available at some locations.[242] In 1933, the LNER introduced 'camping

coaches' at a cost of £2 10s for six people sharing a railway coach for a week.[243] These were located in sidings near stations, and until recently some coaches at Dawlish Warren, in Devon, were still rented out to holidaymakers.[244]

Conclusion

In this chapter the clear relationship between the development of transport and the story of tourism has been explored. The impact of transport has been felt in a number of ways. New, more reliable and cheaper forms of transport increased the volume of tourism, changing its shape, extending its reach into the countryside and transforming the character of existing resorts. Improvements to roads and to the technology of coaches during the 18th century started the process, but this was still a relatively slow, expensive and uncomfortable way to travel. The same could be said of the first services using sailing boats in the 18th century, but with the appearance of steamers during the 1810s the first limited, yet popular, tourism begins to be detected. Mass tourism as we might recognise it today had to wait until the railway network began to coalesce in the mid-19th century and for nearly a century the train was the principal means of travel for business, manufactured goods and tourism. However, the beginning of the decline of rail travel was under way during the mid-20th century. In 1919, there were just over two billion passenger rail journeys per year, but this figure had halved by 1950.[245] In 1945 industrial economist Elizabeth Brunner (1920–83) proclaimed, slightly prematurely, 'The age of the motor car is superseding that of the railway, and is likely to have a profound effect on holiday habits.'[246]

The shift to the privately owned motor car meant that people were no longer restricted to travelling to where there was a railway station and a linked coach service. Now the whole of Britain could be explored. As paid leave and disposable income increased during the 20th century, holidays became universal. However, 300 years ago modern Britain was still waiting to be created and ancient Britain was waiting to be discovered. The next two chapters will tell the story of how pioneering 18th-century tourists began to uncover and record the natural and man-made riches found in these islands. They will also examine how access to new, affordable forms of transport allowed almost all the population by the end of the 19th century to embark on similar private voyages and journeys of discovery.

Fig 5.26
This 1953 photograph by John Gay shows holiday caravans in a field, surrounded by the rural landscape of the area around Bridgnorth, in Shropshire. It nicely illustrates the challenge of trying to accommodate such structures in the countryside.
[AA079452]

6

In search of Britain

Fig 6.1
Many tourists travelled to see romantic ruins, and a site like the late 12th-century Cistercian church at Byland Abbey, in North Yorkshire, which is now cared for by English Heritage, is still a popular visitor attraction. [K981258]

Spas and seaside resorts were the major tourist destinations from the 17th century, but, as had been the case in the Middle Ages, people travelled around Britain for many other reasons. Tourists were inquisitive, sometimes almost formally investigative, and from the 17th century onwards, the increasingly curious intellectual climate was permeating through society. While the antiquarianism of the late Middle Ages might be represented by the works of William Worcestre (1415–c 1485) and John Leland (c 1503–52), by the 17th and 18th centuries dozens of antiquarians were documenting the relics of their own counties and the wider historic remains of Britain. Their published works in turn fuelled curiosity among a growing population who wanted to see the famous sights of Britain. For instance, no self-respecting diarist on the road in southern England could afford to miss Stonehenge in Wiltshire, while the modern architecture of the time – such as Blenheim Palace, in Oxfordshire, Castle Howard, in Yorkshire, and Chatsworth, in Derbyshire – was popular among discerning tourists.

By the 18th century, there were also more reasons to travel. This modern architecture was a growing interest, as was the appearance of the first large-scale industrial sites, Lombe's Mill in Derby leading the way from the 1720s. There was a growing appreciation of beauty, the charms of a baroque palace forming an interesting contrast with a utilitarian industrial site. However, of greater aesthetic significance was a new relationship between man and nature, a Romantic perspective that saw once-daunting craggy hills and mountains as places of sublime beauty. By the end of the 19th century, the natural wonders of the British countryside were being sought by growing numbers of tourists and some places began to feel overwhelmed by the arrival of holidaymakers. This process occurred at different dates in different places: Scotland, due to its remoteness from major English population centres, took longer to enjoy/ endure a form of mass tourism than the Lake District. Access to such beautiful parts of the countryside depended on class, with aristocrats and the wealthy middle-class being able to enjoy the charms of these areas long before convenient, cheap transport opened them to the wider population.

In the next two chapters, the published and unpublished works of a wide variety of travellers will reveal some of their motives. These can be broadly categorised as ranging from the curious and casually inquisitive to the almost formally investigative, documentary works of some writers. There was also a range of reasons for touring, from the antiquarian to the aesthete with an interest in ruins for their poetic beauty rather than their history. Growing numbers of people were travelling to admire the wonders of nature, from the Romantic poets to scientists trying to understand the natural world. In terms of human achievement, people were increasingly searching out Britain's history (Fig 6.1), some diarists seamlessly passing from an ancient Roman ruin to a modern country house and an innovative industrial site within a matter of hours or days. This chapter will concentrate on how rural Britain was the focus of these interests, while Chapter 7 will examine the changing face of urban Britain and how tourists set out in search of the country's past, present and future.

Finding Britain

Underpinning any extension of tourism around Britain was the creation of increasingly accurate and affordable maps and the birth of what would become the guidebook industry. During most of the 18th century, there does not appear to have been a significant improvement in cartography, but the establishment of the Ordnance Survey in 1791 was a key act.[1] In 1801, the first of its one-inch county maps was produced, a series that was completed in 1867. The technical quality of these maps meant that they gradually displaced more unofficial and less accurate maps that had accompanied guidebooks.

Personal journals and diaries were often kept by travellers, describing the sights they had seen. These were usually intended to be private journals on which the author might reflect long after the journey had ended. However, some authors intended, or hoped, that their work would be published. These accounts of travels had an impact on the shape of tourism when they were published. They might serve as templates for other people's adventures and would introduce readers to a huge variety of places worthy of a visit, as the remoter parts of Britain remained to be discovered by the inhabitants of London and southern England.

The ground-breaking *A Tour through the Whole Island of Great Britain*, by Daniel Defoe (1660–1731), described the author's journeys around England, Wales and Scotland in a series of letters. While constructed as a single journal encompassing a series of journeys, its form appears to be the result of many years of travel and research. Initially published in three volumes between 1722 and 1725, fuller versions were published in 1738 and in 1742, by which time a fourth volume had been added.[2] Defoe (Fig 6.2) was able to reach remote parts of Scotland that would have been very unfamiliar, and unwelcoming, before the nation's final subjugation following the Battle of Culloden in 1746. Writer and spy John Macky (d 1726) was also an active traveller in the early 18th century, and ventured apparently as far as Defoe, including within his native Scotland.[3] These substantial works would have been enjoyed in the homes of prospective travellers, but were never intended for use as guidebooks to be taken on a journey, at least not with ease.

As well as journals that were published at the time, some accounts only appeared in print much later due to their historical interest. The

Fig 6.2
A monument to commemorate the life of Daniel Defoe was erected in September 1870 in Bunhill Fields burial ground in London. Funds were raised from 1,700 subscribers who responded to an appeal in the Christian World *newspaper.*
[CC97/00669]

most significant of the early journals subsequently published was kept by Celia Fiennes (1662–1741), who began to travel in order to regain her health 'by variety and change of aire and exercise'.[4] Her first journeys were in England's southern counties, and took in Bath, London and Oxford, but in 1697 she ventured to the north and in the following year she made her 'Great Journey to Newcastle and to Cornwall'. During the first decade of the 18th century, she made further journeys through southern England. In 1702, she reworked the notes she had made during her travels into a journal, but it was not published at length until the late 19th century. The entertaining and informative account by writer Catherine Hutton (1756–1846) of visits to places such as Blackpool in its infancy and Wales during the late 18th century was only published a century after it was written.[5] An interesting, early, unpublished journal was kept by an unnamed student at Cambridge University who embarked on a long and highly informative summer trip around parts of England in 1725, including stays at Bath and Scarborough.[6]

While the various published accounts of Georgian travellers were stimulating and informative, they were not designed to be practical, portable guidebooks. However, during the 18th century guidebooks began to be created for major cities and watering places, though the term does not seem to have been used until 1823.[7] During the 18th century the publishing industry was developing rapidly, but it remained expensive to produce a guidebook for an audience that was still fairly restricted, though literacy rates were rising. Therefore, guidebooks were initially limited to places with larger populations or with sufficient numbers of visitors to make publication profitable. Inevitably London led the way, its first guidebook appearing as early as the end of the 17th century in the form of François Colsoni's *Le Guide de Londres Pour Les Estrangers* (A London Guide for Foreigners, 1693). This is a work arranged in the form of five tours through London, along with advice on where to stay, sights to see, an opportunity to go shopping and information on places of refreshment. The earliest guides published in English, though with parallel French texts, were A *New Guide to London: Or, Directions to Strangers; Shewing the Chief Things of Curiosity and Note in the City and Suburbs* (1726) and *The Foreigner's Guide: or, a Necessary and Instructive Companion* (1729).[8] Other large towns and cities followed London. A local doctor, William Moss,

published a detailed guide to Liverpool in 1797, aimed not just at visitors to the rapidly expanding town, but also at residents and people living in the vicinity.[9] In the same year, the lawyer James MacNayr (*c* 1757–1808) published *A guide from Glasgow to some of the most remarkable scenes in the highlands of Scotland and to the falls of the Clyde*, while Birmingham's first guidebook was written by the noted local publisher and historian William Hutton (1723–1815), who had previously completed *A History of Birmingham*, which was published in 1782.

Seaside resorts and spa towns also published early guidebooks. An early proto-guidebook was published for Scarborough in 1734. In *A Journey from London to Scarborough, in several letters*, the first four letters are devoted to the journey to the town, which at that period was a fairly remote, yet popular, spa town that was already witnessing the new fad for sea bathing.[10] The fifth letter describes the town, the spa, sea bathing and the facilities provided for visitors, including its churches, the Long Room (an early assembly room) and a bookseller's shop, an early form of circulating library. This work ends with a list of all the people who visited the town in 1733. In 1742, Bath became the first spa town to publish a proper guidebook, and other spas and seaside resorts followed its example, though in many instances the guidebook elements appear alongside a lengthy history of the town.[11] The first guidebook to the resorts of the Isle of Thanet was published in 1763 and two years later another version of the guidebook appeared, repeating and expanding much of the content of its predecessor.[12] These early guidebooks describe the rudimentary entertainment facilities and provide a discussion and illustration of bathing machines, which would have been unfamiliar to many visitors.

From the late 18th century onwards, guidebooks were published regularly in leading resorts, often repeating with limited updates the information compiled for a previous edition. They would include details about the main attractions and places to ride out to. Some guidebooks listed accommodation that was available, though more often holidaymakers would be expected to consult lists held in circulating libraries. During the 19th century, guidebooks included information useful for residents as well as visitors, with systematic listings for churches, postal services and local residents of note who provided services, such as bankers, lawyers and doctors.

Initially guidebooks were produced by a local publisher, who was often also the proprietor of a circulating library, but by the end of the 18th century the first national surveys of watering places were beginning to appear. In 1799, entertainer and author George Saville Carey (1743–1807) published *The Balnea*.[13] Its subtitle is somewhat misleading as it claims to be 'Impartial' and to cover 'All the Popular Watering Places'; in fact it often offers a biting criticism or mockery of aspects of the 20 seaside resorts and spa towns he visited. Although each entry is self-contained, there are some anecdotes and descriptions of events on the journey, though it is unclear whether it all took place at one time or was the result of trips to the various watering places over a number of years. A year after *The Balnea* appeared, the first of a series of editions of *A Guide to all the Watering and Sea Bathing Places* was published, providing short descriptions of the most important seaside resorts and spa towns in a number of revised editions until 1825. It was published anonymously, but was said to be written by the editor of *The Picture of London*, which points to the author being John Feltham (fl 1780–1803). This tradition of writing guides to Britain's watering places was continued by Augustus Bozzi Granville, who published *The Spas of England and Principal Sea-bathing Places* in 1841.[14] By this date, guidebooks were becoming less personal and more systematic. Nevertheless, as a doctor his emphasis is on the medical qualities of each place he visited, often including lengthy consideration of the climate of an individual town. A similar, but even more medical approach was taken by Thomas Luke, another doctor. In 1919 he published *Spas and Health Resorts of the British Isles*, a work, unlike Granville's, that embraced Strathpeffer's spa as much as that of Tunbridge Wells, and acclaimed Blackpool as 'one of the wonders of the world'.[15]

During the 18th century, the cost of guidebooks put them beyond the pocket of many tourists.[16] However, prices had fallen by the mid-19th century, as the potential market for them increased. London was welcoming growing influxes of people from provincial towns with limited budgets and little time, who were keen for advice on what to see and do, and the city's rapidly growing population also proved a fertile market for guidebooks. One example is *The Saturday Half-Holiday Guide to London and the Environs*, published in 1868.[17] By this date, the half-day holiday on a Saturday was common in London, though not universal, and the guide promoted two broad ways in which the free afternoon could be spent, namely physical activities, such as sport and exercise, and self-improvement activities of a more educational nature, such as visiting museums and exhibitions (Fig 6.3). A comparable guide for Birmingham followed in 1871 and, perhaps surprisingly, one was also produced for Darlington in 1882. London was sufficiently large and busy in the 18th century to merit at least one specialist guide. From 1757, lists of prostitutes working in

Fig 6.3
This photograph of the central hall of the Natural History Museum, in London, was probably taken soon after it opened to the public in 1881.
[CC97/01699]

A WELSH BORDERLAND CASTLE *Open to the Public*

GOODRICH *In the Wye Valley. Station-Kerne Bridge · G.W.R.*

Fig 6.4
In addition to producing guidebooks, railway companies such as the Great Western Railway also promoted their businesses using posters advertising destinations ranging from historic sights to seaside resorts. This mid-20th-century poster shows the ruins of medieval Goodrich Castle, overlooking the River Wye. [MP/GOC0199]

publications have been made popular again in recent years as the basis for programmes in a BBC TV series entitled *Great British Railway Journeys*. The publishing house of Ward Lock, founded in 1854, took over a series of tourist guides by someone called Shaw in the early 1880s and, by 1900, was eventually responsible for publishing guides to 72 different towns and areas of Britain, as well as European destinations.[23] Many railway companies also issued guidebooks describing the scenery through which their lines passed: the Great Western Railway led the way from 1904, with its guides advertised as '*the Holiday Books of the Holiday Line*' (Fig 6.4). Between 1934 and 1984, the Shell County Guides were published under the general editorship of poet John Betjeman (1906–84) and artist John Piper (1903–92).[24] Unlike their Victorian equivalents, these were not aimed at people travelling by railway, but, as the series title suggests, the growing number of car drivers seeking direction to key sights and attractions. Today, travellers consult series such as *Lonely Planet*, *Michelin Guides* and *Rough Guides*, though increasingly the most widely used sources are internet sites, such as the crowd-compiled Wikipedia and TripAdvisor.

Covent Garden were published and their amusing and titillating descriptions meant the guides sold thousands annually.[18]

By the mid-19th century, the presence of adverts helped to fund the publication of guidebooks, reducing the purchase price. Perhaps most importantly, the market was becoming dominated by large companies publishing guidebooks for destinations throughout Britain and abroad, a phenomenon that also helped to reduce prices. From 1836, the London publisher John Murray (1808–92) began to publish guidebooks for travelling on the Continent, but it was only in 1850 that he produced a guide to London, and in the following year one for Devon and Cornwall.[19] The Continental pioneer was Verlag Karl Baedeker, a firm founded in 1827 by the German publisher Karl Baedeker (1801–59). Baedeker made a worldwide business from publishing travel guides from 1839 onwards.[20] The preface for the first Baedeker handbook for Holland and Belgium acknowledged that Murray's publication of a guide to the Continent was its inspiration. Another popular series was Black's Guides, published by Adam and Charles Black of Edinburgh between 1839 and 1919. Their first guidebook was perhaps inevitably entitled *Black's Economical Tourist of Scotland* in 1839, but soon volumes were available covering tours of England and, from the 1860s, Europe.[21] George Bradshaw (1801–53), a printer and engraver from Manchester, also began a long-term series of travel guides in 1839, followed in 1847 by a Continental series.[22] Both sets of

Visiting England, Wales, Scotland and Ireland

Armed with maps, guidebooks and later train timetables, growing numbers of travellers with an appetite for discovery set off in search of Britain and Ireland. Their targets were varied. Some travelled in search of man-made achievements while others sought natural beauty. Sometimes their motivations were serious, almost formally investigative, but in most cases these new tourists were simply curious about the country in which they lived.

By the 18th century, roads were rapidly improving, allowing people to travel further and faster, and into areas previously largely undocumented. The wild countryside of England, Wales and Scotland was gradually ceasing to be feared and was becoming recognised for its natural beauty, initially by philosophers and artists, but in due course by the wider population.[25] The remoter parts of the British Isles were also being appreciated for their curiosity value, containing people, customs and sights that would have been unfamiliar to travellers from more heavily populated areas.

England

Although there was growing interest in travelling to the various countries within the British Isles, most English travellers nevertheless restricted their individual journeys to England. This was due to time limitations or because the sights, man-made and natural, that interested them lay within their native country. Celia Fiennes was widely travelled from the 1680s until the early 18th century, her favoured destinations being spa towns, recently built country houses and familiar sights such as Stonehenge and Salisbury Cathedral. She rarely ventured beyond the bounds of England, a brief detour to look at the famous shrine at Holywell in north Wales in 1698 being the only recorded instance.[26] In the same year, she skirted the Scottish border, but resisted the urge to head northwards into this still-foreign country for a variety of ill-informed reasons. Fiennes travelled for many years and would have had the time to leave England if she had wished.

The travels recorded in a slightly later diary of an unnamed Cambridge student were limited to England as he only had a summer holiday in which to complete his journey. Beginning on 19 July 1725, this student and two companions left Cambridge and travelled through central England as far north as Scarborough and Manchester before turning south to visit Bath and London. The journal ends on 30 September with two of them returning to the university.[27] A decade later John Whaley (bap 1710, d 1745), with his pupil John Dodd and two other young men, undertook a summer tour of England, covering Kent, the south coast, the West Country, and heading as far north as Manchester. The record of this journey is in a series of letters to his pupil Horace Walpole and in a transcription of his notes. These record visits to see the fleet at Portsmouth, the usual deferential pilgrimage to Salisbury and Stonehenge, and a trip to the mysterious Wookey Hole, in Somerset.[28]

In these last cases, time was the limiting factor, but Daniel Defoe, over several years, was able to travel around the coasts of Wales and Scotland, as well as through much of England. Although he travelled more widely than Fiennes, he nevertheless concentrated on a similar variety of destinations, with large towns and cities, spa towns, contemporary country houses and major historic sights being the main subjects he described. Like Fiennes, he also visited Holywell in north Wales, where he recorded the presence of many 'Romanists' who still believed in the curative spiritual powers of the waters.[29] A slightly later, but even more widely travelled, diarist was Richard Pococke (1704–65), an ordained churchman who later in life was Bishop of Ossory, and subsequently Bishop of Meath.[30] In 1733 and 1734 he toured France and Italy, followed in 1736 and 1737 by the Low Countries, Germany, Austria, Poland and Hungary. Pococke continued to the Near East between 1737 and 1742, where he visited Egypt, Jerusalem, Palestine, Asia Minor and Greece. Pococke also travelled around Ireland while he lived there, and he undertook three trips to Scotland, in 1747, 1750 and 1760, the first of these only a year after the Battle of Culloden.[31] *The Travels through England* illustrates Pococke's wide range of interests, including trade, manufacturing and farming. He visited the dockyards at Plymouth and Portsmouth, in the latter case also examining the new hospital at Gosport (Fig 6.5).[32] At the same time, he took the chance to visit the Roman fortification at Portchester, in Hampshire. Elsewhere in his journals he mentions visits to harbours such as at Ramsgate, in Kent, which was being constructed in 1754, the lighthouse at North Foreland, also in Kent, and

Fig 6.5
Fort Cumberland, built in 1747–8, was also on Richard Pococke's itinerary during his visit to Portsmouth in 1754.
[NMR 26938/024]

fortifications such as Dover Castle, which was still a working military site and prisoner of war camp during the 1750s.[33] At Wareham, in Dorset, in 1750 Pococke met John Hutchins (1698–1773), who was writing *The History and Antiquities of the County of Dorset* (which was still incomplete on his death).[34] Hutchins took time out from his busy schedule to show Pococke around the town.[35] Pococke regularly visited familiar spas, such as Bath and Tunbridge Wells, and was among the earliest documenters of sea bathing at a number of fledgling resorts. Although he was a churchman, he did not record many visits to places of worship beyond the obvious major tourist sights, such as Salisbury Cathedral.[36]

Pococke's journal includes some of the sights that would be staples for any traveller in England, including Blenheim Palace, Oxford, Stonehenge, Bath and, of course, London. He seems at least once to have followed the well-trodden path linking Bath, Wilton House, Stonehenge and Salisbury Cathedral, a cluster of sights that regularly appear in 18th-century itineraries, including one by Mrs Lybbe Powys in 1757.[37] In the north of England, favoured destinations included York and great country houses such as Castle Howard and Chatsworth, both of which were visited by the Cambridge students in 1725.[38]

Wales

During the second half of the 18th century, Wales steadily gained in popularity as the romantic appeal of its ruined castles and abbeys became more widely appreciated. Although Wales was annexed to England in legal terms from 1536, and the Wales and Berwick Act 1746 specified that England included Wales and Berwick-upon-Tweed, during the 18th century it was still felt by English travellers to be a foreign country, with strange customs and a different language.[39] Daniel Defoe visited Wales during the 1720s, his tour following the coast around the country and never venturing into the principality's wilder, more mountainous heartland. However, the lure of novelty, and a desire to see this unspoilt natural beauty, attracted visitors to central Wales, travellers prepared to endure the hardship of poor roads and unsophisticated accommodation. One of the most adventurous was Catherine Hutton and her elderly father, the noted Birmingham publisher and historian William Hutton. They toured Wales on horseback in 1796 and 1799, and when necessary

they walked over what appears to have been tough mountain passes. Catherine Hutton's letters, published in 1891, 45 years after her death, provide a picture of Wales and its inhabitants before industrialisation and improved communications transformed forever the lifestyle of its inhabitants. Her first letter to her brother, written in July 1796, described 'the romantic expedition of riding into Wales'. On reaching the heart of Wales, she found that the 'sublimity of these scenes shook my nerves'.[40] She went on to tell her brother, 'The only way in which I could contemplate these towering hills, wooded glens, and rushing waters was on my feet. We sent the servant on with the horses, and walked nearly four miles before we reached Mallwyd, chiefly in the rain, wholly in the mire, but enraptured at every step we took.'[41] In 1799, in the vicinity of Snowdon, she dismounted so that she could reach a site where she would enjoy a better view of the mountain (Fig 6.6).[42] It is clear that she had steeped herself in the Romantic literature of the period that had prompted poets and artists to head to Wales and the Lake District in search of sublime beauty. But it is also clear from Hutton's letters that she was intrigued by the dress, manners and customs of the people:

> The dress of the women is entirely supplied by the sheep of the country, with the exception of two printed pocket handkerchiefs, one worn on the neck, the other on the head and brought to the throat, and tied behind. Over this head-dress, summer and winter, indoors and out, they wear a black hat, distinguished from the men's only by a riband tied round the crown.[43]

The Welsh diet was also commented on because of its difference to the English one: 'oat cake, bread made of rye and barley, butter and cheese, whey curds and stirup, which is boiled whey thickened with oatmeal'.[44] Hutton also wrote of a Welsh wedding and the lively feasting that followed.[45]

Hutton's main interests were the beauty of the landscape and the curious customs and lifestyle of the people, but many visitors to Wales went in search of the ruins of the country's abbeys and castles. Henry Skrine's *Tour through South Wales …*, published in 1798–1800, is a typical example of someone keen to take in the medieval sights of Wales.[46] Skrine (1755–1803), a wealthy man who travelled around the country, was aware of 'the variety of the picturesque,

Fig 6.6 (facing page) Snowdon, photographed here in 1948, is the highest mountain in Wales, with an elevation of 3,560ft (1,085m). This rugged landscape would have proved a formidable challenge to 18th-century travellers. [WAW020518 © Crown Copyright: Royal Commission on the Ancient and Historical Monuments of Wales: Aerofilms Collection]

the agreeable, the tremendous, and sublime in nature', but his destinations were predominantly the ruined abbeys, churches and ancient sights such as 'the once-famous Caerwent, the Venta Silurum of the Romans'.[47] John Feltham's *A Guide to all the Watering and Sea Bathing Places, with a description of the Lakes; a sketch of a tour in Wales, and Itineraries* ..., published in 1803, might be expected to focus on spas and watering places, but in fact the two Welsh tours are more balanced itineraries where natural beauty and ancient sights both feature prominently.[48]

Scotland

Scotland was an independent country until 1707, though it had shared its monarch with England since 1603. Even after the Act of Union, it retained many of its distinctive institutions, most notably its own church, and legal and education systems.[49] In 18th-century accounts by English visitors, the perceived strangeness of this foreign country is evident. Antiquary and traveller John Loveday (1711–89), writing in 1732, was one of the first visitors, after Defoe, from south of the border to leave a detailed account of his trip.[50] Loveday's antiquarianism is obvious in his descriptions of buildings in Scotland's largest cities, Glasgow and Edinburgh. He shows a great awareness of art, and, unusually for the early 18th century, an interest in Gothic cathedrals, though he was equally concerned about how they were currently being used. Loveday also visited the seat of the Duke of Hamilton, one of Scotland's largest houses, and describes at length Edinburgh Castle, including seeing the Scottish Crown's regalia as well as the room where James VI (James I of England) was born in 1566 (Fig 6.7). The Scotland that Loveday visited would have seemed very different to southern England. He pointed out differences in the organisation of the church and was intrigued by the way that Scots in cities lived in multi-storey tenements. In Glasgow, he saw five- and six-storey buildings with arcaded ground floors, similar to those found in some European cities, but uncommon in England.

The Jacobite Rising in 1745 saw the forces of Bonnie Prince Charlie march southwards as far as Derby, before being turned back and ultimately defeated at the Battle of Culloden, near Inverness, in April 1746.[51] This changed the fundamental relationship between Scotland (especially the Highlands) and the rest of the United Kingdom. Following the defeat of the Jacobites, laws were passed that sought to control Scotland more closely and clan chiefs who had supported the uprising were stripped of their estates. The wearing of tartan was banned except as a uniform for officers and soldiers in the British Army. When the ban was lifted in 1782, it was less favoured by ordinary people and more 'the affectation of their anglicised lairds, the fancy dress of the Lowlanders, and the uniform of the king's Gaelic soldiers.'[52] These measures were an attempt to subjugate the Highlands and to diminish its distinctive identity, but it nevertheless remained a place of interest to English and foreign visitors and became a more popular destination during the second half of the 18th century.[53]

Richard Pococke's journal begins with a description of his two brief visits to southern Scotland, including Edinburgh and Glasgow in 1747 and 1750, before his long 1760 journal in which he headed north to the Highlands and islands. One of his first stops in the north in 1760 was at Inverness, where he saw the newly strengthened Fort George, before visiting the site of the Battle of Culloden and describing the confrontation.[54] He then headed on to Orkney and Shetland, before heading south again to Aberdeen and Edinburgh.

The Scottish Highlands would have seemed remote to most people living in England and it was this that attracted a growing trickle of adventurous travellers. The poet Thomas Gray (1716–71) toured Scotland in 1765, visiting Glamis Castle in Perthshire, before continuing into the Highlands, a journey that marked a shift in Gray's interests from antiquities to natural scenery.[55] In 1769, the naturalist and writer Thomas Pennant (1726–98) undertook a tour of Scotland, particularly visiting the Highlands to explore its natural history.[56] His account was published in 1771, and well received, and therefore he undertook a second tour of Scotland in 1772. His trips inspired the author and lexicographer Samuel Johnson (1709–84) to head to the Highlands in the following year, accompanied by his Scottish friend and biographer James Boswell (1740–95). In August 1773, they embarked on a three-month journey, spending a month on Skye, as well as visiting Scotland's largest cities. Boswell had to persuade Johnson not to take pistols and ammunition with them on their Highland expedition, reassuring him that the roads were free from robbers. Scotland in the 1770s would have still seemed like a foreign country to Johnson, with its own religion,

legal system, distinctive cultural traditions, food, building styles and language, in the northern parts at least.[57] However, he was unimpressed with Scotland's intellectual and literary tradition, but, like Boswell, he was keen to see what he viewed as primitive, formerly war-like people in their native habitat, much as travellers to distant foreign lands were doing at the same time.[58] Writer and headmaster William Gilpin (1724–1804), touring Scotland in 1776 only three years after Johnson, devoted less time to the rebellious Scots, instead concentrating most of his efforts on the Scottish landscape, much as he had done on previous tours of Wales and the Lake District.[59]

The main attractions of the Highlands of Scotland were the natural beauty, the long and distinctive history visible in the ruined castles, and the remains of an ancient culture that survived in Highland villages. While Johnson and other Georgian writers had seen the Scots as a barbaric, bloodthirsty people, later travellers romantically praised their independence and proud fighting traditions. Therefore, a figure such as William Wallace (c 1270–1305), leader of an unsuccessful rebellion against English rule, became a folk hero, and Robert 'Rob Roy' MacGregor (bap 1671, d 1734) enjoyed a status in Scotland similar to Robin Hood in England, largely as a result of Sir Walter Scott's *Rob Roy* (1817) that launched the outlaw's international reputation.[60] In 1803, Dorothy Wordsworth (1771–1855), her brother William (1770–1850) and Samuel Taylor Coleridge (1772–1834) visited Scotland and this inspired William Wordsworth to write poems rooted in Highland history.[61] In 1859–60, French novelist Jules Verne (1828–1905) visited Britain, and while in

Scotland he visited the landscape and sights made famous by Sir Walter Scott (1771–1832), particularly enjoying seeing where Rob Roy had roamed the Highlands.[62] Travelling in search of Rob Roy was not restricted to literary giants. In September 1818, only a year after Scott's novel had been published, the anonymous author of a diary described how he went with his brother to admire Rob Roy's cave.[63]

Although the Highlands were the most obvious attraction for visitors from England, the first parts of Scotland's countryside to be discovered were in the lowlands, such as the Esk Valley and the Falls of Clyde, as they were within easy reach of Edinburgh and Glasgow respectively.[64] The countryside of the Borders was also popular during the early 19th century because it had featured prominently in the works of Sir Walter Scott and its ruined abbeys and castles chimed with both romantic and antiquarian sentiments.[65] Scott's huge popularity led to his home at Abbotsford and the settings used in his books becoming tourist destinations, second only in popularity to locations associated with William Shakespeare.

During the 19th century, a fairly standard tour of Scotland developed, new arrivals beginning in Glasgow or Edinburgh before heading to the lochs of the southern Highlands and then up to the Highlands via Inverness, and sometimes continuing on to the islands off the Scottish coast.[66] Travel within Scotland remained challenging, but innovations such as steamers and later railways would open the country to growing numbers of tourists. In September 1842, Queen Victoria (1819–1901) and Prince Albert (1819–61) made their first visit to Scotland, including spending time in Edinburgh, followed by visits to some of the grandees of the Lowlands and

southern Highlands.[67] They returned to Scotland in 1844 to stay with the Duke and Duchess of Atholl at Blair Castle, in Perthshire, and again in 1847 during a yachting tour. In 1848, Victoria and Albert bought the Balmoral Estate, 40 miles (64km) west of Aberdeen, and during the 1850s a new large house was erected for them (Fig 6.8). Where royalty led, the masses followed, and the presence of the queen, even if only for the summer, prompted tours, and travel agents such as Thomas Cook (*see* p 87), to include Royal Deeside and 'Dark Lochnagar' among their Scottish destinations.[68]

Ireland

To most of the population of England, Ireland was even more remote than Scotland, though links by sea from Wales, Scotland and Liverpool were improving during the course of the 18th century. Ireland had a poor road network until turnpiked roads spread from 1729 onwards. By 1820, there were around 1,500 miles (2,400km) of improved roads and from 1815, mail coaches began to carry passengers and post more rapidly around the island. During the second half of the 18th century, a system of canals began to be cre-

ated, providing the island with its first effective travel network. This had an impact on moving agricultural and manufactured products around the island, but it also allowed a limited form of tourism. However, it was the establishment of the railways from 1834 onwards that stimulated faster, cheaper and more reliable travel, including excursions within the island.[69]

Agricultural reformer and writer Arthur Young (1741–1820) published a *Tour of Ireland* in 1780, directing visitors to attractions such as the spa at Killarney, grand country houses built by Protestant landlords and the many impressive natural sights of the Irish countryside.[70] Irish tourism received a major boost in 1861 when Queen Victoria, Prince Albert and three of their children, accompanied by a retinue of more than 100, visited Killarney (Fig 6.9).[71] Although this trip was widely reported, the potential political instability due to the spread of Fenianism may have acted as a discouragement to many other high-profile visitors in the mid-19th century.

The story of the development of tourism in Ireland follows broadly the story in England, Scotland and Wales. People would travel to the handful of spas and seaside resorts, and of course Dublin, and to a lesser extent Belfast, major cit-

Fig 6.9
This 1933 Aerofilms
photograph shows
Muckross House at
Killarney in County Kerry,
the home of the Earl of
Kenmare. He hosted Queen
Victoria, Prince Albert and
other members of the royal
family on 26 August 1861.
[XPW043519]

ies worthy of the tourist gaze. However, it seems to have been the beautiful countryside of Ireland and a desire to meet its people that particularly attracted visitors in search of the romantic and the picturesque, much as they explored the wilder parts of Wales and Scotland. Antiquary and mineralogist Edward Daniel Clarke (1769–1822), who visited Ireland in 1791, described the mountains of County Wicklow on an excursion out from Dublin, stating grudgingly, 'It is truly a romantic place, although not equal to the scenes of a similar nature in North Wales.'[72] Novelist William Makepeace Thackeray (1811–63), who had visited Ireland in 1842, said:

> What sends picturesque tourists to the Rhine and Saxon Switzerland? Within five miles round the pretty inn of Glengarriff, there is a country of the magnificence of which no pen can give an idea. Were such a bay lying upon the English shores, it would be a world's wonder. Perhaps, if it were on the Mediterranean or the Baltic, English visitors would flock to it by hundreds.[73]

And when it came to wonders, Ireland was well served, with numerous ancient ruined monas-teries, the elegant streets and buildings of Dublin, and the Giant's Causeway, a place celebrated in science, art and literature.

Exploring Britain's countryside

Throughout Britain, travel writers increasingly emphasised the picturesque, unspoilt land-scapes, especially the untamed hills and moors of Wales, the Lake District, the Highlands and the Peak District.[74] This was in marked contrast to early travel writers, who saw barren hills as unproductive, while lowland agricultural land was fertile and valued. Fiennes and Defoe often remarked on agriculture improvement with admiration, while scarcely reflecting on the beauty of the wilder countryside.[75] In 1500, only 45 per cent of agricultural land was enclosed, but by 1760 this figure had risen to more than 75 per cent, a transformation accompanied by a major movement of the population from the countryside to the city. In 1700, less than 20 per cent of the population of England and Wales lived in large towns, and by 1800 over 30 per cent were urban dwellers.[76] However, by 1851 almost half the English and Welsh population were classified as urban and by 1881 this had risen to over 70 per cent.[77]

An interest in Britain's changing agricultural landscape and rural economy, which was already evident at the beginning of the 18th century, was continued by travellers with a professional interest in the subject. The agriculturalist Arthur Young, who wrote detailed reports on English farming, made trips around England at the end of the 1760s.[78] As well as visiting obvious historic landmarks and places, his journals contain comments on agricultural practices, often finding fault with production techniques. In Northamptonshire, he disapproved of the way that hedges were maintained and was critical of how fields were manured, while he considered the New Forest to be a wasteful use of land, rather than a place of natural beauty.[79] Alexander Dennis, a Cornish farmer and miller, described the agriculture he saw during his tour through England and Scotland in 1810.[80] He recorded the crops that were planted, livestock and its condition and even commented on the novelty of drystone walling. At Woburn, in Bedfordshire, he discussed agricultural improvements that had been made by the Duke of Bedford (1765–1802), who had set up the earliest agricultural experimental station to demonstrate modern cultivation methods.[81]

Although there was a continuing interest in agriculture as a human achievement, the emerging Romantic movement preferred to celebrate natural landscapes. Countryside that had once appeared forbidding became sublime or picturesque. The latter term had been used by Thomas Gray as early as 1740 and William Gilpin, touring the Wye Valley and Lake District during the 1770s and 1780s, described the views he saw in terms used in painting.[82] The picturesque was reflected in art, literature and poetry, but it was also led by the arts, particularly through paintings by artists whose depictions of classical scenes in romantic landscapes inspired Grand Tourists, British painters and in turn the wider public.[83] The topographer William Hutchinson (1732–1814), writing in the early 1770s of the Lake District, said, 'The paintings of POUSIN describe the nobleness of ULS-WATER; the works of SALVATOR ROSA express the romantic and rocky scenes of KESWICK; and the tender and elegant touches of CLAUDE LORAINE, and SMITH, pencil forth the rich variety of WINDERMERE.'[84] The beauty of the lakes was firmly aligned with fine art: the quaint villages and their illiterate inhabitants were seen as contributors to poetic

simplicity, rather than evidence of poverty.[85] While painters and poets began the charge to the British countryside, photographers followed. John Muir Wood (1805–92) took one of the earliest photographs of the remarkable geology of the Hebridean island of Staffa in around 1850, and Roger Fenton (1819–69), most celebrated for his pioneering war photography during the Crimean War, captured the picturesque beauty of the Lake District and Wales in the 1850s.[86]

Poetry and literature also had a major impact on travel habits. The works of William Wordsworth, Robert Burns (1759–96) and Sir Walter Scott aroused an interest in the Lake District and the Scottish Highlands, as well as in untamed landscapes in general. The Lake District began to be recognised and promoted as a tourist destination in the third quarter of the 18th century.[87] Among the earliest accounts was one by William Hutchinson in the early 1770s, in which he waxed lyrically about its natural beauty as well as historic sights.[88] The Langton family, flax merchants from Kirkham in Lancashire, also visited in the mid-1770s, with a view to publishing their observations for commercial gain.[89] However, it was William Wordsworth, a figure of national stature, whose writings exposed the nation to the beauty of the Lakes. His first *Guide to the Lakes* was published in 1810 and remained in print in some form for over half a century.[90]

Robert Burns played a similar popularising role for Scotland and its natural beauties, but it was Sir Walter Scott who transformed Britain's view of Scotland's landscape by taking it to a wide public, including the royal family. Another factor in Scotland's growing popularity was its remoteness, meaning that it was not initially being subjected to the impact of the growing crowds of visitors to the Lake District.[91]

With the coming of the railways from the 1830s onwards, large areas of previously difficult-to-visit countryside came within reach of major population centres. Railways ideally required flat countryside and gentle gradients, and therefore the wild mountainous regions of Britain still remained beyond their reach. However, new technologies would open up more of the countryside to more people, beginning with the areas around growing towns and cities within easy reach of cyclists. Specialist maps were published for cyclists, including one for touring north Wales that highlighted the steeper gradients that might have to be avoided.[92]

By the late 19th century, the virtues of rambling through the countryside were being extolled by various travelogues aimed at a mass market. This was in part a response to the perceived low social tone and poor taste of popular amusements that was causing alarm among some social reformers. They felt that more edifying holiday and leisure activities should be available to young working-class people, an expression of the ongoing theme of rational recreation.[93] Beginning in 1891, the Clarion Clubs founded by Robert Blatchford (1851–1943) organised outdoor leisure opportunities, allowing young people to experience a holiday in the open air in a comradely atmosphere.[94] The Cooperative Holiday Association (CHA), established in 1897, organised holidays in reasonably priced accommodation for young cyclists and hikers in unspoilt areas of countryside.[95] The aim was to provide morally and physically improving holidays, through vigorous exercise and serious reading and discussion during the evenings. By 1913, when its offshoot the Holiday Fellowship was formed, the CHA had 30,000 members. After World War I, interest in the outdoors increased. The Youth Hostels Association was founded in 1930 and by 1939 had 80,000 members. The National Council of Ramblers' Federations was formed in 1930 and in 1932 the mass trespass of Kinder Scout in the Peak District demonstrated that the right to roam the hills was strongly felt by ordinary people.[96] During the interwar years, there were more than 600 ramblers clubs, with 50,000 members in total, and the Youth Hostels Association saw an increase from 78,000 overnight stays in its first year to more than 530,000 in 1939.[97]

Country sports and activities

As well as admiring the view, many people set off to the countryside to enjoy country pursuits. These ranged from popular activities such as coarse fishing to pursuits that could be afforded only by the wealthy, such as salmon fishing and grouse shooting. Coarse fishing could be enjoyed on any river or stream where public access was possible, stimulating the creation of many fishing clubs and some railway companies promoted day trips out into the countryside to tempt fishermen to try new stretches of water.[98] At the other end of the economic scale, the ancient tradition of aristocratic and royal hunting grounds had evolved into fishing on a salmon river, deer stalking on a Scottish hillside and shooting on a grouse moor. Estates were transformed to meet the demand not only of traditional customers, but also the rapidly growing number of wealthy industrialists and businessmen who were eager to imitate people from old money (Fig 6.10).[99] Country estates may have evolved to meet the

Fig 6.10
This photograph, taken by Bedford Lemere in April 1892, shows the gallery at Caversham Park, near Reading, with antlers on the walls and deerskin rugs on the floor. The photograph was taken for C J Crawshay, of the family that also owned ironworks in Merthyr Tydfil and the Rhymney Valley, in south Wales.
[BL11452]

Fig 6.11
Gamekeeper Peter Brodie is bringing a stag off the hillside at Glen Tanar, in Royal Deeside, after a day's shooting. He lived in an estate cottage at the foot of Mount Keen. His son, Allan Brodie, the father of this book's author, moved into the bothy in 1926 to train as a gamekeeper.
[Author's collection]

tastes of growing numbers of 'hunters, shooters and fishers', but they were also a vital part of the rural economy – local women served as maids, housekeepers and cooks and men were provided with jobs as gillies and gamekeepers (Fig 6.11).

A number of sports began in the countryside before becoming national, and indeed international, businesses. Golf originated on the east coast of Scotland during the late Middle Ages and arrived in England with the Scottish court at the beginning of the 17th century.[100] Scotland

led the way in codifying the rules of the sport in 1744 and in creating golf clubs. By the late 19th century, golf was an essential part of many people's seaside holiday on the Scottish coast. In 1873, a visitor to Elie, in Fife, was asked what they did on holiday and they replied, 'We golf', and when one Glaswegian visiting North Berwick in 1881 was asked what there was to do, he received the terse reply 'golf'.[101] Between 1880 and 1909, at least 223 golf courses opened in Scotland.[102] England was slow to follow Scotland's example. In 1850, England boasted only one golf club, Blackheath, in London, which had been founded by 1766, but the situation changed dramatically during the late 19th century. By 1880, there were around a dozen golf clubs, rising to 50 by 1887 and to more than 1,000 courses by the outbreak of World War I.[103]

Cricket began to emerge as the modern sport on the village greens of southern England during the mid-18th century, particularly in Surrey and Hampshire, though games with bats and balls had probably taken place for centuries before.[104] From humble roots that are said to be traceable back to Hambledon in Hampshire (Fig 6.12), the sport remains popular with participants and spectators on village greens, while test matches and shorter versions of the game attract thousands to large urban stadia.

Horse racing's roots can be traced back to hunting for sport, an activity that was firmly part of many fairs and traditional holidays by the 18th century.[105] One of Charles II's first acts after the Restoration was to appoint a Master of the Royal Stud and, in 1665, the first race under written rules was held at Newmarket, in Suffolk.[106] A grandstand was certainly in existence there by the 1720s and the Jockey Club was founded in 1750, initially as a high-class social club, though it later had a role in the management of the sport.[107] Other racecourses were laid out during the 18th century, some with architecturally elaborate grandstands, and by the early

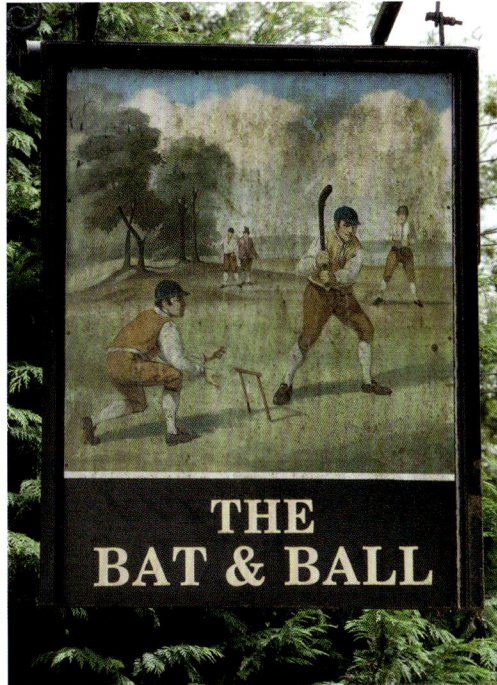

Fig 6.12
This sign for the Bat & Ball Public House at Hambledon, in Hampshire, commemorates this village's key role in the early development of cricket.
[DP064105]

19th century, the five classic flat races had been established.[108] By 1823, there were 95 racecourses, though 87 of these staged only one race per year (Fig 6.13).[109] Jump racing began to gain popularity during the 19th century. A race meeting was first held at Cheltenham, in Gloucestershire, in August 1818, but when flat racing's popularity declined it was replaced by steeplechasing, celebrated meetings being held there annually

Fig 6.13
This pair of stereo photographs shows Epsom racecourse on Derby Day during the late 19th century. Epsom Downs has been a racing venue since the 1770s; the Derby was first run there in 1780 and the course's first grandstand was erected in 1830.
[CC97/00176]

Fig 6.14
The point-to-point
steeplechase on Flagg
Moor, in Derbyshire,
photographed here in 1959
by John Gay, is traditionally
held by the High Peak Hunt
on Easter Tuesday.
[AA069698]

Fig 6.15
The White City Stadium,
in London, which was built
for the 1908 Olympics, was
used for dog racing. This
1929 Aerofilms photograph
shows the stadium during
a race meeting. It was
Britain's leading greyhound
track from its opening in
1927 until 1984.
[EPW031079]

from 1844 until the present day.[110] The racecourse at Aintree, in Liverpool, was set out and a grandstand built in 1829, with the first running of the Grand National taking place in 1836 or 1839.[111] The origins of steeplechasing and point-to-point racing have clear links to hunting, but with the coming of railways, horse racing became the first sport to benefit from access to a mass audience (Fig 6.14).[112]

Another rural pastime has also been transformed into a national sport. The first modern hare coursing club was established at Swaffham, in Norfolk, in 1776 and the National Coursing Club was founded to regulate the sport in 1858.[113] By the late 19th century, it had become a predominantly working-class pursuit, but its popularity declined during the 20th century. Greyhound racing began to take its place and from the 1920s onwards, modern stadia began to be constructed in major population centres (Fig 6.15).[114]

Pressures on the countryside

The charm of the countryside was its unspoilt nature, but growing numbers of people wanting to spend time in it led to significant challenges. The bicycle increased access to countryside within reach of major population centres, but it was the car that first opened up remote parts of Britain to a form of mass tourism between the wars and particularly after World War II. By 1938, there were 1.94 million cars on the road, by which time they were beginning to have a noticeable impact on the shape of tourism, not only to seaside resorts but also into the countryside. Immediately after World War II, the number of visitors arriving in the Lake District was in the tens of thousands, but by 2008 perhaps as many as 7 million visitors arrived in the National Park during the year.[115]

Even before the car and the charabanc had a significant impact on beauty spots, there was already an awareness about the pressures facing the British countryside. In 1792, the soldier and diarist John Byng (1743–1813) bemoaned the fact that the success of Sir Richard Arkwright's Cromford Mill and other factories had 'destroy'd the course, and beauty of Nature'.[116] One of the earliest pressure groups to seek to protect the beauty of the natural rural landscape was the Commons Preservation Society, which was formed in 1865.[117] In cities, the need for open spaces – 'open-air sitting rooms for the poor' as National Trust founder Octavia Hill (1838–1912)

described them – was advocated by the Kyrle Society, which was established in 1878.[118] In 1895, the National Trust for Places of Historic Interest or Natural Beauty was established to protect historic landscapes. The National Trust had acquired 850 acres of countryside in the Lake District, Wales, Derbyshire, Cornwall, Surrey and Cambridgeshire by the time it gained the status of a statutory corporation through the National Trust Act in 1907.[119] A similar National Trust for Scotland was formed in 1931.

Natural wonders

One of the key roles of the National Trust and other conservation bodies was to look after some of the natural wonders that Britain had to offer. Perhaps the most famous single natural sites in Britain are the island of Staffa, in the Inner Hebrides, and the Giant's Causeway, in Northern Ireland. Appreciation of these sites was partly due to their natural beauty, but was especially a result of their intriguingly man-made character. The new and emerging sciences that had demoted the Earth from being the centre of the universe, and through palaeontology and geology were beginning to understand the scientific history of our planet, would change the way that people looked at natural sites such as these.

The 'discovery' by naturalist Sir Joseph Banks (1743–1820) of Staffa and Fingal's Cave in August 1772 first made a wide public aware of its remarkable geology.[120] It had been named after the Norse word for staves, as the columns of polygonal basalt were reminiscent of the way that the Vikings had constructed their houses and churches using vertical tree logs (Fig 6.16). The naming of Fingal's Cave was part of an ancient mythology that had been created by the Scottish writer James MacPherson (1736–96).[121] Fingal was a legendary figure in Ireland who battled the Norse. He was the father of Ossian, someone who many visitors to Scotland came to search for, always unsuccessfully.[122] Among the famous visitors to Staffa was composer Felix Mendelssohn (1809–47) in 1829 who was inspired to write his *Hebrides Overture*. Despite suffering from seasickness, architect Karl Friedrich Schinkel (1781–1841) was still very impressed by the island, with its 'architecture formed by the basalt', including some columns that he assessed to be 50ft (15m) high.[123]

Similar geological formations can be found on the Isle of Mull, also in the Hebrides, and most famously at the Giant's Causeway in Northern

Fig 6.16
This view of Fingal's Cave,
on the island of Staffa,
shows the tall basalt staves
flanking the entrance.
[© Gerry Zambonini,
Flickr (CC BY-SA 2.0)]

Fig 6.17 (facing page)
Most of the columns
that make up the Giant's
Causeway are hexagonal
in section, although there
are also some with between
four and eight sides. The
tallest examples, forming
the Giant's Organ, are about
39ft (12m) high and the
solidified lava in the cliffs is
92ft (28m) thick in places.
[© Author]

Ireland (Fig 6.17). The geological similarity caused writers such as James Johnson to retell the story that Scotland and Ireland had once been joined by 'a gigantic bridge of crystallised basalt pillars' or 'a submarine causeway'.[124] The legend created to explain their remarkable structure was that a giant, Finn McCool, the champion of Ireland, fought a rival Scottish giant, Benandonner. As there were no boats big enough to transport the giants, Finn built a causeway across the sea to Scotland. Finn won the battle, but, after the death of the giants, the causeway fell into the sea, leaving only the two ends of the link.

As well as being a scientific wonder, the Giant's Causeway became a major tourist attraction. In 1830, the geologist Sir Charles Lyell (1797–1875) published the first volume of *Principles of Geology*, which challenged existing ideas about geology and opposed the biblical idea of creation and the Flood as literal history.[125] In the same year, the Irish poet Philip Dixon Hardy (1794–1875) published a guidebook for Northern Ireland in which he noted that there was uncertainty about how the basalt columns

were formed, with one idea being that they were formed underwater, while the other argument was to attribute them to volcanic activity.[126] The Giant's Causeway proved so popular that in 1883 one of the world's earliest electric railways was built to connect it to nearby Portrush. In 1887, the service was extended from Bushmills to the Giant's Causeway, meaning that it covered eight miles (13km). The line last operated in 1949.[127] It is clear from a description of the Giant's Causeway in an 1888 guidebook that the authors regarded this new form of electric railway as a minor wonder, but they were still much more impressed by the Giant's Causeway.[128]

Conclusion

Chapter 5 demonstrated that the development of transport and its increasing affordability had a major impact on the number of people who were able to travel for leisure and for holidays. The successive revolutions in transport extended the range of places that people could visit. They were

no longer limited to a convenient nearby seaside resort or exploring their local countryside. Instead, they could now explore every corner of Britain and were even increasingly able to head abroad.

At the beginning of the 18th century, the countryside that was most celebrated was the one that had been improved by man through modern agricultural practices. However, as the century progressed, the impact of the Romantic movement and the growing power of the idea of the picturesque led to a reinterpretation of the British countryside. The Peak District, the Lake District and the Scottish Highlands became attractive destinations for increasing numbers of tourists. The Lake District particularly benefited from poetic endorsement, while parts of Scotland enjoyed royal recognition. Most people travelled to these locations to celebrate the natural beauty and perhaps the mythological and historical associations of some sites, but places such as Staffa and the Giant's Causeway came to public attention as science began to try to explain their appearance and their existence.

The inquisitiveness that led growing numbers of people to seek the works of mythical giants also prompted tourists to investigate and record the rapidly changing face of the British Isles. As the first country to embrace industrialisation, Britain's towns and cities were transformed during the 18th and 19th centuries. New activities, new architecture and new industries all contributed to their transformation and in the wake of this rapid 'progress', people were also intrigued by what was being lost. In the next chapter, the story of urban tourism will be described, alongside an appreciation of how growing numbers of people set off in search of Britain's past, present and future.

7

Urban tourism and the search for Britain's past, present and future

By the mid-18th century, a fairly standard form of tour and private travel journal had emerged, with a common set of places and themes. As well as an interest in the countryside and natural wonders, the long-standing interest in antiquarianism was growing stronger, and more scholarly. An increasing number of inquisitive and investigative tourists were travelling to witness how Britain was being transformed into a modern industrial state. Therefore, at a time when the romantic and the picturesque were drawing people to the countryside, the nation's rich history and more recent industrialisation were attracting visitors to Britain's cities and growing industrial towns.

This chapter will begin by focusing on urban Britain. London was the capital, but also the heart of Britain's financial world and the centre of an elaborate social scene. Smaller-scale versions of the events and facilities found in the capital also began to appear in provincial towns and cities during the 18th century, and Oxford and Cambridge had become popular tourist destinations. These two seats of learning lured tourists who came to admire their architecture and history, and despite being small towns they were among the earliest in Britain to merit guidebooks.

Growing numbers of people also set out to explore Britain's past, present and future, in a country that was leading the world in transforming itself from a rural economy to an industrial power. As well as seeking out rural ancient monuments, tourists were keen to see historic buildings in towns and cities across the country, but they also wished to see contemporary architecture, country houses we now think of as historic, but were part of their current art scene. They also wished to visit places associated with popular authors and to attend important local and national events while they travelled around the country. There was considerable interest in new industries and some travellers' diaries contain references to visits to mines, tex-

tile mills and factories, sights treated in much the same way as a country house or an old castle. While some tourists saw these new industries as the future of the country, there was also a negative side to this economic success. An early form of 'dark tourism' is evident from the 18th century onwards, with people visiting prisons, orphanages and factories, often with little apparent concern for the hardships being endured by the people they saw there.

Cities, towns and urban life

The most popular urban tourist destination was London. It was both the capital city and by far the largest settlement and therefore was a lure for the provincial rich in search of glamour, prestige and excitement.[1] Fashionable society gathered in and around the royal court and Parliament, and a distinct London season coincided with Parliament sitting in Westminster, the remainder of the year being spent in country houses, at spas and seaside resorts. German author Johanna Schopenhauer (1766–1838) described a busy day in London, which involved the men carrying out their business and visiting coffee houses, while the women wore extravagant hats, went shopping, promenaded and visited art exhibitions, before returning for a fine dinner and a long evening of socialising.[2] By the mid-19th century, the London season was marked by major sporting and social events such as the Boat Race, Henley Regatta (Fig 7.1), the Epsom Derby (see Fig 6.13) and Royal Ascot. It was also peppered with balls held in the London homes of the wealthy. London was also a magnet for the less wealthy, including criminals and prostitutes seeking to exploit the presence of so many rich people.

London was home to major sights that British and foreign tourists wished to see. Czech nobleman Baron Waldstein, in his diary of 1600,

described a visit to the magnificent Royal Palace of Whitehall, predating changes made to it by James I and Inigo Jones:

> We then went on into the nearby Palace, the Royal residence known as Whitehall, ie the White Hall. It is truly majestic ... and it is a place which fills one with wonder, not so much because of its great size as because of the magnificence of its bed chambers which are filled with the most gorgeous splendour.[3]

In 1725, Swiss travel writer César-François de Saussure (1705–83) left Lausanne and arrived in England, where he stayed until October 1729. He documented such obvious landmarks as Westminster Abbey, the recently completed St Paul's Cathedral and the Houses of Parliament.[4] He also visited the Tower of London, which was still an active military site (Fig 7.2), where, as well as being impressed by the Crown Jewels, he enjoyed seeing the King's Menagerie, which at that date included ten lions, a panther, two tigers and four leopards.[5] Nearly a century later, in 1811, the American visitor Louis Simond (d 1831) also visited the menagerie, where he found a tame white tiger imported from India to be the most interesting exhibit.[6] A

menagerie continued to be based at the Tower of London until the 1830s, when the animals were moved to the new zoo at Regent's Park.[7]

By the 18th century, London also offered residents and visitors a wide range of musical and theatrical entertainment. This was often provided in the city's pleasure gardens, which served as a model for provincial towns, spas and seaside resorts to follow. The earliest pleasure garden had been created in London during the 17th century. The most famous of the early pleasure gardens was New Spring Gardens, later called Vauxhall Gardens, which opened soon after the Restoration in 1660. By the 18th century, London was said to be home to more than 60 pleasure gardens.[8] The most important new pleasure gardens in the 18th century were Marylebone, which opened in 1737, and Ranelagh beside Chelsea Hospital, which opened in 1742.[9] Ranelagh's rotunda seems to have been of particular interest to contemporary visitors. German author Carl Philip Moritz (1756–93) visited England in 1782 and described the beautiful chandeliers, large mirrors, paintings and statues, including busts of Britain's leading dramatists.[10] During the early 19th century, new pleasure gardens aimed at a wider audience opened in London, such as the Royal Surrey Gardens at

Walworth in 1831 and the Cremorne Gardens in 1843.[11] Vauxhall survived this new wave of cheaper pleasure gardens by lowering its admission price, but this prompted a decline in the quality of the visitor experience, leading to its closure and the complete dismantling of the gardens in 1859.[12]

London was at the heart of Britain's transport networks, meaning it was an easier place to reach than many nearer provincial towns and cities. By the time of the Great Exhibition in 1851, the capital was at the heart of an emerging, comprehensive national railway network. Visitors came to London to see the works of industry of all nations, including working-class people who had been able to contribute to a savings club to pay for the trip and possibly a stay of a few days.[13] Around six million people visited the Great Exhibition and many of them would also have visited London's museums and other attractions (Fig 7.3).

As the capital city, the main business centre and home to the country's leading social, cultural and entertainment attractions and events, London was visited by huge numbers of tourists. Elsewhere, there were large historic towns and cities, such as York, Bristol and Norwich, that offered provincial equivalents of the range of facilities and attractions that London had to offer. During the 18th century, when most people lived in small settlements with modest, primarily vernacular buildings, the grand, polite, public, private and commercial architecture of major provincial cities would have been very impressive.

Oxford and Cambridge were also popular, with visitors keen to see their colleges, museums and libraries. These were prosperous and interesting places to visit, but they were small, having only 12,000 and 10,000 inhabitants respectively in 1801.[14] Nevertheless, there was sufficient interest to justify producing guidebooks and from 1759 *The New Oxford Guide* was published.[15] As well as obvious historic sights, editions of the guidebook included lengthy descriptions of the main colleges, as well as places to visit outside the city.

In addition to traditional historic towns and cities, many smaller towns that were growing rapidly as a result of increasing trade and industrialisation also became tourist destinations. During the 18th century, Liverpool grew from a small provincial port to a huge town with ships

Fig 7.2
Since its foundation in the 11th century, the Tower of London has been an important military site, yet has welcomed visitors. Today it is a Historic Royal Palace and its vast collection of historic arms and armour are still a major attraction, as it was when this photograph was taken in the late 19th century.
[DD97/00337]

Fig 7.3
This early photograph of the Crystal Palace was probably taken soon after it was relocated to south London, having closed late in 1851 at the end of the Great Exhibition. The building was destroyed by fire in 1936. [DP004607]

sailing from its docks to destinations around the world. In the mid-17th century, it consisted of seven main streets covering only 300 yards from north to south and a similar distance inland from the waterfront.[16] Though it would seem small to modern eyes, author Daniel Defoe (1660–1731), who visited Liverpool at the end of the 17th century, was impressed with the town.[17] Celia Fiennes (1662–1741), visiting in 1698, compared it to the capital:

> LEVERPOOL is built just on the river Mersy, mostly new built houses of brick and stone after the London fashion; ... its a very rich trading town, the houses of brick and stone built high and even, that a streete quite through lookes very handsome, the streetes well pitched; there are abundance of persons you see very well dress'd and of good fashion; the streetes are faire and long, its London in miniature as much as ever I saw any thing.[18]

In 1673, Liverpool had around 1,500 inhabitants, but by 1700 its population was 5,145; 20 years later, it had more than doubled to 11,833 and by the beginning of the 19th century, it had grown to more than 80,000.[19] Liverpool's rapid growth was in large measure due to its location. Like Bristol, it was convenient for the Atlantic trade in slaves, sugar, textiles and tobacco, but it also had a substantial hinterland, including industrial northern England and the canal system of the Midlands.[20] During the 18th century, the town's growing population prompted the creation of new churches and entertainment facilities. Ordained churchman Richard Pococke (1704–65), who visited Liverpool in 1750, recorded the flurry of recent church-building activity in his journal.[21] In 1749–54, an ambitious new exchange, complete with a lavish ballroom, was erected to designs by John Wood the Elder (1704–54).[22] A purpose-built theatre opened in 1772 to replace a smaller one that had opened more than 20 years earlier and by the end of the 18th century there was a Public Concert Room and assemblies were held in the Exchange until it burnt down in 1795 (and was later rebuilt).[23] Walks and pleasure gardens were also established, as Pococke noted: 'At the corner of the town next the sea is a very fine situation, commanding a view of the sea; it is called the Ladies Walk, and is divided into three parts by two narrow slips of grass and two rows of trees.'[24] Another Ladies Walk was created beside Duke Street and was in existence by 1769.[25] The 1766 *Liverpool Directory* listed the professions that would be expected in a major port, but there were also a number of people providing the types of services associated with leisure.[26] These included booksellers and stationers, innkeepers and coffee-house proprietors, as befits both a port and a resort. There were also a number of tradesmen squarely in business for pleasure and leisure, such as wig makers, hatters, hosiers and milliners, as well as Deville Desaubrys, a dancing master in George Street.

Nearby Manchester experienced a similar growth and transformation. When the Cambridge students (*see* p 103) visited in 1725, it was still a small town, its main attraction being its church that would become a cathedral in 1847.[27] Their visit predated any significant signs of industrialisation, but by the time that Johanna Schopenhauer wrote her diary in 1816, Manchester was 'dark with the smoke from the coal fires' and looked like 'a huge forge or workshop'.[28] Schopenhauer also described how 'everywhere the rattling of the looms of the cotton mills can be heard', and she visited one of the largest mills, and recorded how 'a steam engine, placed in the basement, activated the many wheels and spindles in various stories above'. To a modern reader, it seems remarkable that while recording the presence of children working on the looms, she did not think to criticise this.[29] Henry B McLellan, an American visitor to Britain in 1834, also described Manchester's industry and its workforce, unfavourably comparing them to the city of Lowell in Massachusetts.[30] To escape from the noise of the town, McLellan briefly retreated into the cathedral, before again being confronted by the city's huge industrial complexes:

I arrived at an eminence which commanded a view of a part of the city. I looked forth upon the hundred furnace and factory pipes that poured their smoke and fire into the misty canopy of clouds above the city. I saw the massive buildings on every side. I heard the deep murmur of the town, the active working of ten thousand looms, and the unceasing sound of the mighty engines which shake the air.[31]

In 1846, Scottish traveller Hugh Miller described how in the distance 'the looted gloom of the atmosphere that overhangs it' was caused by 'the innumerable chimneys'.[32] Miller found 'whole streets of warehouses – dead, dingy, gigantic buildings' in the centre of the town, but he was also impressed by the magnificence of 'the public buildings devoted to trade'.[33]

During his visit to Britain, Louis Simond visited London, and Scotland's largest cities. In 1811, Edinburgh was home to 103,000 inhabitants, while Glasgow had a population of 101,000.[34] Simond was impressed with Edinburgh, its houses and the prison, but he complained about the amount of rain he endured during August 1810 and criticised the fishwives who prepared the catches at the fish market.[35] He returned to Edinburgh later in the year, when he sat in on a criminal trial that he described in detail. He subsequently discovered that the defendant was found guilty of culpable homicide. The sentence was transportation to Botany Bay, but the convict would have to wait for two years in prison until 'a full cargo' was ready.[36] After his initial visit to Edinburgh, he headed to Glasgow via New Lanark, and his journal returned to one of his main interests, documenting the major factories that he visited. At both places he saw a wide range of mills and, interestingly, like Schopenhauer, he mentions the presence of children without any sense of concern that they were working alongside their parents.[37]

During the 18th century, the arts and architecture flourished in Dublin. The city's population was over 100,000 and by 1831 it had doubled in size (Fig 7.4). From 1758, a major reconstruction programme led to the demolition of the narrow streets of medieval Dublin and their replacement with grand new roads lined with elegant Georgian buildings. Antiquary and mineralogist Edward Daniel Clarke (1769–1822), who visited during his summer tour in 1791, was impressed with the architecture. He saw a range of buildings and sights comparable to those that might be found in London. At Trinity College he saw its three quadrangles, hall, chapel, spacious library and the recently established museum. He moved

Fig 7.4
This 1884 photograph shows the General Post Office in Dublin, which was built in 1814–18. During the Easter Rising of 1916, it served as the headquarters for the uprising's leaders. Nelson's Pillar of 1809 was destroyed by Irish republicans in an explosion in 1966 and has been replaced by the Spire of Dublin (2002–3).
[© HES]

on to the Houses of Parliament, then the barracks, which he described as a 'noble and useful structure' capable of housing 6,000 soldiers. Beside the 'Lying-Inn-Hospital', a rotunda similar to Ranelagh (*see* p 120) had been built.[38] Clarke was also able to visit Dublin's Foundling Hospital, the House of Industry, the new prison, the Royal Hospital, the lunatic asylum founded by Dean Jonathan Swift and the Asylum for Magdalens, a place for reformed prostitutes.[39] Although Clarke was highly complimentary about the buildings of Dublin, he was critical of its people. His unhappy and insanitary stay in a hotel coloured his opinion of the entire city, prompting him to conclude, 'The streets are filled with wretchedness and grandeur, idleness and extravagance.'[40]

Events

As well as visiting places, people travelled to witness or participate in events or accidentally came across them during their journeys. While César-François de Saussure was in London between 1725 and 1729, he saw royal processions, the coronation of George II (1683–1760) and the regular executions taking place at Tyburn.[41]

Catherine Hutton (1756–1846) on her journey to Wales in 1796 came across the sitting of the Assizes. She recorded, 'At Shrewsbury it was the Assizes, and a bishop was to be tried for a riot. The novelty of the case had filled every house.'[42] (The Bishop of Bangor was tried for riot at Shrewsbury Assizes on 16 July 1796.)

For the poorer members of society, leisure was usually enjoyed at home in small, informal get-togethers, playing in the streets, at markets and in gatherings of friends and relatives to celebrate births, deaths and marriages. Pleasure had to wait until a day's hard work in the fields had been completed. There were also festivals and other celebrations in the agricultural calendar and in some places there were wakes holidays lasting up to a week. In a county such as Northamptonshire, local communities enjoyed a range of rustic pleasures, such as dancing, wrestling, bull-baiting, racing and music on these occasions.[43] In many counties, industrialisation led to an erosion of these traditional festivities. However, in Lancashire and Yorkshire they survived into the 19th and 20th centuries, though by then the week or fortnight holiday was usually being taken at seaside resorts.

Most local communities had access to fairs, annual events that people might travel to, at least short distances (Fig 7.5). In town centres, or in designated locations in or beside towns, an annual fair would take place where goods were traded. As late as the early 19th century, the main business of the Nottingham Goose Fair was still trading in lace, willow baskets, cheese, poultry and, of course, geese.[44] Fairs also provided opportunities for England's rural population to gather and enjoy entertainment, and during the 18th and 19th centuries the emphasis shifted from commerce to pleasure.[45] St Bartholomew's Fair in London began as a commercial fair, but from the 17th century offered satirical theatre, puppet shows, jugglers, comedians and fire eaters.[46] By the 1780s, this fair was described as being 'purely devoted to the entertainment of the populace and the diversions of children'.[47] Increasingly there was concern among reformers and local government about the behaviour of adults, fairs increasingly being associated with drunkenness and sexual licence.[48] Therefore, the Fairs Act 1871 allowed for the abolition of fairs if they were deemed to be unnecessary, causing immorality or were harmful to the inhabitants of towns.[49] Although more than 150 fairs were suppressed, most remained popular, galvanised by the introduction of steam power from the 1860s to create new types of rides.[50] The internal combustion engine and electricity continued the transformation of fairgrounds, allowing larger, faster and brilliantly illuminated rides. However, the introduction of this new technology required significant investment and therefore showmen increasingly concentrated on larger fairs, resulting in the decline of the smaller, traditional village fair.[51]

Traditional fairs not only spawned events and sites that would lead to the creation of the modern amusement park, but were also the roots of many modern sporting occasions. In some parts of England there were local sports gatherings which, along with Highland Games in Scotland, influenced Pierre de Coubertin (1863–1937) when he founded the modern Olympics in 1896.[52] In horse racing, some racecourses and meetings can be traced back to events held at the traditional fairs. A number of more urban sports and events also had their origins at fairs, including rugby, wrestling and boxing, which were regulated, codified and commercialised during the late 19th century. For instance, prize fights had been popular from the late 1780s, but the Marquess of Queensberry Rules were published in 1867 and in 1880 the Amateur Boxing Association was formed.[53]

Fig 7.5
This photograph by Henry William Taunt shows the August Fair at Bampton, in Oxfordshire, in 1904. A small swing ride can be seen among the adjacent stalls and booths.
[CC57/00458]

The most popular sport to have at least part of its roots in traditional fairs is football. Author and painter George Keate (1729–97) published a lively description of his travels in Kent during the 1760s. On one occasion he visited Ramsgate, where he encountered the village fete during a 'running match'. In the afternoon, he described how he saw two teams playing a football match using their clothes as goalposts.[54] Football grew in popularity during the 19th century, but it was the coincidence of improved rail links, growing individual income and the increasing incidence of the Saturday half-day holiday that stimulated the creation of professional association football from the 1860s onwards. Prior to the formation of the Football Association in 1863, there were local variations in the sport and its rules, but within a few years professional football clubs were being formed in England and Scotland.[55] Football stadia, among the largest structures being built in many towns, appeared from the late 19th century onwards (Fig 7.6). In 1888, the most commercially minded clubs formed the Football League, which during its first season attracted 600,000 spectators.[56] By 1951, 416 professional clubs were attracting nearly one million spectators each week.

In search of the past

As well as enjoying the beauty of the country-side and discovering the changing character of historic towns and cities, tourists also travelled to marvel at, and sometimes to study, Britain's long history. The key tourist attractions for people with an interest in prehistory were Stonehenge and Avebury, in Wiltshire, monuments that attracted both scholarly interest and tourist curiosity. Stonehenge was regarded as a particular marvel and regularly featured in private journals and later travel guides, particularly as it was conveniently located between Salisbury and Bath. The mineral water springs at Bath had been revered since Roman times and its ancient bath was still a working therapeutic site, as well as a historic curiosity. Roman sites, such as Hadrian's Wall, in the north of England, and Caerleon, in south Wales, also regularly feature in the works of antiquaries, many of whom still travelled on roads that began life during the Roman Empire. The Dissolution of the Monasteries by Henry VIII had deprived England of its complex religious infrastructure, but by the 18th century, the decaying remnants of this rich heritage were proving of interest to antiquarians

Fig 7.6
The original Wembley Stadium was built in 1922–3 for the 1924 British Empire Exhibition. This Aerofilms photograph shows it on 25 April 1925 during the FA Cup Final between Sheffield United and Cardiff City. [EPW012731]

and people with an eye for the sublime beauty of ruins (Fig 7.7).

The railway served as a major stimulus to popular archaeology, allowing local societies to arrange trips for their members to archaeological sites and historic monuments.[57] Most excursions undertaken inevitably focused on churches, as they were the most common form of historic monument available to visit, there being relatively few active archaeological sites available in any given year.[58] In 1871, members of the Suffolk Archaeological Society met at Needham Market station before looking at local churches, ending with a gathering in the new school room at Earl Stonham, where they examined finds that had been excavated nearby. In the same year, the Sheffield Architectural and Archaeological Society placed less emphasis on churches, taking time to visit Wentworth House, near Rotherham, the old Roman fort at Templeborough and the new hospital that was being erected.

These excursions benefited from the new transport infrastructure, but antiquarians and archaeologists were also increasingly aware of the threat that Britain's heritage faced in the wake of industrialisation. Therefore, the Ancient Monuments Protection Act 1882 allowed for a

Fig 7.7
Ruined abbeys such as Rievaulx Abbey and Fountains Abbey, in Yorkshire, and particularly Tintern Abbey, in Monmouthshire (shown here), were often inspirations for poets and painters, and in their wake came growing numbers of tourists. [DP031971]

range of archaeological sites to be placed on the schedule, and, with the consent of the owner, to be placed under the guardianship of the state or a local authority (Fig 7.8).[59] A second Act in 1900 extended the scope of the legislation to include buildings that were not occupied as a dwelling place.[60] The National Trust had initially concentrated on acquiring open spaces, but by its tenth birthday in 1905 it was already caring for six historic buildings.[61]

As well as historic sites, tourists were increasingly able to enjoy museums and art galleries that illustrated Britain's rich history, as well as displaying artefacts from distant, ancient civilisations. Museums were being created by the 18th century to house the collections assembled by travellers, scientists, anthropologists and art lovers. These institutions were encouraged by reformers as they could be enjoyed by the whole family and provided a wholesome alternative to activities such as gambling and drinking.[62] By the late 19th century, museums were even seen as a way of diverting working people from sinful pursuits on the Sabbath, and Charles Hill (d 1910), secretary of the Working Men's Lord's Day Rest Association, was advocating their opening as an alternative to drinking.[63]

The earliest collections were in Oxford, where portraits and curiosities owned by Oxford University were based in the Upper Reading Room of the Bodleian Library from the 1620s. As the collection grew, it became too large for its origi-

Fig 7.8
By 1907, the Commissioners of Works had scheduled 86 monuments, including Silbury Hill and Stonehenge, both in Wiltshire. Prehistoric Silbury Hill, shown here at dusk with its reflection in the water around it, has been a key tourist attraction for centuries.
[DP057662]

nal home and was rehoused in a purpose-built facility in 1845. The Ashmolean Museum opened in Oxford in 1683 to house the collection of curiosities and antiquities of government official Elias Ashmole (1617–92) in a specially created building. In London, the British Museum was founded in 1753 to house historic collections of books, manuscripts and curiosities acquired for the nation from Sir Hans Sloane (1660–1753), Sir Robert Cotton (1571–1631) and the Harleys, the Earls of Oxford (Fig 7.9). Louis Simond described a visit to the museum in April 1810, the main object of his interest being the recently acquired Rosetta Stone, though he also remarked on Greek sculpture and some of the manuscripts he saw.[64] Major provincial towns and cities also opened art galleries and museums. The Manchester Art Gallery came into being following a public meeting in 1823. It led to the foundation of the Manchester Institute for the Promotion of Literature, Science and the Arts, which raised £16,000 to build a gallery, designed by Charles Barry (1795–1860), which opened in 1834.[65]

Country houses

During the summer travels of the group of Cambridge students in 1725, their main destinations, apart from churches, were country houses, where they admired the gardens, furniture and paintings. However, the main reason for visits to such illustrious houses as Blenheim,

in Oxfordshire (Fig 7.10), Castle Howard, in Yorkshire, and Chatsworth, in Derbyshire, was to marvel at the architecture.[66] Today country houses are considered, alongside the remains of ruined abbeys and castles, as part of the heritage industry, these great houses being revered old masterpieces. However, to the 18th-century tourist these mansions represented modern architecture. As the anonymous Cambridge

Fig 7.9
The Reading Room of the British Museum was designed by Sydney Smirke (1798–1877) and opened in 1857. Located in the centre of the museum site, this stunning rotunda ceased to be used when the new British Library opened in 1997.
[AA98/05954]

Fig 7.10
This 1886 photograph by Bedford Lemere shows Blenheim Palace, which was built between 1705 and c 1722 and was designed by Sir John Vanbrugh (1664–1726) and Nicholas Hawksmoor (c 1661–1736). Now a World Heritage Site, it is still a very popular tourist destination.
[BL06805]

student diarist noted in 1725, when visiting Easton Neston, in Northamptonshire, 'This is a modern building (its date 1701)' (Fig 7.11).[67]

People who visited country houses might be doing so as guests, as tourists or as an amateur/critic seeking to investigate contemporary projects. It was common for an aristocrat undertaking a major development to send their architect or mason, or visit in person, to see works that had been completed recently or were in progress. For instance, the Dowager Countess of Shrewsbury in 1592 visited Holdenby, in Northamptonshire, and Wollaton, in Nottingham, while her own house at Hardwick, in Derbyshire, was in progress.[68] However, most visitors to country houses were simply there to admire the art and architecture. At Warwick Castle, visiting architect Karl Friedrich Schinkel (1781–1841) explored the old fortifications and the gardens, but he was particularly impressed by the lavish interiors containing old master paintings, especially the 'Great hall of weapons' with its 'furniture … in labour brass'. He noted, 'Etruscan vases, cinquecento bronze, wood panelling', as well as 'the great and famous Warwick vase' that had been brought to Britain from Hadrian's Villa in Tivoli.[69] The ultimate in country house visiting would

have been a trip to a royal palace. In June 1826, Schinkel enjoyed a visit to the Royal Pavilion at Brighton, where he was impressed by the elaborate culinary technology employed in the kitchen (Fig 7.12). He also took the opportunity to visit the circular stable block built by William Porden (1755–1822) in 1803–8, which incorporated a riding arena.[70]

During the 17th and 18th centuries, many country houses put in place procedures to deal with strangers arriving to admire the house. Senior members of the domestic staff, often the housekeeper, would decide whether a new arrival was a suitable and safe guest to entertain, and of course a fee was levied in exchange for a tour.[71] At Kedleston Hall, in Derbyshire, in 1777, author and lexicographer Samuel Johnson (1709–84) and his Scottish friend and biographer James Boswell (1740–95) were taken round by a 'most distinct articulator', namely Mrs Garnett the housekeeper, and in Jane Austen's *Pride and Prejudice*, Elizabeth Bennet's tour of Pemberley was also provided by the housekeeper.[72] Soldier and diarist John Byng (1743–1813) visited Apethorpe House, Northamptonshire, in 1790. After ringing the front door bell, and waiting for a long time, he was shown around by the

Fig 7.11
The visits to country houses made by the Cambridge students in 1725 are more akin to a modern tourist exploring the cutting-edge skyscrapers of the City of London or Canary Wharf. Easton Neston, in Northamptonshire, a work by Nicholas Hawksmoor, was built in the contemporary baroque style, the modern style of its day.
[CC001835]

Fig 7.12
Karl Friedrich Schinkel was also impressed by the lavish Chinese-inspired interiors of Brighton's Royal Pavilion, which were created as part of the refurbishment programme undertaken in 1815–22 by John Nash (1752–1835). [FF98/00157]

Fig 7.13
Gardens such as at Stourhead, in Wiltshire, were attempts to create a classical vision in modern-day England. As well as containing the finest classical monuments, these landscapes were huge engineering projects in which lakes were created and large areas of woodland planted. [AA98/05115]

housekeeper. At Chatsworth in the previous year he was under the guidance of the gardener and the housekeeper, who proudly showed off their respective parts of the estate.[73] At Burghley House, near Stamford in Lincolnshire, the Earl of Exeter regularly greeted visitors himself, in the case of Horace Walpole (1717–97) opening up everything he wanted to see.[74] Although Byng simply turned up at country houses and industrial sites, Horace Walpole took the precaution of writing to property owners in advance to ensure that he would be welcomed.[75]

Gardens were a popular attraction for tourists seeking to enjoy the latest creations of landowners and fashionable gardeners. Celia Fiennes saw the now long-lost garden at Wilton House, in Wiltshire, designed by Isaac de Caus (1590–1648), and Byng visited Blenheim Palace in 1785 under the guidance of 'a park keeper', where he admired the grounds laid out by Lancelot 'Capability' Brown (bap 1716, d 1783).[76] Particularly popular were the contrived, Claude-Lorrain and Grand-Tour inspired landscapes of the first half of the 18th century, with their temples, grottoes and carefully designed vistas, such as at Stowe, in Buckinghamshire, and Stourhead, in Wiltshire (Fig 7.13).[77] During the 1740s, Henry Hoare II

(1705–85) opened his garden at Stourhead to visitors of all classes and Mrs Lybbe Powys, who visited a quarter of a century later, found the gardens full, and therefore had to return the following day.[78]

From the second half of the 18th century onwards, there was a growing interest in visiting country houses and an increasing willingness to open them to the general population. As early as 1760, Chatsworth opened to the public two days per week, and by the 1780s Blenheim was open daily from 2pm until 4pm, while Fonthill Abbey, in Wiltshire, was open from noon until 4pm.[79] By 1784, Horace Walpole at Strawberry Hill, Twickenham, had established a set of rules for visitors, who could visit between noon and 3pm between 1 May and 1 October; children were not allowed. As the house was so near London and so very popular, he required people to obtain tickets in advance (Fig 7.14).[80]

Increasing visitor numbers can be explained by an acceptance that country house visiting was no longer restricted to the wealthiest in society, foreshadowing the profound democratisation of tourism that would take place during the second half of the 19th century. Although this would bring in more income, increased access could also lead to problems regarding the behaviour of visitors. Lady Beauchamp Proctor (1760–1848) poked a fresco at Wolterton, in Norfolk, with her stick to ensure that it was genuine, and delicate china at Blenheim Palace had to be kept under lock and key because so many pieces had been broken by tourists.[81] By the early 19th century, Hampton Court Palace had introduced a formal ticketing system for admission to some of the

Fig 7.14
Strawberry Hill House is a small but highly influential Gothic villa built in stages during the mid-18th century in Twickenham by Horace Walpole (1717–97). In 1923, it was bought by St Mary's University, Twickenham, and it is now open to the public again after a major restoration. [BB94/05718]

state apartments, but with the death of the housekeeper in 1838, the one-shilling entrance fee was abolished. This led to a sharp rise in admissions, from a few hundred per year in the 1830s to 122,339 in 1840, with peaks of more than 350,000 and almost 370,000 in 1851 and 1862 respectively.[82] One anonymous writer in *The Gentleman's Magazine* in 1840 felt that this was a disaster, as police had to guard the rooms, but other people recorded that generally the large crowds were well behaved and appreciative.[83]

The appetite for country house visiting was being felt more widely as a result of the spread of railways. Organised excursions to country houses began during the mid-19th century. Thomas Cook (1808–92; *see* p 87) regularly arranged excursions for groups of around 300 people to country houses during the late 1840s and 1850s, including Burghley House, Belvoir Castle, in Leicestershire, and Chatsworth House, where a trip of 500 'respectable, orderly and well-dressed individuals' arrived in June 1849.[84] The opening of the line from Derby in that year meant that Chatsworth was visited by around 80,000 tourists per year, and this number increased when the same line reached Manchester in 1863. Some excursions were organised by tourist societies, such as the York Tourist Society, which arranged visits to houses as far away as Chatsworth, Belvoir and Alnwick, in Northumberland.[85] Faced with large numbers of visitors, country house owners were naturally nervous, but it demonstrates that enlightened house owners recognised that this was an important new revenue stream.

Industrial Britain and 'dark' tourism

Diaries and journals reveal that many inquisitive travellers were conscious of the rapid changes that were going on in Britain, whether these changes were reflected in great houses, new agricultural practices or increasingly in the industrialisation of the British economy.[86] Britain was a work in progress in the 18th and 19th centuries, on a path to an uncertain future.

As early as 1725, the Cambridge students visited a contemporary industrial wonder. Lombe's Mill in Derby was a revolutionary industrial building: a water-powered, silk-spinning mill built in 1721 by John Lombe (*c* 1693–1722) and his brother Sir Thomas Lombe (1685–1739).[87] Daniel Defoe also visited the site, as it

was unique when it was built, and wondered 'whether it answers the expense or not', failing to see that it was the way forward for the country's economy.[88] During the summer of 1735, tutor John Whaley (bap 1710, d 1745) visited Lombe's Mill; Thomas Quincey (1753–1793), visiting in 1775, recounted his impressions of the 'great silk-mill' that employed three to four hundred people, mostly women and girls.[89] As well as being powered by water, the mill was also, incredibly, partially powered by children, who shared the turning of a capstan with an ass.

Nearby, the Derwent Valley, in Derbyshire, had a pioneering role in industrialisation during the 18th century, featuring the water-powered spinning mills owned by Sir Richard Arkwright (1732–92), modern mineral mines and canals. Cromford Mill, dating from 1771, introduced technological advances in spinning machines, but of greater importance was Arkwright's new organisation of production (Fig 7.15).[90] Byng attempted to visit it in 1790, but was refused access as he was likely to disturb the girls at work.[91] Housing, and places of recreation and worship were also required for the mill workers, meaning that Arkwright was also a pioneer of education for workers' children, including a school in the village. The most famous example of creating a new industrial community was New Lanark, in Lanarkshire, founded by David Dale (1739–1806) and Richard Arkwright in 1786. Dale sold the mills, land and village in the early 19th century to a partnership that included his son-in-law Robert Owen, who continued the philanthropic approach to industrial working. New Lanark was a regular stop for tourists in general and featured in guidebooks. An 1822 example described the benevolent aims of the 'Great Cotton Manufactory and village of New Lanark', which was highly praised: 'Mr Owen, the proprietor and manager, a man of much benevolence, has devised sundry plans for the improvement of the young people, and his efforts have been crowned with as much success as many of his friends anticipated.'[92] However, writer James Johnson, returning from touring the Highlands in 1834, was hostile to the social experiment, commenting, 'But if I hold Mr Owen's UTOPIA very cheap, I greatly admire his mill.'[93]

In terms of popularity with tourists, the Soho foundry, in Birmingham, can be ranked alongside Lombe's Mill and New Lanark. It was founded in 1795 by Matthew Boulton (1728–1809) and James Watt (1736–1819) for the manufacture of steam engines. James Boswell

Fig 7.15
This 1947 aerial photograph shows the rural setting of Sir Richard Arkwright's highly influential Cromford Mill. It was this building that earned him the accolade of being the 'father of the factory system'.
[EAW011494]

visited the recently opened factory, which employed 700 people, and said, 'I wish [Samuel] Johnson had been with us: for it was seen which I should have been glad to contemplate by his light. The vastness and the contrivance of some of [the] machinery would have "matched his mighty mind"'. During his visit, Boswell met Boulton, who told him, 'I sell here, Sir, what all the world desires to have – POWER.'[94] Another place of considerable public interest was Stoke-on-Trent, and particularly the Etruria factory of Josiah Wedgwood (1730–95). In 1792, John Byng arrived and sent his card up to 'Mr W'. While he waited, he sauntered around the grounds until he could be shown the workshops, where 300 men were employed, followed by a visit to where women undertook the 'painting business', which he described as 'an hot, unwholesome, employ'.[95]

As well as new factories, other manifestations of the transformation of Britain were attracting curious visitors. Elderly Miss Wyndham Portman and her companion Miss Philippa Grove, while visiting Cornwall, naturally went to see St Michael's Mount and the cartographic curiosity of Land's End. They also took the chance to look at the Botallac Copper Mine near Land's End, admiring the machinery built onto the side of the rocks.[96] When Edward Daniel Clarke toured south Wales in 1791, he visited a coal mine, providing an interesting portrait of the use of horse-drawn, railed tramways and pit ponies underground.[97] Another important development in the early 19th century was the introduction of gas lighting (Fig 7.16). Louis Simond described a number of industrial sites and processes, including gas production at a factory in Birmingham.[98]

Transport was also changing. In 1792, John Byng came across the new canal from Leeds to Liverpool, 'where they are now building locks for the advantage of increasing trade'.[99] Although impressed by it, he was unhappy about how the excavated earth was simply dumped on top of nearby hedges rather than being placed in the adjacent fields. If canals were impressive, railways were revolutionary. Henry B McLellan's journal, published in 1834, described the recently opened Liverpool to Manchester railway:

The rail-road commences just at the mouth of a dark gallery, into which we rapidly darted. We passed on for some time through the dark with fearful velocity, when the daylight began once more to glimmer on us, and we soon were flying along, the green fields on either side of us. It was nearly evening when we started, so that the shades of night soon darkened the scene. The motion was both new and agreeable to me. We scarce seemed to touch the earth, whilst the passing objects appeared to whirl by with dizzy swiftness. Occasionally carriages coming from the other direction shot by us with their sparkling furnaces, leaving a train of smoke and fire behind them. We had scarce time to take note of their presence before they had passed with the *whir* and speed of a sky rocket; *a mist of wagons and faces,* visible for a moment, then gone. They govern these highly accelerated machines with surprising facility. Their speed is not abated until very near the stopping place, yet they *bring up* just before the door, as exactly as if with a coach and horses. We completed the thirty miles in about ninety minutes, including twelve or fifteen stoppages.[100]

Britain was popular with foreign tourists eager to learn from the world's first industrialising country. Reinhold Rücker Angerstein (1718–60), a Swedish metallurgist, civil servant and entrepreneur who visited England between 1753 and 1755, was investigating how coal was used in the manufacture of wrought iron. He also travelled widely, looking at many aspects of industrial and agricultural life, and found time to record the new fad for sea bathing that he witnessed at Weymouth, in Dorset, and Scarborough, in Yorkshire.[101] Jabez Maud Fisher, an American Quaker who visited Britain in the 1770s, was interested in the usual tourist sights such as Bath and Chatsworth House, but he also had a keen eye on new developments, such as the docks at Hull, the harbour at Scarborough and the ground-breaking industries in Derbyshire.[102] Joshua Gilpin (1765–1840), an American papermaker, travelled around Britain and the Continent between 1795 and 1801 and again from 1811 to 1814.[103] During his travels around Britain, he visited a variety of industrial sites, including the canal and docks at Gloucester, as well as lead and iron works.[104]

Many commentators also recorded the darker side of Britain's growing economic success. Agricultural reformer and writer Arthur Young (1741–1820) visited the Nacton Poor House, in Suffolk, during the 1760s, a model workhouse for 144 paupers. There were separate rooms for men and their wives, single women and single men. There were also rooms in which different trades were carried on, including spinning, weaving and making twine and sacks, and there were also facilities for baking and brewing.[105] Daniel Benham (1789–1873), secretary to the City of London Gaslight Company, visited the Royal Sea Bathing Infirmary at Margate, in Kent,

Fig 7.16
This engraving from William Kidd's 1831 guidebook to Margate shows the neo-classical-style gasworks in King Street. Built in 1824 to provide gas for Margate's street lighting, it was both an industrial wonder and a tourist destination. [By kind permission of the Society of Antiquaries of London]

in August 1829, apparently just another site to take in. However, his diary, with its very detailed accounts, does include an entry for ten shillings donated in the infirmary's charity box.[106]

In London, tourists could visit contemporary buildings housing prisoners, the mentally ill and orphans. Prisons were regularly visited by people ranging from social reformers to curious teenage boys. Here, the division between formally investigative tourists and the merely inquisitive is particularly obvious. Writer and spy John Macky (d 1726) was an example of the latter when he visited the Bridewell House of Correction in 1714. He spoke harshly of the workhouse inmates:

> BRIDEWELL was formerly a Royal Palace, but is now converted into a Work-house, like the Rasp-House at Amsterdam. Many a pretty Girl is brought into it with their fine Cloaths, but for all that is forc'd to receive Correction here for Night-Walking; of which Sort of Cattel this City abounds more than any City in the World; it being impossible to walk the Streets, and especially about the Play-Houses, without being picked up by this Sort of Vermine.[107]

While César-François de Saussure was in London between 1725 and 1729, he visited Bridewell, where 140 poor boys in green coats and large grey hats were still being taught trades. There were also rooms for lazy servants, robbers and 'other bad people' who were given punitive work and were fed only on bread and water. The inspector, 'Captain Whip'em', 'had a surly, repulsive countenance' and carried a cane 'about the thickness of my little finger'.[108]

William Pitt, the Keeper of Newgate, in London, made more than £3,000 from people who wanted to see Jacobite prisoners being held there after the 1715 uprising, while visitors to see the highwayman Jack Shephard in 1716 paid £200.[109] On 3 May 1763, James Boswell decided to visit Newgate out of simple curiosity. He wrote:

> I then thought I should see prisoners of one kind or other, so went to Newgate. I stepped into a sort of court before the cells. They are surely most dismal places. There are three rows of 'em, four in a row, all above each other. They have double iron windows, and within these, strong iron rails; and in these dark mansions are the unhappy criminals confined. I did not go in, but stood in the court, where were a number of strange black-guard beings with sad countenances, most of them being friends and acquaintances of those under sentence of death.[110]

Fig 7.17
Significant parts of Daniel Asher Alexander's vast prison of 1809–23 still survive within the modern HMP Maidstone. It had been built to allow the segregation of offenders according to the seriousness of their crimes, but its accessibility to tourists must have made the maintenance of good order more complicated. [AA95/05933]

John Byng sarcastically described Lincoln's new prison, and prisons in general, as 'what ornaments to a country!', while at York the felons 'live in state' in the grand prison buildings.[111] James Wallace, writing in 1795, refers to Liverpool's Borough Gaol in the chapter on 'Buildings and Institutions of amusement and recreation'![112] Teenager Charles Powell visited Maidstone Gaol, in Kent, less than a year after the monumental detached-radial plan structure by Daniel Asher Alexander (1768–1846) had been completed (Fig 7.17).[113] On 19 September 1823, he recounted: 'Arrived at Maidstone at 4 o'clock to Bell Inn, Papa came in soon after us, then we all walked to the New Jail a fine stone building – went into the wards and chapel – saw the prisoners spinning, weaving, making mats, string, ropes, etc., then we came in to dinner.' At the end of his day's journal, he concluded, 'Maidstone seems a large town and the Jail a large, strong, melancholy and clean place of punishment.'[114] It is clear from Powell's diary that he and his father were inquisitive about a range of places and activities, but it is also evident that Maidstone Prison, like a Martello Tower and the steamships in the harbour, was simply part of the family's entertainment while on holiday.

At the other extreme of 'prison tourism' was John Howard (1726–90). Following his election as High Sheriff of Bedfordshire in 1773, he set out to record the state of prisons in England, Wales and Europe.[115] In total he made seven journeys around Europe, reaching as far as Moscow, Constantinople, Lisbon and Malta, and between these longer trips he continued to visit British prisons. His resulting publication, *The State of the Prisons*, is rightly celebrated as a biting indictment of prisons, but it is also a tribute to Howard's stamina and tenacity in travelling so extensively. It rarely, and almost certainly deliberately, gives insight into the process of his visit to an individual site, each entry being put forward in a dry, factual way. However, in his entry for Newgate he does mention that he attended prayers there on one occasion. There are more insights into his personal experiences during his foreign visits. In Paris his visit to the Bastille in the mid-1770s proved difficult. After knocking on the door he was allowed to enter and looked around the outside of the building: 'But whilst I was contemplating this gloomy mansion, an officer came out of the Castle much surprised, and I was forced to retreat through the mute guard, and thus regained that freedom, which for one locked up within those walls it is next to impossible to obtain.'[116]

The life of prisoners could provide amusement for visitors, but their deaths were also part of the Georgian entertainment landscape. Executions at Tyburn were often riotous and caused the authorities concern and therefore in 1783, once repairs had been completed following the Gordon Riots in 1780, Newgate Prison became the site for public executions in London. Despite being transformed into a modern prison, it was still possible for tourists to visit it (Fig 7.18). In 1811, Louis Simond was shown around Newgate by a turnkey, and his visit included a tour of the area where felons sentenced to death were playing a game of fives against the wall while chained down on one leg.[117]

As well as criminals, mentally ill people and orphans could also be a tourist attraction. The Bethlehem Hospital, colloquially known as Bedlam, had been rebuilt in 1675–6 to designs by Robert Hooke (1635–1703). The long galleries allowed sightseers to watch the patients on display, as a means of encouraging donations to fund the work of the institution.[118] The types of scenes that visitors might witness were captured forever in 'Scene in Bedlam', the eighth of a series of paintings entitled *The Rake's Progress* (1733–4), by William Hogarth (1697–1764). Cornish farmer and miller Alexander Dennis, on a trip to London from his native Penzance in 1810, visited the Foundling Hospital, a home for

Fig 7.18
Newgate Gaol became the site for public executions in 1783. This late 19th-century photograph, one of a stereo pair, shows it before it was demolished and replaced by the Central Criminal Court. [CC97/00507]

abandoned children, and joined in the Sunday worship.[119] Dennis's description suggests that it was regarded more as entertainment than as a charitable or spiritual experience.

It is perhaps even more remarkable that tourists could wander around working military sites. Antiquary and traveller John Loveday (1711–89) visited Edinburgh Castle in 1732, where he saw the troops and the artillery that formed the garrison of the castle. He wrote:

On This, yᵉ Castle with it's several Batteries &c. is thought impregnable; 'tis properly a Citadel, for It both hang's over & commands yᵉ Town. It is kept in most excellent repair, yᵉ Whole of large Compass ... A Garrison is kept here, and all yᵉ Stores for North-Britain ... The Field-Train is kept in a place, once a Kirk, and of great Antiquity ... The officers & Soldiers lie within yᵉ Castle; for yᵉ latter in a large room, wᶜʰ was formerly yᵉ Parliament-house, it's roof of Irish oak.[120]

In September 1754, Richard Pococke visited Dover Castle, in Kent, admiring the Roman remains and the medieval castle. He also noted the accommodation provided for officers and the barracks for foot soldiers, and the fact that prisoners of war 'have usually been kept in this castle'.[121] Within a couple of years, Britain would again be at war with France and Dover Castle would be pressed into use as a prisoner of war camp (Fig 7.19). From 1793 until 1815, Britain was almost continuously at war with France. Nevertheless, inquisitive tourists recorded the defences that were being built to protect the

Fig 7.19
This aerial photograph of Dover Castle shows the Inner Bailey, with its buildings that were used as barracks, and the central Great Tower, which housed French prisoners of war during the mid-18th century.
[NMR 27304/036]

country, particularly in the south-east of England. An anonymous tourist travelling around Kent in 1809 was able to see the recently constructed Martello towers, Shorncliffe Barracks and the Royal Military Canal, constructed between 1804 and 1809.[122] William Cobbett (1763–1835), the political writer and farmer, visited the same Kentish coastal defences during the early 1820s and concluded that Martello towers were a ridiculous investment.[123] Teenager Thomas Lott, in July 1815, also travelled around Kent, a month after the final French defeat at Waterloo. Dover Castle was still an active military site, but Lott was able to be shown around the site, seeing the barracks, bake houses and cannons.[124] Dover Castle, which remained in the front line of Britain's defences even in the mid-20th century, was a popular destination through the 19th century and a number of guidebooks included detailed descriptions of visits to the site.[125]

Literary destinations

Since the 18th century, people have also travelled around Britain to see sites associated with important literary figures. The most important destination was Stratford-upon-Avon, in Warwickshire, the birthplace of William Shakespeare (1564–1616), which featured many buildings that could be associated with the Bard (Fig 7.20). Fans of his work first arrived during the 1760s 'and they never stopped coming'.[126] In 1785, John Byng visited and saw sights such as 'Shakespears old chair', surprisingly purchasing a tiny slice of it as a souvenir.[127] He also visited the Bard's birthplace, saw a commemorative head, and in the town hall enjoyed Thomas Gainsborough's portrait of actor David Garrick embracing a bust of the playwright.[128] The main attraction at Stratford-upon-Avon was a timber-framed building reputed to be Shakespeare's birthplace. It was purchased by a private trust in 1847, and within five years it attracted more than 2,000 visitors annually. In 1874, the Shakespeare Memorial Trust established a theatre and other buildings, such as Mary Arden's house, also became key attractions.[129] Five years later, the first ten-day Shakespeare Festival attracted 1,500 visitors, a number that grew steadily so that in 1894 the event drew 4,000 people and 14,000 a decade later.[130] The cult of Shakespeare has grown apace in recent years, particularly on the South Bank of the Thames in London, where

the Globe Theatre provides a tourist attraction, as well as a great performance venue (Fig 7.21).

A similar personality cult was based around the birthplace of the poet Robert Burns (1759–96) at Alloway, in Ayrshire, a place endlessly celebrated in souvenirs, from transfer-printed Mauchline Ware to tastefully produced tea towels. Novelist Sir Walter Scott (1771–1832) popularised the Highlands, particularly with the publication of *Waverley*, a novel set at the time of the Jacobite Rising and first published in 1814. He sold more novels than any other contemporary author and his works became a staple of circulating libraries. Scott used Scotland, its countryside and its history to create a new romantic image that stimulated tourism.[131] George IV (1762–1830) was an admirer of the novelist – Scott was the first baronet to be created after the king's accession in 1820.[132] During the king's first visit to Scotland in 1822, Scott had a leading role in the ceremonials, and as the monarch wore tartan during his visit, it grew in popularity.[133] Scott himself was a tourist attraction: Louis Simond counted 'the Caledonian Bard' among Edinburgh's sights and described seeing him and listening to him speaking 'with

Fig 7.20
This 1950s photograph shows two smartly dressed visitors admiring Anne Hathaway's Cottage at Shottery, at Stratford-upon-Avon. It is the farmhouse where Shakespeare's wife had been brought up. This indirect connection with the Bard still proves popular with visitors. [AA002207]

Fig 7.21
The modern Globe Theatre is a monument to the dedication and vision of the actor and director Sam Wanamaker (1919–93). It opened in 1997 and is a reconstruction of how the short-lived 1599 and 1614 Globe Theatres would have looked.
[AA034531]

Fig 7.22
Poets' Corner is the name traditionally given to a part of the south transept of Westminster Abbey where a large number of literary figures are buried and commemorated. This late 19th-century photograph shows the monument to William Wordsworth (1770–1850), which was erected four years after his death.
[CC97/00576]

all a poet's exstasy'.[134] Scott's home at Abbotsford, in the Scottish Borders, also became a popular attraction for tourists. In Henry B McLellan's journal, published in 1834, he visited the house twice. A few years later, the poet Chauncy H Townshend (1798–1868) visited his guide's house in nearby Melrose and realised that he had collected 'prints, pictures, casts and curiosities' inspired by the example of Scott's nearby house at Abbotsford.[135] Scott's impact was felt elsewhere, settings for scenes in his books inspiring visits by growing numbers of travellers during the 19th century. For instance, the Trossachs and Loch Katrine, about 30 miles (48km) north of Stirling, became popular destinations following the publication of *The Lady of the Lake* in 1810.[136]

In London's Westminster Abbey, Poets' Corner, a term first coined in the mid-18th century, became a popular destination for people seeking the final resting places of, or memorials to, Britain's great literary figures (Fig 7.22). This was regardless, in the case of Thomas Hardy (1840–1928), of whether they wished to be buried there. In the end, Hardy's body was buried in Westminster Abbey, but his heart was laid to rest in Dorset.[137] Lord Byron (1788–1824), despite being prepared for a funeral at Westminster

Abbey or St Paul's Cathedral, was refused burial due to his scandalous life, and instead his funeral cortege made a four-day journey up to Nottinghamshire.[138] To these illustrious names can be added Jane Austen (1775–1817), who still attracts people to Bath and to her home at Chawton, in Hampshire, and the Brontës at Haworth parsonage, in Yorkshire. A new form of literary tourism also exists today, many tourists setting off in search of film locations such as those used in the *Harry Potter* films (including Lacock Abbey, in Wiltshire, and Gloucester Cathedral), and in the *Star Wars* series (Fig 7.23).

Conclusion

Improved and more affordable means of transport from the 18th century onwards began to allow people to explore Britain's towns and cities, as well as discovering its countryside. In the 19th century, increased national and personal prosperity, and the extension of the number of days available as holidays, helped to open up Britain to its people. A growing percentage of the population was becoming more literate and publishing costs were decreasing dramatically, leading to a growth in inquisitive travel, which had been limited to the few in the 17th and 18th centuries.

Tourists, therefore, set out in growing numbers to discover Britain's past, present and future. Britain's history was of particular interest, illustrated by prehistoric monuments and the ruined legacy of monasteries and castles dating from the Middle Ages. Many people also travelled to learn more about the contemporary country in which they lived. Country house visiting grew in popularity during the 18th and 19th centuries, and while we now consider such visits in similar terms to poking around an ancient ruin, in fact these excursions were more akin to visiting Docklands' modern skyscrapers today. There was also a growing interest in the new industries and technologies that were developing during the 18th and 19th centuries, and transforming Britain into the world's first industrial nation. Diaries regularly record visits to textile mills, mines and new harbours, but what is also interesting is the ease with which people could visit working prisons and military sites, the latter even during times of war. In modern terms, this would be described as 'dark' tourism, but in the 18th and 19th centuries, it was simply part of mainstream tourism.

Improving transport transformed the nature of travel within Britain, opening up every corner of the nation to the inquisitive eye of the tourist. As will be seen in the next chapter, it would also have a profound effect on the seaside, the once genteel, socially restricted world of the Georgian seaside being transformed during the second half of the 19th century into a mass form of leisure.

Fig 7.23
Fans of the 2015 film Star Wars VII: The Force Awakens *have good reason to seek out the Forest of Dean, in Gloucestershire, and Skellig Michael, on the west coast of Ireland. They might also glimpse the (fenced-off) former cruise-missile bunkers at Greenham Common, in Berkshire, pictured here, which were used as the rebel base in the film. [AA000528]*

8

The seaside holiday 1837–1939

By the early 19th century, an elaborate infrastructure had been created to provide seaside holidays and deliver improved health to tens of thousands of visitors each year. Significant areas of new, high-quality housing were beginning to transform many resorts in the south of England and increasingly prestigious entertainment venues were being erected, including many assembly rooms, circulating libraries and theatres, the staples of Georgian social life. Seafronts were becoming lined with bathing machines and bathhouses had been erected. During the early 19th century, with the introduction of steamers, a form of mass tourism was beginning to be recognisable at a few places, but nevertheless the seaside holiday remained something usually restricted to the wealthiest members of society. In many ways, the seaside holiday in the early 19th century – its participants, its locations, its facilities and accommodation – would have been recognisable to the first sea bathers almost a century earlier. The same cannot be said of what happened during the subsequent century. Holidays and seaside resorts were transformed, with millions instead of thousands enjoying them each year. This had a huge impact on accommodation, establishing grand hotels for the rich and huge areas of housing for working-class residents and visitors. The small, sociable, respectable and exclusive entertainment venues of the Georgians were soon supplanted by new, large facilities, some on an industrial scale in the largest resorts.

Behind this transformation lay a technological revolution in terms of the handling of materials and the provision of power. Initially, innovations had been applied to driving a revolution in manufacturing, through the use of iron and steel in buildings and the application of water then steam power to increasingly large factories. During the 19th century, these new technologies were beginning to have an impact first on transport and soon on forms of enter-

tainment. By the 1810s, steamers were running along the Clyde and Thames, while during the following decade the first piers were being built, though the earliest pier with iron piles appeared only in the 1830s. During the mid-19th century, there was an increase in pace in seaside resort expansion and the extension of access to the seaside once the initially fragmentary railway lines began to meld into a national network.

As discussed in Chapter 5, railways increased the number of places that could be reached and extended access to the coast to the bulk of the population of rapidly growing industrial towns, as well as London. Organised trips, affordable excursion tickets and the travel agent all resulted from the new means of transport. The growing number of trippers also stimulated middle-class visitors and residents to move from the centres of popular resorts into the suburbs, or to move to more distant resorts, and even abroad to the south of France. Railways also had an indirect impact on seaside tourism, through their contribution to greater national and individual wealth.

The central focus of the Georgian seaside, as discussed in Chapter 4, had been health, though visitors to a resort had expectations of good living and more or less refined and genteel entertainment. The pursuit of health continued through the 19th century, but it was increasingly secondary to the pursuit of pleasure. And these pleasures were changing as a result of new technology. In London at the beginning of the 1850s, the Great Exhibition and the first aquarium at London Zoo showed the way forward for the seaside in the 1870s, the decade when huge entertainment venues began to appear in seaside resorts. During the 1860s, steam power was beginning to be applied to fairground rides and once the internal combustion engine and electricity were added by the early 20th century, the modern fairground had been invented. Electricity also spawned street lights, and Blackpool's famous illuminations, and it also revolutionised transport along many seafronts and powered the projectors of new cinemas.

Railways increased access to the seaside and they inevitably concentrated arriving visitors in town centres, within easy reach of the station, driving genteel residents and visitors outwards. However, the charabanc, bus and car allowed visitors to go anywhere, meaning resorts could sprawl outwards and new resorts and residential seaside towns could also be created, prompted by this new flexibility. But of course with progress came problems. By the interwar years, the negative impact of urban sprawl and the blight of cheap development on previously unspoilt coastlines were already causing concern. The most prominent contributor to the expansion along coastlines was the holiday camp, providing all the facilities for wholesome holidays at a price that families could afford. This was the antithesis of the exclusivity of the Georgian seaside of a century earlier and helps to define what many people consider to be the heyday of the British seaside holiday.

New entertainments, new technology and new customers

The Georgian seaside was enjoyed by a privileged, wealthy elite, with facilities aimed at this small, genteel market and with access to entertainment controlled by large fees. However, from the mid-19th century onwards the seaside was increasingly something enjoyed by a mass market, leading to a change of tone, as well as a change in the types and sizes of facilities that were demanded and expected.

The Assembly Room, once at the heart of the Georgian social scene, gradually disappeared, so that a resort like Teignmouth, in Devon, saw its assembly room becoming the East Devon and Teignmouth Club around 1870.[1] However, some resorts, like Great Yarmouth, in Norfolk, were still building them in the 1860s, and Bognor Regis, in West Sussex, constructed a new, larger one in the 1880s, a building subsequently converted into a cinema.[2] Technology trumped sociability! Theatre, which was often a far-from-polite experience during the Georgian period for performers and audience members alike, continued through the 19th century. Music hall emerged as a distinct new form of entertainment, often with its own venues, but there was felt to be a certain vulgarity about this type of entertainment. In 1872, Westward Ho!, in Devon, boasted that visitors would never be 'annoyed by the vulgar discordant songs of Ethiopian serenaders'.[3] However, while music hall was not well regarded, the minstrel show seems to have gained a reputation as a respectable form of entertainment.[4] Minstrels remained a prominent feature of resorts until the beginning of the 20th century, when an invasion of pierrots (entertainers who dressed like the *commedia dell'arte* figure, all in white) drove them from the beaches and music halls (Fig 8.1).

Fig 8.1
This view of the beach at Margate, in Kent, dating from c 1900, shows a troupe of minstrels entertaining holidaymakers. This form of entertainment, as well as pierrots and other types of musical performers, was a common sight on beaches at this date.
[OP00621]

The new markets opened by the railways led to influxes of holidaymakers deemed to have less refined tastes. They also had shallower pockets, and therefore, during the course of the 19th century, entertainment venues had to be both less expensive and larger to deal with the growing numbers of lower-wage tourists. A comparison of a Georgian theatre with the first Opera House in Blackpool Winter Gardens, or a genteel assembly room with Blackpool Tower Ballroom, immediately illustrates that the size of venues had multiplied, in extreme cases many times. These new venues also had a different economic model. Upfront, large fees, sometimes for a season-long subscription, were consciously designed to limit access, while the new model involved smaller fees aimed at getting as many people as possible through the doors. Blackpool Tower offered visitors a wide range of entertainments for 6d and, if they paid extra, they could ascend the Tower or enjoy a show in the 3,000-seat Circus.

Along with the growing size of venues came a new attitude to technology. It was required to build the vast structures that could cope with millions of visitors each year, but it also contributed to creating new forms of entertainment. This began with the application of iron and steel, as well as steam power, but by the late 19th century, electricity, the combustion engine and a new appreciation of natural sciences created a range of new attractions, from piers and winter gardens to fairgrounds, cinemas and aquaria.

The development of piers

The first seaside piers were primarily jetties for steamers to land passengers, though they often also sought to cater for the promenading holidaymaker. Initially constructed using timber piles supporting a wooden deck, iron piles had made their first tentative appearance during the 1830s. The major technological change took place when Eugenius Birch's Margate Jetty (1853–6; see p 81) established the use of the iron screw pile at the heart of thinking about pier construction, though other engineers would also employ alternative techniques, sometimes to overcome particular local problems (Fig 8.2).

Like other piers being built during the 1850s and 1860s, Margate Jetty originally had a fairly plain superstructure to maximise the area for promenaders and passengers disembarking from steamships. Such sparseness can still be experienced on the piers at Saltburn-by-the-Sea, in Yorkshire, and Clevedon, in Somerset, both of which, coincidentally, opened in 1869 (Fig 8.3). However, prior to their construction, changes were already under way in the presentation of the seaside pier. Birch erected Blackpool's first pier, which opened in 1863, and he included a series of kiosks on its deck. Three years later he completed Brighton's West Pier using a similar formula, but he included the first hint of exotic detailing inspired by the nearby Royal Pavilion. This vocabulary would eventually dominate

Fig 8.2
This W & Co photograph of c 1900 was probably intended to become a postcard. It shows Margate Jetty with the new polygonal pier head that was added to the original Birch structure in 1875–7. See also Fig 5.10. [OP00650]

Fig 8.3
*Clevedon Pier opened to the
public in 1869. It is Grade I
listed due to its elegant
cast-iron structure.*
[DP081827]

thinking about the detailing of piers and culminate in the extravagance of Eastbourne Pier, in East Sussex, and Brighton's Palace Pier at the end of the 19th century. It also introduced exotic forms as a mainstream theme in seaside architecture and paved the way for the lavish detailing found in major entertainment venues.

During the 1860s, more than 20 piers were begun, with a similar number being constructed during the following decade. This boom was based on the belief that there was money to be made from piers. Blackpool's first pier was created for a select clientele, but the reality was quite different. In 1863, it attracted 275,000 visitors, and during the following year 400,000 people paid to walk along the pier (Fig 8.4). This was at a time when the town was growing from a population of around 4,000 in 1861 to 7,000 a decade later, and suggests the huge popularity of this new type of attraction. In 1875, Brighton's West Pier entertained 600,000 visitors and by 1890, Blackpool's Central Pier had around a million visitors annually, figures guaranteeing profits for investors.[5]

Piers were increasingly offering more than simply a place for promenading. By the 1840s, the Chain Pier at Brighton offered its customers refreshment rooms, shops, a reading room and a camera obscura, while Southport Pier, in Merseyside, was so long that it provided its customers with a waiting room and refreshment room.[6] During the 1870s, some piers incorporated large pavilions in their design. Hastings Pier, in East Sussex, which opened in August 1872 on the first ever August Bank Holiday, included a pavilion capable of seating 2,000 people.[7] Existing piers were also expanded and extended. The Indian Pavilion was constructed at the seaward end of Blackpool's North Pier in 1874–7, a superficially lavish structure apparently inspired by an actual Indian temple.[8] Some piers also began to provide fairground rides. As early as 1876, Birnbeck Pier at Weston-super-Mare, in Somerset, had swings and by the early 20th century it offered its customers a switchback, a water chute, a helter-skelter and a short-lived flying machine, attractions made possible as the pier incorporated an island in its structure.[9] By the outbreak of World War I, Britain had more than a hundred piers, ranging from the quiet, plain, promenade pier to the fully developed pleasure pier with pavilions, rides and amusements. No other country has embraced the promenade pier and pleasure pier so enthusiastically as Britain, Europe boasting only a handful of examples, mostly derived directly from British models.

Travel on the seafront

The pier had begun as a practical means of landing passengers and soon became a pleasure venue for visitors. Elsewhere on the seafront, there was a practical need to overcome tall cliffs and allow people to move across increasingly large seaside

Fig 8.4
This photograph of Blackpool's North Pier was taken between its opening in 1863 and the creation of the new Indian Pavilion in 1877. The number of people thronging around its entrance suggests the popularity of Blackpool and this novel feature.
[BB88/00110]

Fig 8.5
This rather flimsy looking
structure at Shanklin was
the original cliff lift that
linked the beach and
seafront with the
accommodation on
the clifftops.
[BB82/13476B]

resorts, the former challenge being met by cliff lifts and funicular railways, the latter by trains and trams. All these forms of transport were practical solutions to problems, but all have subsequently become part of the holiday industry.

By the second half of the 19th century, technology in the form of the cliff lift and the cliff or funicular railway was coming to the aid of holidaymakers and residents. In 1869, a hoist is recorded at Saltburn 'for raising and lowering people thus avoiding the toilsome ascent by road' and in the following decades a few resorts installed lifts.[10] The first lift at Shanklin, on the Isle of Wight, was built in 1892, but was replaced in 1957 by a new lift that still operates today (Fig 8.5).[11] The Isle of Thanet is well supplied with lifts: Ramsgate has two cliff lifts that opened in 1910 and 1926, Margate has a lift dating from 1934, and Broadstairs constructed its Millennium Lift to greet the 21st century.[12] Blackpool's cabin lift dates from 1930 (Fig 8.6). In 1901, instead of a lift, Southend-on-Sea, in Essex, asked the American engineer Jesse W Reno (1861–1947) to design a moving walkway, a predecessor of the modern escalator.[13] It did not survive long and was replaced by a cliff railway, the most popular solution to the problem of commuting between a seafront and a cliff top.

Fig 8.6
Lifts were popular
wherever there were cliffs
to overcome. The cabin
lift at Blackpool of 1930
provided access to the sea
and a new model boating
lake for visitors staying on
the cliffs of the North Shore.
[AA053285]

Fig 8.7
A second cliff railway at West Cliff in Bournemouth (pictured here) opened on 1 August 1908 and originally used the same kind of motor as the earlier railway. The third cliff railway, at Fisherman's Walk, opened in 1935. [DP001300]

descent of carriages. When the weight of the top carriage of a pair of linked, counterbalanced carriages was increased by pumping water into a tank beneath the upper carriage, it descended, pulling up the lower carriage on the adjacent track, which had an empty tank. This was the favoured method until the beginning of the 20th century, but by the early 20th century this system had been superseded by the use of a counterweight and electric motors, eliminating the need to have a second, counterbalancing carriage. In Dorset, Bournemouth East Cliff Railway, the oldest of Bournemouth's three funicular railways, opened on 16 April 1908, and is the oldest surviving cliff railway originally powered by electricity (Fig 8.7).

The seafront was occasionally also the location for a narrow-gauge railway. On 4 August 1883, Volk's Electric Railway, built by Magnus Volk (1851–1937), opened on the seafront at Brighton, the first electric railway providing a regular service in Britain (Fig 8.8).[15] This short line was extended in 1884, and in 1901 a further length of line took the service as far as Kemp Town at the east end of Brighton. Volk also wished to extend his railway to Rottingdean. Therefore, he invented the 'Pioneer' or the 'daddy-long-legs', which could go through the sea at high tide, a hybrid of 'an open-top tramcar, a pleasure yacht and a seaside pier'.[16] This service began on 28 November 1896, but it was not financially viable and had closed by 1901.[17]

By 1876, the earliest cliff railway was opened at Scarborough, in Yorkshire, by Mr Hunt of the Prince of Wales Hotel for his guests.[14] The South Cliff Railway, like the nearby Central Cliff Railway that opened a few years later, used water to provide the weight to power the ascent and

Fig 8.8
Volk's Electric Railway in Brighton also enjoys the accolade of being the oldest electrically driven railway service still in use in the world. It got its power from the third rail running between the main rails. [DP153079]

Many resorts also had seafront tram services, including Morecambe, in Lancashire, Margate and Hastings, but the most famous and the longest lasting is at Blackpool. The initial two-mile-long (3km) tram service, running on a single track with a number of passing places, was in use by September 1885.[18] It drew its power from a conductor rail in a conduit between the rails, but there were problems caused by sea-water earthing the electrical supply and sand collecting in the conduit. Therefore, Blackpool followed other towns in employing overhead collectors to draw the tram's power; a new line with overhead wires opened in 1898 between central Blackpool and Fleetwood. The switch-over of power transmission systems in the original line accompanied the doubling of the tracks that took place between 1899 and 1905.

Grand venues

Piers demonstrated the new command of metal-lurgy and the ability to handle materials on an industrial scale, skills and knowledge that had been pioneered in textile mills. Another inspiration for seaside venues was the Crystal Palace, which was erected for the 1851 Great Exhibition in Hyde Park, in London (*see* Fig 7.3). The tech-nological origins of the Crystal Palace and Winter Gardens can be traced back ultimately to small, glass-roofed, cast-iron greenhouses at country houses that began to appear during the early 19th century. By the 1820s, some huge structures were being erected as confidence in construction techniques grew.[19] Horticultural writer Henry Phillips (1779–1840) designed a large glass conservatory called the Athenaeum near his home in Brighton.[20] Work began in June 1827, but was abandoned due to a lack of funds. A revised version was erected in 1833: the Antheum, at the west end of Hove, was a glazed, domed structure reminiscent of William Porden's Dome beside the Royal Pavilion. It was to be an early winter garden housing exotic plants, as well as a museum and lecture rooms. However, major flaws in its design were not rectified during construction, meaning that it collapsed when its scaffolding was removed. This early failure may have contributed to a dearth of any new constructions in the mid-19th century, though the success of the Palm House at Kew (1844–8), the Winter Garden in Regent's Park (1846) and the Crystal Palace began to rekindle interest.

It was not until the 1870s that winter gardens began to appear at seaside resorts. Southport's Winter Gardens, built in 1874 by the Manches-ter architectural practice Maxwell and Tuke, who would later build the Blackpool Tower com-plex, was the earliest and one of the largest built at a seaside resort (Fig 8.9). Morecambe also had a Winter Gardens, the earliest part of which began life as the People's Palace in 1878, with the more ornate oriental-style facade being created in 1896. Blackpool's Winter Gardens opened in 1878 as a direct response to the new complex at Southport and as an indoor alterna-tive to the attractions of Raikes Hall pleasure gardens.[21] The Winter Gardens is now an unri-valled complex of entertainment venues, including some of the largest and grandest in Britain. Surviving from the initial 1870s phase is the foyer, topped with its tall rotunda and dome, which leads through the Floral Hall to the horse-shoe and the Grand Pavilion. The Fernery, which had an iron-and-glass roof, provided a perfect environment for exotic plants and a sedate promenade. In 1889 the first Opera House, capable of holding 2,500 people, was added. To compete with the newly opened Blackpool

Fig 8.9
Southport's Winter Gardens, with a steel, glazed structure, is clearly derived from the Crystal Palace. Its concert hall catered for 2,000 people and it also contained an aquarium and later a fairground behind. The Winter Gardens was demolished in 1962. [BB83/05801]

Fig 8.10
The Spanish Hall in Blackpool Winter Gardens was designed by Andrew Mazzei (1887–1975), an art director in the British film industry. He also created the adjacent Baronial Hall, based on a Jacobean hall, and the Galleon Bar, with its plaster walls and ceiling designed to mimic oak timbers. [DP117417]

Tower, a series of new attractions was built in 1896, including the huge Empress Ballroom, the adjacent Indian Lounge, an elegant refreshment room and the Great Wheel, inspired by the Ferris wheel at the Chicago World's Fair in 1893. In 1911, the second Opera House was built, and while it has been replaced, its magnificent foyer has survived on the first floor. In 1930, the Olympia indoor amusement park and exhibition hall opened and in the following year a series of themed rooms, including the Spanish Hall, were

created opening off the Floral Hall (Fig 8.10). At the end of the 1930s, the 3,000-seat Opera House designed by Charles MacKeith opened in a streamlined Moderne style.

By 1900, the major rival to the Winter Gardens was Blackpool Tower, which opened in May 1894. It was the ultimate expression of the new role of technology in entertainment and was a reflection of the scale of the town's holiday industry (Fig 8.11). Included in the complex was an aquarium, a menagerie, the Monkey House

Fig 8.11
This c 1900 photograph taken from the North Pier at Blackpool shows Blackpool Tower, with the lavish Alhambra beside it. Behind, the large Ferris wheel at the Winter Gardens is visible. [OP00480]

and Aviary, the Seal Pond and Bear Cage, and Roof Gardens. There was also the Circus, the Grand Saloon, a refreshment bar, billiard saloon and the Grand Pavilion, which became the Tower Ballroom (Fig 8.12). The complex exemplified the mass production of fun, providing customers with opulent interiors at an affordable price, relying on attracting millions of visitors to make a profit. The Tower, which was Britain's tallest structure when it was built, measuring 518ft 9in (158m) to the top of the flagstaff, was constructed in less than three years at a cost of £300,000.[22] Blackpool Tower and Watkin's Tower were both technologically and visually inspired by the Eiffel Tower in Paris. Watkin's Tower was an ambitious and incomplete project to create a 1,175 ft (358m) high tower at Wembley. The foundations were laid in 1892, but it was never completed and was demolished in 1907.

Fig 8.12
Blackpool Tower contained a ballroom from the outset, which was refurbished and rearranged in 1899 by Frank Matcham (1854–1920). A fire in 1956 led to a restoration programme. [AA048180]

Maxwell and Tuke, who had built Blackpool Tower, also designed New Brighton Tower, at Wallasey, in Cheshire, which was 567ft (173m) high. It was the tallest building in Britain from its opening in 1898–1900 and its dismantling, which began in 1919.[23] A tower was also built at Morecambe in 1898 and there was a plan to erect a 530ft-high (162m) tower at the Kursaal entertainment complex, at Southend-on-Sea, but this was never built.

Blackpool's huge entertainment complexes would not be matched in other resorts as none had to cater for visitor numbers on the same scale. However, many other resorts did offer appropriately sized venues and complexes suitable for their visitor numbers, variously called Winter Gardens, People's Palaces and, from around 1900, Kursaals. Kursaals were, and remain, the centrepieces of the seafronts of many European resorts, such as Ostend, in Belgium, and San Sebastian, in Spain. The earliest use of the name in Britain seems to have been at Southend, but in fact this was simply a new brand for a multifunctional entertainment complex. The Kursaal at Southend contained a theatre, a circus, the grand ballroom, dining hall, oriental arcade and a menagerie with a trotting track and 'a football enclosure' behind.[24] In 1910, a building called the Kursaal opened at Bognor, which was an entertainment palace with a roller-skating rink, a

theatre, shops and tearoom.[25] It was demolished in 1975. Great Yarmouth's Winter Garden, erected in 1903, had originally been built at Torquay, in Devon, in 1878–81, but was successfully dismantled and sailed around the coast.[26] Margate's Winter Garden officially opened on 3 August 1911 and contained a large concert hall and an amphitheatre, as well as cloakrooms, offices and refreshment rooms.[27] In 1924, the Winter Gardens opened at Rothesay, on the Isle of Bute, on the site of a former bandstand. With the contraction of the holiday market during the 1960s, it closed and lay derelict until the 1990s, when it was redeveloped as a tourist information and exhibition centre.[28] As late as 1927, the Winter Gardens at Weston-super-Mare opened and, while it stood within lavish gardens, it was effectively just another indoor entertainment venue for the resort.[29] Perhaps the last of the multipurpose venues erected before the outbreak of World War II was the De La Warr Pavilion at Bexhill-on-Sea, in East Sussex. The need for a new entertainment venue had been recognised for many years and in 1933 it was decided that the Corporation should develop a seafront site.[30] The influence of the Earl De La Warr (1900–76) led to the design brief specifying that the building 'should be simple in design' with large windows and a 'Modern steel-framed or ferro-concrete construction' (Fig 8.13).[31]

Fig 8.13
As modernist architect Thomas Tait was appointed as the assessor of the competition to design the De La Warr Pavilion at Bexhill, a Modern Movement design was inevitably going to be selected. Serge Chermayeff and Erich Mendelsohn's winning design was built in 1935. [DP217884]

New attractions

As well as providing entertainment complexes, seaside resorts also offered specialised single venues. Every large town in Britain might have offered its residents at least a theatre and/or a music hall, but at seaside towns the number of visitors meant that many such venues could be sustained and in some resorts more specialised venues could be economically viable.

In 1853, the world's first public aquarium opened in Regent's Park in London and by the 1870s the first aquaria at seaside resorts had opened.[32] The first of these was at Brighton (Fig 8.14). In 1871 a book on aquaria included a description of the recently completed facility, designed by Eugenius Birch (1818–84).[33] Its tanks ranged in size from 11ft 6in (3.5m) by 20ft (6.1m) to the largest, at the centre of the main corridor, which measured 103ft (31.4m) by 40ft (12.2m). The structure was rebuilt externally in the 1920s and is still in use today as an aquarium, though the internal arrangements have been transformed. An aquarium was built in Southport in 1874, followed by examples in 1875 at Tynemouth and Blackpool, and at Great Yarmouth in 1876 (Fig 8.15).[34] A large but short-lived aquarium, designed, like that at Brighton, by Eugenius Birch, was built at Scarborough in 1877, in an Indian style, with the fish tanks set among caves and grottoes.[35]

Fig 8.14 (above) Brighton's aquarium resembled a modern interpretation of a Roman basilica, executed in brick, iron and glass. Its style is in marked contrast to modern aquaria, which almost universally employ high-tech forms. [BB78/07043]

Fig 8.15 (left) The Aquarium at Great Yarmouth, designed by Messrs Bottle and Olley at a cost of around £10,000, originally had a large, galleried hall with 18 tanks measuring up to 50ft (15.2m) in length around the central space. Its plan made it relatively easy to convert into a cinema, though it still retains traces of where the tanks were located. [CC76/00349]

Swimming was a novelty activity that grew in popularity during the later years of the 19th century. The earliest examples of purpose-built pools were in major towns and cities, or at places of learning, and date from between the late 17th century and the early 19th century. Spa towns and seaside resorts were well supplied with bathhouses from an early date, and while these were usually equipped with small or individual baths, some did have plunge pools that would have allowed some swimming. However, the Cleveland Baths at Bathwick, near Bath, originally featured a D-shaped pool measuring 137ft (41.8m) by 38ft (11.6m), with a crescent of changing rooms surrounding its curved end.[36] In 1823, a building containing a large, circular, public bath that was used for swimming, affectionately known as 'the Onion', opened at Brighton and the baths on Knightstone Island at Weston-super-Mare included an outdoor tidal pool by the mid-1820s.[37] In the 1870s, swimming came to the forefront of the public imagination. On 24–25 August 1875, Captain Matthew Webb (1848–83) successfully swam the English Channel and duly became a national hero.[38] His fame coincided with, but also stimulated, major developments in the spread of swimming. The Public Health Act 1875 included clauses allowing funding for swimming pools and this was expanded by the 1878 Baths and Washhouses Act, which empowered local authorities to provide covered swimming baths.[39]

Even before legislation came into effect, some pools were beginning to be built at seaside resorts. In 1859, seawater baths were built on Blands Cliff at Scarborough, while a decade later at Brighton, Brill's Baths were built near where the Palace Pier would be erected at the end of the 19th century.[40] This new facility had a circular pool, 65ft (19.8m) in diameter.[41] Designed by George Gilbert Scott (1811–78), it resembled a Gothic, polychrome-brick version of the Pantheon and cost £90,000 to build. It was demolished in 1929. The saltwater baths on the Promenade at Southport opened in 1871 (Fig 8.16). At Blackpool, swimming baths on Cocker Street opened at the beginning of the 1870s and the facility was refitted in 1873. In the early 1880s, the Prince of Wales Baths was created in Central Beach between the North and Central piers, providing bathers and performers in aquatic shows with a large plunge pool. In May 1878 a large swimming baths opened on the seafront at Hastings, containing a pool measuring 180ft (54.9m) by 40ft (12.2m), while another smaller one (90ft/27.4m by 40ft/12.2m) opened for ladies the following year.

Seaside resorts also invested in outdoor pools, especially between the wars. They provided swimming and spectating facilities for hundreds and even thousands of people at a time. They also fitted in with the new themes of sun worship and the body beautiful being increasingly embraced by holidaymakers and allowed people

Fig 8.16
At Southport, the Victoria Salt Water Baths opened in July 1871 on the Promenade; one of the baths was large enough for swimming. [AA053222]

to enjoy playing in the water as much as formally swimming. One of the first erected was at Scarborough. The South Bay Pool by Harry W Smith, the town's Borough Engineer from 1897 to 1933, was begun in April 1914 and the pool opened on 21 July 1915. With a budget of £5,000, Smith created an oval pool 350ft (106.7m) by 180ft (54.9m), which was refilled at each high tide.[42] The Open Air Baths at Blackpool, which opened on 9 June 1923, was reputedly the largest such facility in the world. It cost £80,000, 16 times as much as the pool at Scarborough, despite having a pool approximately the same size (376ft/114.6m by 172ft/564.2m).[43] This was because of its grand architecture, which incorporated 574 dressing rooms for bathers and tiers of seating able to accommodate around 3,000 spectators (Fig 8.17).

During the 1920s, around 50 outdoor pools were built across the country, while in the following decade another 180 opened. The 1930s saw a shift from civic classicism to increasingly Moderne versions of Art Deco as the decade progressed. Among the earliest of these new-style outdoor baths was at Tarlair, in Aberdeenshire, which was built on the chilly northern coast of Scotland in 1930–31. St Leonard's Bathing Pool at Hastings, which opened in 1933, had tiered seating for 2,500 spectators around the curved, landward side of the pool.[44] In 1934, the pool at New Brighton opened, providing a Moderne reinterpretation of the Blackpool Open Air Baths of a

Fig 8.17
On some days at the height of the season there were over 20,000 visitors at Blackpool's Open Air Baths and by the end of its first full season in 1924, more than 500,000 people had gone through the turnstiles. Interestingly, only 94,403 were actual bathers, the remainder paying to sit, watch and relax.
[Afl03/lilywhites/blp43]

Fig 8.18
The lido at Penzance opened in 1935. One of a plethora of new Art Deco pools, it was designed by the Borough Engineer and Surveyor Frank Latham, apparently to reflect the shape of a seagull alighting on water.
[AA031412]

decade earlier, with a pool of almost the same size.[45] In 1935 the unusually shaped lido in Penzance, Cornwall, opened (Fig 8.18). In 1937, the Bathing Pool at Weston-super-Mare allowed people to swim when the sea was unavailable, because it recedes so far at low tide. Many of these pools were on an enormous scale, much larger than Olympic-size pools, but at Saltdean, in East Sussex, the last of the interwar Moderne seaside lidos, the pool was a mere 140ft (42.7m) by 50ft (15.2m).[46] What distinguished this design was the elegant, curved structure that almost embraced the pool's landward side, architecture reminiscent of the De La Warr Pavilion at Bexhill-on-Sea.

During the 1930s a few seaside resorts decided that they required an indoor pool. Brighton erected the SS Brighton (Super Swimming) in 1934, an indoor pool with seating for 1,900 and a pool measuring 165ft (50m) by 80ft (24m), which was claimed to be the world's largest indoor seawater pool.[47] Another indoor pool opened on the seafront at Bournemouth in 1937, designed by the architect Kenneth Cross

(1890–1968).[48] Blackpool's Derby Baths, which unofficially opened in 1939, contained a competition-size pool at which swimming events were held after the war.[49]

As well as swimming pools, the aquarium at Scarborough staged swimming displays and aquatic elements featured in shows staged at Blackpool Tower Circus and at the Hippodrome at Great Yarmouth. The Hippodrome was built in 1903 with an elaborate facade decorated with terracotta tiles with art nouveau detailing. These circuses could stage aquatic performances as the arena floor sank into the huge water tank beneath the ring, a transformation still accompanied at Great Yarmouth by vigorous fountains.

Great Yarmouth's circus is a rare survivor, but another class of venue for a type of once-popular entertainment has almost entirely disappeared. Roller-skating began to be a popular activity with the development of a new form of skate in the 1860s. It prompted a fad nicknamed 'rinkomania' or 'rollermania' in the mid-1870s for skating at new public rinks, so that at its

Fig 8.19
Ayr's Roller Skating Rink was designed by the Glasgow architect James Campbell Reid (1879–1923) in the early 1900s to cater for the resurgent craze for roller skating. It was photographed soon after it opened by the distinguished architectural photographer Bedford Lemere.
[© HES (Bedford Lemere and Company)]

height in 1876 Brighton had six rinks.[50] These structures often combined their skating function with other uses, such as being concert venues, which would prove to be a saviour for some rinks as within a couple of years the craze soon passed, though there were regular, though usually short-lived, revivals during the late 19th and early 20th centuries (Fig 8.19).

Amusement parks

Roller skating was just one of many fads enjoyed by the Victorians as a result of new technology, but one of the longest-lasting has been the fairground ride. During the 1860s, steam power was applied to fairground rides and by the end of the 19th century these would be further revolutionised by the application of power from the internal combustion engine.[51] Blackpool is the most important destination in the world for historic rollercoaster enthusiasts. The town has been offering its visitors fairground rides since at least the early 1890s, and in 1896 a large Ferris wheel was constructed at the Winter Gardens.[52] By the 1890s, a proto-amusement park had emerged at Raikes Hall Gardens. Originating as a pleasure garden in 1872, during the next 25 years a series of new attractions was added, including a tricycle track, a camera obscura and a switchback railway.[53]

At the south end of Blackpool, Britain's first enclosed seaside amusement park, the Pleasure Beach, had been established by the early 20th century.[54] Its immediate inspiration was in the amusement parks created along the beach at Coney Island at the south end of Brooklyn, in New York.[55] Today, little survives at Coney Island to celebrate this illustrious history, but Blackpool Pleasure Beach still retains a rich fairground heritage. Sir Hiram Maxim's Captive Flying Machine, the oldest ride in continuous use in Europe, first operated on 1 August 1904 at Blackpool and actually predates the foundation of the Pleasure Beach, early photographs showing it standing among the sand dunes (Fig 8.20).[56] It consists of rotating steel arms from which cables hang to support cars that were originally in the shape of boats holding several people each. The River Caves opened in 1905, a ride consisting of boats taking customers through a series of 'caverns' with tableaux lit by electric lights. In 1906, more than 3 million people visited the Pleasure Beach, where they could

Fig 8.20
This photograph of Blackpool Pleasure Beach in c 1905 shows the 1905 River Caves in the distance (in the centre of the photograph) and to the right the upward arms of Sir Hiram Maxim's Captive Flying Machine of 1904.
[From Anon 1926, image 235, author's collection]

Fig 8.21
This aerial photograph of
Blackpool Pleasure Beach,
taken in the early 2000s,
shows the complexity of the
site, with dozens of historic
and modern rides and
attractions woven together.
The circular casino is at the
top of the photograph.
[NMR 17760/20]

enjoy dozens of rides and attractions.[57] In 1913, the first casino was erected by the local architect R B Mather and contained a billiard hall, the park's first cinema, a grill room, restaurant and shop. Its white concrete facade was decorated with white electric lights and was modelled on some of the orientalism of Continental casinos, as well as echoing the exotic style of the nearby Victoria Pier.[58]

Between the wars, a number of the modern park's rollercoasters were constructed, including the Big Dipper (1923), the 1933 Roller Coaster (now the vibrant-orange Nickelodeon Streak) and the 1934 The Little Dipper (later known as the Zipper Dipper, now the Blue Flyer). A year later, the Grand National was erected. It is a Mobius-loop coaster that allows competing cars to race around a track with features named after jumps on the Aintree racecourse.[59] The 1930s also saw the park adopting a Moderne style as a house style to unify the appearance of the disparate rides and attractions. In July 1937, the 2,000-seat Ice Drome opened, with its rink beneath a wide, unsupported roof. The 1913 casino was demolished and the new casino opened in May 1939 at a cost of £300,000.[60] Although called a casino, like its predecessor, it was not a venue for gaming, instead containing a series of restaurants and bars, as well as a banqueting hall seating 700 (Fig 8.21).[61]

Blackpool Pleasure Beach served as an inspiration and a model for other seaside amusement parks. The Kursaal at Southend opened in July 1901, evolving from pleasure grounds that had opened in 1894.[62] Faced with continuing financial difficulties, the site changed ownership in 1910 and became Luna Park, a dedicated amusement park featuring the Harton Scenic Railway, a Figure of Eight coaster, a miniature railway, Astley's Circus and a cinema.[63] At Great Yarmouth, the first amusement ride, an L A Thompson Switchback Railway, was erected on the seafront in 1887 and remained there until the early 20th century. In 1909, the Pleasure Beach was established further to the south and included a Scenic Railway set within a mountainous terrain fashioned from plaster.[64] The lease of the Scenic Railway ended in 1928 and the ride was rebuilt at Aberdeen Beach Amusement Park, but a new Scenic Railway was purchased from Paris, and opened in 1932. In 1920, the Hall-by-the-Sea at Margate, which had once been the base for the circus and menagerie of 'Lord' George Sanger (1825–1911), reopened as Dreamland, offering customers a large amusement park and cinema.[65] It had been bought by John H Iles (1871–1951), who was marketing

rollercoasters for L A Thompson's Scenic Railway Company in Britain and Europe, and in 1920 he installed at Margate what is now the oldest surviving Scenic Railway in England.[66]

Electricity and entertainment

It was the application of electricity to the lighting of fairgrounds that created their magical atmosphere. Electric street lights first began to appear during the 1870s, including at Blackpool. In September 1879, the town installed nine Siemens lamps, each producing 6,000 candlepower, mounted on 60ft-high (18m) lampposts along the central seafront. These were some of the earliest street lights in the world, but the adoption even of an improved form of arc lighting proved premature, as by 1880 the invention of incandescent lighting would soon render these arc lights redundant (Fig 8.22). Electric lights were

Fig 8.22
Blackpool's illuminations are probably the ultimate example in Britain of using electricity to entertain holidaymakers. Fully illuminated in the autumn, they serve to lengthen the resort's tourist season. [DP129901]

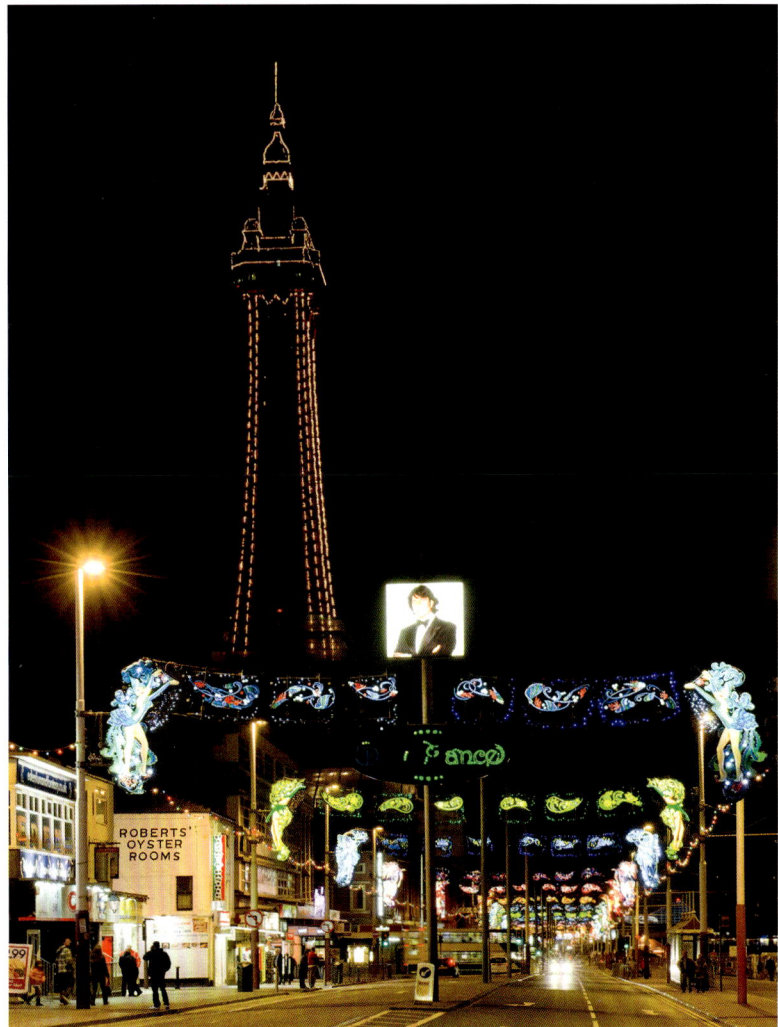

also being used to decorate buildings. The facade of the Gem Cinema at Great Yarmouth was lit by 1,500 light bulbs, a modest reflection of Coney Island's Luna Park, which in 1903 had 500,000 light bulbs.[67]

During the early 20th century, electricity and the invention of practical systems for projecting moving pictures came together to create cinema. Prior to this, seaside visitors had enjoyed visual treats such as the camera obscura, the earliest being one on the Steine at Brighton in 1807, while another was created on the town's Chain Pier.[68] Magic lantern shows became more sophisticated and more popular as the technology of their lights improved and at the end of the 19th century the mutoscope, including the celebrated 'What-the-Butler-Saw' machine, provided a simple way of creating the impression of moving pictures.[69] The first films were shown in 1894 using the Kinetoscope, designed by Thomas Edison (1847–1931). This new contraption was a cabinet in which a short film was shown and only one viewer at a time could watch it.[70]

The earliest seaside film show seems to have occurred on 25 March 1896 at the Pandora Gallery in Brighton, a few weeks after the first exhibition in London.[71] The first films were shown to an audience in Blackpool on 29 June 1896 at the Prince of Wales Theatre. The follow-

ing summer, a half-hour show of the Lumières' Cinématographe was available to visitors at the Theatre Royal in Talbot Square. A few Mitchell and Kenyon films from the beginning of the 20th century were filmed at north-west English seaside resorts and shown to the people captured in them, the technology rather than the storyline being the thrill of the attraction.[72]

The first purpose-built cinemas probably appeared between 1904 and 1906, but it was the Cinematograph Act 1909 that regulated the safety of cinemas and enabled hundreds to be built in the following years.[73] The earliest survivor at the seaside is probably the Gem Cinema at Great Yarmouth, which opened in 1908, though it was apparently originally intended to be a venue for a wild-animal show.[74] Prior to World War I, Blackpool had more than a dozen venues showing films. These were a mixture of cinemas within existing entertainment complexes, theatres and other buildings showing films occasionally, as well as a few purpose-built cinemas. The earliest surviving, purpose-built cinema at Blackpool opened in 1909 as the Royal Pavilion Cinema on Rigby Road. The former Princess Cinema on the Promenade originally opened in 1912, and was significantly enlarged when it re-opened in 1922. The Imperial Picture Palace on Dickson Road opened in July 1913 and accommodated

Fig 8.23
The Central Picture Palace on Central Drive, Blackpool, opened in 1913. It was a single-storey building with a barrel-vaulted ceiling and had a more elaborate facade than any of the other early surviving cinemas. [AA052999]

731 customers in its two-tier auditorium. The Central Picture Palace on Central Drive also opened in 1913 (Fig 8.23). Margate boasts two early, surviving cinemas. The Parade Cinema opposite the pier opened in 1911, but its facade has panels decorated with masks and musical instruments, suggesting that the building may have been conceived as a music hall. The former Cinema de Luxe was built at the top of the High Street in 1914–15.

As the 20th century progressed, increasingly complicated films required larger screens for growing audiences. The small picture house of the early 20th century was superseded during the interwar years by much larger, city-centre cinemas. Cinemas probably reached the peak of their popularity during the 1930s when resorts like Brighton and Bournemouth could each boast 16.[75] The most famous cinema chain was Odeon, the largest example at the seaside being the 1939 Odeon in Blackpool, designed by Robert Bullivant of Harry Weedon and Partners, with an auditorium containing more than 3,000 seats (Fig 8.24).[76] Other local and national businesses were also erecting new cinemas to exploit the growing popularity of British and (particularly) Hollywood films, including the new cinema fronting Margate's Dreamland amusement park (Fig 8.25).

Holiday camps – fun for all the family

Large areas of new housing and the continuing practice of providing lodgings in any suitable houses were responses to growing working-class access to seaside holidays, but perhaps the most iconic British solution to this new market was the creation of holiday camps. Their roots lie in Victorian philanthropy: concern about the welfare and morality of children prompted the creation of temporary tented camps by organisations such as the Catholic Church, the Children's Country Holidays Fund, the Boys' Brigade and the Ragged School Union (Fig 8.26).

Joseph Cunningham's camp near Douglas on the Isle of Man is credited as Britain's first permanent holiday camp.[77] He had been a superintendent of the Florence Institute in Toxteth, Liverpool, since 1889 and every August he and his wife Elizabeth took the boys camping in tents for a week.[78] In 1894, he leased land on the Isle of Man in his own name and the camp began to attract young men during the summer from a number of Sunday Schools, clubs and temperance leagues in and around Liverpool. At first, the 600 campers slept in tents, cooked their own food and washed their own dishes, but to broaden the appeal of the camp, and to make it

Fig 8.24 (above left)
The structure of Blackpool's Odeon Cinema consisted of a steel frame clad in brick, with coloured faience cladding. Throughout Britain this chain of cinemas helped to introduce a splash of modernist architecture into the heart of towns and cities.
[AA053269]

Fig 8.25 (above)
One of the most impressive of the new cinemas was the 2,200-seat Dreamland Cinema at Margate of 1935. Its design included the striking central fin, which was based on Berlin's highly influential 1928 Titania Palast. The building survives but is not currently in use as a cinema.
[OP13149]

Fig 8.26
This photograph shows a
Ragged School Union
holiday camp being held at
New Hall Farm, Upper
Dovercourt, in Essex, in
1933. It consists of little
more than a group of tents
in the corner of a large
playing field.
[EPW042621]

more economically viable, Cunningham raised its prices, which allowed the abolition of doing chores. This shifted the emphasis from discipline to leisure and fun, though his fervent stance against alcohol continued. In 1904, Cunningham bought a permanent site, allowing him to create a camp consisting of 1,500 tents, a large dining room and facilities such as billiards, mini golf, tennis, a bowling green, a 90ft-long (27m) covered swimming pool and a concert hall. There were also shops, a bank, a post office, a bake-house and a chaplain.[79] Nevertheless, the camp remained a temperance institution run on quasi-military lines with set mealtimes and lights-out marked by bugle calls. By 1939, more than one million campers, all male and at least temporarily teetotal, had stayed at Cunningham's camp. After wartime service as a prisoner-of-war camp, the holiday camp alas never reopened.

Other early, permanent camps were designed to allow children from industrial cities the opportunity to breathe fresh, sea air and enjoy an improved diet. In 1897, the Wood Street Mission established a holiday camp at St Anne's-on-Sea, in Lancashire, for children from central Manchester and Salford and by around 1900 a boys' club in Leicester was arranging holidays for deserving boys and girls at Mablethorpe, in Lincolnshire, where the boys initially slept in tents, while a hut was erected for girls.[80] Local authorities could also be behind the creation of holiday camps for children and the City of Salford opened one at Prestatyn, in north Wales, in 1928.[81] A number of early camps were also created as a result of political convictions. John Fletcher Dodd established a camp at Caister-on-Sea, in Norfolk, in 1906 for the Independent Labour Party. Roseland Summer Camp at

Rothesay, which opened in 1911, was a non-profit-making cooperative camp.[82] During the 1930s, the trade union NALGO ran a camp at Scarborough and at Croyde Bay, in Devon, and the Workers Travel Association established Rogeston Hall Camp at Corton, in Norfolk, in 1938.[83] In 1939, a holiday centre for Derbyshire miners and their families opened beside the convalescent home for miners at Indgoldmells, near Skegness, in Lincolnshire.[84]

Holiday camps were not limited to left-wing politics. Each summer between 1933 and 1937, the British Union of Fascists held summer camps in the Bognor Regis area.[85] The 1937 camp catered for up to 1,000 campers for two months, paying up to two guineas a week.[86] However, unlike those arising from left-wing politics, the fascist camps were, thankfully, only temporary.

By the outbreak of World War II, there were 116 permanent holiday camps and 59 temporary ones in Britain.[87] Most were commercial ventures providing family holidays. In 1920, Herbert Potter and his brother Arthur opened a camp at Caister-on-Sea, with Herbert opening a second site in 1924 at Hopton-on-Sea near Great Yarmouth.[88] Captain Harry Warner opened his first holiday camp on Hayling Island in 1931, and by 1939 he owned four camps.[89]

These first commercial camps were relatively small scale, at least initially, but one man began to dare to take holiday camps to a larger and wider audience. William 'Billy' Heygate Edmund Colborne Butlin (1899–1980) began his career in 1921 with a single hoop-la stall. In 1928, he invested £2,000 in the first batch of dodgem cars to arrive in Britain, as well as securing the exclusive rights to operate them in Europe.[90] By 1934, Butlin was running eight seaside amusement parks and operated most of the attractions at several big Christmas fairs.[91] Although already a successful entrepreneur in the amusement industry, he decided to diversify into providing holiday camps. He saw the potential in opening a self-contained holiday village for middle-income families for whom no one seemed to be catering. It would have chalets, rather than tents, set in landscaped gardens and indoor and outdoor sports and entertainment facilities would be available.[92] His first camp – at Ingoldmells, near Skegness – welcomed its first 500 visitors at Easter 1936 (Fig 8.27).[93] Butlin's holiday camps sought to attract visitors by emphasising the comfort of the accommodation. Adverts extolled the virtues of its 'electric light, carpeted

Fig 8.27
A homely, mock-Tudor style was employed for the timber chalets at Butlin's and one of those at the Ingoldmells camp, near Skegness, is now a Grade II listed building. [© Author]

floors, running water, baths and first-class sanitary arrangements'.[94] The communal buildings of the camps were often just utilitarian boxes, industrial in scale in the case of Butlin's camps, but some were decorated with superficial flourishes. His first two camps – at Ingoldmells, near Skegness, and at Clacton, in Essex – employed some Art Deco forms, one building at the latter being embellished with toy soldiers. By the late 1960s, Butlin's had nine camps in Britain and Ireland (*see* p 179).

The other major name in the post-war story of holiday camps was Fred Pontin (*see* p 179). Warner's, Butlin's and Pontins were, at their peak, large chains offering accommodation at a number of sites, but many holiday camps before and after World War II were small, family-run businesses (Figs 8.28 and 8.29).

Conclusion

During the century following Queen Victoria's accession to the throne in 1837, technology transformed tourism. The rapid growth of a national railway network increased access to seaside resorts and, combined with growing individual wealth and the increasing availability of holidays, led to a transformation of the holiday habit. A shift occurred from being a small-scale, exclusive experience limited to the wealthiest in society to a genuinely mass-market phenomenon, something that could be experienced and enjoyed by almost everyone. Technology transformed the small-scale, sociable entertainment institutions of the Georgian period into the large-scale popular venues of the late 19th century. Instead of dozens of couples dancing in an assembly room, thousands could now take to

Fig 8.28 (facing page)
This 1952 Aerofilm's
photograph shows Squires
Gate Holiday Camp at
Lytham St Anne's,
Lancashire, before it was
taken over by Pontins in
1961 and redeveloped.
It closed in October 2009
as a result of falling
visitor numbers.
[EAW047516]

Fig 8.29 (above)
Brighstone Camp on the
Isle of Wight, which opened
in 1932, provided visitors
with chalets set around a
large grassy area. It is
on a rapidly eroding cliff
and some of its original
buildings have fallen into
the sea.
[DP005028]

the floors of Blackpool's ballrooms and for modest fees the same holidaymakers could enjoy the Circus or ascend the Tower. As well as scale, the tone of entertainment changed. The theatre of the Georgian period, often a rowdy experience at best, became a more serious art form, while for mass entertainment music hall and variety grew in importance. By the early 20th century, the application of new technology had created the cinema, which would contribute to a marked decline in all types of live theatre.

The beach as a holiday venue seems to have grown in significance during this period. It had always featured in holidays, sometimes being used as a promenade and other times employed for horse racing. During the 19th century, it was now common to see entertainers, such as pierrots and minstrels, performing on the beach to appreciative crowds. The beach also became a place to sit, with the invention of the deckchair in 1894, a phenomenon that coincided with a growing relaxation of rules for bathing in the sea. In 1837, polite society demanded the use of a bathing machine, an etiquette often reinforced by local bylaws. By the end of the 19th century, these rules were being relaxed, permitting people to change for bathing in their lodgings and later leading to the beach huts that began to line the seafront of many resorts. By World War II, more revealing swimsuits were common and would culminate in the invention of the bikini. This was a realisation of a change in attitude to the seaside. Where bathing in seawater had been the focus of a visit, increasingly it was the sea air and the tanning sunshine that was attracting holidaymakers. In 1837, visitors to seaside resorts were often considered to be patients who needed to bathe in the sea, but by 1939, holidaymakers were filling seaside resorts in search of relaxation and fun.

Changes in the numbers and the character of seaside visitors also transformed the accommodation market at seaside resorts. In 1837, the number of visitors was modest and could be accommodated in small hotels and in homes adapted for use as lodging houses. With the arrival of the railways, there was a need for more and cheaper overnight accommodation and seaside resorts often grew quickly to meet this challenge. Another response to this change was the invention of the Grand Hotel, an expensive, and therefore, exclusive, place reserved for small numbers of wealthy visitors. In contrast, during the early 20th century the holiday camp began to transform the way that many people took their annual holidays and helped to change the image of popular seaside holidays and entertainment.

By 1939, increasing disposable income, statutory paid holidays, affordable accommodation, thrilling rides and electrifying entertainment combined to create popular and prosperous seaside resorts. With the outbreak of war, this stopped abruptly, though Blackpool remained busy as it was away from the front line. The seaside resumed entertaining Britain's population after the war and while visitor numbers reflected its continuing popularity, sustained lack of investment and the lure of foreign holidays would lead to its decline during the last decades of the 20th century.

9

Spas and health resorts: traditional and new therapies 1800–1939

In the mid-18th century, at the height of their success, spa towns faced a new rival. By the 19th century, the seaside resort would contribute to their decline and transformation. The reason for this significant shift was in part due to new medical thinking and a belief that seawater bathing was more effective than drinking spa waters. Related to this was a growing appreciation of the sea and a decline in fearing it. Having acknowledged the sea as the country's 'bath', a series of small towns had begun to welcome wealthy 'patients' who had previously been limited to visiting fashionable spa towns. In their wake, new, more elaborate and fashionable entertainment venues and lodging houses began to be constructed. With suitable facilities in place, aristocrats and eventually members of the royal family began to visit, their patronage serving as a mark of approval and respectability for the seaside in general, as well as for specific seaside resorts. In 1788, George III (1738–1820) spent several weeks in Cheltenham, in Gloucestershire, on the recommendation of his doctors, but uncured by his stay, he went to Weymouth, in Dorset, in the following year and returned there most years until 1805. Brighton, in East Sussex, became the seasonal home for the Prince Regent, the future George IV (1762–1830), and other members of the royal family could on occasion be found elsewhere around the coast.

This new fashion for the seaside did not mean that spas ceased to attract royalty and substantial numbers of visitors. At the end of the 18th century, Cheltenham had become popular following the visit of George III, and other newer spas, such as Leamington Spa in Warwickshire, also grew in popularity. However, during the first half of the 19th century, spa towns increasingly became more residential in nature. They welcomed people who were retiring and some spa towns also began to host a commuting population using the growing railway network. Tensions emerged in some spa towns, as well as at seaside resorts,

between the growing number of residents and people who were seeking to make their living from tourism. Residents might be seeking peace and quiet, whereas hoteliers and shopkeepers wanted to attract as many customers as possible.

During the late 19th century, spa centres such as Bath and Harrogate enjoyed a form of revival due to a renewed interest in using waters as part of new approaches to hydropathy. Scotland proved particularly enthusiastic in embracing this new approach to mineral waters, focusing on what could be done with water, rather than what was in the water. This led to the creation of many hydropathic hotels in towns and in the countryside.

By the 20th century, spa towns throughout Britain were still attractive to visitors, less often as places for medical treatment, but more commonly as tourist destinations with fine facilities that might include bathing and treatments as part of an offer of relaxation and entertainment. Bath now also welcomes a substantial international audience, who come to see its important Roman remains, its historic baths and its imposing Georgian architecture. Nevertheless, the opening of Thermae Bath Spa in 2006 marked a revival of interest in the city's hot mineral waters and allowed bathers to use a rooftop outdoor pool while admiring the surrounding cityscape.[1] Today the term spa more often refers to pampering treatments available at luxurious country establishments, the aim being to promote the well-being of wealthy clients rather than treating the ailments of patients.

Spa towns in the early 19th century

During the early 19th century, spa towns continued to offer patrons treatments by drinking and bathing in local mineral waters. Tunbridge Wells, in Kent, remained popular because of its good facilities, healing waters, royal endorsement and convenient location for London. As detailed in Chapter 3, by the early 19th century, it had an elegant promenade, the Pantiles, two assembly rooms, libraries, a playhouse and a chapel that was a key part of each morning's routine for visitors.[2] A cold bath was built in 1780, and in 1802–4 a bathhouse was constructed over the springs.[3] In 1849, this building was modified to include a lodge for the dippers (the women who helped bathers), and in 1865 a new basin was created, which survives today. A pump room was constructed in 1877 at the south end of the Pantiles, but it was demolished in 1964. As well as improved facilities in the town, visitors could also enjoy pleasant excursions into the countryside, which was still on the growing town's doorstep (Fig 9.1). Although sea bathing was attracting leading members of the royal family and aristocrats, the future Queen Victoria (1819–1901) and her mother, the Duchess of Kent (1786–1861), visited the town at least five times between 1822 and 1835.[4]

Harrogate was also growing in size and reputation during the first half of the 19th century, a process that was obvious by 1843, when Alfred Hargrove included it in his curiously selective guidebook featuring places within 26 miles (42km) of the city of York.[5] A total of 88 springs existed within a two-mile (3km) radius of the town, a rare example in Britain of a town that was well provided with accessible sources, allowing treatments for a wide range of medical conditions.[6] The Royal Pump Room was built where the waters of one of the sulphur wells could be enjoyed, while the Royal Chalybeate Well, designed in 1835 by John Clark (1798/9–1857), was on the site of the original Tewit Well (Fig 9.2).[7] The newest major spring had been discovered in 1819, providing saline chalybeate water that was christened the Cheltenham Water, while another source was called the Montpellier Cheltenham Water in an effort to attract customers by associating the waters with more celebrated health resorts. As well as having plentiful drinking waters, people also bathed at Harrogate. In 1832, John Clark also built the Victoria Baths, combining bathing facilities with a large circulating library to attract subscribers, while the Montpellier Baths and Gardens were laid out in 1835 by Joseph Thackwray, owner of the Crown Hotel. The Bath Hospital was built and enlarged through public subscription during the 1820s.[8]

Throughout the 19th century, Bath remained the largest and busiest spa centre in Britain. When the war with France ended in 1815 it was hoped that Bath's prosperous leisure economy would revive, but the shape of the country's and the city's tourism market was changing. In 1801, the city had a population of 33,000 and by 1841, when the railway was beginning to open, it had risen to just over 50,000, where it hovered until the eve of World War I.[9] Bath was one of Britain's largest towns at the beginning of the 19th century, but had slipped down the ranks significantly a century later as other towns grew and

Fig 9.1
This postcard shows people relaxing on the Common that still exists today beside Tunbridge Wells. It was the proximity of the countryside that attracted visitors, particularly during the summer. Just behind the buildings lies the Pantiles, the social centre of this spa town.
[PC08200]

Fig 9.2
Harrogate's Royal Pump
Room consists of a stone
rotunda built in 1842 to
designs by Isaac Shutt and
a glazed annexe of 1913.
Visitors to the town could
drink the water from the
Old Sulphur Well. Today it
houses the town's museum.
[DP033121]

its spa function declined in significance. Part of the reason for its declining spa trade was its large size. Although this meant that it had more accommodation and a wider range of entertainments, many visitors were deterred by its urban character, preferring to relax in the new, smaller, quieter spas such as Cheltenham and Leamington Spa, as well as enjoying the still rural charms of Tunbridge Wells.[10] Instead Bath became more dependent on industrial activity and a shift occurred from providing baths and pump rooms for visitors to building churches and schools for local residents.[11] Despite changes in taste and the popularity of its seaside rivals, Bath nevertheless remained a place that attracted visitors, leading to the construction of new hotels and entertainment facilities. During the second half of the 19th century, a revival in the spa took place, so that between 1864 and 1886 the number of customers at the baths doubled from 42,000 to more than 86,000, a growth in part due to a new, more scientific interest in hydropathy.[12]

A similar shift of emphasis from leisure to residential can be seen at other spa towns. In 1799, entertainer and author George Saville Carey (1743–1807) was scathing about Tunbridge Wells, describing its visitors as mostly being 'peevish old maids', 'bloated old dowagers' and 'a frisky young tit or two'.[13] As early as 1766, the town was beginning to be recognised as a place for retirement and by the end of the 19th century, a guidebook claimed, 'Unbeneficed clergymen, gentlemen who have served their country in the army, in the navy, or in colonial appointments, and retired merchants, have settled in large numbers in this quiet, healthy,

and lovely spot. It is also a favourite residence for widows and maiden ladies of independent means.'[14] In 1800, probably fewer than 1,200 people lived in Tunbridge Wells, which was still effectively a large village, but by 1831 the population had risen to around 6,000, a decade later it was over 8,000 and in 1851 almost 11,000.[15] A railway line linking the town to London had been proposed as early as 1835, but a route was established in 1846, though it took until 1869 for a more direct line to be created.[16]

A considerable part of Tunbridge Wells' growing population was made up of retired people and people of independent means, and the size and quality of the new houses reflected the growing wealth of its residents. Foremost among the new developments was the Calverley Estate, designed by Decimus Burton (1800–81). Work began in the late 1820s on a 60-acre site and consisted of substantial villas set in parkland, an arrangement that Burton brought from Regent's Park and repeated at St Leonards, on the Sussex coast, at the same date.[17] During the late 1840s, medical reform writer and spa physician Edwin Lee (d 1870) recognised that this was the most desirable part of the town. He stated, 'The most eligible spot for a few weeks residence is the elevated Calverley quarter, consisting of a splendid hotel, the terrace of which commands a beautiful prospect, a crescentic promenade, with colonnade, detached villas, an extensive park, &c. The environs abound in picturesque and varied walks and drives.'[18] By 1891, more than 29,000 people lived in the prospering town, with its affluent residents catered for in large areas of housing, with many new churches, luxury shops and hotels, including a hydropathic hotel.[19]

Cheltenham witnessed a similar, but even more marked shift from being a town with its economy focused on leisure during the early years of the 19th century to a residential settlement later in the century. In 1801, Cheltenham consisted of concentrations of development around the historic settlement and the Old Well, but with the discovery and exploitation of new springs at the beginning of the 19th century, a series of new estates were developed. The Montpellier Spa began in the house of local entrepreneur Henry Thompson in 1804, which was known as Hygeia House and later Vittoria House, while a chalybeate spring was discovered at Cambray in 1803–4, though it did not acquire a pump room until the 1830s.[20] In 1809, another spring was tapped at Alstone, followed by the Sherborne Spa, which had a pump room by

1818.[21] As well as pump rooms for drinking waters, there were attempts to promote bathing, including the Montpellier Baths, which by 1809 was attracting more than 100 bathers per week.[22] The town had a number of circulating libraries and in 1810 its first museum was established.[23] In 1816, an assembly room almost as large as the one in Bath was opened in great ceremony by the Duke of Wellington.[24] A race meeting was first held in August 1818, but with the decline of flat racing it was replaced by steeplechasing, celebrated meetings being held there from 1844.[25]

Cheltenham's Master of Ceremonies, Simeon Moreau, died in 1801 and was succeeded by James King, who combined this duty with his responsibilities at Bath.[26] Sharing a master of ceremonies with another spa town had been possible since the times of Richard 'Beau' Nash (1674–1761; see p 35) because Bath was not popular with visitors during the hottest part of the summer, but in 1809 Cheltenham also tried to tap into the winter market, though progress was initially slow in part due to difficulties in obtaining coal.[27] However, the opening of a horse-drawn railway in 1811 from the docks at Gloucester meant that supplies such as coal and building materials could be transported easily to the town.[28] Accompanying the proliferation of springs and the increase in visitor numbers there was a growth in the town's population, so that by 1821 Cheltenham had more than 13,000 residents.[29]

Fig 9.3
The Montpellier Pump Room in Cheltenham was designed by the architect J B Papworth (1775–1847). The Rotunda's proportions, though not its size, are almost the same as its inspiration, the Pantheon in Rome.
[AA98/04306]

The construction of facilities for spa visitors continued during the 1820s, including the provision of an improved Montpellier Pump Room and the creation of a new development, Pittville, named after the rich private banker, property developer and politician Joseph Pitt (1759–1842; Fig 9.3).[30] In 1826, the Pittville estate plan was published. It included two central gardens with a road on each side, with terraces and villas, and a crescent, along with a third garden with lakes.[31] A Pump Room, set within the pleasure gardens, opened in July 1830 (Fig 9.4). If it had been

Fig 9.4
The Pittville Pump Room, completed in 1830, stands in a prominent location in parkland laid out as part of the Pittville development, in Cheltenham.
[AA98/04298]

completed, Pittville would have provided 600 houses, though it took until 1853 for 505 to be erected.[32]

These large, new estates were designed to cater for the growing residential population as well as visitors, but as early as the 1820s there were the first signs of a concerted shift from leisure to a residential economy. In 1824, the new curate of Holy Trinity Church arrived in Cheltenham. Francis Close (1797–1882), later Dean of Carlisle Cathedral, sought to confront the excesses of the spa culture, even praising the destruction by fire of the town's theatre as a sign from God.[33] In December 1839, he founded the Cheltenham Society for the Prevention of the Desecration of the Sabbath, which soon secured the closing of most of the shops that had previously opened on Sundays.[34] Where Regency pump rooms had once been the largest structures being erected in Cheltenham, now churches began to appear, reflecting a change in the tone and the main focus of the town.[35] St Mary's Church, the medieval parish church, remained at the heart of the town, but other later Church of England churches were erected to deal with the town's growth. Baptists worshipped in an old chapel that was demolished in 1820 and rebuilt as the Bethel Chapel. Roman Catholics had a substantial church capable of holding a congregation of 500 worshippers, which was built in 1810, but this was replaced by a new, larger church, completed in 1857.

As the spa declined in importance, Cheltenham increasingly became a residential town, popular with retired people, a town promoted because of its location in the Cotswolds and as 'The Garden Town of England'.[36] The opening of the railway in 1840 – first to Bromsgrove, then Birmingham and eventually, in 1845, to London – allowed Cheltenham to become a place for commuters to live, but it also became a centre for education, especially after the creation of Cheltenham College in 1841 (Fig 9.5).[37] Although the town's focus had shifted from its spa during the mid-19th century, it still proved popular with visitors, as is demonstrated by its hotel accommodation. The leading hotel in the mid-19th century was the Queen's Hotel, which was built in 1861 and was described as 'one of the finest and most complete establishments of the kind in this country'. It contained '70 best bed-chambers, 30 servants' sleeping apartments, 16 elegant sitting rooms, and two excellent suites of apartments' on the main and upper floors, while on the ground floor there was an elegant hall, coffee rooms, drawing rooms, billiard rooms and services.[38] Today Cheltenham is a popular place to live, shop, dine and be educated, the spa buildings that survive forming a pleasant reminder of the town's colourful past.

Fig 9.5
Cheltenham Ladies College moved to its current site, a short distance from the town centre, in the 1870s and in the following decades a large complex of school buildings was constructed, as can be seen in this photograph of 1928.
[EPW024138]

New thinking on hydropathy

By the 19th century, more scientific analyses of mineral waters were taking place as a greater understanding of chemistry developed. The matching of a particular mineral in solution, such as copper, iron or sulphur, to a particular condition, such as rheumatism, gout or neuralgia, became the province of spa doctors. The ways in which water was used also became more complex due to a greater understanding of its curative value, or, perhaps more plausibly, due to the need for doctors to make their treatments seem distinctive. In the early 19th century, Deen Mahomed (1759–1851) introduced the Indian treatment of shampooing, using oils to massage patients during bathing.[39] He resigned from the Bengal Army's 3rd European Regiment and emigrated to Ireland in 1784 and by 1807 he had moved to London, where he worked for the Hon Basil Cochrane (1753–1826).[40] Cochrane established a charitable steam bath in his Portman Square mansion, with Mahomed providing the 'shampooing' body massage therapy. In 1810, Mahomed opened the Hindostanee Coffee House nearby, a restaurant serving Indian food in an Indian-furnished setting, but despite attracting interest from epicures as Britain's earliest Indian restaurant, the business went bankrupt. Therefore, he moved to Brighton, where he worked in a bathhouse attached to the New Steine Hotel in 1814. By December 1815, he had opened his own Battery House Baths, at the foot of the Steine, and during 1820–21 he and his silent partner, Thomas Brown, built Mahomed's Baths on King's Road, overlooking the sea. His celebrity grew, leading to his appointment as the shampooing surgeon to George IV and William IV and he also published a book on his shampooing therapy in 1822.[41] His sons Deen (c 1812–36) and Horatio (1816–73) followed him into the bathhouse business. In 1843, Horatio published *The Bath*, in which he described the history of bathing and the variety of techniques that he and his father used.[42] As well as shampooing, their bathhouses included warm-water baths, showers and steam baths, tracing the last of these back to the late 17th-century works of John Colbatch (c 1666–1729) who had set up a steam bath near the salt mines in Cheshire.[43]

Deen Mahomed's bathhouse, and his writings, in some ways anticipated the full-blown development of hydropathy – the scientific, therapeutic application of water in baths and showers to treat a range of medical conditions and ailments by using changing temperature and pressure to stimulate blood circulation. This was ultimately inspired by the bathing practices of the ancient Egyptians, Greeks and Romans, who built bathhouses containing a series of rooms with varying water and air temperatures. A growing awareness of the archaeology of these ancient bathhouses seems to have been a factor in the development of complicated hydropathic establishments during the 19th century and in the appreciation of new approaches to using water for medical cures.

The pioneer of hydropathy was the 'Silesian peasant' Vincenz Priessnitz (1799–1851) during the 1820s.[44] Having successfully treated the brother of the Austrian Emperor Francis I, dozens of wealthy patients and doctors flocked to his clinic at Gräfenberg in Silesia, which opened in 1829. In it he offered structured programmes of water treatment, as well as barefoot walks on grass and a strict diet and sleep regime. Among suggested items in the diet were cod-liver oil, beef tea and ice cream and a basic tenet of hydropathy involved avoiding the use of alcohol.[45] Inspired by his own experience, Priessnitz developed a range of baths and showers, and techniques involving wrapping people in sheets. Among the treatments at Gräfenberg were the sponge bath, foot and arm baths, the douche, stream bath, the dripping sheet, dry blanket packing and the sitz, a warm hip bath used to relieve discomfort and pain in the lower part of the body. A distinctive treatment of wrapping the patient in a wet sheet so as to sweat out impurities was a key technique of the early hydropathic movement, but it gradually lost its place. Although Priessnitz claimed to have similar success with patients in their own homes, the mountainous location, with its fresh and invigorating air, was identified by many practitioners as a key factor in successful hydropathic treatments.

Priessnitz's ideas first became widely known in the English-speaking world through the lecture tours and publications of Captain R T Claridge (c 1797/99–1857) after he visited Gräfenberg in 1841. After a three-month stay, during which he took 800 baths, drank 1,500 glasses of water, spent 200 hours of perspiring and enjoyed walks totalling 1,000 miles (1,600km), he claimed to have been cured of his chronic rheumatism.[46] His book *Hydropathy; or The Cold Water Cure, as practiced by Vincent Priessnitz, at Grafenberg, Silesia, Austria* was first published in 1842 and by the following year was already in its eighth edition.[47] Claridge, like

Priessnitz, was not a medical professional and this undoubtedly contributed to the poor reputation of hydropathy in general, as well as a withering attack by the medical journal *The Lancet* on his book, which it denounced as quackery.[48] However, not all physicians condemned the new techniques and hydropathy attracted many wealthy and influential supporters, including Charles Dickens (1812–70) and Florence Nightingale (1820–1910). The emphasis on water and the rejection of alcohol secured the movement the backing of the temperance cause; indeed temperance and hydropathy were sometimes felt to be two sides of the same coin.

The Hydropathic Society was formed in London in March 1842 and in the same year Dr James Wilson, who had studied under Priessnitz, opened a hydropathic establishment in a former hotel at Malvern.[49] He was soon joined by Dr James Manby Gully (1808–83) and in 1845 they moved to Priessnitz House, a larger and better-equipped establishment with 72 bedrooms, offering a wide range of treatments and facilities.[50] Dr Edward Johnson, following a meeting with Claridge during 1842, spent the winter at Gräfenberg. On his return he established a hydropathic establishment at Stansteadbury, in Hertfordshire, and from 1847 onwards at Umberslade Hall at Hockley Heath, near Birmingham. Major centres of hydropathy in England were established at Ilkley, in Yorkshire, and Matlock, in Derbyshire, where patients benefited from being up in the hills (Fig 9.6). Ben Rhydding, on the outskirts of Ilkley, which

Fig 9.6
This Aerofilms photograph shows Smedley's Hydropathic Establishment at Matlock Bank, in Derbyshire, in 1921. It was originally founded by John Smedley in 1853, following his visit to Ben Rhydding, and grew rapidly during the late 19th century. [EPW005811]

opened in March 1844, became popularly known as 'the Yorkshire Malvern' or 'Northern Gräfenberg'.[51]

Claridge also travelled around Ireland during the summer of 1843. Within two weeks of his visit to Cork, a hydropathic establishment had been opened by Dr Wherland, while Dr Richard Barter (1802–70), who had also heard him speak, opened the Hydro at St Ann's, at Blarney, County Cork, which proved to be the longest lived in Ireland.[52] A number of other ventures were established in Ireland, including near Dublin, though hydropathy did not have a similar impact around Belfast. Scotland took to hydropathy with enthusiasm, with early small centres at Rothesay, on the Isle of Bute, and Dunoon, in Argyll. These were followed by a surge of larger ventures from the 1860s onwards, of which Crieff Hydro, in Perthshire, was, and is, the best known. The rise of hydropathy reflected a failure of conventional medicine to achieve cures for many conditions. While surgery was advancing apace, orthodox medicine was still stuck with bloodletting and chemical treatments, meaning that mineral and seawater cures seemed both sophisticated and effective.

The creation of hydropathic establishments

During the course of the 19th century, a blueprint for a hydropathic establishment gradually developed and was described at length by Robert Owen Allsop in his 1891 book *The Hydropathic Establishment and its Baths*.[53] He outlined how such establishments should be designed, the type of accommodation to be provided and how the baths should be arranged. Allsop included the types of room that would be found in a large, comfortable Victorian hotel, including a smoking room, though he was aware that smoking would undermine the potential benefit of hydropathic treatments. After describing the hotel accommodation, he turned to a detailed discussion of the wide range of bathing and treatment facilities that would be needed in a hydropathic establishment. Patients would be treated using a variety of baths, including many incorporating sprays or showers, and there would also be rooms in which poultices and other types of medicated coverings and plaster could be applied to a patient's body.

Hydropathic hospitals and hotels appeared all over the country during the second half of

the 19th century, including at traditional holiday destinations such as seaside resorts and spa towns. One of the grandest seaside hydropathic hotels, 'by far the finest building in Bournemouth', was the Mont Dore Hotel, which was built in 1881–5 to the designs of Alfred Bedborough (Fig 9.7).[54] Located inland from the seafront beside the gardens that flanked the Bourne river, it consisted of a 120-bed hotel in a Franco-Italianate style with a separate baths building, set in acres of grounds planted with Bournemouth's characteristic pine trees. As well as seawater and mineral water baths, the treatments included Turkish baths, pine inhalation and vapour baths, and shower, needle, sitz and douche baths.[55] The hotel accommodation included an indoor tennis court, a roller-skating rink, winter gardens, a reading room, a smoking room, a basement billiard room and a first-floor ballroom.[56]

As well as constructing new facilities, some existing hotels were converted into hydropathic establishments. The Imperial Hotel at Blackpool was built in 1866–7 with 100 beds in 120 rooms, as well as restaurants, dining rooms, billiard rooms and coffee rooms. In 1881, after an expansion during the 1870s, it was converted into a hydropathic hotel and behind it a seawater pumping station was established to provide the hotel and subscribers in the town with a supply of seawater.[57]

Fig 9.7
The former Mont Dore Hotel is now the Town Hall at Bournemouth. The baths on the left, which were connected to the hotel by a glass walkway, were supplied with seawater. There were also treatments based on those practised at Mont Dore in the Auvergne, France, from where spring water was imported for bathing and drinking.
[DP001306]

There were also many hydropathic hotels and hospitals in spa towns (Fig 9.8). Harrogate offered patients the Royal Bath Hospital, which treated 1,200 patients during 1910. Proof of the specialist nature of this facility was the fact that it was open only from March to November and admission was by subscriber's ticket. St John's Brine Bath Hospital at Droitwich Spa, in Worcestershire, established in 1877, was also funded by subscriber's tickets, at a cost of 5s per week. Llandrindod Wells, in Powys, had a hospital and convalescent home with 22 beds, though only a proportion of these were used for patients sent for the special mineral water treatment.[58]

As well as being established in traditional holiday destinations, hydropathic institutions and new spa facilities began to be created in the countryside, including on hills and mountains, and these enjoyed particular favour in Scotland.[59] A quiet, rural, unpolluted and elevated position echoed the location of the original Priessnitz clinic at Gräfenberg and reflected the findings of researchers who were studying the links between the environment and health. Sir James Clark (1788–1870) was a key figure in understanding the link between climate and health, including climate being a cause of, or cure for, certain medical conditions. After practising in Europe, he published a book in 1820 on the relationship between the climate of southern Europe and pulmonary consumption.[60] Six years later, Clark was in London and by the end of the decade he had published his major work

on climate and health, *The Influence of Climate in the Prevention and Cure of Chronic Diseases*, which ran to a number of editions.[61] As well as suggesting the obvious idea that people's health would be improved by moving from large, polluted cities to the countryside or the seaside, he examined the varying climate of different parts of the country to establish their key characteristics and therefore who might benefit from spending time there. He also became a physician to, and a close friend of, Queen Victoria and Prince Albert, his works perhaps influencing them in the choice of Balmoral, in Aberdeenshire, as their summer seat.[62]

By the 1890s, there were 75 hydropathic establishments around the country, ranging from seaside resorts to the Scottish Highlands.[63] Twenty had been established in Scotland, though only two remain in existence: Crieff Hydro and one at Peebles, in the Scottish Borders. Although many hotels still bear the name of hydro, most now offer only conventional hotel facilities. The large hydropathic hotel at Peebles was originally built in 1878–81 but was destroyed by fire in 1905, 'only to be rebuilt on a more extensive and elaborate scale' (Fig 9.9).[64] Thomas Davy Luke described this Georgian-style building set in a beautiful, natural location and he praised the elaborate bathing equipment and other facilities that this hotel provided. This fulsome praise should not come as a surprise, as Luke (*see* p 176) was the Physician-in-Charge at Peebles. As well as a bewildering range of baths and treatments, patients might have to endure Metchnikoff's sour milk treatment, the Johann Schroth diet, the grape cure, the Koumiss cure or the Salisbury system, a high-protein weight-loss diet using Salisbury steak.[65] Outdoor recreations were also available for residents, ranging from otter hunting to tennis, shooting, croquet and cycling, as well as a wide range of activities for inclement weather and the evenings.

Many of the hydropathic establishments were in new locations, but some existing rural spas also felt the benefit of a renewed interest in water treatments. Strathpeffer, which lies to the north-west of Inverness, enjoys a mild climate due to the Gulf Stream bringing warm water to the north-west coast of Scotland. Mineral water springs provided chalybeate and sulphur waters that had been used by local people for centuries, but these began to be noticed by the wider population at the beginning of the 19th century, following Dr Monroe's paper to the Royal Society in 1772.[66] A small pump room was built over

Fig 9.9
This 1894 photograph of Peebles Hydropathic Hotel, by Bedford Lemere, shows the hotel prior to the devastating fire of 1905. Located on a commanding position overlooking the River Tweed, it was designed by the architect John Starforth (1822–98) in a French Renaissance style, the style most in favour for contemporary hotels.
[© HES (Bedford Lemere and Company)]

the 'Strong Well' in 1819, when there were said to be a 100 visitors; this small wooden building was replaced in 1861 by a new stone Pump Room.[67] A second storey, containing bathrooms, was added in 1871, and a decade later the range known as the Ladies' Baths was erected. In 1879, a pavilion for concerts was also added and in 1909 an Upper Pump Room was erected. Underpinning the growth of the spa was the increasing ease of access by railway, allowing visitors even from England to come to the spa. By 1885, there was a service from Strathpeffer to Inverness, from where there was access to the national network. Growing numbers of visitors led, in due course, to the construction of a substantial hotel (Fig 9.10).

In 1889, Dr Robert Fortescue Fox (1858–1940) published a book describing Strathpeffer spa and its regime. As well as its range of medical treatments, patients could 'enjoy good music, pleasant company, light literature; or better still, discover an interest in investigating the antiquities or natural curiosities of the district; or, if strong enough, find pleasurable excitement in a little mountaineering'.[68] The timetable of the day began with patients rising early to take their first glass of sulphur water at least an hour and a half before breakfast, preferably fresh from the spring at the wells. After breakfast, which should be eaten at half past eight or nine, and a short rest, moderate exercise was recommended, including playing golf, bowling, horse riding or tennis. A small lunch at about 1pm would be

followed by a dinner at 6pm or 7pm, before retiring to bed early so that the patient would be well rested to start drinking the waters again the next morning.

Strathpeffer's regime echoed that of Georgian spas, more than Priessnitz's system, with its emphasis on drinking mineral water, an improved diet, fresh air and exercise. However, by the early 20th century, the range of techniques advocated

Fig 9.10
Although there were numerous lodging houses and small hotels in Strathpeffer, it was not until 1911 that the Highland Hotel was built to provide grander accommodation for visitors.
[© Dr J Close-Brooks]

originally in hydropathy was being supplemented by a range of other therapeutic treatments. Neville Wood, in his 1912 survey of health resorts of the British Isles, provided a lengthy account of the art of hydropathy, covering the range of baths, showers, wet sheets and wraps advocated by Priessnitz almost a century earlier.[69] However, it is also clear that technology had moved on, allowing more elaborate forms of bath and shower, including what appear to be saunas and hot vapour baths, as well as using heat from electric lamps as part of the therapy. This reflected a new appreciation of how the environment had an impact on health. Initially patients had benefited from using water and air to improve their health, but by the end of the 19th century, the sun had been recognised as an important factor in improving well-being, and the science of heliotherapy and its artificial counterpart, phototherapy, grew in popularity. In the 1770s, ulcers and tumours were first treated with sunlight, but it took until 1859 for neurologist Jean-Martin Charcot (1825–93) to demonstrate that the sun had a therapeutic effect that was not dependent on its heat. In 1893, Dr Niels Finsen (1860–1904) began experiments that would lead to the creation of phototherapy.[70] By the 1890s, scientists had discovered that heliotherapy could help children with rickets and the victims of tuberculosis.[71] It was also used in some cases of rheumatism, renal disease and syphilis.[72] By the beginning of the 20th century, the Alexandra Bromo-Iodine Spa at Woodhall Spa, in Lincolnshire, offered a wide variety of hydropathic treatments, ranging from some that Priessnitz would have recognised to more terrifying modern therapies employing X-rays, as well as high-frequency and static electricity.[73]

Spas and hydros in the early 20th century

Thomas Davy Luke was the author of a survey of the *Spas and Health Resorts of the British Isles*, published in 1919. He was also the author of *A Manual of Natural Therapy* (1908) and *Manual of Physio-therapeutics* (1922), as well as works on anaesthesia in dentistry and a book about massage and Swedish gymnastics.[74] He was the Physician-in-Charge at Peebles Hydropathic Hotel and, while it was under Royal Navy control during World War I, he was also Surgeon Lieutenant Commander of the RNA Hospital at Peebles.

His involvement with the hydropathic hotel at Peebles may explain why it was given such a lengthy entry in his national survey. It begins with the statement, 'The Town of Peebles – It would indeed be difficult to find a more beautiful spot, or one more suited for an inland health resort, than Peebles.'[75] Other hydropathic hotels also provided valuable, wartime medical facilities. Edinburgh's Craiglockhart Hydro, renamed the Slateford War Hospital, treated the poets Siegfried Sassoon (1886–1967) and Wilfred Owen (1893–1918) following its requisition late in 1916.[76] With the cessation of hostilities, the various requisitioned hydropathic hotels were returned to their owners in a more or less fit state to operate. The Atholl Palace Hotel at Pitlochry, in Perthshire, had been looked after reasonably well by the armed forces, but the other hydro in the town had suffered 'a good deal of damage'.[77]

When Luke published his survey of spas in 1919, he would not have been aware that it would effectively mark the beginning of the end of the heyday of spa and hydropathy treatments. At the end of World War I, there were already some signs of the troubles ahead. Craiglockhart Hydro briefly reopened after the war, but due to its condition it was not viable to operate as a medical facility and was therefore sold. Luke's national survey showed that spas were still very active medically, with some establishments offering the whole range of hydropathic treatments. Some, such as at Llandrindod Wells, also featured treatments such as stimulation using electrical current, radioactive mud, sun baths and the inhalation of pine fragrance.[78] Luke's survey also recorded a range of dietary cures to complement the waters available at spas around the country. He also tackled an issue of great importance today, obesity, which he considered a grave condition, as serious as heart disease and tuberculosis.[79]

Hydropathic hotels, spas and their towns still welcomed visitors during the interwar years, but compared with seaside resorts their numbers were tiny. Business records reveal that their heyday was passing, many institutions suffering declines in visitor numbers and therefore income. There were also some notable losses of facilities, Moffat Hydro, in Dumfries and Galloway, being destroyed by fire in 1921, followed by Callander Hydro, in Perthshire, three years later.[80]

In 1900, Lloyds Bank bought and demolished the Assembly Rooms at Cheltenham, but the new town hall of 1903 provided visitors with a musical venue, other smaller rooms for entertainment and a central octagonal 'spa' supplying four of the waters from the town's mineral springs.[81] Between the wars, interest in the spa declined. The Winter Gardens, designed by J T Darby in 1878–9, was in use only as a temporary theatre by the 1930s and was demolished in 1942 as it was beyond repair. The Cambray Spa had ceased to perform its original function and was demolished in the late 1930s.[82]

The assembly rooms at Bath were in financial trouble at the beginning of the 20th century, resulting in the sale of one of their paintings, a Gainsborough portrait, in 1903. During World War I they were occupied by the Royal Flying Corps, and in 1921 the ballroom became a cinema.[83] In 1927, the Royal Bath at Bath was redesigned in a neo-Georgian style, but receipts between 1928 and 1932 nevertheless fell by 10 per cent.[84] Although visitors to Droitwich Spa could enjoy the recently constructed Imperial Hydro, by the early 1920s visitor numbers were in decline.[85] Harrogate bucked the general trend of decline: the number of treatments given at the Royal Baths was 96,000 in 1901 and had risen to 120,207 in 1927 (Fig 9.11).[86]

Conclusion

In the 19th century, spas were still prominent in wealthier people's thinking about health – places where they could escape from the growing crowds thronging seaside resorts. However, during the interwar years, health become synonymous with sunshine, swimming and bathing at the seaside. Spas were identified more as places of illness for old people, rather than suitable places for well-being and good health, the image being so actively promoted by seaside resorts. After World War II, spas, like seaside resorts, felt increasingly old-fashioned and people instead turned to modern medicine, epitomised by the National Health Service, which was established in 1948 and incorporated many existing hydropathic institutions into its portfolio.

The hydropathic movement had gradually lost its focus on the cure and instead its hotels became a place for respectable people to find good company, enjoy fine food and gentle leisure facilities such as swimming pools, tennis courts and golf courses. Many leading hotels still bear the name of hydro today, though they offer only conventional hotel facilities, with perhaps a massage salon and a jacuzzi. While spas and sea bathing facilities with the medical dimension remain common in parts of Europe, in Britain they have been sidelined by the pursuit of well-being through pampering at spa hotels dotted around the countryside.

10

Tourism challenges since 1939

In 1939, millions of people enjoyed seaside holidays each year and holiday camps were emerging as a major draw for holidaymakers, Butlin's offering a week's holiday for a week's wages. If this proved too expensive, working people might still enjoy day trips or working holidays, many of London's East Enders hop-picking in the fields of Kent.[1] Spas were still enjoyed by a small number of wealthier patrons, who might also opt for a touring caravan holiday. And for the very wealthy, there were luxury hotels, cruises and holidays in the warm Mediterranean sun. They might motor down through France, though a small but growing number were beginning to fly from emerging airports such as Croydon and Shoreham.

During World War I, the Continent had been closed to holidaymakers. In Britain, a few resorts on the east coast had been shelled or bombed and facilities such as spas and hotels taken over for use as hospitals and convalescent homes. World War II had a more profound and longer-term effect on holidays and tourism. The threat of invasion closed off most of the country's popular seaside resorts, though Blackpool, safe on the west coast, still welcomed holidaymakers, as well as influxes of civil servants and tens of thousands of military personnel.

After the war, the landscape of tourism began to be transformed. Seaside resorts reopened almost immediately, but national economic priorities meant years of rationing and underinvestment in facilities. Some resorts had their decline compounded by the impact of the storm surge of 1953 that killed 300 people, but also damaged the fabric of resorts along the east coast. And if their piers survived this onslaught, they might later succumb to another major storm in 1978.

Until World War II, seaside resorts had a near monopoly on popular tourism, the strictures of a railway network inevitably directing people towards suitably connected destinations. However, during the post-war years, car ownership grew rapidly, coinciding with increased national and individual wealth. The near monopoly of the two-week annual seaside holiday was soon being challenged by other tourism options at home and abroad. By the 1960s, the increasingly old-fashioned, cold, wet and even 'scruffy' British seaside resort was being unfavourably, and unfairly, compared and contrasted with the bright, new, warm and affordable, sun-kissed resorts of the Mediterranean, despite regular media stories featuring their embarrassing incompleteness. Just as in the 19th century, increases in wealth and changes in transport contributed to altering the landscape of tourism. In the 19th century it was in favour of the seaside resort, but by the late 20th century, the same factors were drawing people away from the British coast.

As well as competition from abroad, there was competition from within Britain for people's disposable income. While a two-week holiday might still be the centrepiece of a family's year, now often taken abroad rather than exclusively in Britain, many people also enjoyed a plethora of mini breaks, long weekends, day trips and winter sports breaks, most of the last inevitably being taken abroad. Traditional seaside holidays were increasingly being challenged by new types of attractions and the growth of leisure pursuits that did not require a week-long stay. Disposable income also took people with free time to theme parks, spa hotels for a day of pampering, a meal at a fine-dining restaurant, a romantic weekend, a weekend taking in a football match and city breaks at home and abroad. Simple pleasures like walking in the countryside and visiting Britain's rich natural and man-made heritage, once enjoyed by small numbers of tourists, had become mass activities by the early 21st century.

After the 2008 financial crisis and the prolonged period of austerity in the UK which followed, media reports of 'staycations' nostalgically looked back to earlier troubled times. However, the reality was that people were still going on holiday. They were also following other pursuits and year-round activities, ranging from sailing to skydiving, from Civil War re-enactments to car rallies.

Although the shape and character of the tourism industry may have changed dramatically, it has continued to grow, providing a considerable number of direct or indirect jobs and injecting a huge boost of money into the national and local economies. In 2016, the travel and tourism sector was directly responsible for £66.3 billion (3.4 per cent) of UK GDP. When its indirect impact is included, it added £209 billion to the economy in 2016 (10.8 per cent of GDP). Foreign tourists alone contributed £22 billion to the British economy in 2016. Travel and tourism is one of the fastest-growing sectors in the UK economy in employment terms, providing 1.6 million jobs directly (4.6 per cent of all employment) and 4 million jobs indirectly (11.9 per cent).[2]

Holidays during and after World War II

During World War II, seaside holidays remained an occasional, but, in some places, still a popular form of holiday, or, more frequently, a short excursion to provide a brief diversion from the hardships endured by the population. Blackpool's population increased from 128,000 in 1939 to almost 144,000 in 1945, as the town was still able to function as a resort, but it also benefited from an influx of civil servants and military personnel, who worked and lived in the town during the war. More than 750,000 RAF recruits passed through the town during the war, with as many as 45,000 being in residence at any one time.[3] Some of Devon's seaside resorts were also deemed far enough from the conflict to welcome influxes of evacuees and relocated military and civilian personnel.[4] However, in the south and east of England there were significant restrictions on access and beaches were officially no-go areas.

Seaside holiday camps had an interesting war. Middleton Tower Holiday Camp, near Morecambe, in Lancashire, was opened with great ceremony on Saturday 19 August 1939, in time for the camp to be requisitioned by the government when war broke out a fortnight later.[5] At Butlin's, on the outbreak of war, visitors were sent home to make way for the military, which

paid Billy Butlin (1899–1980; *see* p 163) a rent based on 25 per cent of his 1938 profits. In 1939, construction of his third holiday camp at Filey, in Yorkshire, was in progress, but as the War Ministry wanted to use the site, Butlin shrewdly agreed to complete it at a cost of £175 per person to be accommodated, but with the stipulation that he could buy it back after the war, for three-fifths of the cost.[6] During the war, Butlin worked on improving accommodation for factory workers in hostels, as well as organising travelling fairgrounds and running clubs for troops in liberated towns after D-Day.[7]

After the war there was a large and immediate demand for holidays. Weary service personnel, along with millions of civilian workers (who had, in theory, enjoyed statutory holidays with pay since the 1938 Holidays with Pay Act), formed a huge and hungry new market.[8] By 1945, 18.5 million working people earning less than £250 per annum were entitled to holidays with pay.[9] Butlin's camps were in a more or less good state of repair when they reverted to civilian use after VE Day. Half of the camp at Filey was handed back immediately in good condition. With the assistance of RAF personnel, it opened as a holiday camp on Saturday 2 June 1945, catering for 50,000 visitors that year. The pre-war sites at Ingoldmells, near Skegness, in Lincolnshire, and Clacton, in Essex, reopened in 1946.[10] In January 1946, the government de-requisitioned 50 holiday camps and planned to release a further 70 later in the year.[11] Butlin had concluded agreements similar to the one at Filey during the war to build new camps at Pwllheli, in north Wales, and Ayr, in Ayrshire, and in 1947 they both opened, followed in 1948 by a camp at Mosney, near Dublin.[12] Butlin's had nine camps in Britain and Ireland by the late 1960s.

Other patriarchal holiday camp entrepreneurs followed a similar plan. By 1939, Harry Warner (*see* p 163) had four camps and after the war he and his three sons expanded the business so that by 1960 they were operating eight camps.[13] In 1946, Fred Pontin (1906–2000) bought Brean Sands, in Somerset, a 1930s holiday camp that had been used by the US Army. His aim was to cater for demobbed members of the armed forces seeking affordable family holidays. Within weeks he had added Osmington Camp near Weymouth, in Dorset. In the following year, he opened another four camps, taking his capacity to 1,300, a tiny but growing empire when compared to Butlin's five camps that could hold more than 30,000 patrons.[14] By the end of the 1940s, more than 1.2 million people per year stayed at holiday camps; these visits accounted for more than 7 per cent of the total holidays taken by the British population at the time.[15]

The success of holiday camps in the immediate post-war years demonstrates Britain's continuing love affair with the seaside, but also reflects a lack of affordable alternatives. Despite a concerted return of holidaymakers to the beach, many traditional resorts were still trying to recover from the depredations caused by wartime closure and enemy action in an economic environment where there were more pressing investment priorities. During World War I, Margate, in Kent, was attacked 42 times from the sea and air, but it soon recovered and attracted huge numbers of visitors in the interwar years.[16] However, in World War II, the town suffered more severe damage, as well as being run down through depopulation. More than 2,700 bombs and shells hit the town, destroying 238 buildings, severely damaging 541 and damaging 8,391 others (Fig 10.1).[17] There were an estimated 14,000 properties in Margate before the war yet at one time during the war more than 7,000 were unoccupied. With the threat of invasion in 1940, the population dropped to less than 10,000 from a pre-war figure of over 36,000, though it rose to around 19,000 by 1944.

As well as damage and neglect from enemy action, Margate was among the resorts that were a victim of nature. The storm surge of 31 January to 1 February 1953 resulted in 307 deaths around the UK and 24,500 houses were destroyed or damaged. Prime Minister Winston Churchill called it a 'National Disaster'.[18] At Margate, gaps were torn in the concrete facing of the promenade, the railway line flooded, boats were washed into the streets of the Old Town and the lighthouse at the end of the pier fell into the sea. The storm also caused severe damage to Margate's resort infrastructure. The Westbrook Pavilion, the Marine Terrace Bathing Pavilion, the Jetty and the Lido were all damaged, and the bathing pavilions and cafes in the bays of Cliftonville were completely destroyed. Nearby at Herne Bay, hundreds of tons of shingle was washed onto the promenade, boats were smashed and houses and shops flooded.[19] However, it was further up the east coast of England that was worst affected, especially in Essex, where 112 people died.[20] The village of Jaywick suffered flooding up to 6ft (1.8m) deep in places, leading to 35 deaths, and at nearby Canvey Island there were 58 deaths, some people drowning while in bed.[21] In Lincolnshire, at Mablethorpe, an estimated 860,000 tons of sand was washed into the town, stripping the beach back to its black

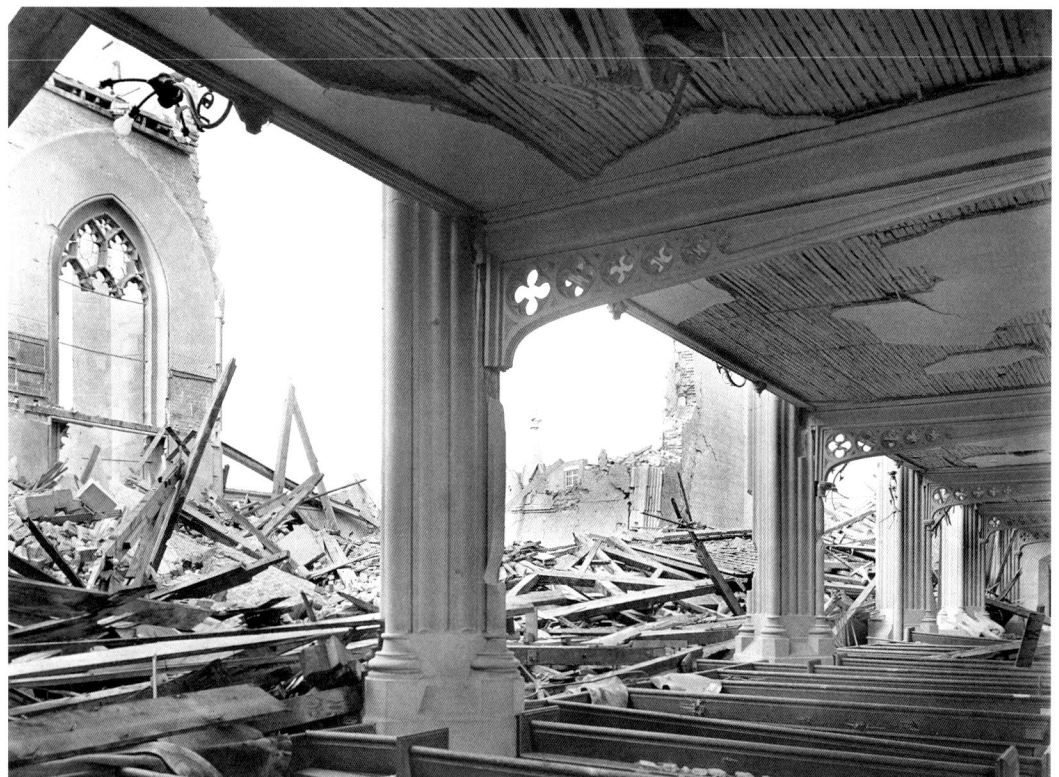

Fig 10.1
Built in 1825 as the centrepiece to the Trinity Square residential development, Holy Trinity Church at Margate had a 57ft-high (17m) nave and a tower that rose to a height of 136ft (41m). This evocative image, taken shortly after the air raid of 1 June 1943, shows the extent of the damage it suffered. [AA43/07427]

clay, while near Skegness sea defences were destroyed, damaging many properties, as well as flooding an amusement park and gardens with up to 5ft (1.5m) of water. At Cleethorpes, huge sections of concrete were displaced from the North Promenade, a hole was scoured beneath the railway line and around 1,000 homes were flooded, along with damage to, and the destruction of, many seafront buildings.[22] The 1953 storm surge highlighted years of underinvestment in sea defences, and the same lack of funding was obvious in the entertainment facilities and accommodation in resorts all around the coast. Nevertheless, during the 1950s the relatively captive British market made the best of what was available, enjoying the type of holidays lampooned gently in the 1980s BBC TV series *Hi-de-Hi*.

Although 1950s holidays appear broadly similar to those from before the war, profound changes in the character and shape of the holiday market were beginning to become obvious. This had been recognised even during the war when the industrial economist Elizabeth Brunner (1920–83), who was a member of the Nuffield College Post-War Reconstruction Survey, published a book in 1945 entitled *Holiday Making and the Holiday Trades*.[23] Her study looked into areas of the tourist industry that she thought had capacity to absorb the expected increase in numbers of holidaymakers. These ranged from traditional seaside resorts to holiday camps and camping coaches (train carriages that had been converted into accommodation and parked on sidings by the sea or in the countryside).[24] One of the last vestiges of this innovative solution survived at Dawlish Warren, in Devon, where each year during the summer months 'eight converted railway carriages with many original features' offered 'spacious accommodation at competitive prices'.[25] Unfortunately, their website announced that the summer of 2016 was the last time that this experience would be on offer. However, the same type of accommodation is still available from the Caledonian Camping Coach Company, which markets the Loch Awe Carriage, and the North Yorks Moors Railway offers two coaches in idyllic locations.[26]

Shortly after Brunner's book appeared, John Pimlott's seminal history of *The Englishman's Holiday* was published in 1947.[27] Pimlott (1909–69) concluded his book with a summation of the state of holidays immediately after the war and their likely future in the face of having to react to the effect of the Holidays with Pay Act.

He was particularly concerned with how seaside resorts would cope during the short summer season. Like Brunner, he identified a number of means to relieve this pressure, such as greater use of camping and caravans, the key role that holiday camps would play, and the fact that access to holidays abroad would absorb some of the demand, through cruises and winter sports.[28] Pimlott also believed that the countryside would open up more as a leisure destination. However, he was acutely aware that any such invasion would be likely to create tensions, and that spas might also make a useful, if limited, contribution to meeting demand.[29] Most of Pimlott's futurology seems, from the perspective of the early 21st century, to have been sound. However, one aspect of his vision, which was grounded in an era when collectivism and nationalisation had come to dominate thinking, now seems very far from the mark. He claimed, 'The road from [Richard "Beau"] Nash to Butlin has been winding and long, but as the crow flies the distance is not great. The individualistic holiday may prove to have been the aberration, and communal holiday the norm.'[30] However, he recognised, slightly contradictorily, that there would be no 'reason to suppose that the individually organised holiday will cease to be important' and that 'in a free society, the new holidaymaking will reflect the diversity of tastes and standards of the whole community'.[31] In the early 21st century, the tourism and leisure market clearly reflects 'the diversity of tastes' that Pimlott foresaw, as will be examined at the end of this chapter.

Transport and tourism during the late 20th century

Post-war Britain saw not only an increase in the number of holidaymakers but also a change in the character of holidays, particularly in the way that people went on holiday and, therefore, where they could go. In 1952, all forms of transport within the UK, apart from sea travel, accounted for 135 billion miles (218 billion kilometres), but by 2001 this had more than trebled to 456 billion miles (734 billion kilometres).[32] During this same half century, Britain's population only increased from 50.2 million to 59.1 million, therefore 18 per cent more people were travelling 336 per cent more miles. While the mobility of Britain's population was increasing rapidly, there was also a profound shift from people going on holiday by train to using the private car. In 1951, 14 per cent

of households owned one or more cars, but by 2001 this had risen to 74 per cent.[33] In 1951, 27 per cent of people went on holiday by car, the same number as those using coaches, while railways accounted for 47 per cent of travellers.[34] In 2002, 73 per cent of people went by car, only 6 per cent by coach and 12 per cent by rail.[35] During the half century between 1951 and 2002, there was a profound reorganisation of the railways, including the streamlining resulting from Dr Richard Beeching's reports of 1963 and 1965 (Fig 10.2).

Although trains are still a key way of travelling for work and business, the car is at the heart of modern domestic holidaymaking. It allows greater access to the countryside, celebrated beauty spots and natural wonders. It also creates congestion on routes to the very same attractions, as well as on major roads into, and out of, Britain's cities (Fig 10.3).[36] The most profound impact has been felt at seaside resorts, their geographical location limiting routes to them and creating at times legendary traffic jams. To improve road travel, a network of motorways was constructed. The M1 from London to Birmingham opened in 1959 and the completion of the M5 brought an extra 18 million people to within a 3½-hour drive of Devon's seaside resorts.[37] However, despite this major road-building programme, the rate of increase of car ownership has far outstripped the capacity of Britain's road network at key times of the day and year.

The proliferation of cars and motorways encouraged more people to visit familiar tourist destinations, resulting in dramatic changes to their size and form. Early photographs show quiet, seafront promenades where pedestrians and horse-drawn vehicles are scattered along the seafront, but during the course of the 20th century they record the dramatic increase in traffic until today, when esplanades are dominated by lines of parked and slow-moving cars. While the train had concentrated development in the areas around railway stations, leading to relatively compact town plans, the car and bus allowed the rapid expansion of the suburbia of many resorts along the seafront between the 1930s and the 1960s. Spa towns, although their spa function declined significantly, remained attractive places to visit for shopping and sightseeing, as well as to live in, and this also prompted significant suburban growth and high-class retail development.

The private car increased personal freedom and changed the size, shape and infrastructure of towns throughout the country. Blackpool, as one of the largest resorts in Britain, experienced one of the most visible changes. Before World War II, the town already provided a primitive form of park-and-ride and had one of the earliest multistorey car parks. The central railway station closed in 1964 and the site became a surface car park, alongside a new police station and law courts. The route of the railway line from Preston was turned into Seasiders Way and Yeadon Way, the latter running on the former railway viaduct to join the end of the M55 motorway, which opened in 1975.

The coach tour also became a popular means of holidaymaking, particularly among the growing number of older tourists. This lucrative market was recognised by Sidney De Haan (1919–2002), who founded Saga in the 1950s. Half a century later it had become a billion-pound business with more than two million customers.[38] Although many of these holidays and shorter excursions are taken within Britain, Saga has developed a worldwide portfolio of destinations and cruises to suit every taste and pocket, as long as its customers are over 50, the slice of the market with the highest disposable income and most leisure time.

Air travel

The rapidly expanding rail network opened seaside resorts to the masses. Similarly, the aeroplane ushered in an era of foreign package holidays and cheap flights, first to the sunshine of the Mediterranean and subsequently to more distant parts of the world. However, before aircraft would transform the holiday market, they were viewed as a novelty and a tourist attraction, with the first rival air shows being held in October 1909 at Doncaster, in Yorkshire, and Blackpool.[39] People could not have anticipated that aeroplanes would be a major contributing factor to the British seaside's decline during the late 20th century, making travel abroad affordable to a mass market that had once flocked to resorts such as Blackpool.

Fig 10.2 (facing page) Dr Beeching's programme of railway line closures inadvertently launched a new stream of tourism and leisure through the creation of heritage railways. The Sir Nigel Gresley steam locomotive, pictured here, still runs on the North Yorkshire Moors Railway. [DP064586]

Fig 10.3 This photograph of 28 July 1951 shows the A6 south of Lancaster (to the right of the railway track) before the M6 motorway had been built. The congestion is only on one side of the road, suggesting people are heading towards a popular event or destination. [Afl03/aeropictorial/ r15159]

Initially, air travel contributed to the domestic tourism market, increasing the range of British destinations that could be reached more quickly and comfortably. In 1919, Sir Edwin Alliott Verdon Roe (1877–1958) introduced Britain's first scheduled daily air service between Manchester and Blackpool and, a decade later, the Blackpool Municipal Aerodrome opened at Stanley Park.[40] In 1931, a hangar and a clubhouse and offices with an observation tower on top were constructed and the new facility was officially opened as Blackpool's municipal airport on 2 June by Prime Minister Ramsey McDonald.[41]

In West Sussex, Shoreham Airport's terminal building opened in June 1936 (Fig 10.4).[42] The terminal was designed by the architect R Stavers Hessell Tiltman (1888–1968), who had offices in Brighton and was the architect to Southern Aircraft Ltd. Tiltman was responsible for other major commercial airport designs in Britain, including Belfast Harbour Airport (1939) and the Leeds Bradford Joint Municipal Airport at Yeadon (1939). Although some people undoubtedly flew to Shoreham to enjoy a holiday on the south coast, the net effect was to begin the process of improving access to the Continent for the upper end of the British market, as well as to other parts of Britain.

The aeroplane has also had a key role in connecting the mainland with the numerous islands and groups of islands off the British coast. It is a lifeline to many Scottish island communities and serves as a convenient route for tourism to otherwise difficult-to-reach, beautiful destinations, ranging from Shetland and Skye in Scotland to the Channel Islands and the Isles of Scilly in the south. Scilly was first served by Channel Air Ferries in September 1937 from an aerodrome at Kelynack, near Land's End in Cornwall, and the airfield on St Mary's, Scilly, was transferred to its present site in 1939. A new terminal was constructed in 1949 when the Ministry of Transport and Civil Aviation assumed responsibility for the airfield. On 1 May 1964, British European Airways (BEA) introduced Britain's first scheduled helicopter service from Land's End to St Mary's and by July 1979 it had carried its millionth passenger.[43] The helicopter service ended in 2012, leaving the islands to be served by fixed-wing aircraft from Exeter, in Devon, and from Newquay and Land's End, in Cornwall, as well as the *Scillonian III* ferry. However, a new helicopter service was launched in May 2018.

By the time World War II broke out, Imperial Airways was carrying nearly a quarter of a million passengers on routes to connect the Empire, while other airlines were beginning to offer flights to Europe.[44] One of the first post-war initiatives for tourism by aircraft occurred on

Fig 10.4
The terminal building at Shoreham Airport (now renamed Brighton City Airport), in West Sussex, was built using contemporary Art Deco forms. It is steel-framed, with cement-rendered block and reinforced concrete. [DP054459]

Sunday 13 June 1948, when Billy Butlin officially opened his own airport, 'Butlin's Skegness (Ingoldmells) Aerodrome' close to his holiday camp in Lincolnshire.[45] It dealt with air charters for passengers and freight, and local pleasure and sightseeing trips, as well as providing facilities for owners of aircraft. This was just a small-scale facility, more a novelty than a practical long-term option, but it does suggest that air travel was at the forefront of the thinking of even a well-established, domestic tourism business.

In 1951, the first terminal opened at London Airport (renamed Heathrow Airport in 1966; Fig 10.5). In the following year the Comet provided the first jet service from London to Johannesburg, in South Africa, a service that would usher in the era of long-distance air travel, even though this plane's lifespan proved short due to major technical problems.[46] In 1970, the first Boeing 747 entered service and six years later Concorde made its inaugural commercial flight between the USA, France and Britain.[47]

Fig 10.5
This 1960s photograph shows a Bentley parked on the runway in front of the British European Airways buildings at London Airport. This wonderful photograph by John Gay captures something of an era of stylish, if not rapid, international travel.
[AA087930]

In 1950, there were 195,000 landings and take-offs at British airports, but by 2002 this had risen to just over two million, in much larger aircraft. Consequently, over the same period the number of passengers passing through British airports rose from just over two million to almost two hundred million.[48]

Foreign holidays

Although aeroplanes provided important new links within Britain's islands, their main impact was to bring cheap foreign travel to within the reach of most holidaymakers. Nevertheless, a major part of the shift from domestic to foreign tourism can also be attributed to the motor car. It opened up western Europe to holidaymakers and second-home owners. France particularly benefited from an influx of British tourists arriving by car after the first roll-on/roll-off ferry service began in 1953. Ferries in 1960 handled 5.7 million cars, but this had risen to 20.1 million by 1992.[49] Today the annual congestion at the Port of Dover and the approach to the Channel Tunnel at Folkestone at the beginning of the summer holidays serves as testimony to the numbers of people fleeing abroad each summer (Figs 10.6 and 10.7).

Spain, in contrast, enjoyed the benefits of flights from major cities across Europe. In the early 1930s, 266,000 foreign tourists visited the country, a figure that rose in the 1950s to 2 million and increased to 12 million during the 1960s, a decade when huge national, and international, investment began to manifest itself in new resorts along its Mediterranean coast.[50] Britons led the way, with 709,000 people visiting Spain in 1964 and 2,775,000 heading there in 1974.[51] Shortly after World War II, there had been around 15 million domestic holidays of four or more nights in Britain; by 1955 this had risen to 25 million and to 34.5 million by 1970.[52] British Travel Association figures recorded that in 1951, 1.5 million people took holidays abroad, a figure that rose to around 5 million during the 1960s and to 8.5 million in 1972.[53] In the late 1960s, British holidaymakers holidaying in Britain spent £600 million but the smaller number who were going abroad spent almost £400 million.[54] Despite growing foreign competition, the peak of domestic holidays seems to have occurred in the early 1970s. One writer placed it in 1973, using evi-

Fig 10.6
Dover, in Kent, is the busiest passenger port linking the UK to the Continent, with dozens of ferries making the short crossing each day.
[DP093158]

dence from holiday camps, while in 1974 40.5 million British people took a holiday in Britain of four days or longer, perhaps exacerbated by the 'Oil Crisis'.[55] From the mid-1970s onwards, tourism to foreign destinations increased rapidly. In 1978, British tourists took 9 million holidays of four nights or more abroad but nine years later this had risen to 20 million.[56]

The rapid growth in the number of Britons holidaying abroad was largely due to modern providers updating the package holiday formula of Thomas Cook (1808–1892; *see* p 87). However, increasingly in the 21st century, the High Street travel agent and package holiday companies have been facing significant competition from websites and airlines that offer holidays as well as flights. As well as package holidays, low-cost flights opened up recreational travel within Europe and across the Atlantic, ushering in the era of the city break and, when the rate of exchange is favourable, even shopping trips to New York. The pioneer was Freddie Laker (1922–2006), who established Laker Airways in 1966, with his innovative no-frills airline 'Skytrain' beginning operation in 1977.[57] Interestingly, this new service was based on buying

tickets to fly on the day, much as people would buy a railway ticket, hence the 'train' in the name. It was short-lived, going bankrupt in 1982, but it established that there was demand for cheap air travel independent of package holidays and led to the founding of Ryanair in 1984 and easyJet in 1995.[58]

Ease of travel encouraged Britons to travel abroad, but it also allowed foreign travellers easier access to Britain. Their impact is felt most strongly in London and a small number of major historic towns and cities, ranging from Canterbury to York and Edinburgh.[59] In years with major events, such as jubilees or royal weddings, the draw of London is even greater, but foreign tourists are also drawn to a few other must-see locations, such as Stonehenge, in Wiltshire, and Stratford-upon-Avon, in Warwickshire. Where foreign tourists are unlikely to be found in large numbers are traditional British holiday spots, such as historic spa towns and seaside resorts. In 1974, 8 million foreign tourists came to Britain and four years later this figure had risen to 12.5 million.[60] By 2003, the number of visits was 24.7 million, and by 2015 it had risen to 36 million.[61]

Fig 10.7
The Channel Tunnel, a rail tunnel 31.4 miles (50.5km) long, linking the UK to France, opened in 1994. It provides an alternative means of crossing the English Channel for vehicles (which board Le Shuttle trains) and for Eurostar trains. This photograph shows the tunnel's UK terminal, at Folkestone, in Kent. [NMR 26135/005]

Challenges in the late 20th and early 21st centuries

The impact of affordable package holidays, no-frills flights and easier travel by car to the near-Continent has had the most profound impact on the traditional, fortnight-long, summer seaside holiday in Britain. British tourists found Continental resorts to be modern, comfortable, affordable and with guaranteed sunshine. Despite frequent media reports of arrivals at incomplete hotels, Mediterranean seaside resorts were soon providing tourists with a mixture of the familiar and the exotic, chip shops and pubs against a backdrop of palm trees and deep-blue seas. The glamour of foreign climes was increasingly promoted by new forms of media, the increasing use of colour in magazines and films, such as the James Bond series, tempting more people abroad. Television had a dramatic impact, too. The television career of Sir Roger Moore (1927–2017) illustrates a shift from the short-lived black-and-white series *Ivanhoe* (1958–9), through *The Saint* (1962–9) that was filmed initially in black and white, largely in and around Elstree Studios, to *The Persuaders* (1971–2), shot on location in the French Riviera, Spain, Switzerland, Rome and Stockholm.[62] Ultimately Moore became Bond, a byword for exoticism and glamour. And where Bond went, tourists followed. Europe was no longer the ultimate destination for many travellers, who preferred, and could afford, to visit Africa on safari, sun themselves on a Caribbean beach or cruise around the world.

In contrast, British seaside resorts had 'the constraints of decaying infrastructure, designed for one era and not evolving, or not physically able to evolve, to accommodate the demands of another'.[63] In addition, the decline of many traditional industries, and linked holidays such as the Lancashire Wakes Weeks and Glasgow Fair, had an impact on some towns, such as Blackpool, Scarborough and the resorts on the Clyde Estuary. And seaside resorts also suffered in the late 20th century from long-term economic problems arising from the seasonal and casual nature of their leading industry. Accompanying the legion of economic challenges came more or less severe social problems. The book on Blackpool published in 1998 by Professor John Walton (b 1948) described a town that he loved, but he was acutely aware of the severe problems that it faced.[64] Since World War II, Blackpool had suffered from high rates of crime, seasonal

unemployment, the poverty of old age, low wages and a poor standard of housing. It also had an image problem, often being portrayed as a town with benefits claimants filling its bed-and-breakfasts, polluted beaches, drunkenness and litter. The town's population peaked in 1961 at 153,185, but during the next 30 years it declined to a post-war low of just under 140,000.[65]

Multiple Deprivation Indices examining a range of economic and social factors, prepared every few years by the government, reveal that a number of resorts feature among the 100 most deprived local authorities.[66] Of 326 local authorities in England, Blackpool ranks 4th, Hastings 20th, Great Yarmouth 25th and Thanet, which includes Margate, as well as more prosperous resorts and residential areas, is 35th. This ranks seaside resorts alongside inner-city boroughs of London and major industrial cities, where economic deprivation is widespread. When the more detailed figures for the Lower-layer Super Output Areas (LSOA) are examined, the picture of deprivation in some seaside resorts is even more striking. Of the 32,844 LSOAs, each with approximately 1,500 residents in 650 households, local authorities with significant seaside resorts are prominent in the list of most deprived places. Of Blackpool's LSOAs 5 are in the top 10 most deprived list and the town occupies 13 of the top 100 places, while Thanet DC and Great Yarmouth DC both have 3 in the 100 most deprived. In Wales, in 2014, the industrial cities of south Wales and the towns of the Valleys dominate the list, but Rhyl, on the north coast, has 5 LSOAs in Wales's top 100.[67] In Scotland, the list is dominated by the cities of the central belt, though this is less likely to indicate that resorts do not face problems and is more probably a testament to severe inner-city deprivation.[68] Northern Ireland has also faced the inevitable deterrent effect of The Troubles. However, with the success of the Peace Process following the Good Friday Agreement, it is now fully open for tourism, with Derry/Londonderry having been the UK City of Culture in 2013. Belfast has made a virtue of disaster in promoting the Titanic Quarter. The natural beauty of Northern Ireland's countryside and the wonder of the Giant's Causeway all act as major draws for domestic and foreign tourists.[69] The travel guide publisher Lonely Planet has awarded Belfast and the Causeway Coast the accolade of being the best region in the world to visit in 2018.[70]

While the Deprivation Indices appear gloomy, a study by Sheffield Hallam University has suggested that seaside towns prospered more in the early 21st century than some statistics might suggest, though the prominence of Brighton, in East Sussex, and Bournemouth, in Dorset, may be disguising issues felt more acutely further north and in smaller resorts.[71] This research revealed that employment was relatively strong in resorts and that there was a net outward flow of people from resorts to work in nearby towns. Commuting from seaside resorts and spa towns has taken place in some form since the 19th century, and part of the growth in residential populations in some resorts can be explained by commuters. Southport, in Merseyside, began to serve as a dormitory for wealthy Liverpool businessmen during the second half of the 19th century and Brighton came within reach of London through the reduction of the train journey time to 1½ hours.[72] By the end of the 19th century, commuters to Bradford, in Yorkshire, were prompting the development of their own suburb at Morecambe, in Lancashire.[73] Some spa towns have also morphed from being primarily tourist destinations into commuter towns. Tunbridge Wells, in Kent, is a favoured place to live for commuters to London, and Cheltenham, in Gloucestershire, has become a residential town, popular with retired people and commuters to London and Birmingham.[74]

Some seaside resorts have enjoyed investment as companies, particularly those in the service sector, have recognised that a coastal location with poor road and rail links is no longer a hindrance due to modern communications. One of the first was American Express, which set up its European customer service and card accounting operations at Brighton during the 1960s (Fig 10.8). By 2010, American Express was the largest private-sector employer in the city, employing approximately 3,000 people.[75] Brighton, like Bournemouth, also benefits economically from the presence of higher education institutions. Brighton's economy grew from £2.7 billion in 1996 to £3.2 billion by 2004 and has thriving universities with 30,000 students.[76]

Nevertheless, a potentially vicious circle began to be evident at some resorts in which decreasing popularity led to less private income and public funding. This in turn led to poorly maintained and underoccupied buildings, sea defences in need of renewal, low-quality facilities and therefore fewer visitors. This was magnified by negative media reports that gave the British seaside an unappealing image for anyone planning their well-earned family

holiday. The legendary confrontations between the Mods and Rockers in the mid-1960s left a lingering legacy of uncertainty about the wholesomeness of some resorts, despite decades of trouble-free family fun. American-born author Bill Bryson (b 1951), a great fan of Britain, was unimpressed by some of the seaside resorts he saw and at Blackpool he was particularly scornful of the famed illuminations, which he described as 'several miles of paltry decorations on lampposts' and 'a rumbling procession of old trams decorated as rocket ships or Christmas crackers' (see Fig 8.22).[77]

As well as man-made issues, seaside resorts are increasingly facing the challenge of survival in the face of nature and by the early 21st century this was reaching a crisis point. The storm surge of 1953 had been a salutary reminder of the awesome power of nature and considerable investment in sea defences followed. Further major storms occurred in 1976 and in 1978, when there was severe damage to piers at Herne Bay, in Kent, Southwold, in Suffolk, and Skegness and Cleethorpes, and the destruction of the piers at Hunstanton, in Norfolk, and at Margate.[78] Brighton's West Pier has suffered from both the power of the sea and fire damage (Fig 10.9). The winter of 2013–14 was one of the most extreme in British meteorological history and included a major storm surge in the North Sea on 5–6 December 2013.[79] Storms damaged sea defences at resorts including Newquay, in Cornwall, and

Fig 10.8
American Express set up its European customer service and card accounting operations in Brighton in the 1960s and moved to this purpose-built office block in the city in 1977. It was demolished in 2016 and replaced with a larger office building on the site. [DP054420]

Fig 10.9
This 2003 photograph of the West Pier at Brighton shows a lone kiosk standing apparently untouched amid twisted, fire-damaged girders. Since its closure in 1975, this Grade I pier has been the victim of neglect, storm damage in 1987 and a series of fires.
[AA044831]

Teignmouth and Dawlish, in Devon. In Dawlish, the ground beneath the railway line was washed away, resulting in the closure of the main route into Cornwall for two months. In December 2013, the North Pier at Blackpool was damaged and had to close for several weeks. In January 2014, the sea walls at Aberystwyth, in Mid Wales, were breached, surfaces damaged and a shelter destroyed, and the same stormy period also had an impact on the coast of Ayrshire, where the older sea defences of many resorts were over-topped by significant amounts of water.

Storm events have troubled Britain's seaside resorts since their inception. However, by the 21st century, Britain's long coastline was feeling the impact of climate change. The fifth report of the Intergovernmental Panel on Climate Change (IPCC), published in 2013, provided clear evidence of climate change during the past century.[80] Evidence published by the UK Climate Impacts Programme demonstrates that sea level has risen around 1mm per year during the 20th century, though the rate has increased during the past two decades.[81] Projections suggest that sea level will rise around Britain by between 0.12m and 0.76m between 1990 and 2095, if the medium emissions scenario occurs. Any rise may be disproportionately felt in the south-east of England, as this part of the country is sinking slowly, while Scotland is rising, a continuing consequence of the loss of the ice sheet that once burdened northern parts of the country.[82] The

rate of increase in extreme weather events is less easy to quantify, though the consensus is that Britain can expect more frequent and more severe storms.

Climate change projections are leading to a greater focus on coastal defences. The most comprehensive programme of new defences has taken place at Blackpool in recent years. New sea defences were needed to protect the central part of the town and this prompted the start of a proposed £1 billion programme of regeneration in several districts. On the seafront, a modern tram system was created behind a new set of sea defences that improved the town's connection with the sea, rather than building a barrier. The stepped defences were a solution to removing energy from the sea but also acted as a space for seating. And by creating a series of projecting headlands, Blackpool has moved the sea further from its buildings, but also created public spaces for entertainments and events (Fig 10.10).

Diversification and the changing face of tourism and leisure

Think of tourism in Britain today and its image is still dominated by the family beach holiday. Seaside resorts are still the most visible and widespread manifestation of tourism, though the beach holiday can today be as easily taken abroad as at home. While foreign competition has undoubtedly undermined domestic tourism, perhaps a greater challenge to the traditional British holiday is a combination of access to more affordable air travel, changing lifestyles at home, an increase in portfolio careers and the consequent shift from one major seaside holiday to year-round short breaks and leisure activities that can be enjoyed from home. A recent survey found that the wealthiest were enjoying eight holidays per year, while the poorest quarter of the population took none at all.[83]

During the late 20th century, Britain saw the growth of the High Street travel agency. Some of the large chains had their own integrated airlines and travel businesses, and these contributed to an increase in foreign travel. However, by the early 21st century, their primacy was increasingly being challenged by the internet, which has made everyone their own travel agent. The ease of booking travel and accommodation has also been extended in recent years by the development of smartphones, thanks to apps such as Airbnb and

Fig 10.10
The design of the new
promenade and sea
defences at Blackpool
means there is no need
for a high sea wall. The
stepped defences, subtle
shaping of grassed banks
and lengths of contoured
seating, are designed to
redirect any over-topping
by the sea away from
seafront properties.
[DP157253]

Booking.com, as well as airline and train companies' booking apps. Another recent development has been the challenge to the guidebook due to smartphones giving access to travel information on websites such as Wikipedia and TripAdvisor.

As a result, in the early 21st century, the landscape of British tourism has been changing rapidly. City breaks now extend beyond Paris and Amsterdam to Prague, Istanbul and Cairo. Coach trips are no longer limited to excursions to seaside resorts and natural beauty spots in Britain, but encompass Europe, much as American travellers had first conquered Austria on Monday, Switzerland on Tuesday and Italy on Wednesday. Cruises at sea and along rivers have also grown in popularity, moving from being the ultimate treat for the super-rich on the *Queen Mary* or the *QEII* to a genuine mass-market experience on some of the largest ships on earth. Schools have organised more adventurous trips for pupils. No longer is a day out in a local big city or a two-week educational exchange the limit of their ambition, but skiing trips to Colorado, netball trips to Spain and cricket tours of Barbados have come within reach of better-off students. Similarly, a hen and stag party is no longer limited to a boozy night at the pub, but could involve a pirate-themed weekend in Newquay, a golf-themed break in Blackpool or a binge in Berlin. The growth of second-home ownership has also increased the number of people who regularly travel to their country or seaside bolt-holes, while some people have invested in rural properties in France. And while summer is inevitably the main season for holidaymaking, the growing popularity of winter sports sees millions of people travelling abroad in search of ever-diminishing snowfalls. However, Scotland still offers popular skiing resorts when winter sets in, such as the Aviemore ski centre, which opened in the Scottish Highlands in 1963, and Glenshee, in Aberdeenshire.[84]

What these examples indicate is that the near monopoly of seaside holidays has been challenged and supplemented by a huge range of tourism options. Some are familiar revivals of older themes, but many others are new pursuits. The Visit England annual survey of visitor attractions in 2016 showed the range of attractions enjoyed by domestic tourists.[85] The most popular destinations were country parks, farms, gardens, historic houses and heritage sites, theme parks, heritage railways, wildlife parks and zoos. The list of leading free attractions in the survey was still dominated by London's museums and art galleries, the British Museum

attracting 6.4 million visitors, the National Gallery 6.2 million and the Tate Modern 5.8 million. Brighton Pier, with an estimated 4.6 million visitors, was the only one of the top-ten free attractions located outside London, although the piers of Blackpool and some other large resorts are likely to have featured high on the list, if figures had been available.[86] Any visitor figures for free attractions inevitably have to be treated with caution, but more reliable figures can be assembled for locations charging an admission fee. The most popular paying attractions were the Tower of London, with 2.8 million visitors, and Westminster Abbey, the Royal Botanic Gardens at Kew and St Paul's Cathedral, each with 1.6 million visitors. Chester Zoo, in Cheshire, was the most popular visitor attraction outside London, with 1.5 million visitors, though Blackpool Pleasure Beach might have featured at the top of this list if visitor admission figures had been available. In 2007, the last year for which visitor numbers have been published, Blackpool Pleasure Beach had 5.5 million visitors, while Great Yarmouth Pleasure Beach entertained 1.4 million customers.[87] In Scotland, Edinburgh's two main attractions – the National Museum of Scotland and Edinburgh Castle – each attracted just over 2 million visitors in 2017, while the Scottish National Gallery welcomed 1.6 million visitors. Northern Ireland's biggest attractions in 2017 were the Giant's Causeway, with 1 million visitors, and Titanic Belfast, with 770,000.[88]

The range of modern tourist attractions includes both traditional and new types of destinations. Visits to country houses and heritage sites have grown in popularity during recent decades. Once limited to a small number of wealthy, inquisitive tourists, the advent of the National Trust, National Trust for Scotland and national heritage bodies have encouraged huge numbers of people to visit country houses, castles and ruined abbeys regularly, as well as while on holiday. The National Trust has more than four million members and relies on 60,000 volunteers to make visits memorable, while the National Trust for Scotland has a third of a million members.[89] English Heritage, which became a registered charity in 2015, has more than one million members who enjoy visits to a range of historic sites and organised events, from seaside strolls to festivals featuring jousting.[90] Britain also boasts an impressive range of privately owned grand houses, some of which are open to the public. While it was possible to visit these houses even in the 17th and 18th centuries, the modern phenomenon of mass tourism to private houses began after World War II, with the opening of Longleat, in Wiltshire, in 1949, then Wilton, also in Wiltshire, in 1951 and Beaulieu, in Hampshire, in 1952.[91] Some owners realised that a historic home may not be a sufficient enticement for tourists. Therefore, a number have used part of their grounds to create safari parks, while Lord Montagu's car collection at Beaulieu was transformed into the National Motoring Museum from humble beginnings when the butler sold tickets and the cook made sandwiches.[92]

Modern tourism has seen a revival of interest in its very roots: in pilgrimage and visiting spas. Although Britain officially broke with the tradition of pilgrimage in the 16th century, Walsingham, in Norfolk, is still a site for veneration and people seek to experience the serene piety of Iona, in the Inner Hebrides. Pilgrimage has always taken Britons abroad, Santiago de Compostela, in Spain, being the most popular destination during the Middle Ages, and today thousands of pilgrims still walk along the Camino. Newer Christian pilgrimage destinations have also become popular, including Knock, in County Mayo, Lisieux, in Normandy, and Lourdes, near the Pyrenees, while Jerusalem, Bethlehem and other sites in the Holy Land are high on the list of revered destinations in the Middle East. For

Muslims, the Hajj – the pilgrimage to Mecca, in Saudi Arabia – is a key part of their religion. Pilgrimage is also significant for the Hindu faith, the Kumbh Mela, in India, attracting millions of pilgrims, including many Britons. In contrast to the vast scale of these events, religious retreats within Britain enjoy a small but faithful following.

Spas remained popular in Europe during the 20th century and seawater bathing, once a key part of British medicine, has continued around Europe's coastline in dedicated thalassotherapy businesses and institutions. However, in Britain interest in both for medicinal purposes has declined in the face of the strength of the NHS and the supreme popularity of the seaside holiday. There has been a revival since the late 20th century in 'spas' in the pampering, rather than strictly medical, sense.[93] A day at a hotel spa with beauty treatments has now replaced the medicinal consumption of mineral waters in Britain, any water that is being drunk acting as a curiosity rather than the cure. Moffat, in Dumfriesshire, for example, has reinvented itself as a centre for wellbeing rather than purely medicinal treatments.

Newer forms of attraction are also proving popular, ranging from collections of re-erected historic buildings such as at Weald and Downland Living Museum, in West Sussex, or Beamish Museum, in County Durham, to Dreamland

Fig 10.11 Museums have been identified as an important means of regenerating towns across the country. The Jerwood Art Gallery, on the Stade at Hastings, in East Sussex, which opened in 2012, was designed to reflect the size and colour of the adjacent historic net lofts. [DP153081]

amusement park at Margate and Dingles Fairground Heritage Centre in Devon, where historic fairground rides tap into Britain's love of nostalgia. Art galleries and museums have been recognised as potentially valuable drivers for economic regeneration, including at traditional seaside resorts, such as Margate or Hastings (Fig 10.11), and in former industrial towns and cities, such as the National Space Centre in Leicester or the Big Pit National Coal Museum at Blaenavon, in south Wales. A 1998 survey found that nearly half of all England's museums opened between 1970 and 1989, along with a third of historic properties and 46 per cent of wildlife sites.[94] Could anyone in 1945 have imagined that the Museum of Brands, Packaging and Advertising (in Notting Hill) would prove to be a popular attraction?[95]

Inquisitive tourists of yesteryear sought out the natural beauties of the British countryside and today, a quarter of people each year holiday in the countryside, rambling, cycling and birdwatching being the most popular pastimes. Walking is one of Britain's most popular leisure pursuits, ranging from gentle Sunday afternoon strolls to ambitious long-distance hikes. *The Pennine Journey* of Alfred Wainwright (1907–99) popularised walking in the Lake District during the 1960s and 1970s and The Ramblers, formerly known as the Ramblers Association, sees thousands taking to the countryside of Britain every weekend.[96] And people also hunt, shoot and fish throughout Britain, a range of activities enjoyed by millions in terms of angling, while smaller numbers of wealthy people enjoy grouse shooting and salmon fishing on Scottish estates. Boat trips to Britain's islands are also a popular activity, either as a means of getting there on holiday or as a pleasant day out (Fig 10.12). PS *Waverley*, the last seagoing passenger-carrying paddle steamer in the world, was built in 1946, and is based on the Clyde, providing a regular service and excursions during the summer. As well as seagoing services, trips along Britain's canal network and on the Norfolk Broads are popular with tourists and people who own or hire boats for holidays. The UK's inland waterway industry is large enough to keep more than 12,000 cruisers afloat, including more than 4,000 boats for hire.[97]

As well as enjoying nature, people now often spend free time and disposable income at events. The British summer is dominated by festivals, ranging in size from small local gatherings celebrating motorbikes or steam engines to city-sized music festivals such as at Reading and

Fig 10.12
The harbour at Hugh Town, on St Mary's in the Isles of Scilly, connects the archipelago to the mainland via the Scillonian III, *which is moored by the quay. It is also a base for the regular boat trips to the 'off islands' and provides moorings for a wide variety of leisure and working craft.*
[DP085176]

Glastonbury (Fig 10.13). Britain's largest celebration of the arts and culture is the Edinburgh Festival Fringe, which claims to be the largest arts festival in the world, providing '50,266 performances of 3,269 shows in 294 venues across Edinburgh'.[98] It was established in 1947 as an alternative to the Edinburgh International Festival, which provides three weeks of music, theatre, opera and dance during August each year.

Sports events are year-round attractions, some football fans following their team around the country, sometimes making weekends of this when matches are played in a new or interesting place. Test matches and shorter games of cricket attract large crowds, as do tennis tournaments, particularly Wimbledon (Fig 10.14). The highlight of the motor racing calendar is the Formula One Grand Prix at Silverstone, in Northamptonshire. Britain has been favoured with holding three Olympic Games, in 1908, 1948 and 2012. The 1948 Games served as a welcome distraction from post-war austerity, and the 2012 event was a major tourist attraction for London and a boost for east London's economy. The success of the *grand départ* of the Tour de France in Yorkshire in 2014 has spawned the Tour de Yorkshire, a race but also a celebration of Britain's new affection for cycling. Golf remains, despite high

Fig 10.13 (above)
This aerial photograph shows the T in the Park festival at Balado, Kinross-shire, in July 2013 before it moved to Strathallan Castle in Perthshire. This three-day event attracts up to a quarter of a million people annually.
[© Crown copyright: HES]

Fig 10.14 (left)
The All England Lawn Tennis and Croquet Club is the venue for the Wimbledon Championships, the only Grand Slam tennis event still held on grass. This aerial photograph of 2010 shows the rectangular Centre Court, with its retractable roof, which was completed in 2009, and the circular No 1 Court of 1997.
[NMR 26626/001]

green fees, one of the most popular sports in Britain and players often arrange trips to new unfamiliar courses to test their skills. In Scotland, the highlight of the year for villages such as Aboyne, Braemar and Lonach are their Highland Games, Braemar's gathering enjoying the patronage of the Queen. Head to the coast and windsurfing and surfing have become popular leisure pursuits, a town like Newquay being a favoured destination for surfing and enjoying the economic benefits of this activity, which is year-round thanks to wetsuits. Such is the popularity of surfing that an artificial surfing facility has been established in Snowdonia, in north Wales.[99]

Today, there is likely to be something for any interest somewhere in Britain, from painting courses in the Scottish countryside to diving with seals on St Martin's in the Isles of Scilly or a punk rock festival in Blackpool's Winter Gardens. There is always somewhere for concerted retail therapy, from a small town like Hay-on-Wye renowned for its books, or Malton, which is marketing itself as Yorkshire's food capital. Major shopping malls – such as Westfield at Stratford, in east London, beside the former Olympic Park, and the Metro Centre at Gateshead – are popular all year round (Fig 10.15). More sedately, many people enjoy dining at fine restaurants, spending time in rented rural cottages or enjoying a romantic night at a luxury hotel. And if five-star luxury isn't your cup of tea, caravan sites and campsites are popular places to enjoy a week or a weekend away.

The holiday camp market has changed dramatically in recent years. Butlin's, the most famous brand, operates three 'Family Entertainment Resorts', with tented 'Skyline Pavilions' at their heart linking existing and new entertainment buildings to create a central forum where visitors can congregate regardless of the weather. In addition to traditional holidays, the sites offer themed weekends, and they now also have self-catering facilities. The Bognor Regis site, in West Sussex, has three hotels and a range of restaurants. Center Parcs entered the British market in 1987, providing undercover facilities in a futuristic glazed structure that contains a large pool and high-quality accommodation for people who may not have traditionally stayed at holiday camps. Warner's has moved from the traditional holiday camp market into providing a child-free environment for couples, in hotels and on sites that were once traditional holiday camps. Potters Leisure Resort, near Great Yarmouth, has invested heavily in recent years in its indoor facilities, including extensive indoor bowling rinks. Therefore, annually in January, it hosts the World Indoor Bowls Championships and has the facilities to offer holiday breaks based around the sport. Like Saga, this is a deliberate strategy to target an older demographic, people with the time, disposable income and appetite for breaks all year round.

So, today, the character of tourism is more complex and varied than at any time in the past. The beach holiday, or at least a holiday at the coast, is still the centrepiece of modern British tourism, whether taken in Britain or abroad, but alongside it is a huge range of alternative tourist offers and leisure pursuits. The variety of attractions available is amusingly captured in a modern, humorous book, catchily named *Crap Days Out*. Among the visitor attractions that it mocks is Sellafield Power Station, in Cumbria, the World Black Pudding Throwing Championship at Ramsbottom, in Lancashire, and the Bog Snorkelling Championship and Man v Horse race, both of which are held at Llanwrtyd Wells, in Powys.[100]

Fig 10.15
Shopping centres, such as the White Rose Shopping Centre at Leeds, pictured here, are no longer simply a place for retail therapy, but have increasingly become leisure destinations and places to socialise. [AA022521]

Looking ahead

What about the future? In response to short-term fears regarding Britain's departure from the European Union, and in an attempt to encourage foreign tourists to leave London and enjoy the rest of the country, the government published in August 2016 its Tourism Action Plan, with £40 million being devoted to a Discover England Fund.[101] And since the creation in the 1990s of stronger, separate identities for each national tourist board, campaigns have sought to lure domestic and foreign tourists to all four corners of the United Kingdom. To cater for tourists from emerging economies, and particularly China, tourist destinations and facilities will have to adapt to meet their needs and tastes. There has also been a need to adapt to a new, greater threat from terrorism. Anyone boarding a plane or trying to enter a national museum or landmark in Britain or abroad will be acutely aware of new procedures required to ensure safety, sometimes meaning even longer waits for admission.

New portable, personal technology has already had a significant impact on tourism and although televisions are getting larger and cheaper and offer clearer pictures, more people are spending time on their tablets and phones, allowing them to enjoy home entertainment wherever they are travelling. Within a few weeks of its launch in 2016, the worldwide, but seemingly short-lived, phenomenon of Pokémon GO, an augmented reality game, captivated children of all ages, who went in search of characters that are generated as overlays on the real world. Some fairground rides are making use of virtual reality to turn a terrifying rollercoaster ride into a hair-raising trip through space, and affordable virtual reality headsets may allow people to experience the world in any number of ways. On Southwold Pier in 2002, artist, cartoonist and engineer Tim Hunkin (b 1950), perhaps presciently, installed Microbreak, which allows a person to 'sit in the chair and travel on holiday, moved by the magic carpet. After manic flight and coach ride, arrive in tropical paradise and get brief suntan from heatlamp.'[102] Why leave the comfort of your home, when your holiday can be brought to you? Fortunately, this dystopian vision of future holidays is unlikely to become reality and, regardless of the impact of Brexit, tourism at home and abroad will continue to be a major part of British life.

While the sky was the limit in the past, the expected advent of 'affordable' space travel means that the trip of a lifetime may be a weightless jaunt in a Virgin Galactic ship or a night in a Bigelow habitation in an orbiting space hotel.[103] However, for most people it will continue to be the seaside holiday that offers their main holiday of the year, whether it is at Aberdeenshire's bracing Cruden Bay, at a scorching Costa or on a Caribbean island.

Notes

Abbreviations

NHLE: National Heritage List for England
*ODNB: Oxford Dictionary of National
    Biography*

1 Introduction

1   Furlong 2009, 183.
2   Wells 2014, 176–7.
3   Brodie 2018 discusses in detail the issues
    facing seaside resorts today.
4   Pimlott 1976, 150.
5   Urry 2003.
6   Perkin 1976.
7   Miller 1888, 77.
8   Pimlott 1976, 78–9; Cunningham 1980, 57.
9   August 2013, 29.
10 August 2013, 30, 35; Oldham's Wakes are
    covered in detail in Poole 1983, 71–98.
11 Boulton 1971, 2, 44.
12 Cunningham 1980, 15.
13 Pimlott 1976, 79–80.
14 Ibid, 83.
15 Ibid, 80; Walvin 1978, 6–7; Cunningham
    1980, 66.
16 http://hansard.millbanksystems.com/
    commons/1832/jul/03/observance-of-
    the-sabbath [accessed 9 December 2017].
17 Pimlott 1976, 82.
18 Barton 2005, 89; Barton and Brodie 2014,
    I, 269.
19 Pimlott 1976, 142.
20 Barton and Brodie 2014, I, 270.
21 Barton 2005, 89.
22 Smee 1871, 3–4.
23 Act of Parliament 34 Vict c17; Simmons
    and Biddle 1999, 151.
24 Pimlott 1976, 144–5; *ODNB.*
25 Act of Parliament 38 & 39 Vict c13.
26 Kelly 1846, 103. Three of his diaries are
    known and published, though the
    destinations of two of his other holidays
    can be inferred from these sources. Palmer
    1943; Palmer 1944; Whyman 1980, 185–
    225.
27 Pimlott 1976, 155; Barton 2005, 113–4.
28 Barton 2005, 93–7.
29 *Report of the Committee on Holidays with
    Pay* 1937–8 Cmd 5724, 7; Pimlott 1976,
    215; Act of Parliament 18 & 19 Geo 5, c33.
30 *ODNB.*
31 Barton 2005, 127.

32 Act of Parliament 1 & 2 Geo 6 c70.
33 Brunner 1945, 13; Pimlott, 1976 221–2;
    Demetriadi 1997, 58.
34 Barton 2005, 219–20.
35 Ibid, 220.
36 Morgan and Pritchard 1999, 42.

2 The origins of tourism in Britain

1   Margary 1973, 18–33.
2   Stenton 1936, 1, 9.
3   Wise to the volume of people passing along
    some routes, some enterprising locals were
    known to try to exact tolls from pilgrims.
    Stenton 1936, 15.
4   Jennett 1971, 10, 15; Addison 1980, 60,
    63; Hindle 1998, 13.
5   Chaucer 1951, 25, 130, 305, 473; Margary
    1973, 34–52.
6   Wright 1988, 71–6.
7   Stenton 1936, 6; Hindle 1976, 208, 211,
    217–20; Wright 1988, 88–9; Hindle 1998,
    43–5; Taylor 2012; Salter 2015.
8   Stenton 1936, 16–17; Woolgar 1999, 187;
    Harvey 1969, xvii–xviii.
9   Anon 1750?, 7.
10 Stenton 1936, 18–19.
11 Addison 1980, 91.
12 Hindle 1998, 131.
13 Woolgar 1999, 187–8.
14 Chandler 1999, 226.
15 Addison 1980, 59.
16 Ibid, 59–60, 73.
17 Hindle 1993, 72.
18 Hindle 1976, 211, 213; Stenton 1936,
    19–20.
19 Heal 1990, 236; Bettey 1989, 30.
20 Heal 1990, 236. NHLE 1097028 and
    1240669.
21 Heal 1990, 201.
22 Ibid, 201–2.
23 Woolgar 1999, 23, 25.
24 Gabel 1988, 31; Heal 1990, 201.
25 Lewkenor 1693, 7–8.
26 Heal 1990, 206.
27 Heal 1990, 215–6; for example Chandler
    1999, 17, 19, 21, 23.
28 Chandler 1999, 110.
29 Heal 1990, 203.
30 Hindle 1976, 212.
31 Woolgar 1999, 188; Sellar and Yeatman
    1999, 34.

32 Hindle 1998, 17.
33 Woolgar 1999, 181–2.
34 Stenton 1936, 4.
35 Neild 1972, 3.
36 Neild 1972, 41.
37 Rosen 1981, 152, 158.
38 Jamieson and Lane 2015, 255–71.
39 Bazeley 1910; Warren 1961, 152.
40 Poole 1955, 29; Powicke 1962, 512–3.
41 http://avalon.law.yale.edu/medieval/excheq.
    asp#b1p11 [accessed 9 December 2017].
42 Colvin 1963, II, for example 671, 899, 937,
    938–9, 988–9, 1009–10.
43 James and Robinson 1988, 1, 267.
44 Ibid, 4, 267; Colvin 1963, II, 910.
45 Colvin 1963, I, 121; Colvin 1963, II, 912;
    James and Robinson 1988, 7–8.
46 James and Robinson 1988, 40ff, 268.
47 Robinson 1998, 10.
48 Norton and Park 1986, 40–1, 68.
49 Ibid, 76–8, 85.
50 Hindle 1998, 27.
51 Spencer 2010, 13–14.
52 Addison 1980, 60; *ODNB.*
53 For example 28 September 1443 (vol 2, 55),
    18 November 1456 (vol 3, 112), 15 Sept-
    ember 1471 (vol 5, 109) *in* Gardiner 1987.
54 Spencer 2010, 135.
55 Pritchard 2009.
56 Walsham 2011, 52.
57 Webb 2001, 213. Aeneas Sylvius visited
    Scotland in the 1440s and encountered the
    administrative and practical difficulties of
    travelling between the countries. Gabel
    1988, 28–32.
58 Webb 2001, 214, 221–2.
59 Ibid, 214–5.
60 Spencer 1990, 7; Spencer 2010, 16.
61 Spencer 2010, 10–11.
62 Gerald of Wales 1978; Gerald of Wales
    1982.
63 *ODNB.*
64 Harvey 1969, 316–7, 333. This is one of
    the earliest drawings of medieval
    mouldings anywhere in Europe.
65 Ibid, 53–7.
66 Ibid, 99–103. The submersion myth may
    be a reflection of the rising sea levels that
    occurred at the end of the last Ice Age, and
    eventually created the modern archipelago
    of the Isles of Scilly from a single or pair of
    larger islands.
67 Ibid, 181–5.

68 Ibid, 181.
69 Ibid, 283, 291.
70 Ibid, 31–3.
71 *ODNB*; Toulmin Smith 1964, vii–xx.
72 Hindle 1998, 17.
73 Saunders 2012, 24–7.
74 Steinke 1974, 505–6; Crossley 1981.
75 Crossley 2003, 73ff.
76 Morris 1984, 69.
77 Walsham 2011, 105.
78 Morris 1984, 158–9; Tyrer 1968, I, 40, 60, 142–3.
79 Hindle 1998, 17.
80 Act of Parliament 2 & 3 Ph & M, c8; Addison 1980, 86–7; Wright 1988, 90; Taylor 2012, 58.
81 Addison 1980, 87; Act of Parliament 5 Eliz I c13.
82 Addison 1980, 91.
83 Ibid, 92.
84 Osborne 1989, 18.
85 Heal 1990, 307–8; Osborne 1989, 19.
86 Osborne 1989, 20.
87 Wright 1988, 100.
88 Osborne 1989, 129.
89 Ibid, 48.
90 Ibid, 72–4.
91 Ibid, 74ff, 110; Keay and Watkins 2013, 6–7, 48.
92 Keay and Watkins 2013, 48 citing Kuin 1983, 16.
93 Davis and Bonsall 1996, 24; Cunliffe 1969, 112; Wroughton 2006, 89–93.
94 Hembry 1990, 27, 29–31; Manco 1992, 29; Shakespeare may be referring to the town in sonnet 153:
    And grew a seething bath, which yet men prove
    Against strange maladies a sovereign cure.
95 Hembry 1990, 6–7; Turner 1562.
96 Wood 1969, 71–7; Quinn 1999, 74–5.
97 Cunliffe 1969.
98 Scwell 1846, 38; Osborne and Weaver 1996, 239–40.
99 McIntyre 1981, 201; Manco 1992, 26; Fawcett and Bird 1994, 17–20.
100 McIntyre 1981, 201.
101 Chapman 1673, 3; Hembry 1990, 2; Fawcett and Bird 1994, 26–8.
102 Havins 1976, 28–9; Davis and Bonsall 1996, 22; Cunliffe 1986, 109–10.
103 Hembry 1990, 26, 27, 29; Cunliffe 1986, 108; Manco 1992, 27.
104 McIntyre 1981, 202.
105 Hembry 1990, 32, 33, 39; Davis and Bonsall 1996, 24.
106 Turner 1562; Jones (1) 1572; Hembry 1990, 27, 54.
107 Hembry 1990, 31–2; Davis and Bonsall 1996, 27; Wroughton 2006, 121; Act of Parliament 14 Eliz 1, c5.
108 Wood 1969, 207; Fawcett and Bird 1994, 30.
109 Hembry 1990, 57–8.
110 McIntyre 1981, 204; Manco 1992, 29.

111 Tyrer 1968–72, 38 (23 June 1703); Atkins *c* 1730, 32.
112 Jones 1572 (1); Jones 1572 (2).
113 *ODNB*; Hembry 1990, 10.
114 CSP Scotland 1907, 21.
115 Heape 1948, 22–4.
116 Thornes and Leach 1991; Thornes and Leach 1994.
117 *ODNB*; Toulmin Smith 1964, 86.
118 Grainge 1871, 109–10; Alderson 1973, 73; Denbigh 2000, 5.
119 Mitchell 1986, 189.
120 De Seta 1996, 13.
121 Brennan 2002, 7; *ODNB*.
122 *ODNB*.
123 Stoye 1989, 73; Chaney 1996, 95; Watkin 2000, 50; *ODNB*.
124 Watkin 2000, 51; *ODNB*.
125 Ringler 1962, xx–xxiii; Trease 1967, 22–5; Duncan-Jones 1991, 63–85; Brennan 2002, 10; *ODNB*.
126 Trease 1967, 35–43; Stoye 1989, 73; Brennan 2002, 11; *ODNB*.
127 Moryson 1617.
128 Stoye 1989, 74. Despite major European wars, the 18th century proved more peaceful and easier for travellers; Ingamells 1996, 21.
129 De Seta 1996, 14; *ODNB*.
130 Harris *et al* 1973, 17, 55–6; Stoye 1989, 74–5; Worsley 2007, 19–30; Hart 2011, 11–14; *ODNB*.
131 Brennan 2002, 16.
132 *ODNB*; Jones 1971; Hart 2011, 50–55.

3   The spa 1500–1800

1   Scott 1894, 14.
2   Burr 1766, 5–6.
3   Ibid, 6–14.
4   Ibid, 23–5.
5   Rowzee 1632; Chalklin 2008, 2.
6   Havins 1976, 25; Hembry 1990, 48.
7   Wittie 1667, 5.
8   Wittie 1660, 7–8.
9   Wroughton 2004, 24–9, 163–5; Davis and Bonsall 1996, 22; Fawcett and Bird 1994, 34–6.
10 Hembry 1990, 53, 59; Fawcett and Bird 1994, 36; Quinn 1999, 82.
11 Hembry 1990, 66.
12 Wood 1969, 217–19; Barbeau 2009, 19, 25; Davis and Bonsall 1996, 25; Fawcett and Bird 1994, 41; Addison 1951, 61, 63.
13 McIntyre 1981, 202.
14 Hembry 1990, 56; Osborne and Weaver 1996, 237.
15 Osborne and Weaver 1996, 237; Manco 1992, 36.
16 Osborne and Weaver 1996, 236.
17 Ibid, 235–6.
18 Hembry 1990, 89, 91; Cunliffe 1986, 111.
19 Manco 1992, 36, 39; Osborne and Weaver 1996, 236.

20 Hembry 1990, 91.
21 Borsay 2014, 51–2.
22 Burr 1766, 38, 44–5.
23 Farthing 1990, introduction.
24 Burr 1766, 47.
25 *ODNB*; Gregg 1980, 46–7, 55–61; Somerset 2012, 56–9, 69, 91, 93.
26 Burr 1766, 55–6; Anon 1993, 4. Chalklin 2008, 7, says the fire took place in June 1688.
27 Lewkenor 1693, 46–7.
28 Hembry 1990, 105.
29 Addison 1951, 14, 16.
30 Morris 1984, 238.
31 Macky 1714, 113, Havins 1976, 27.
32 Hembry 1990, 99–100; Curl 2010, 32–3, 39, 43–5.
33 Hembry 1990, 99–100; Curl 2010, 49–55.
34 Hembry 1990, 97.
35 Floyer 1697, 4.
36 Hembry 1990, 96; Denbigh 2000, 7.
37 Hembry 1990, 50.
38 Morris 1984, 93.
39 Digby 1994, 209; Borsay 2000 (1), 783.
40 Anon 2003, 51, 49.
41 Defoe 1986, 532.
42 Anon 1893, 134.
43 Hembry 1990, 98; Tyrer 1968–72, 1, 142 (24 June 1707), 2, 50 (21 June 1712), 3, 50 (10 July 1721).
44 Tyrer 1968–72, 1, 142 (24 June 1707).
45 Morris 1984, 158.
46 Defoe 1986, 388.
47 Mitchell 1986, 189; Deane 1626; Rowzee 1632
48 Hinderwell 1811, 201ff; Rowntree 1931, 249.
49 Simpson 1669; Tunstall 1670; Poynter 1953, vol 2, 72–81; Rowntree 1931, 248–50.
50 Simpson 1679.
51 Chapman 1673, 9.
52 Wood 1742, 90.
53 Floyer 1697.
54 Allen 1711, 2.
55 King 1737; Cheyne 1724.
56 Atkins *c* 1730.
57 Brodie 2012 (2), 131–2.
58 Lewkenor 1693, 75–6.
59 Burr 1766, 7.
60 Ibid.
61 Addison 1951, 121–2; Short 1734.
62 Hembry 1990, 92–3, 113; Wood 1969, 221; Fawcett and Bird 1994, 45; Cunliffe 1986, 112.
63 Hembry 1990, 114, 143; Cunliffe 1986, 115.
64 *ODNB*; Goldsmith 1762; Barbeau 2009, 36ff; Davis and Bonsall 1996, 41; Eglin 2005.
65 Anon 1725, 117–18.
66 Eglin 2005, 63–4.
67 Barbeau 2009, 40.
68 Hembry 1990, 114–15.

69 Anon 1725, 114–15.
70 Ison 1991, 25; Davis and Bonsall 1996, 29; Morriss 1993, 59.
71 Anon 1725, 117.
72 Anstey 1994, 59–62.
73 Wood 1742; Anon 1734.
74 Neale 1981, 131.
75 Wood 1742, 19–20.
76 Neale 1981, 151; Ison 1991, 115–20; Fawcett and Bird 1994, 50; Morriss 1993, 19–21, 79.
77 Davis and Bonsall 1996, 31; Fawcett and Bird 1994, 55; Mitchell and Penrose 1983, 7–8; Borsay 2000 (2), 104ff.
78 Ison 1991, 141ff; Neale 1981, 155; Mitchell and Penrose 1983, 11.
79 Neale 1981, 183; Cunliffe 1986, 132.
80 Ison 1991, 27ff, 148–51; Fawcett and Bird 1994, 61; Morriss 1993, 59, 88.
81 Ison 1991, 41ff; Hembry 1990, 126.
82 Neale 1981, 228–34; Ison 1991, 46ff; Davis and Bonsall 1996, 29, 32–3; Borsay 2000 (2), 202–6.
83 Neale 1981, 260, 262–3; Cunliffe 1986, 145; Ison 1991, 15; Fawcett and Bird 1994, 67, 69; Davis and Bonsall 1996, 46.
84 Carey 1799, 136–43.
85 Hembry 1990, 134–5.
86 Neale 1981, 31–2; Hill 1989; Davis and Bonsall 1996, 43; Fawcett and Bird 1994, 62.
87 Hembry 1990, 156.
88 Neale 1981, 266; Ison 1991, 17; Morriss 1993, 69; Jackson 1991, 35–7.
89 Hembry 1990, 141–2.
90 Burr 1766, 62–3.
91 Ibid, 64–5.
92 Macky 1722, 1, 94–6.
93 Ibid, 1, 96.
94 Goldsmith 1762, 45–6.
95 Burr 1766, 100–101.
96 Ibid, 101.
97 Goldsmith 1762, 49.
98 Chalklin 2008, 32.
99 Carey 1799, 51ff.
100 Anon 1993, 5. Chalklin 2008, 43, says this took place between 1801 and 1805.
101 Carey 1799, 52.
102 Defoe 1986, 469.
103 Heape 1948, 28–30; Pigot 1976, 25; Stroud 2002, 10–11.
104 Hembry 1990, 203.
105 Smollett 1995, 149.
106 Hembry 1990, 208–9.
107 Smollett 1995, 150.
108 Ibid.
109 Hembry 1990, 205; ODNB.
110 Hembry 1990, 208; Hargrove 1801.
111 Hembry 1990, 207.
112 ODNB.
113 Hembry 1990, 172; Curl 2010, 92.
114 Bevis 1760.
115 Curl 2010, 94–5.
116 Ibid, 99.
117 Hembry 1990, 180.

118 Little 1952, 28; Havins 1976, 34; Blake and Beacham 1982, 33; Hembry 1990, 179. Hart 1981, 115, dates its discovery to 1718.
119 Anon 1783, 374.
120 Little 1952, 32–3.
121 Addison 1951, 113; Hart 1981, 117; Blake and Beacham 1982, 33; Hembry 1990, 181.
122 Little 1952, 34; Hart 1981, 117; Humphris and Willoughby 2008, 31–3.
123 Little 1952, 35; Hembry 1990, 182, 184–5, 189.
124 Fothergill 1785; Little 1952, 35–6; Hembry 1990, 186, 188; Hart 1981, 125. Moreau's appointment took place in 1780 according to Little 1952, 35, while Hembry 1990, 185, states it occurred in 1781. Hembry 1990, 187.
125 Act of Parliament 26 Geo III, c116; Blake and Beacham 1982, 103; Hembry 1990, 190; Hodsdon 1997, ix–x. An Act in 1806 extended the powers of the Improvement Commissioners. Hart 1981, 243–4.
126 Hembry 1990, 189.
127 Hart 1981, 123.
128 Williams 1788; Humphris and Willoughby 2008, 50ff; Little 1952, 35, 39–41, 186, 191–2.
129 Addison 1951, 114; Hembry 1990, 186.
130 Little 1952, 51–2; Hembry 1990, 195, 198; Hart 1981, 137, 140.
131 Hembry 1990, 193–4.
132 Anon 1787, 171.
133 Durie 2003, 66.
134 Boyd 1987, 6.
135 Mawman 1805, 195.
136 Anon 1734, 47–68.
137 Whittaker 1984, 69; Hembry 1990, 211; Binns 2003, 102.
138 Whittaker 1984, 52.
139 Smollett 1995, 166–9.

4 The Georgian seaside

1   Vicary 1587, 55; http://www.france-thalasso.com/XVIe-siecle [accessed 9 December 2017].
2   Mulcaster 1581, 95; Markham 1610, 167; Vicary 1613, 194–5.
3   Manship 1854, 104.
4   Wittie 1660, 46–50; Wittie 1667, 172.
5   Floyer 1702, 191.
6   Floyer and Baynard 1706, 26.
7   Floyer 1702, 193.
8   Walton 1974, 234–5; Walton 1983, 10.
9   Tyrer 1968–72, I, 181.
10 Ibid, 225.
11 Jones 1718.
12 Neller 2000, 13, citing Lincolnshire Record Office LAO, MASS 13/16.
13 Anon 1734; John Setterington, *View of the antient Town, Castle, Harbour, and Spaw of Scarborough* 1735; Anon 1732.
14 Anon 1734, 36.

15 Evans 1821, 37.
16 Whyman 1985, 160.
17 A detailed discussion can be found in Brodie 2012 (1).
18 Tyrer 1968–72, III, 52, 2 August 1721.
19 Shaw 1735, 35–6.
20 John Setterington, *View of the antient Town, Castle, Harbour, and Spaw of Scarborough* 1735.
21 Peet 1908, 55-6; Touzeau 1910, 358–9, 398.
22 British Library Maps K.Top.18.76.a. This was the site of a bathhouse shown on a 1765 map, the first to depict this area of the town in any detail. Liverpool's 18th-century maps are reviewed in Stewart-Brown 1911, 143–74.
23 Temple Patterson 1966, 39; Brodie 2012 (1).
24 Simpson 1997, 40; Hasted 1800, 517; Anon 1810, 261; Gill 1993, 193; Rolf 2011, 51; Miskell 2011, 115–7.
25 Bread 1859, 4.
26 Parkin 1776, 13.
27 Cartwright 1888–9, I, 102.
28 Moule 1883, 125.
29 Angerstein 2001, 69.
30 Simpson 1997, 40; Durie 2003, 67.
31 Durie 2003, 66; Simpson 2013, 17.
32 Simpson 1997, 38; Durie 2003, 67, says 1778.
33 Durie 2003, 67.
34 Borsay 2011, 87–8.
35 Cartwright 1888–9, II, 6, 2 June 1754.
36 Hutton 1789, 20; Baines 1824, 526.
37 Hutton 1789, 5, 34–7.
38 Bailey 1955, 29, 34; Glazebrook 1826, 59–64; Alsop 1832, 39; Robinson 1848, 25.
39 Smith 1991, 3.
40 Pevsner 1989, 619; Robinson 1981, 57.
41 Lackington 1974, 312.
42 Henstock 1980, 71.
43 Neller 2000, 14; Kime 2005, 21–2.
44 Park (nd) 1.
45 Floyer and Baynard 1706, 222.
46 Russell 1752, 65.
47 Shaw 1735, 36–8.
48 Russell 1752, v–vi.
49 Anderson 1795, 15.
50 Anon 1732, 7; Brodie 2012 (2), 144–8.
51 Keate 1779, I, 81.
52 Reid 1795, 8; Crane 1795, 87.
53 Cole 1828, 109.
54 Rymer 1777, 17.
55 Anderson 1795, 32.
56 Lewis 1736 in the Society of Antiquaries Library.
57 Cartwright 1888–9, II, 86.
58 Angerstein 2001, 227–8.
59 Awsiter 1768, 4.
60 For instance, Anon 1765, 67-8; Smollett 1995, 166–7.
61 Anon 1770a, 22–3.
62 Anderson 1795, 29, 56, 57.
63 Bulley 1956, 143–62, 146; Griffiths 2001, 57; Griffiths and Griffiths 1965, 46.

64 Anon 1794, 69; Anon c 1830, 34; Whereat c 1855, 42.
65 Lyons 1763, 12; Hall 1790, 9; Cozens 1793, 3.
66 Kent Archives and Local History Service R/U696/T12/1.
67 Kent Archives and Local History Service R/U696/T12/2; Lyons 1763, 12.
68 Anon 1770b, 15–16; Anon 1797a, 61; Anon 1800, 86.
69 Anon 1809, 50; Anon 1822, 38–9.
70 Reid 1795, 70.
71 British Library Maps K.Top.17.7.d.
72 Anon 1797a, 104; Anon 1797b, 70.
73 Whyman 1985, 160.
74 *The Kentish Post, or Canterbury News Letter*, 27 April 1737 cited in Whyman 1985, 161.
75 *The Kentish Post, or Canterbury News Letter*, May 1740 cited in Whyman 1985, 161.
76 Awsiter 1768, 15; Reid 1795, 15–17.
77 Awsiter 1768, 17–18; Anon 1780, 27; Farrant 1980, 15, 19, 21; Berry 2002, 103–4.
78 Anon 1780, 28.
79 Anon c 1830, 34; Lewis 1840, II, 377; Baines 1986, 305.
80 Osborne 1860, 61.
81 Whyman 1985, 170–2.
82 Historic England Archive File 86314.
83 Mahomed 1822, opposite 37.
84 Anon 1846, 35–6; Boddy and West 1983, 139; Anon 1859a, 673.
85 Bruyn Andrews 1934–5, I, 87.
86 Macky 1722, I, 50; Lewis 1736, 123.
87 Anon 1732, 1ff.
88 Sympson 1679, 5–6.
89 Anon 1734, 38–9; Brodie 2012 (2), 140–4.
90 Whyman 1985, 268; Anon 1822, 36.
91 Hall 1790, 10; Cozens 1793, 25.
92 Hall 1790, 10–11.
93 Cozens 1793, 25.
94 Lyons 1763, 16; Clarke 1975, 76; Baines 1986, 304–5; Moss 1824, 168.
95 Colvin 1995, 281–2 (a plaque on the building dates the facade to 1766); Walton 1983, 158.
96 Berry 2005, 27.
97 Schopenhauer 1988, 133.
98 Anon 1797a, 57; Anon 1822, 34.
99 Anon 1770b, 13–14.
100 Cozens 1793, 24.
101 Berry 2002, 105; Hutton 1789, 37–8.
102 Staelens 1989, 31; Lee 1795, 536–7.
103 Parkin 1776, 400; Anon 1806, 20, 61.
104 Hembry 1990, 210.
105 Relhan 1761, 15.
106 Anon 1785, 57.
107 Hunter 1998, 135–8.
108 Miele 1998, 149, 156.
109 Berry 2002, 99.
110 Schopenhauer 1988, 130.

111 Morley 1984, 13, 32ff; Brighton Polytechnic School of Architecture and Interior Design 1987, 26–30; Berry 2005, 46–62.
112 Brodie et al 2008, 9.
113 Anon 1797c, 16.
114 Bread 1859, 5; Hern 1967, 57.
115 Keate 1779, II, 200–1.
116 Ibid, I, 104–5.
117 Ison 1991, 5–6.
118 Anon 1809, 14; Anon undated [1770s].
119 Berry 2009, 124–5; Berry 2015, 213.
120 Hay 1794, 45; Anon 1838, 5; Butler 1984, 2; Young 1983, 1–8.
121 Young 1983, 47; Butler 1984, 2.
122 Brannon 1867, 9.
123 Sherry 1972, 129.
124 Anon 1837, 37.
125 Ibid, 39.
126 Dale 1967, 113–19.
127 Berry 2015, 219.
128 Anon 1825.
129 Pevsner 1967, 281.
130 Colvin 1995, 47. However, according to Colvin 1995, 252 ,William Barnard Clarke is another name associated with Hayling Island.
131 Anon 1843, 17–18. The library was bought in 1867 by G R Divett who enlarged the building and converted it into a house, named on the 1872 map as 'The Lodge'. Trigg 1892, 37.
132 Anon 1843, 16, 18.
133 Anon 1817, 71; Morrice 2001, 94.
134 Moss 1824, 146; Morrice 2001, 96–7, 102.
135 Baines 1956, 50.
136 Ibid, 23.
137 Baines 1990, 9, 11.
138 Baines 1956, 28, 37; Baines 1990, 28–9.
139 Bulley 156, 150.
140 Colvin 1995, 717.
141 Anon 1841, 92.
142 Colvin 1995, 456–7.
143 Kent Archives and Local History Service, K/Herne Bay, Herne Bay Pier Company Prospectus 1831.
144 Anon 1835, 5.
145 Anon 1859b, 2; Gough 2002, 10.
146 Anon 1835, 12.
147 Kelly 1855, 394.
148 Colvin 1995, 470.

5 Transport and tourism 1500–1939

1 Copeland 1968, 85; Pawson 1977, 282; Baker and Gerhold 1995, 35.
2 Addison 1980, 93–5.
3 Copeland 1968, 16; Act of Parliament 14 Cha c6.
4 Copeland 1968, 16; Taylor 1979, 155; Wright 1988, 143; Wright 2008, 5.
5 Wright 2008, 5.
6 Dyos and Aldcroft 1969, 33; Wright 1988, 143; Wright 2008, 5.

7 Copeland 1968, 24; Wright 2008, 22–23.
8 Dyos and Aldcroft 1969, 72; Albert 1972, 44, 49; Pawson 1977, 136, 141, 143, 152, 158.
9 Albert 1972, 14.
10 Taylor 1979, 155; Moore-Colyer 2007, 139.
11 Moore-Colyer 2007, 139.
12 Addison 1980, 102; Pawson 1977, 144.
13 Taylor 1979, 169; Wright 2008, 10.
14 Durie 2012, 31.
15 Pawson 1977, 153; Wright 2008, 12.
16 Taylor 1979,155.
17 Dyos and Aldcroft 1969, 78–9.
18 Smollett 1995, 151.
19 Ibid, 294, 173.
20 Copeland 1968, 97–8.
21 Austen 1997, 1.
22 Wright 1988, 143.
23 Ibid, 120.
24 Bruyn Andrews 1934–5, 1, 72, 23 August 1782.
25 Ibid, 1, 6, 3 June 1781.
26 Ransom 1984, 20.
27 Pawson 1977, 285.
28 Ibid, 289.
29 Grosley 1772, 11.
30 Austen 1981, 27; Ransom 1984, 29, 110; Baker and Gerhold 1995, 37.
31 Dyos and Aldcroft 1969, 76; Dodd and Dodd 1980, 133.
32 Copeland 1968, 86, 88.
33 Hutton Beale 1891, 130.
34 Dodd and Dodd 1980, 132.
35 Copeland 1968, 85.
36 Pawson 1977, 289; Dodd and Dodd 1980, 131.
37 Austen 1981, 27.
38 Baker and Gerhold 1995, 37.
39 Walton 1983, 21.
40 Ransom 1984, 108.
41 Barker and Savage 1974, 27.
42 Wright 1988, 120.
43 Turnbull 1977, 19; Gerhold 1993, 69.
44 Freeman 1977, 69; Harvey 1800, 83; Ryall 1800, 67–8.
45 Schopenhauer 1988, 45–8.
46 Tower 1871–4, 365–6.
47 Gray 1996, 75.
48 Morris 1984, 185.
49 Albert 1972, 37, 44; Wright 1988,147–8.
50 Morris 1984, 127.
51 Smith 1982, 201ff.
52 Hembry 1990, 212.
53 Albert 1972, 205.
54 Ibid, 206, 211.
55 Ibid, 214.
56 Pawson 1977, 277.
57 Gough 1983, 3; Anon 1835, 18. By the 1830s, the road brought in around £500 per year and it remained in the control of the turnpike trust until November 1887.
58 Anon 1859b, 2.
59 Copeland 1968, 100.
60 Moore-Colyer 2007, 137.

61 Taylor 1979, 161; Dodd and Dodd 1980, 131.
62 Dodd and Dodd 1980, 131–2; Wright 1988, 17, 21.
63 Wright 2008, 17.
64 Taylor 1979, 162.
65 Bagwell 1974, 138.
66 Ibid, 45.
67 Miller 1888, 124.
68 Taylor 1979, 163.
69 Barker and Savage 1974, 123–4.
70 Keate 1779, I, 104–5, II, 200–1.
71 Anon 1770b, 22; Whyman 1981, 114; Scurrell 1982, 60.
72 Anon 1810, 304; Whyman 1993, 35.
73 Lyons 1763, 15.
74 Durie 2012, 72ff.
75 Greswell 1807?, 69–72.
76 For instance, by sea to Scarborough from London (Anon 1734) or on canals and rivers in central Scotland (Guthrie 1822, 11–21, 33–44, 59–68).
77 Wright 2008, 12.
78 Bagwell 1974, 30.
79 Walton 1983, 21–2.
80 Phillips 1970, 244.
81 Bagwell 1974, 30.
82 Cleland 1816, 2, 393–4.
83 Ibid, 396.
84 Durie 2003, 47.
85 Whyman 1981, 117.
86 Durie 2003, 49; Whyman 1981, 122.
87 Stafford & Yates 1985, 75.
88 Clarke 1975, 26; Whyman 1985, 65; Whyman 1981, 124, 127.
89 Whyman 1985, 25.
90 Ibid, 24.
91 Bagwell 1974, 45.
92 Towner 1996, 195.
93 Information supplied by Alastair Durie.
94 Thomas 1971, 161–3, 166, 183; Towner 1996, 195.
95 http://www.waverleyexcursions.co.uk [accessed 9 December 2017].
96 Cleland 1816, 2, 395.
97 Durie 2003, 48.
98 Fry 1826–9, 70–1.
99 Watts 1820, 16.
100 Durie 2003, 50–1.
101 Anon 1806, 22.
102 Wills and Phillips 2014, 173.
103 Kidd 1831, 46; Fischer and Walton 1987, 12.
104 *ODNB*; http://www.grantonhistory.org/ buildings/chain_pier.htm [accessed 9 December 2017].
105 Bishop 1896, 6–18, 40–7.
106 Anon 1834, 4. Although this form of design was closely associated with Samuel Brown, two other examples were erected: at Greenhithe on the Thames in the 1840s (demolished in 1875) and at Seaview on the Isle of Wight in 1880, which survived into the 1950s. Easdown 2007, 11, 13. A company was formed by a Mr Birch in

1842 to build Greenhithe pier. Adamson 1977, 28.
107 Armstrong and Bagwell 1983, 163.
108 Lewis 1840, 226; Clarke 1975, 25; Easdown 2007, 60.
109 Fischer and Walton 1987, 35; Anon 1835, 5.
110 Easdown 2007, 19, 35.
111 Fischer and Walton 1987, 49; *ODNB*.
112 *ODNB*.
113 Adamson 1974, 47.
114 Easdown 2007, 60–73.
115 Walton 1983, 31.
116 Turnock 1998, 54.
117 Searle 1982, 12.
118 Whishaw 1969, 78; Pearson 1968, 284.
119 Walton 1980, 124.
120 Clapham 1967, 400.
121 Simmons and Biddle 1999, 207.
122 Ibid, 51; Turnock 1998, 94.
123 Simmons and Biddle 1999; Walton 1998, 23–4.
124 Turnock 1998, 227; Millward 2003, 212–3.
125 Baker 1990, 161.
126 Millward 2003, 220.
127 Walton 1980, 129.
128 Parry 1983, 177.
129 Aston and Bond 2000, 179.
130 Simmons 1986, 252; Biddle 1990, 131; Turnock 1998, 228.
131 Millward 2003, 214.
132 Simmons 1986, 258–9; Turnock 1998, 228; Simmons and Biddle 1999, 207, 212; http://www.norfolk-on-line.co.uk/ hunstanton-norfolk/new-hunstanton [accessed 9 December 2017].
133 Simmons 1986, 257: Biddle 1990, 132.
134 Simmons 1986, 257; Simmons and Biddle 1999, 207, 212; Biddle 2003, 381–3.
135 Jordan and Jordan 1991, 233; Biddle 1990, 132; Ekberg 1986, 60.
136 Cannadine 1980, 410–11.
137 Walton 1979, 195; Biddle 1990, 132.
138 Biddle 1990, 132–3.
139 Walton 1980, 125.
140 Walton 1979, 201.
141 Ibid, 197–8, 200–201, 205, 208; Simmons 1986, 255; Biddle 1990, 132–3.
142 Simmons and Biddle 1999, 212.
143 https://en.wikipedia.org/wiki/Cruden_ Bay_Hotel_Tramway [accessed 9 December 2017].
144 Turnock 1998, 229.
145 Carter 1989, 36.
146 Clonmore 1933, 94.
147 Simmons 1986, 244–5.
148 Ibid, 245.
149 Turnock 1998, 228.
150 Butt 1995, 100.
151 Cannadine 1980 237–8: Biddle 1990, 130.
152 Turnock 1998, 228.
153 Walton 1980, 121.
154 Anon 1876, X, 512.

155 Walton 1974, 234–5.
156 Kellett 1969, 90.
157 Walton 1983, 22.
158 Ekberg 1986, 60.
159 Walton 1983, 23; Walton 1998, 139.
160 Morgan and Pritchard 1999, 106, 111.
161 Ibid, 121.
162 Turnock 1998, 263.
163 Thomas 1980, 195.
164 Thomas 1971, 45, 54.
165 Ibid, 89.
166 Jordan and Jordan 1991, 41.
167 Thomas 1980, 196.
168 Simmons and Biddle 1999, 150.
169 Bagwell 1974, 127–8; Pimlott 1976, 161.
170 Simmons and Biddle 1999, 207, 516.
171 Jordan and Jordan 1991, 110; Simmons and Biddle 1999, 151.
172 Anon 1977; Brodie and Winter 2007, 181–2.
173 Jordan and Jordan 1991, 115; Simmons and Biddle 1999, 151.
174 Simmons and Biddle 1999, 150; Walton 1983, 28.
175 Thomas 1980, 197.
176 Jordan and Jordan 1991, 112.
177 *The Stirling Observer*, 18 June 1929.
178 Simmons and Biddle 1999, 112; Horn 1999, 127; Jordan and Jordan 1991, 13; Turnock 1998, 261; *ODNB*.
179 Simmons and Biddle 1999, 150.
180 Durie 2003, 72.
181 Ekberg 1986, 61.
182 Verne 1992, 89–90; Durie 2003, 72.
183 Kilvert 1977, 266.
184 Jordan and Jordan 1991, 24–5.
185 Perkin 1976, 184.
186 Jordan and Jordan 1991, 35.
187 Turnock 1998, 261.
188 *Dunfermline Sunday Press*, 14 September 1867, 4.
189 Jordan and Jordan 1991, 41.
190 White 1998, 79; Simmons 1986, 252; Biddle 1990, 131.
191 Bagwell 1974, 150; Watson and Gray 1978, 111–4, 116–8; Barton and Brodie 2014, 143–5; *ODNB*.
192 Watson and Gray 1978, 16–17, 119–20; http://www.makingthemodernworld.org. uk/icons_of_invention/technology/ 1880-1939/IC.025 [accessed 9 December 2017]; *ODNB*.
193 Watson and Gray 1978, 120–2; Barton and Brodie 2014, 143–4.
194 Watson and Gray 1978, 131.
195 Greene 1889; Gotch 1889.
196 Pimlott 1976, 167; Watson and Gray 1978, 22, 114–5.
197 Walvin 1978, 93.
198 Watson and Gray 1978, 133–4.
199 Ibid, 134–9; Barton and Brodie 2014, 144.
200 Walvin 1978, 93.
201 Pimlott 1976, 167 n1.
202 Ibid, 196.

203 Bobbitt 2000, 29–31.
204 Durie 2017, 37–8.
205 Ibid, 38.
206 Bagwell 1974, 90, 150.
207 Barker and Savage 1974, 131; Bagwell 1974, 151, 199.
208 Act of Parliament 41 & 42 Vict c58.
209 Morrison and Minnis 2012, 7.
210 Ibid, 8–9.
211 Ibid, 8; Zuelow 2016, 115; Act of Parliament 59 & 60 Vict c36.
212 Morrison and Minnis 2012, 9; http://www.veterancarrun.com [accessed 9 December 2017]; https://en.wikipedia.org/wiki/London_to_Brighton_Veteran_Car_Run [accessed 9 December 2017].
213 Thorold 2003, 51; Strange and Carnevali 2007, 112.
214 Barker and Savage 1974, 136; Act of Parliament 3 Edw 7 c36.
215 Miller 1888, 104.
216 Anderson and Edmund 1978, 35.
217 Walton 2010a, 75–6.
218 Morton 1927, vii.
219 Bagwell 1974, 228.
220 Roberts 1976, 212.
221 Walvin 1978, 141.
222 Morrison and Minnis 2012, 391.
223 Ibid, 392.
224 Maitland 1936, 19.
225 Morrison and Minnis 2012, 194–5.
226 Thorold 2003, 108; Morrison and Minnis 2012, 186–7.
227 Morrison and Minnis 2012, 174; 185–7.
228 Ibid, 277ff.
229 Minnis 2014, 156–9, EPW007656.
230 Morgan and Pritchard 1999, 74.
231 https://en.wikipedia.org/wiki/Motorail_%28British_Rail%29 [accessed 9 December 2017].
232 Roberts 1976, 212.
233 Barton 2005, 163–4.
234 Anon 1938, 240. Another writer in 1936 described the first Butlin's holiday camp as 'a remarkable venture', but cautioned against the spread of Elizabethan-style chalets to Dorset cliffs or a Cornish cove. Brenan 1936, 15.
235 Hardy and Ward 1984, 72; Joad 1957, 88.
236 Hardy and Ward 1984, 90.
237 Mills 1989, 175.
238 Jenkinson 2003, 6; Jenkinson 1998, 7.
239 Jenkinson 1998, 34.
240 Braggs and Harris 2000, 39.
241 Whiteman 1973, 208–12.
242 Barton 2005, 165.
243 Braggs and Harris 2000, 39.
244 Barber 2001, 24.
245 http://webarchive.nationalarchives.gov.uk/20080108051731/http://www.dft.gov.uk/pgr/statistics/datatablcspublications/tsgb/edition2006.pdf (table 6.1) [accessed 9 December 2017].
246 Brunner 1945, 6.

6 In search of Britain

1 Vaughan 1974, 81.
2 Defoe 1986, 16.
3 Macky 1714; Macky 1722; Macky 1723; Macky 1725.
4 ODNB.
5 Hutton Beale 1891.
6 Anon 1725.
7 Vaughan 1974, 62.
8 O'Byrne 2003, 22–3.
9 Moss 2007.
10 Anon 1734.
11 Wood 1742; Hembry 1990, 150. Relhan 1761 is an early seaside history/guide for Brighton.
12 Lyons 1763; Anon 1765.
13 Carey 1799.
14 Granville 1841.
15 Luke 1919, 165–8, 273.
16 Vaughan 1974, 87.
17 Anon 1868.
18 Rubenhold 2005, 11; Linane 2003, 85–6.
19 Zuelow 2016, 78.
20 Vaughan 1974, 47; https://en.wikipedia.org/wiki/Baedeker [accessed 9 December 2017].
21 Barton and Brodie 2014, I, 25–7; https://en.wikipedia.org/wiki/Black%27s_Guides [accessed 9 December 2017].
22 Vaughan 1974, 70.
23 Liveing 1954.
24 https://en.wikipedia.org/wiki/Shell_Guides [accessed 9 December 2017].
25 Towner 1996, 138.
26 Morris 1984, 158–9.
27 Anon 1725.
28 Letter – Add MS 71125; 1775 transcription – Add 5842, ff 122v–136.
29 Defoe 1986, 388.
30 ODNB.
31 Pococke 1887.
32 Cartwright 1888–9, I, 106; II, 114, 116.
33 Ibid, II, 116–7, 87, 92.
34 Ibid, I, 91.
35 ODNB.
36 Cartwright 1888–9, II, 132–5.
37 Lybbe Powys 1899, 50–4.
38 Anon 1725, 43, 64.
39 Barton and Brodie 2014, I, 343–5; Act of Parliament 20 Geo II, c42.
40 Hutton Beale 1891, 118.
41 Ibid, 120.
42 Ibid, 127–30.
43 Ibid, 120.
44 Ibid.
45 Ibid, 124–5.
46 Mavor 1798–1800, V, 137–72.
47 Ibid, V, 140–1, 142.
48 Feltham 1803.
49 Williams 1964, 273–4, 284–7.
50 Loveday 1890.
51 Prebble 1973, 298–301.
52 Ibid, 301–2.
53 Durie 2003, 34.
54 Pococke 1887, 105–8.
55 ODNB.
56 Ibid.
57 Withey 1998, 33–4.
58 Ibid, 35–6.
59 Ibid, 37.
60 ODNB.
61 Clyde 1995, 119.
62 Verne 1992, 81–3, 144–7.
63 Durie 2012, 127–8.
64 Towner 1996, 155.
65 Ibid, 156.
66 Withey 1998, 53. For instance Jules Verne in 1859–60, Verne 1992.
67 ODNB.
68 Cook 1861, 80–3.
69 Furlong 2009, 13–15; Barton and Brodie 2014, I, 363–6.
70 Furlong 2009, 18.
71 Ibid, 16.
72 Clarke 1793, 308.
73 Furlong 2009, 20.
74 Andrews 1990.
75 Moir 1964, 37–9.
76 Towner 1996, 146.
77 Ibid, 219.
78 Trench 1990, 138ff; Barton and Brodie 2014, I, 304.
79 Trench 1990, 157, 163.
80 Dennis 1816; Barton and Brodie 2014, I, 304, 307–10.
81 Brown 1999, 183.
82 Withey 1998, 42.
83 Andrews 1990, 26–9; Rutherford 2010, 203.
84 Hutchinson 1776, 191.
85 Withey 1998, 48.
86 Anon 1989, 122–3; Fenton 1988; Baldwin, Daniel and Greenough 2004, 33ff, 41–6.
87 Walton 2010a, 32.
88 Hutchinson 1776.
89 Walton 2010a, 32; Wilkinson 1994, 23.
90 Withey 1998, 51.
91 Ibid, 52.
92 For instance, *Bacon's Large Scale Map for Cyclists and Tourists of North Wales, c 1900*.
93 Taylor 1997, 191.
94 Barton 2005, 143.
95 Ibid, 144; Huggins and Gregson 2010, 186.
96 Middleton 2005, 5: Barton and Brodie 2014, I, 305–6.
97 Tinniswood 1998, 163.
98 Barton and Brodie 2014, I, 275–8.
99 Durie 2017, 67–8.
100 An alternative suggestion is that golf originated from an activity that took place in the Low Countries during the Middle Ages, though the modern game can trace its origins to the Scottish ancestry. https://en.wikipedia.org/wiki/History_of_golf [accessed 9 December 2017].
101 Durie 2003, 83, 125.

102 Durie 2017, 69.
103 http://www.historytoday.com/john-lowerson/scottish-croquet-english-golf-boom-1880-1914 [accessed 9 December 2017].
104 Brailsford 1999, 41–2.
105 Griffin 2007; Cunningham 1980, 142.
106 Roberts and Taylor 2013, 18.
107 Ibid, 20–1; https://en.wikipedia.org/wiki/Jockey_Club [accessed 9 December 2017].
108 Cunningham 1980, 19. (The five classic flat races are the 2,000 Guineas Stakes, 1,000 Guineas Stakes, Epsom Oaks, Epsom Derby and St Leger Stakes.)
109 Cunningham 1980, 19; Brailsford 1999, 25.
110 Hembry 1997, 35; Blake and Beacham 1982, 48; Hart 1981, 182–3, says the races began in 1819.
111 https://en.wikipedia.org/wiki/Grand_National [accessed 9 December 2017].
112 Walvin 1978, 24.
113 https://en.wikipedia.org/wiki/Hare_coursing [accessed 9 December 2017]; https://web.archive.org/web/20090407134901/http://www.defra.gov.uk/rural/hunting/inquiry/evidence/coursingclub1.htm [accessed 9 December 2017].
114 NGRC and Genders 1990, 19, 21, 33, 40, 44, 53, 72.
115 Walton 2010b, 80, 83.
116 Bruyn Andrews 1954, 417.
117 Hall 2010, 104–5.
118 Tinniswood 1998, 172–3.
119 Denyer 2010, 17; Act of Parliament 7 Edw 7 c136.
120 http://www.vulcanospeleology.org/sym14/papers/Mills-Staffa.pdf [accessed 9 December 2017]; Durie 2003, 22.
121 ODNB.
122 For instance, Leyden 1903, 250; Townshend 1840, 51.
123 Bindman and Riemann 1993, 167–8.
124 Johnson 1834, 95–6.
125 Lyell 1830–3; ODNB.
126 Hardy 1830, 294–5; http://en.wikipedia.org/wiki/Philip_Dixon_Hardy [accessed 9 December 2017].
127 http://en.wikipedia.org/wiki/Giant's_Causeway_and_Bushmills_Railway [accessed 9 December 2017].
128 Black and Black 1888, 302–20.

7 Urban tourism and the search for Britain's past, present and future

1 Pimlott 1976, 23.
2 Schopenhauer 1988, 148–61.
3 Tinniswood 1998, 16.
4 De Saussure 1902, 49–57, 74–8.
5 Ibid, 84–91.
6 Simond 1968, 135–6.
7 Porter 2015, 236–7.
8 Simpson 1896; Edelstein 1983, 11; Black 2005, 198; Sands 1987, 11; Downing 2009, 11; Coke and Borg 2011, 18.
9 Brewer 1997, 66; Downing 2009, 27; Curl 2010, 144–9, 154–7.
10 Moritz 1965, 42.
11 Cunningham 1980, 95, 165.
12 Edelstein 1983, 15; Coke and Borg 2011, 353–6.
13 Barton 2005, 41–72.
14 Mitchell 1962, 24, 26.
15 Barton and Brodie 2014, I, 291.
16 Chalklin 1974, 98–100; Sharples and Stonard 2008, 3–4.
17 Defoe 1986, 540–2.
18 Morris 1984, 160–1.
19 Chalklin 1974, 20; Enfield 1773, 28; Mitchell 1962, 24.
20 Porter 1982, 199–200; Chalklin 1974, 19–20, 49–5; Ascott et al 2006, 16; Longmore 1989, 117–19.
21 Cartwright 1888–9, I, 4; Brown and Figueiredo 2008, 9–10.
22 Borsay 1991, 109, 157; Sharples and Stonard 2008, 7.
23 Moss 2007, 125–6, 128–9.
24 Cartwright 1888–9, I, 5.
25 Layton-Jones and Lee 2008, 7.
26 Shaw 1987.
27 Anon 1725, 51–6.
28 Schopenhauer 1988, xv, 36.
29 Schopenhauer 1988, 37.
30 McLellan 1834, 112–3.
31 Ibid, 116.
32 Jennings 1987, 230.
33 Ibid, 231.
34 Mitchell 1962, 24.
35 Simond 1968, 76–7.
36 Ibid, 86–9.
37 Simond, 1968, 77–8.
38 Clarke 1793, 312, 315–7, 320–2.
39 Ibid, 319–22.
40 Ibid, 305.
41 De Saussure 1902, 57–62, 239–70, 123–7.
42 Hutton Beale 1891, 119.
43 Towner 1996, 46–7.
44 Starsmore 1975, 16.
45 Williamson 1973, 20; Braithwaite 1976, 19.
46 Starsmore 1975, 12–14.
47 Ibid, 16; Cunningham 1980, 30.
48 Williamson 1973, 77; Cunningham 1980, 25.
49 Williamson 1973, 149; Act of Parliament 34 & 35 Vict c12.
50 Starsmore 1975, 46–9; Cunningham 1980, 174; Wilkes 1989, 42, 47.
51 Cunningham 1980, 174; Wilkes 1989, 47.
52 Polley 2011, 88ff.
53 Cunningham 1980, 25–7; Lowerson 1995, 170.
54 Keate 1779, I, 112–4.
55 Cunningham 1980, 127–9.
56 Reid 2000, 773–5.
57 Hudson 1981, 43–4.
58 Ibid, 46–7.
59 Sargent 2001, 58; Act of Parliament 45 & 46 Vict c73.
60 Act of Parliament 63 & 64 Vict c34.
61 Tinniswood 1998, 180.
62 Ibid, 145.
63 August 2013, 191 ff.
64 Simond 1968, 43–4.
65 Hylton 2010, 194–5; Barton and Brodie 2014, I, 414.
66 Ousby 1990, 69.
67 Anon 1725, 12.
68 Tinniswood 1998, 20.
69 Bindman and Riemann 1993, 124.
70 Ibid, 108–11.
71 Tinniswood 1998, 63.
72 Ibid, 102, 108; Austen 1975, 180.
73 Bruyn Andrews 1954, 277, 177.
74 Ousby 1990, 76.
75 Tinniswood 1998, 63.
76 Bold 1988; Bruyn Andrews 1954, 106.
77 Tinniswood 1998, 74.
78 Ibid, 77, citing Lybbe Powys 1899, 168.
79 Ousby 1990, 79; Tinniswood 1998, 96.
80 Tinniswood 1998, 96–99.
81 Ibid, 94.
82 Ibid, 139.
83 Ibid, 141.
84 Ousby 1990, 88–9.
85 Tinniswood 1998, 152.
86 Moir 1964, 31–3.
87 Anon 1725, 78–9; Calladine 1993.
88 Defoe 1986, 458.
89 British Library Add MS 5842 f134; Quincey 1775, 59–60.
90 Cannon 1997, 47.
91 Bruyn Andrews 1954, 249.
92 Guthrie 1822, 67.
93 Johnson 1834, 201.
94 Jennings 1987, 73.
95 Bruyn Andrews 1954, 440–1.
96 North 1991, 272.
97 Clarke 1793, 196–201.
98 Simond 1968, 119–20.
99 Bruyn Andrews 1954, 425.
100 McLellan 1834, 110.
101 Angerstein 2001, 68–9, 227–8; ODNB.
102 Morgan 1992, 116ff, 187, 38–39, 190.
103 Woolrich 1973, 169.
104 Ibid, 181, 185, 187.
105 Trench 1990, 161.
106 Whyman 1980, 200, 207.
107 Macky 1714, I, 195.
108 De Saussure 1902, 299–300.
109 McConville 1981, 71.
110 Pottle 1950, 250–1.
111 Bruyn Andrews 1954, 370, 397.
112 Wallace 1797, 178.
113 Brodie et al 2002, 67–70.
114 Hull 1966, 109–17, 110.
115 Ramsay 1977, 4; Brodie 2014.
116 Howard 1777, 93.
117 Simond 1968, 159.
118 Richardson 1998, 154–5; Porter 1997, 127; Cannon 1997, 92.

119 Dennis 1816, 77.
120 Loveday 1890, 146.
121 Cartwright 1888–9, II, 92–4.
122 Whyman 1983, 178–83.
123 Cobbett 1958, 182–4.
124 Grandfield 1989, 73.
125 For instance, Lyon 1813–14; Batcheller 1828; Anon 1851; Anon 1861a.
126 Zuelow 2016, 83.
127 Bruyn Andrews 1954, 99.
128 Ibid, 100.
129 Zuelow 2016, 83.
130 Pimlott 1976, 258.
131 Clyde 1995, 102.
132 Anon 1876, 12, 860.
133 Clyde 1995, 27–9.
134 Simond, 1968, 89–90.
135 McLellan 1834, 130; Townshend 1840, 394–5.
136 Withey 1998, 55–6.
137 Ousby 1990, 28–32.
138 Ibid, 29–31.

8 The seaside holiday 1837–1939

1 Kelly 1889, 545, states 1869; Griffiths 2001, 88, offers the date of 1871.
2 Nall 1867, 150; Kelly 1887, 1750; Anon 1892, 23.
3 Horn 1999, 137.
4 Pickering 2008, 5, 24.
5 Fischer and Walton 1987, 16, 18.
6 Easdown 2009, 68.
7 Foote Wood 2008, 76.
8 Easdown 2009, 103.
9 Fischer and Walton 1987, 18.
10 Gordon 1869, 25.
11 http://www.iwhistory.org.uk/timeline [accessed 9 December 2017].
12 NHLE 1391989.
13 https://en.wikipedia.org/wiki/Southend_Cliff_Railway [accessed 9 December 2017].
14 Gale 2000, 93.
15 Pulling 1983, 3–7; Jackson 1993. A few months after Volk's Electric Railway opened, an electric-powered train service from Portrush to the Giant's Causeway, in Northern Ireland, was inaugurated.
16 Jackson 1993, 16–18.
17 Pulling 1983, 20; Jackson 1993, 45.
18 Johnson c 1986, 4.
19 The title of the oldest glass-roofed, cast-iron greenhouse in Britain appears to belong to Chiselhampton, in Oxfordshire, which dates from c 1800. Woods and Warren 1990, 88.
20 Hix 1974, 114.
21 Walton 1998, 87–90.
22 Brodie and Whitfield 2014, 65–71.
23 https://en.wikipedia.org/wiki/New_Brighton_Tower [accessed 9 December 2017].
24 Kelly 1906, 459.
25 Young 1983, 204–5; http://www.localhistories.org/bognor.html [accessed 9 December 2017].
26 Lewis 1980, 21–2.
27 Williams and Salvage nd, 3–4.
28 http://www.theatrestrust.org.uk/resources/theatres/show/2337-winter-gardens-rothesay [accessed 9 December 2017]; https://en.wikipedia.org/wiki/Rothesay,_Bute [accessed 9 December 2017]; http://canmore.org.uk/site/143522/bute-rothesay-winter-gardens [accessed 9 December 2017].
29 Avon County Council Planning Department 1991, 46; Harding and Lambert 1994, 99.
30 Brook 1987, 24; Fairley 2001, 33–34.
31 Bexhill Observer, 16 September 1933, cited in Brook 1987, 25, 30.
32 Humphreys 1857, 19; Blunt 1976, 86; Kisling 2000, 40–1, 70.
33 Anon 1871, 11–8.
34 Kelly 1883, 574; Lewis 1980, 22; Walton 1983, 170–1.
35 Anon 1890, 1043.
36 Smith 2005, 13, 176.
37 Hassan 2003, 40; Smith 2005, 13; Historic England Archive Buildings File 86314.
38 ODNB; Love 2007, 577–8.
39 Act of Parliament 38 & 39 Vict c55; 41 & 42 Vict c14.
40 Gordon and Inglis 2009, 278.
41 Ibid, 45.
42 Binns 2003, 213.
43 Walton 1998, 127–9; Smith 2005, 45, 62–7.
44 Smith 2005, 80–1.
45 Ibid, 86–9.
46 Ibid, 146–51.
47 Gordon and Inglis 2009, 180.
48 Ibid, 176.
49 Ibid, 180.
50 Pearson 1991, 66.
51 https://content.historicengland.org.uk/images-books/publications/iha-historic-amusement-parks-fairground-rides/heag057-historic-amusement-parks-iha.pdf [accessed 21 September 2018].
52 Ordnance Survey Maps; Walton 2007, 16.
53 Walton 1998, 88. The 1893 Ordnance Survey map shows the substantial facilities available at the renamed Royal Palace Gardens.
54 Bennett 1998, 23; Preedy 1992, 8; Walton 2007, 16ff; Kane 2007, 74–5; Toulmin 2011, 11, 15; Kane 2013, 31–2.
55 Cross and Walton 2005.
56 Bennett 1996, 19–21.
57 Kane 2007, 79.
58 Bennett 1996, 35–6; Walton 2007, 33–4; Toulmin 2011, 27, 53.
59 Bennett 1996, 45, 63, 65; Bennett 1998, 40; Walton 2007, 47, 50, 61, 64; Toulmin 2011, 33, 43, 127; Kane 2013, 148.
60 Bennett 1996, 77–8, 81–4; Walton 2007, 48, 70; Toulmin 2011, 55, 57; http://www.c20society.org.uk/botm/joseph-embertons-blackpool-pleasure-beach [accessed 9 December 2017].
61 Toulmin 2011, 57.
62 Crowe 2003, 7; Kane 2007, 104; Kane 2013, 59.
63 Kane 2007, 108–10; Kane 2013, 63.
64 Goate 1994, 17–19; http://en.wikipedia.org/wiki/Great_Yarmouth_Pleasure_Beach [accessed 9 December 2017].
65 Morley 1966, 137.
66 Clements 1992, 126; Bennett 1998, 23.
67 Gray 1996, 18; Bennett 1998, 21.
68 Hammond 1981, 116.
69 https://en.wikipedia.org/wiki/Magic_lantern [accessed 9 December 2017].
70 Brodie and Whitfield 2014, 83.
71 Gray 1996, 10.
72 Brodie and Whitfield 2014, 83.
73 Gray 1996, 17, 22–3; Act of Parliament 9 Edw VII c30.
74 Gray 1996, 18.
75 Braggs and Harris 2000, 86.
76 Brodie and Whitfield 2014, 101–2, 144.
77 Drower 1982, 9–10.
78 www.isle-of-man.com/manxnotebook/tourism/ccamp [accessed 9 December 2017]; http://www.theflorrie.org [accessed 9 December 2017]; https://en.wikipedia.org/wiki/Florence_Institute [accessed 9 December 2017].
79 Drower 1982, 15–16; Kniveton et al 1996, 37; www.isle-of-man.com/manxnotebook/tourism/ccamp [accessed 9 December 2017].
80 http://www.library.manchester.ac.uk/search-resources/guide-to-special-collections/atoz/wood-street-mission-archive [accessed 9 December 2017]; http://leicesterchildrensholidaycentre.co.uk [accessed 9 December 2017].
81 Wilkinson 2002, 35, plate opposite 39.
82 Barton 2005, 146–9.
83 NALGO was the National Association of Local Government Officers.
84 The Times, 17 May 1939, 9; Gration 2000, 11, 13.
85 Booker 1999, 1. In 1937 Joachim von Ribbentrop (1893–1946), German ambassador to London, stayed at Bognor Regis.
86 Booker 1999, 13.
87 Hardy and Ward 1984, 119.
88 http://www.pottersholidays.com/potter-family [accessed 9 December 2017].
89 http://www.butlins-memories.com [accessed 9 December 2017].
90 Butlin and Dacre 1993, 88–9.
91 Ibid, 29.
92 Ibid, 31.
93 Ibid, 105.
94 Read 1986, 32.

9 Spas and health resorts: traditional and new therapies 1800–1939

1   https://www.thermaebathspa.com [accessed 9 December 2017].
2   Carey 1799, 51ff.
3   Anon 1993, 5. Chalklin 2008, 43, says this took place between 1801 and 1805.
4   Chalklin 2008, 39.
5   Hargrove 1843.
6   Hembry 1990, 203.
7   Colvin 1995, 249–50.
8   http://www.harrogatepeopleandplaces. info/publications/hollins1866/013-Harrogate%20Bath%20Hospital.htm [accessed 9 December 2017].
9   Mitchell 1962, 24–5; Davis and Bonsall 1996, 75; Fawcett and Bird 1994, 71, 80–1; Cunliffe 1986, 154.
10 Hembry 1990, 283; Hembry 1997, 54.
11 Davis and Bonsall 1996, 63ff, 87ff.
12 Hembry 1997, 155–6; Davis and Bonsall 1996, 77.
13 Carey 1799, 52.
14 Thomson 1893, 49–50.
15 Chalklin 1984, 385; Cunningham 2007, 58.
16 Cunningham 2007, 58–61; Chalklin 2008, 63.
17 Chalklin 1984, 393–4; Cunningham 2007, 44–57.
18 Lee 1848, 85.
19 Chalklin 2008, 63, 67, 71–3.
20 Little 1952, 45–6.
21 Ibid, 46–9; Hembry 1990, 258; Hart 1981, 164; Blake and Beacham 1982, 34.
22 Hembry 1990, 257; Hart 1981, 139.
23 Hembry 1990, 255, 262–3.
24 Little 1981, 59.
25 Hembry 1997, 35; Blake and Beacham 1982, 48; Hart 1981, 182–3, says the races began in 1819.
26 Hembry 1990, 201; Blake and Beacham 1982, 48.
27 Hembry 1990, 260.
28 Little 1952, 51.
29 Ibid, 49.
30 Ibid, 71.
31 Chalklin 1984, 399; Blake and Beacham 1982, 78; Hart 1981, 171.
32 Little 1952, 78; Hart 1981, 172; Hembry 1997, 37, 43. Blake and Beacham 1982, 34–5, 71, says that only a third were completed by 1860.
33 Little 1952, 56, 87; Hart 1981, 190; ODNB.
34 Hembry 1997, 43–4; Havins 1976, 45.
35 Anon 1861b, 28–44, 45–61; Hembry 1997; Hart 1981, 173–4, 216–19.
36 Blake and Beacham 1982, 35; Havins 1976, 39, 41, 48.
37 Hembry 1997, 49, 53; Hart 1981, 214–15; Blake and Beacham 1982, 113.
38 Anon 1861b, 94.
39 Mahomed 1822.
40 Fisher 1997, 135ff; ODNB.
41 Mahomed 1822.
42 Mahomed 1843.
43 His work was known through his book, Colbatch 1696. Mahomed's lengthy discussion and quotation from this book suggests that he owned a copy.
44 Anon 1876, VII, 236; Wood 1912, 125; https://en.wikipedia.org/wiki/Vincenz_Priessnitz#cite_ref-Hydropathy3rded_2-0 [accessed 9 December 2017].
45 Durie 2006, 3, 9.
46 Ibid, 3.
47 Claridge, RT 1842.
48 Durie 2006, 11.
49 Anon 1876, VII, 236; Havins 1976, 59–60.
50 ODNB.
51 Durie 2006, 14.
52 Ibid, 18–21.
53 Allsop 1891, 12–29, 48–58, 81–97.
54 Curtis 1888, 31.
55 Anon 1891, 32; Anon 2002, 2.
56 Anon 1891, 32; Anon 2002, 3.
57 Blackpool Herald, 25 February 1881; Brodie and Whitfield 2014, 45–6.
58 Wood 1912, 133.
59 Durie 2006, 14.
60 Clark 1820.
61 Clark 1829.
62 ODNB; Wood 1912, 25.
63 Durie 2002, 38–9.
64 Luke 1919, 160.
65 https://en.wikipedia.org/wiki/Peebles_Hydro [accessed 9 December 2017].
66 Hembry 1997, 207–10.
67 Durie 2003, 92.
68 Fox 1889, 90.
69 Wood 1912, 121–34.
70 Rollier 1927, 1.
71 Saleeby 1928, xi.
72 Rollier 1927, 263–5, 269, 271–3; Miller 1926, 143–5.
73 Wood 1912, 1325–31; https://www.lincstothepast.com/Download/1359 [accessed 9 December 2017].
74 Luke 1908; Luke 1922; Luke 1903; Luke 1913.
75 Luke 1919, 152.
76 Durie 2006, 114.
77 Ibid, 116.
78 Luke 1919, 139–41.
79 Ibid, 50–7.
80 Durie 2006, 118, 120.
81 Hembry 1997, 229.
82 Ibid, 229; Whiting 1986, 12, 26.
83 Forsyth 2003, 42.
84 Hembry 1997, 226.
85 Ibid, 231–2.
86 Ibid, 237.

10 Tourism challenges since 1939

1   Barton 2005, 93–7.
2   https://www.wttc.org/-/media/files/reports/economic-impact-research/countries-2017/unitedkingdom2017.pdf [accessed 17 May 2018]; https://www.ons.gov.uk/peoplepopulationandcommunity/leisureandtourism/timeseries/gmaz/ott [accessed 9 December 2017].
3   Walton 1998, 137.
4   Morgan and Pritchard 1999, 72.
5   http://www.butlins-memories.com/pontins/camps/middleton.htm [accessed 9 December 2017].
6   Butlin and Dacre 1993, 130; RAF Hunmanby Moor, as it was known during the war, housed up to 6,000 military personnel.
7   Butlin and Dacre 1993, 138, 140, 148.
8   Act of Parliament 1 & 2 Geo 6, c70.
9   Brunner 1945, 9.
10 Butlin and Dacre 1993, 154; notes from a typescript history of Butlin's by the Butlin's archivist Roger Billington, 13.
11 Dawson 2011, 160.
12 Butlin and Dacre 1993, 134, 156–9, 162; Ferry 2016, 77.
13 http://www.butlins-memories.com/warners/index.htm [accessed 9 December 2017].
14 http://www.butlins-memories.com/pontins/index.htm [accessed 9 December 2017].
15 Dawson 2011, 177.
16 Hern 1967, 169.
17 Humphreys 1991, 248.
18 Murphy 2009, 128.
19 Summers 1978, 93–5.
20 Murphy 2009, 182.
21 Summers 1978, 60, 84–5.
22 Ibid, 67–9.
23 Brunner 1945; Anon 1983.
24 Brunner 1945, 39.
25 http://www.dawlishwarren.info/accommodation/railway-carriages [accessed 26 June 2016]. Site discontinued by 2017. See also http://www.dawlishwarren.info/accommodation/brunel-camping-coaches/
26 http://www.scotlandrailholiday.com; https://www.nymr.co.uk/Pages/Category/accommodation [accessed 21 September 2018].
27 Pimlott 1947.
28 Pimlott 1976, 222, 231, 235, 261–6.
29 Ibid, 256–261.
30 Ibid, 267.
31 Ibid.
32 http://webarchive.nationalarchives.gov.uk/20050301192906/http://dft.gov.uk/stellent/groups/dft_transstats/documents/page/dft_transstats_023381.pdf (table 9.1) [accessed 9 December 2017].

33 Ibid (table 9.4) [accessed 9 December 2017].
34 Lavery 1974, 100; Cosgrove and Jackson 1972, 119.
35 https://www.visitbritain.org/sites/default/files/vb-corporate/Documents-Library/documents/England-documents/england_tourism_facts_2002.pdf [accessed 9 December 2017].
36 Pimlott 1976, 231–2, 256–8; Morrison and Minnis 2012, 285, 291–2; Minnis 2014, 222–3, 240–1.
37 Morgan and Pritchard 1999, 74.
38 Middleton 2005, 116–17.
39 *Flight*, 28 August 1909, 516; Anon 1909.
40 Brodie and Whitfield 2014, 84; https://en.wikipedia.org/wiki/Blackpool_Airport [accessed 9 December 2017].
41 http://www.madeinpreston.co.uk/Aviation/StanleyAir.html [accessed 9 December 2017].
42 Braggs and Harris 2000, 40; NHLE 1353731.
43 Notes provided by Isles of Scilly Museum curator Amanda Martin, from a display panel.
44 Middleton 2005, 13, 190.
45 http://www.butlins-memories.com/skegness/index.htm [accessed 9 December 2017].
46 Middleton 2005, 34, 97–8.
47 Ibid, 39, 202–3.
48 http://webarchive.nationalarchives.gov.uk/20050301192906/http://dft.gov.uk/stellent/groups/dft_transstats/documents/page/dft_transstats_023381.pdf (table 9.13) [accessed 9 December 2017]. In 1950 there were 195,000 landings or take-offs; in 2002 there were 2,023,000 landings or take-offs. In 1950 there were 2,133,000 passengers; in 2002 there were 188,761,000 passengers.
49 Middleton 2005, 106.
50 Lavery 1974, 171.
51 Walvin 1978, 144.
52 Middleton 2005, 20, 23, 29.
53 Walton 2000, 63.
54 Middleton 2005, 23.
55 Ibid, 81; Demetriadi 1997, 50.
56 Demetriadi 1997, 59.
57 Middleton 2005, 103–4, 119–21; https://en.wikipedia.org/wiki/Freddie_

Laker#Skytrain [accessed 9 December 2017].
58 Middleton 2005, 126–7; https://en.wikipedia.org/wiki/Ryanair [accessed 9 December 2017]; https://en.wikipedia.org/wiki/EasyJet [accessed 9 December 2017].
59 Urry 2003, 47.
60 Middleton 2005, 41, 43.
61 https://www.visitbritain.org/2015-snapshot [accessed 9 December 2017].
62 http://www.imdb.com [accessed 9 December 2017].
63 English Tourism Council 2001, 4.
64 Walton 1998, 157–61.
65 Ibid, 148.
66 https://www.gov.uk/government/statistics/english-indices-of-deprivation-2015 [accessed 9 December 2017].
67 http://gov.wales/statistics-and-research/welsh-index-multiple-deprivation/?lang=en [accessed 9 December 2017].
68 http://www.gov.scot/Topics/Statistics/SIMD [accessed 9 December 2017].
69 Furlong 2009, 154, 156, 208, 221–2.
70 https://www.lonelyplanet.com/best-in-travel/regions [accessed 9 December 2017].
71 Beatty and Fothergill 2003.
72 Baker 1990, 154; Walton 1980, 128; Simmons and Biddle 1999, 51.
73 Walton 1980, 129.
74 Barton and Brodie 2014, II, 332.
75 https://en.wikipedia.org/wiki/Amex_House [accessed 9 December 2017].
76 Crockett [2004].
77 Bryson 1993, 291.
78 Summers 1978, 153–5; https://en.wikipedia.org/wiki/Gale_of_January_1976 [accessed 9 December 2017]; Steers *et al* 1979; http://en.wikipedia.org/wiki/1978_North_Sea_storm_surge [accessed 9 December 2017]; Wills and Phillips 2014.
79 https://www.metoffice.gov.uk/climate/uk/interesting/2013-decwind [accessed 9 December 2017].
80 IPCC Climate Change 2013, 3, 7, 9; Nicholls, R J *et al* 2011, 161–81.
81 UK Climate Projections: Briefing report December 2010, 5–6; http://ukclimateprojections.metoffice.gov.uk/22530 [accessed 9 December 2017].

82 Ibid, 8, 50.
83 *The Times*, 14 October 2015.
84 Middleton 2005, 37.
85 https://www.visitbritain.org/annual-survey-visits-visitor-attractions-latest-results [accessed 17 May 2018].
86 Ibid.
87 http://www.visitengland.org/Images/Visits%20to%20Visitor%20Attractions%20Survey%2007%20-%20Top%20Attractions%20-%20Top%20Free%20Attractions_tcm30-19640.pdf [accessed 9 December 2017].
88 http://www.alva.org.uk/details.cfm?p=423 [accessed 17 May 2018].
89 https://en.wikipedia.org/wiki/National_Trust_for_Places_of_Historic_Interest_or_Natural_Beauty [accessed 9 December 2017]; https://www.nationaltrust.org.uk/lists/fascinating-facts-and-figures [accessed 9 December 2017].
90 https://en.wikipedia.org/wiki/English_Heritage [accessed 9 December 2017]; http://www.english-heritage.org.uk/visit/whats-on/members-events [accessed 9 December 2017].
91 Middleton 2005, 74.
92 Ibid, 74.
93 Ibid, 11.
94 Ibid, 84–5.
95 http://www.museumofbrands.com/about-us/robert-opie.html [accessed 9 December 2017].
96 http://www.wainwright.org.uk/pennine_journey.html [accessed 9 December 2017]; https://en.wikipedia.org/wiki/The_Ramblers [accessed 9 December 2017].
97 Turnock 1998, 262.
98 https://www.edfringe.com [accessed 9 December 2017].
99 https://www.surfsnowdonia.com [accessed 9 December 2017].
100 Rubin 2011, 177, 192, 242.
101 https://www.gov.uk/government/publications/tourism-action-plan [accessed 17 May 2018].
102 http://www.underthepier.com/10_current_machines.htm [accessed 9 December 2017].
103 https://bigelowaerospace.com [accessed 9 December 2017].

Bibliography

Adamson, S H 1977 *Seaside Piers.* London: Batsford

Addison, W 1951 *English Spas.* London: Batsford

Addison, W 1980 *The Old Roads of England.* London: Batsford

Albert, W 1972 *The Turnpike Road System in England 1663–1840.* Cambridge: Cambridge University Press

Alderson, F 1973 *The Inland Resorts and Spas of Britain.* Newton Abbot: David & Charles

Allen, B 1711 *The Natural History of the Mineral-waters of Great-Britain. To which are added, some observations of the cicindela, or glow-worm.* London: Benjamin Allen

Allsop, R O 1891 *The Hydropathic Establishment and its Baths.* London: E & F N Spon

Alsop, W 1832 *A Concise History of Southport, etc.* Southport: William Alsop

Anderson, J 1795 *A Practical Essay on the Good and Bad Effects of Sea-water and Sea-bathing.* London: C Dilly, etc

Anderson, J and Swinglehurst, E 1978 *The Victorian and Edwardian Seaside.* London: Country Life Books

Andrews, M 1990 *The Search for the Picturesque.* Palo Alto, CA: Stanford University Press

Angerstein, R R 2001 *R R Angerstein's Illustrated Travel Diary, 1753–1755: Industry in England and Wales from a Swedish Perspective.* London: Science Museum

Anon 1725 *An account of a tour in several English counties in 1725, Bath, Nottingham, Oxford, Lincoln, etc.* (Manuscript held at Bath Local Studies Collection, ref TOU1/1)

Anon 1732 *The Scarborough Miscellany for the Year 1732.* London: J Wilford

Anon 1734 *A Journey from London to Scarborough, in Several Letters …* London: Caesar Ward and Richard Chandler

Anon 1750? *The Tradesman's and Traveller's Pocket Companion or the Bath and Bristol Guide.* Bath

Anon 1765 *A Description of the Isle of Thanet, and Particularly of the Town of Margate.* London: J Newbery and W Bristow

Anon 1770a *The New Brighthelmstone Directory: or, Sketches in Miniature of the British Shore.* London: T Durham

Anon 1770b *The Margate Guide. Containing a particular account of Margate, … to which is prefix'd, a short description of the Isle of Thanet … Illustrated with a map of the Isle of Thanet, etc.* London

Anon 1780 *A Description of Brighthelmston and the Adjacent Country.* London: J Bowen

Anon 1783 *The European Magazine: And London Review.* 3 May 1783

Anon 1785 *The Weymouth Guide.* Weymouth

Anon 1787 *The Gentleman's Magazine.* August 1787

Anon 1794 *The Hastings Guide …* London: I Stell

Anon 1797a *The Margate Guide, a descriptive Poem, with … notes.* Margate

Anon 1797b *The Hastings Guide …* Hastings: J Barry

Anon 1797c *A New Weymouth Guide, etc.* Dorchester

Anon 1800 *A Companion to the Watering and Bathing Places of England …* London: H D Symonds

Anon 1806 *An Historical Guide to Great Yarmouth, in Norfolk.* Yarmouth

Anon 1809 *Picture of Margate, being a Guide to all Persons Visiting Margate, Ramsgate, and Broadstairs.* London

Anon 1810 *A Guide to all the Watering and Sea Bathing Places, with a description of the Lakes; a sketch of a tour in Wales, and Itineraries …* London

Anon 1817 *An Historical Guide to Great Yarmouth.* Great Yarmouth

Anon 1822 *The Thanet Itinerary.* Margate

Anon 1825 *Prospectus Bognor New Town Company.* London: Whiting in British Library

Anon *c* 1830 *Hastings Guide.* Hastings: P M Powell

Anon 1834 *Holidays at Brighton; or, Sea-Side Amusements.* London: Darton & Harvey

Anon 1835 *A Picture of the New Town of Herne Bay, its Beauties, History, and the Curiosities in its Vicinity, including some particulars of the Roman town called Reculver.* London: John Macrone

Anon 1837 *Historical and Descriptive Account of the Town and Borough of Christchurch; comprehending a guide to the watering places of Mudford and Bournemouth, etc.* Christchurch: C Tucker & Son

Anon 1838 *The Bognor Guide, containing the history of Bognor, and the history and antiquities of several adjoining parishes, including an account of Goodwood, Arundel Castle, etc., etc., and the Roman remains at Bignor.* Petworth: John Phillips

Anon 1841 *The New Portsmouth, Southsea, Anglesey, and Hayling Island.* Portsmouth

Anon 1843 *The Guide to Hayling Island.* Hayling

Anon 1846 *A Guide Book to Weymouth and Melcombe Regis, with the adjacent villages and the Island of Portland.* Weymouth

Anon 1851 *A Day's Ramble about Dover Castle.* Dover: W Brett

Anon 1859a *Post Office Directory for Dorset.* London

Anon 1859b *The Visitors Guide to Herne Bay.* London

Anon 1861a *A Guide to Dover, Ancient and Modern.* Dover: The Chronicle

Anon 1861b *The New Cheltenham Guide: resources of Cheltenham as a place of residence, its spas and educational establishments …* Cheltenham: FC Westley; London: Simpkin, Marshall & Co

Anon 1868 *The Saturday Half-Holiday Guide to London and the Environs.* London: The Saturday Half-Holiday Committee

Anon 1871 *Life beneath the Waves, and a Description of the Brighton Aquarium. With numerous illustrations, etc.* London

Anon 1876 *The Popular Encyclopedia.* London: Blackie and Son

Anon *c* 1889 *Souvenir of Scotland, its Cities, Lakes and Mountains.* London: T Nelson & Sons

Anon 1890 *History, Topography, and Directory of North Yorkshire.* Preston: T Bulmer & Co

Anon 1891 *Bright's Illustrated Guide To Bournemouth, Christchurch, New Forest, Poole, Wimborne, Swanage, Corfe Castle, Etc.* Bournemouth: Bright & Son

Anon 1892 *A New Illustrated Guide to Bognor … With a guide to the fossil deposits and lists of plants.* Bognor

Anon 1893 'Letter from Edmund Withers to his Brother Revd William Withers Vicar of Tunstall'. *The Yorkshire Archaeological Journal* **12**, 133–5

Anon 1909 *Blackpool Aviation Week. October 18th to 23rd, 1909, etc. Official programme-souvenir.* Manchester: John Heywood

Anon 1926 *Blackpool's Progress.* Blackpool: Blackpool Borough Council

Anon 1938 'Leisure as an architectural problem'. *The Architectural Review* **LXXXIV** December 1938, 231–310

Anon 1977 *Bass, Ratcliff & Gretton Limited Excursion to Scarborough.* Burton Upon Trent

Anon 1983 'Obituary: Professor Elizabeth Brunner'. *The Journal of Industrial Economics* **32**/2 (December 1983), i–iv

Anon 1989 *Our Photographic Legacy.* Cheltenham: Shutter Press

Anon 1993 *The Chalybeate Springs at Tunbridge Wells.* London: Kings College

Anon 2002 *Hotel in the Glen: A History Of The Town Hall (1881–2002).* Bournemouth: Bournemouth Borough Council

Anon 2003 *A Guide To Historic Scarborough.* Scarborough: Scarborough Archaeological and Historical Society

Anon undated [1770s] *A Summer Trip to Margate.* British Library

Anstey, C 1994 *The New Bath Guide.* Bristol: Broadcast Books

Armstrong, J and Bagwell, P S 1983 'Coastal shipping', *in* Aldcroft, D H and Freeman, M J (eds) *Transport in the Industrial Revolution.* Manchester: Manchester University Press

Ascott, D E, Lewis F and Power, M 2006 *Liverpool 1660–1750: People, Prosperity and Power.* Liverpool: Liverpool University Press

Ashton, J 1990 *Chapbooks of the Eighteenth Century.* London: Skoob Books

Aston, M and Bond, J 2000 *The Landscape of Towns.* Stroud: Sutton

Atkins, J c 1730 *A Compendious Treatise on the Contents, Virtues, and Uses of Cold and Hot Mineral Springs in General.* London: A Dodd

August, A (ed) 2013 *The Urban Working Class in Britain, 1830–1914.* London: Pickering & Chatto

Austen, B 1981 'The impact of the mail coach on public coach services in England and Wales'. *The Journal of Transport History.* Ser 3, **2**/1, 25–37

Austen, J 1975 *Pride and Prejudice.* London: Pan Books

Austen, J 1997 *Sanditon.* London: Mandarin Paperbacks

Avon County Council Planning Department 1991 *Gazetteer of Historic Parks & Gardens in Avon.* Bristol: County of Avon Public Relations and Publicity

Awsiter, J 1768 *Thoughts on Brightelmston. Concerning sea-bathing, and drinking sea-water. With some directions for their use. In a letter to a friend.* London: J Wilkie

Bagwell, P S 1974 *The Transport Revolution from 1770.* London: Batsford

Bailey, F A 1955 *A History of Southport.* Southport: A Downie

Baines, E 1824 *History, Directory, and Gazetteer of the County Palatine of Lancaster*, 2 vols. Liverpool: William Wales

Baines, J M 1956 *Burton's St Leonards.* Hastings: Hastings Museum

Baines, J M 1986 *Historic Hastings.* St Leonards-on-Sea: Cinque Port

Baines, J M 1990 *Burton's St Leonards.* Hastings: Hastings Museum

Baker, M H C 1990 *Railways to the Coast: Britain's Seaside Lines Past and Present.* Wellingborough: Stephens

Baker, T and Gerhold, D 1995 *The Rise and Rise of Road Transport, 1700–1990.* Cambridge: Cambridge University Press

Baldwin, G, Daniel, M and Greenough, S 2004 *All the Mighty World: Photographs of Roger Fenton, 1852–1860.* New Haven and London: Yale University Press

Barbeau, A 2009 *Life & Letters at Bath in the Eighteenth Century.* Stroud: The History Press

Barber, C 2001 *The Story of Dawlish Warren.* Exeter: Obelisk Publishers

Barker, N 1993 'The Building Practice of the Board of Ordnance' *in* Bold, J and Cheney, E *English Architecture Public and Private.* London: The Hambledon Press, 199–214

Barker, T C and Savage, C I 1974 *An Economic History of Transport in Britain.* London: Hutchinson and Co

Barton, S 2005 *Working-class Organisations and Popular Tourism.* Manchester: Manchester University Press

Barton, S and Brodie, A 2014 *Travel and Tourism in Britain, 1700–1914.* London: Pickering & Chatto

Batcheller, W 1828 *New History of Dover Castle, during the Roman, Saxon, and Norman Governments.* Dover: W Batcheller

Bazeley, M L 1910 'The Forest of Dean and its relations with the Crown during the twelfth and thirteenth centuries'. *Transactions of the Bristol and Gloucestershire Archaeological Society* **33**, 153–286

Beatty, C and Fothergill, S 2003 *The Seaside Economy: The Final Report of the Seaside Towns Research Project.* Sheffield: Sheffield Hallam University, Centre for Regional Economic and Social Research

Bennett, D 1998 *Roller Coaster.* London: Aurum Press

Bennett, P 1996 *A Century of Fun.* Blackpool: Blackpool Pleasure Beach

Berry, S 2002 'Myths and reality in the representation of resorts'. *Sussex Archaeological Collections* **140**, 97–112

Berry, S 2005 *Georgian Brighton.* Chichester: Phillimore & Co Ltd

Berry, S 2009 'Thomas Read Kemp and the Shaping of Regency Brighton c 1818–1845'. *The Georgian Group Journal* **XVII**, 125–40

Berry, S 2015 'A Resort Town transformed c 1815–1840'. *The Georgian Group Journal* **XXIII**, 213–30

Bettey, J H 1989 *Suppression of the Monasteries in the West Country.* Gloucester: Sutton

Bevis, J 1760 *An Experimental Enquiry concerning the … Mineral Waters lately discovered at Bagnigge Wells, near London; with directions for drinking them, etc.* London: J Clarke

Biddle, G 1990 *The Railway Surveyors: The Story of Railway Property Management 1800–1990.* London: Ian Allen: British Rail Property Board

Biddle, G 2003 *Britain's Historic Railway Buildings: An Oxford Gazetteer of Structures and Sites.* Oxford: Oxford University Press

Biddle, M and Clayre, B 1983 *Winchester Castle and the Great Hall.* Winchester: Hampshire County Council

Bindman, D and Riemann, G 1993 *'The English Journey': Journal of a Visit to France and Britain in 1826.* New Haven and London: Yale University Press

Binns, J 2003 *The History of Scarborough.* Pickering: Blackthorn Press

Bishop, J G 1896 *The Brighton Chain Pier: In memoriam. Its history from 1823 to 1896, with a biographical notice of Sir Samuel Brown, its designer and constructor, etc.* Brighton: John George Bishop

Black, A and Black, C 1888 *Black's Guide to Belfast, the Giant's Causeway and the North of Ireland.* Edinburgh: Adam and Charles Black

Black, J 2005 *A Subject for Taste.* London: Hambledon

Blackpool Borough Council, 1897 *Blackpool: The Unrivalled Seaside Resort for Health and Leisure.* Blackpool: Blackpool Borough Council

Blake, S and Beacham, R 1982 *The Book of Cheltenham*. Buckingham: Barracuda Books

Blunt, W 1976 *The Ark in the Park: the Zoo in the Nineteenth Century*. London: Hamilton: Tyron Gallery

Bobbitt, M 2000 'William Ireland: Bicycle maker and pioneer motorist'. *Archive* **27**, September 2000, 28–35

Boddy, M and West, J 1983 *Weymouth: An Illustrated History*. Wimborne: Dovecote

Bold, J 1988 *Wilton House and English Palladianism*. London: HMSO

Booker, J A 1999 *Blackshirts On-Sea: A Pictorial History of the Mosley Summer Camps 1933–1938*. London: Brockingday

Borsay, P 1991 *The English Urban Renaissance*. Oxford: Clarendon Press

Borsay, P 2000a 'Health and Leisure Resorts 1700–1840', *in* Clark, P (ed) *The Cambridge Urban History of Britain*, 2 vols. Cambridge: Cambridge University Press, 2, 775–803

Borsay, P 2000b *The Image of Georgian Bath 1700–2000*. Oxford: Oxford University Press

Borsay, P 2011 'From port to resort: Tenby and the narratives of transition', *in* Borsay, P and Walton, J (eds) *Resorts and Ports: European Seaside Towns since 1700*. Bristol: Channel View Publications, 86–112

Borsay, P 2014 'Town or country? British spas and the urban-rural interface', *in* Walton, J K *Mineral Springs Resorts in Global Perspective*. Abingdon: Routledge, 45–59

Boulton, W B 1971 *Amusements of Old London*, 2 vols. London: Frederick Muller Ltd

Boyd, J I 1987 *Moffat 17th to 20th Century*. Moffat: Moffat Museum

Braggs, S and Harris, D 2000 *Sun, Fun and Crowds: Seaside Holidays between the Wars*. Stroud: Tempus

Brailsford, D 1999 *A Taste for Diversions: Sport in Georgian England*. Cambridge: Lutterworth Press

Braithwaite, D 1976 *Fairground Architecture*. London: Hugh Evelyn

Brannon, P 1867 *The Illustrated Historical and Picturesque Guide to Bournemouth and the Surrounding Scenery*. London

Bread, O 1859 *Bread's New Guide and Hand-Book to Worthing and its Vicinity*. Worthing: Owen Bread

Brennan, M G 2002 *English Civil War Travellers and the Origins of the Western European Grand Tour*. London: Hakluyt Society

Brewer, J 1997 *The Pleasures of the Imagination*. London: Harper Collins

Brighton Polytechnic School of Architecture and Interior Design 1987 *A Guide to the Buildings of Brighton*. Macclesfield: McMillan Martin for the South East Region of the Royal Institute of British Architects

Brodie, A 2012a 'Liverpool and the origins of the Seaside Resort'. *The Georgian Group Journal* **XX**, 63–76

Brodie, A 2012b 'Scarborough in the 1730s – spa, sea and sex'. *Journal of Tourism History* **4**/2, 125–153

Brodie, A 2014 'The Georgian prison: inquisitive and investigative tourism'. *Prison Service Journal*, November 2014, 44–49

Brodie, A 2018 *The Seafront*. Swindon: Historic England

Brodie, A and Whitfield, M 2014 *Blackpool's Seaside Heritage*. Swindon: English Heritage

Brodie, A and Winter G 2001 *The Law Court 1800–2000: Developments in Form and Function*. Report for Court Service and English Heritage

Brodie, A and Winter, G 2007 *England's Seaside Resorts*. Swindon: English Heritage

Brodie, A *et al* 2002 *English Prisons*. Swindon: English Heritage

Brodie, A *et al* 2008 *Weymouth's Seaside Heritage*. Swindon: English Heritage

Brook, J 1987 'The story of the De La Warr Pavilion', *in Erich Mendelsohn 1887–1953: A Touring Exhibition Organised by Modern British Architecture*. London: Modern British Architecture, 23–33

Brown, D 1999 'Reassessing the influence of the aristocratic improver: the example of the fifth Duke of Bedford (1765–1802)'. *Agricultural History Review* **47**/2, 182–195

Brown, S and de Figueiredo, P 2008 *Religion and Place: Liverpool's Historic Places of Worship*. Swindon: English Heritage

Brunner, E 1945 *Holiday Making and the Holiday Trades*. Oxford: Oxford University Press

Bruyn Andrews, C 1934–5 *The Torrington Diaries 1781–1794*. 4 vols, London: Eyre & Spottiswoode

Bruyn Andrews, C 1954 *The Torrington Diaries*. London: Eyre & Spottiswoode

Bryson, B 1993 *Notes from a Small Island*. London: Transworld

Bulley, J A 1956 'Teignmouth as a seaside resort'. *Reports and Transactions of the Devon Association* **LXXXVIII**, 143–62

Burr, T B 1766 *The History of Tunbridge-Wells*. London: M Hingeston

Butler, C 1984 *The Property of Sir Richard Hotham in Aldwick, Bognor, Felpham & Flansham*. [Bognor Regis]: Bognor Regis Local History Society

Butlin, B and Dacre, P 1993 *The Billy Butlin Story: 'A Showman to the End'*. London: Robson

Butt, R V J 1995 *The Directory of Railway Stations*. Sparkford nr Yeovil: PSL Ltd

Calladine, A 1993 'Lombe's Mill: an exercise in reconstruction'. *Industrial Archaeology Review* **16**/1, 82–99

Cannadine, D 1980 *Lords and Landlords: The Aristocracy and the Towns 1774–1967*. Leicester: Leicester University Press

Cannon, J (ed) 1997 *The Oxford Companion to British History*. Oxford: Oxford University Press

Carey, G S 1799 *The Balnea, or, an impartial description of all the popular watering places in England: interspersed with original sketches and incidental anecdotes, in excursions to Margate [etc.] …* London: W West

Carter, O 1989 *An Illustrated History of British Railway Hotels, 1838–1983*. St Michael's: Silver Link

Cartmell, R 1987 *The Incredible Scream Machine*. Bowling Green, OH: Amusement Park Books

Cartwright, J J (ed) 1888–9 *The Travels Through England of Dr Richard Pococke*, 2 vols. London: Camden Society

Chalklin, C W 1974 *The Provincial Towns of Georgian England*. London: Edward Arnold

Chalklin, C W 1984 'Estate development and the beginning of modern Tunbridge Wells, 1800–1840'. *Archaeologia Cantiana* **100**, 385–99

Chalklin, C W 2008 *Royal Tunbridge Wells*. Chichester: Phillimore

Chandler, J 1991 'Accommodation and travel in pre-turnpike Wiltshire'. *Wiltshire Archaeological and Natural History Magazine* **84**, 83–95

Chandler, J 1999 *Travels through Stuart Britain: The Adventures of John Taylor, the Water Poet*. Stroud: Sutton

Chaney, E 1996 'The grand tour and the evolution of the travel book', *in* Wilton, A and Bignamini, I (eds) *Grand Tour: The Lure of Italy in the Eighteenth Century*. London: Tate Gallery, 95–7

Chapman, H 1673 *Thermae Redivivae: The City of Bath described: with some observations on those sovereign waters, etc.* London

Chaucer, G, with Coghill, N (ed) 1951 *The Canterbury Tales*. Harmondsworth: Penguin

Cheyne, G 1724 *An Essay of Health and Long Life*. London: George Strahan

Clapham, J H 1967 *The Early Railway Age 1820–1850*. Cambridge: Cambridge University Press

Claridge, R T 1842 *Hydropathy; or The Cold Water Cure, as practiced by Vincent Priessnitz, at Grafenberg, Silesia, Austria*. London: James Madden and Co

Clark, J 1820 *Medical Notes on Climate, Diseases, Hospitals, and Medical Schools, in France, Italy, and Switzerland; comprising an inquiry into the effects of a residence in the South of Europe, in cases of pulmonary consumption, etc*. London: T & G Underwood

Clark, J 1829 *The Influence of Climate in the Prevention and Cure of Chronic Diseases, more particularly of the chest and digestive organs ...* London: T & G Underwood

Clarke, E D 1793 *A Tour through the South of England, Wales and part of Ireland, made during the summer of 1791*. London: R Edwards

Clarke, G E 1975 *Historic Margate*. Margate: Margate Public Libraries

Cleland, J 1816 *Annals of Glasgow*. Glasgow: James Hedderwick

Clements, R 1992 *Margate in Old Photographs*. Stroud: Sutton

Clonmore, Lord 1933 'London, Morecambe and elsewhere'. *The Architectural Review* **LXXIV** September, 93–9

Clyde, R 1995 *From Rebel to Hero: The Image of the Highlander 1745–1830*. East Linton: Tuckwell Press

Cobbett, W 1958 *Rural Rides*. London: MacDonald

Cocke, R and Cocke, S 2013 *Public Sculpture of Norfolk and Suffolk*. Liverpool: Liverpool University Press

Coke, D and Borg, A 2011 *Vauxhall Gardens: A History*. New Haven and London: Yale University Press for the Paul Mellon Centre for Studies in British Art

Colbatch, J 1696 *A Physico Medical Essay, concerning Alkaly and Acid, so far as they have relation to the cause or cure of distempers*. London: Dan Browne

Cole, J 1828 *The History and Antiquities of Filey in the County of York*. Scarborough: John Cole

Colvin, H M 1963 *The History of the King's Works*. I & II, London: HMSO

Colvin, H M 1995 *A Biographical Dictionary of British Architects, 1600–1840*. 3 edn. New Haven, London: Yale University Press for the Paul Mellon Centre for Studies in British Art

Cook, T 1861 *Cook's Scottish Tourist Official Directory: A guide to the system of tours in Scotland, under the direction of the principal railway, steamboat, & coach companies*. London: W Tweedie, W H Smith & Son

Copeland, J 1968 *Roads and their Traffic 1750–1850*. Newton Abbot: David & Charles

Cosgrove, I and Jackson, R 1972 *The Geography of Recreation and Leisure*. London: Hutchinson and Co

Cozens, Z 1793 *A Tour through the Isle of Thanet, and some other parts of East Kent, etc*. London

Crane, J 1795 *Cursory Observations on Sea-bathing; the use of sea-water internally, and the advantages of a maritime situation, as conducing to health and longevity*. Weymouth: S Margrie

Crockett, T [2004] 'The story of Brighton – is it a model for the south coast?' Unpublished conference paper at The First Annual South Coast Towns Conference, 9 July 2004

Cross, G (ed) 1990 *Worktowners at Blackpool: Mass-Observation and Popular Leisure in the 1930s*. London: Routledge

Cross, G S and Walton, J K 2005 *The Playful Crowd: Pleasure Places in the Twentieth Century*. New York: Columbia University Press

Crossley, P 1981 'Wells, the West Country, and Central European Late Gothic'. *Medieval Art and Architecture at Wells and Glastonbury, British Archaeological Association Conference Transactions 1978*. British Archaeological Association, 81–109

Crossley, P 2003 'Peter Parler and England: new thoughts on old problems'. *Wallraf-Richartz Jahrbuch* **64**, 53–82

Crowe, K 2003 *Kursaal Memories: A History of Southend's Amusement Park*. St Albans: Skelter Publishing

CSP Scotland 1907 *Calendar of State Papers, Scotland: Volume 5, 1574–81*. London: HMSO

Cunliffe, B 1969 *Roman Bath*. London: Society of Antiquaries

Cunliffe, B 1986 *The City of Bath*. Gloucester: Sutton

Cunningham, H 1980 *Leisure in the Industrial Revolution, c 1780–c 1880*. New York: St Martin Press

Cunningham, J 2007 (ed) *An Historical Atlas of Tunbridge Wells*. Royal Tunbridge Wells Civic Society

Curl, J S 2010 *Spas, Wells and Pleasure – Gardens of London*. London: Historical Publications Ltd

Curtis, B 1988 *Blackpool Tower*. Lavenham: Dalton

Curtis, C H O (ed) 1888 *Bright's Illustrated Guide To Bournemouth, Christchurch, New Forest, Poole, Wimborne, Swanage, Corfe Castle, Etc*. London

Dale, A 1967 *Fashionable Brighton 1820–1860*, 2 edn. Newcastle upon Tyne: Oriel Press

Davis, G and Bonsall, P 1996 *Bath: A New History*. Newcastle under Lyme: Keele University Press

Dawson, S T 2011 *Holiday Camps in Twentieth-century Britain*. Manchester: Manchester University Press

De Saussure, C 1902 *A Foreign View of England in the Reigns of George I and George II*. New York: E P Dutton & Co

De Seta, C 1996 'Grand tour: the lure of Italy in the eighteenth century', *in* Wilton, A and Bignamini, I (eds) *Grand Tour: The Lure of Italy in the Eighteenth Century*. London: Tate Gallery, 13–19

Deane, E 1626 *Spadacrene Anglica*. London: John Grismand

Defoe, D 1986 *A Tour through the Whole Island of Great Britain*. London: Penguin

Demetriadi, J 1997 'The golden years: English seaside resorts 1950–1974', *in* Shaw, G and Williams, A (eds) *The Rise and Fall of British Coastal Resorts: Cultural and Economic Perspectives*. London: Mansell, 49–75

Denbigh, K 2000 *Harrogate, the Yorkshire Spa*. Tadworth: Spas Research Fellowship

Dennis, A 1816 *Journal of a Tour, through great part of England and Scotland, in the year 1810*. Penzance: T Vigurs

Denyer, S 2010 'The Lake District landscape: cultural or natural', *in* Walton, J K and Wood, J *The Making of a Cultural Landscape: The English Lake District as Tourist Destination 1750–2010*. Farnham: Ashgate, 3–29

Digby, A 1994 *Making a Medical Living*. Cambridge: Cambridge University Press

Dodd, A E and Dodd, E M 1980 *Peak Land Roads and Trackways*. Ashbourne: Moorland Publishing Co Ltd

Downing, S J 2009 *The English Pleasure Garden 1660–1860*. Oxford: Shire Publications

Drower, J 1982 *Good Clean Fun: The Story of Britain's First Holiday Camp*. London: Arcadia Books

Duncan-Jones, K 1991 *Sir Philip Sidney: Courtier Poet*. London: Hamish Hamilton

Dunn, T 2014 'Top models'. *C20 Magazine*. 3, 2014, 30–5

Durie, A J 2002 'The business of hydropathy in the North of England, *c* 1850–1930'. *Northern History* **39**/1 37–58

Durie, A J 2003 *Scotland for the Holidays: A History of Tourism in Scotland, 1780–1939*. East Linton: Tuckwell Press

Durie, A J 2006 *Water is Best: The Hydros and Health Tourism in the 1840s–1940*. Edinburgh: John Donald

Durie, A J 2012 *Travels in Scotland 1788–1881*. Woodbridge: Scottish History Society

Durie, A J 2017 *Scotland and Tourism: The Long View, 1700–2015*. London and New York: Routledge

Dyos, H J and Aldcroft, D H 1969 *British Transport: An Economic Survey from the Seventeenth Century to the Twentieth*. Leicester: Leicester University Press

Easdown, M 2007 *Piers of Kent*. Stroud: Tempus

Easdown, M 2009 *Lancashire's Seaside Piers*. Barnsley: Wharncliffe Books

Edelstein, T J 1983 *Vauxhall Gardens*. New Haven, CT: Yale Center for British Art

Eglin, J 2005 *The Imaginary Autocrat Beau Nash and the Invention of Bath*. London: Profile Books

Ekberg, C 1986 *The Book of Cleethorpes*. Buckingham: Barracuda

Enfield, W 1773 *An Essay Towards the History of Leverpool …* Warrington

English Tourism Council 2001 *Sea Changes: Creating World-class Resorts in England: A Strategy for Regenerating England's Resorts*. London: English Tourism Council

Evans, J 1821 *Recreation for the Young and the Old. An excursion to Brighton, with an account of the Royal Pavilion, a visit to Tunbridge Wells, and a trip to Southend*. Chiswick

Fairley, A 2001 *Bucking the Trend: The Life and Times of the Ninth Earl De La Warr, 1900–1976*. Bexhill-on-Sea: The Pavilion Trust

Farrant, S 1980 *Georgian Brighton 1740–1820*. Brighton: Centre for Continuing Education, University of Sussex

Farthing, R 1990 *Royal Tunbridge Wells: A Pictorial History*. Chichester: Phillimore

Fawcett, T and Bird, S 1994 *Bath*. Stroud: Sutton

Feltham, J 1803 *A Guide to all the Watering and Sea Bathing Places, with a description of the Lakes; a sketch of a tour in Wales, and Itineraries …* London

Fenton, R 1988 *Roger Fenton: Photographer of the 1850s*. London: South Bank Board

Ferry, K 2016 *The Nation's Host: Butlin's and the Story of the British Seaside*. London: Viking

Fischer, R and Walton, J 1987 *British Piers*. London: Thames and Hudson

Floyer, J 1697 *An Enquiry into the Right Use and Abuses of the Hot, Cold, and Temperate Baths in England, etc*. London: R Clavell

Floyer, J 1702 *The Ancient Ψυχρολουσια Revived: Or, the History of Cold Bathing: Both Ancient and Modern* . London: S Smith and B Walford

Floyer, J and Baynard, E 1706 *Ψυχρολουσια: Or, the History of Cold Bathing: Both Ancient and Modern*. London: S Smith and B Walford

Foote Wood, C 2008 *Walking over the Waves*. Dunbeath: Whittles Publishing

Forsyth, M 2003 *Bath*. New Haven and London: Yale University Press

Fothergill, A 1785 *A New Experimental Inquiry into the Nature and Qualities of the Cheltenham Water, etc*. Bath

Fox, R F 1889 *Strathpeffer Spa, its Climate and Waters*. London: H K Lewis

Freeman, M J 1977 'The carrier system of south Hampshire, 1775–1851'. *The Journal of Transport History,* New Series **IV**/2, 61–85

Fry, W 1826–9 *Excursions*. Leicester University Library MS 149

Furlong, I 2009 *Irish Tourism 1880–1980*. Dublin: Irish Academic Press

Gabel, L C (ed) 1988 *Secret Memoirs of a Renaissance Pope: The Commentaries of Aeneas Sylvius Piccolomini Pius II*. London: The Folio Society

Gale, A 2000 *Britain's Historic Coast*. Stroud: Tempus

Gardiner, J (ed) 1987 *The Paston Letters*. Gloucester: Sutton

Gerald of Wales 1978 *The Journey Through Wales/The Description of Wales*. London: Penguin

Gerald of Wales 1982 *The History and Topography of Ireland*. Harmondsworth: Penguin

Gerhold, D 1993 *Road Transport before the Railways – Russell's London Flying Waggons*. Cambridge: Cambridge University Press

Gill, C 1993 *Plymouth: A New History*. Tiverton: Devon Books

Glazebrook, T K 1826 *A Guide to Southport, North Meols in the County of Lancaster: With an Account of the Places in the Immediate Neighbourhood*. London

Goate, E 1994 'The old Switchback and the Hotchkiss Bicycle Railway'. *Yarmouth Archaeology*, 17–19

Goldsmith, O 1762 *The Life of Richard Nash, of Bath, Esq; Extracted principally from his original papers*. London: J Newbery, etc

Gordon, I and Inglis, S 2009 *Great Lengths*. Swindon: English Heritage

Gordon, S 1869 *The Watering Places of Cleveland; being descriptions of these and other attractive localities in that Interesting District of Yorkshire. With observations on sea-bathing, etc*. Stockton

Gotch, J A 1889 *Holiday Journeys in Northamptonshire*. Northampton: Taylor

Gough, H 1983 *A Picture Book of Old Herne Bay*. Rainham: Meresborough

Gough, H 2002 *Herne Bay's Piers*. Herne Bay: Pierhead

Grainge, W 1871 *The History and Topography of Harrogate and the Forest of Knaresborough*. London: John Russell Smith

Grandfield, Y 1989 'The holiday diary of Thomas Lott; 12–22 July, 1815'. *Archaeologia Cantiana* **107**, 63–82

Granville, A B 1841 *The Spas of England and Principal Sea-bathing Places*, 2 vols. London: Henry Colburn

Gration, G 2000 *The Best Summer of our Lives: A Photographic History of the Derbyshire Miners' Holiday Camp*. Derby: Breedon

Gray, R 1996 *Cinemas in Britain: One Hundred Years of Cinema Architecture*. London: Lund Humphries

Gray, T 1996 'The travels of Mrs Parry Price through Devon in 1805'. *Transactions of the Devon Association for the Advancement of Science* **128**, 65–89

Greene, R 1889 *Northampton as a Cycling Centre, etc*. Northampton: Taylor & Son

Gregg, E 1980 *Queen Anne*. London: Routledge & Kegan Paul

Greswell, J 1807 *An Account of Runcorn and its Environs: Hatton Castle, Rock-Savage, Norton Priory, etc*. Manchester

Griffin, E 2007 *Blood Sport: Hunting in Britain since 1066*. New Haven and London: Yale University Press

Griffiths, G 2001 *History of Teignmouth*. Bradford on Avon: ELPS

Griffiths, G D and Griffiths, E G C 1965 *History of Teignmouth*. Teignmouth: Brunswick Press

Grosley, P J 1772 *A Tour to London, or New Observations on England and its Inhabitants*. London

Guthrie, C 1822 *The Tourist's Companion: or A Guide to the Steam and Canal Boats, Edinburgh and London Smacks, and other Vessels connected with Scotland.* Edinburgh

Hall, J 1790 *New Margate and Ramsgate guide … : and a general account of the Isle of Thanet.* Margate

Hall, M 2010 'American tourists in Wordsworthshire', *in* Walton, J K and Wood, J *The Making of a Cultural Landscape: The English Lake District as Tourist Destination 1750–2010.* Farnham: Ashgate, 87–109

Hammond, J H 1981 *The Camera Obscura: A Chronicle.* Bristol: Hilger

Harding, S and Lambert, D (eds) 1994 *Parks and Gardens of Avon.* Bristol: Avon Gardens Trust

Hardy, D and Ward, C 1984 *Arcadia For All: The Legacy of a Makeshift Landscape.* London: Mansell

Hardy, P D 1830 *The Northern Tourist; or, Stranger's Guide to the North and North West of Ireland With a Map and views.* Dublin

Hargrove, A F 1843 *A Brief Description of Places of Public Interest in the County of York, within Twenty-Six Miles of the City.* York

Hargrove, E 1801 *A Catalogue of Hargrove's Circulating Library at Harrowgate.* York

Harris, J, Strong, R and Orgel, S 1973 *The King's Arcadia: Inigo Jones and the Stuart Court.* London: Arts Council of Great Britain

Hart, G 1981 *A History of Cheltenham.* Gloucester: Sutton

Hart, V 2011 *Inigo Jones: Architect of Kings.* New Haven and London: Yale University Press

Harvey, J 1800 *Harvey's Improved Weymouth Guide, etc.* Dorchester

Harvey, J H 1969 *William Worcestre Itineraries.* Oxford: Clarendon Press

Hassan, J 2003 *The Seaside, Health and the Environment in England and Wales since 1800.* Aldershot: Ashgate

Hasted, E 1800 *The History and Topographical Survey of the County of Kent*, Vol 9. Canterbury, 517

Havins, P J N 1976 *The Spas of England.* London: Robert Hale and Co

Hay, A 1794 *The Chichester Guide: Containing, an Account of the Antient and Present State of the City of Chichester and its Neighbourhood, etc.* Chichester: J Seagrave

Heal, F 1990 *Hospitality in Early Modern England.* Oxford: Clarendon Press

Heape, R G 1948 *Buxton under the Dukes of Devonshire.* London: Robert Hale

Hembry, P 1990 *The English Spa 1560–1815: A Social History.* London: The Athlone Press

Hembry, P 1997 *British Spas from 1815 to the Present: A Social History.* London: The Athlone Press

Henstock, A (ed) 1980 *The Diary of Abigail Gawthern of Nottingham 1751–1810.* Nottingham: Thoroton Society

Hern, A 1967 *The Seaside Holiday: The History of the English Seaside Resort.* London: Cresset Press

Hill, M K 1989 *Bath and the Eighteenth-Century Novel.* Bath: Bath University Press

Hinderwell, T 1811 *The History and Antiquities of Scarborough, and the Vicinity.* York

Hindle, B P 1976 'The road network of medieval England and Wales'. *Journal of Historical Geography* **II**, 207–21

Hindle, P 1993 *Roads, Tracks and their Interpretation.* London: Batsford

Hindle, P 1998 *Medieval Roads and Tracks.* Princes Risborough: Shire

Hix, J 1974 *The Glass House.* London: Phaidon

Hodsdon, J 1997 *An Historical Gazetteer of Cheltenham.* Bristol and Gloucestershire Archaeological Society

Horn, P 1999 *Pleasures and Pastimes in Victorian Britain.* Stroud: Sutton

Horsfield, T W 1835 *The History, Antiquities and Topography of Sussex.* Lewes: Sussex Press

Howard, J 1777 *The State of the Prisons in England and Wales.* Warrington: William Eyres

Hudson, K 1981 *A Social History of Archaeology: The British Experience.* London: MacMillan

Huggins, M and Gregson, K 2010 'Sport, tourism and place identity in the Lake District, 1800–1950', *in* Walton, J K and Wood, J *The Making of a Cultural Landscape: The English Lake District as Tourist Destination 1750–2010.* Farnham: Ashgate, 181–197

Hull, F (ed) 1966 'A Kentish holiday, 1823'. *Archaeologia Cantiana* **81**, 109–17

Humphreys, H N 1857 *Ocean Gardens: The History of the Marine Aquarium, and the Best Methods … for its Establishment and Preservation.* London

Humphreys, R 1991 *Thanet at War 1939–45.* Stroud: Sutton

Humphris, E and Willoughby, E C 2008 *Georgian Cheltenham.* Stroud: The History Press

Hunter, M 1998 'The first seaside house?'. *The Georgian Group Journal* **VIII**, 135–42

Hussey, C 1968 'Tunbridge Wells, Kent – III'. *Country Life*, 12 December 1968, 1594–7

Hutchinson, W 1776 *An Excursion to the Lakes in Westmoreland and Cumberland: with a tour through part of the northern counties in the years 1773 and 1774.* London: J Wilkie

Hutton Beale, C (ed) 1891 *Reminiscences of a Gentlewoman of the last Century Birmingham by Catherine Hutton.* Birmingham: Cornish Brothers

Hutton, W 1789 *A Description of Blackpool in Lancashire; frequented for sea bathing.* Birmingham: Pearson and Rollason

Hylton, S 2010 *A History of Manchester.* Chichester: Phillimore

Ingamells, J 1996 'Discovering Italy: British travellers in the eighteenth century', *in* Wilton, A and Bignamini, I (eds) *Grand Tour: The Lure of Italy in the Eighteenth Century.* London: Tate Gallery, 20–30

IPCC Climate Change 2013 *The Physical Science Basis final report – policy maker summary*, http://www.ipcc.ch/pdf/assessment-report/ar5/wg1/WG1AR5_SPM_FINAL.pdf [accessed 9 December 2017]

Ison, W 1991 *The Georgian Buildings of Bath.* Bath: Kingsmead Press

Jackson, A A 1993 *Volk's Railways, Brighton: An Illustrated History.* Brighton: Plateway Press

Jackson, E 1885 *Jackson's Illustrated Guide to Cleethorpes.* Grimsby: E Jackson

Jackson, N 1991 *Nineteenth-Century Bath.* Bath: Ashgrove Press

James, T B and Robinson, A M with E Eames, 1988 *Clarendon Palace: The History and Archaeology of a Medieval Palace and Hunting Lodge near Salisbury, Wiltshire.* London: Society of Antiquaries Research Report No XLV

Jamieson, E and Lane, R 2015 'Monuments, mobility and medieval perceptions of designed landscapes: The Pleasance, Kenilworth'. *Medieval Archaeology* **59**/1, 255–71

Jenkinson, A 1998 *Caravans: The Illustrated History – 1919–1959.* Dorchester: Veloce

Jenkinson, A 2003 *Motorhomes – The Illustrated History.* Dorchester: Veloce

Jennett, S 1971 *The Pilgrims' Way.* London: Cassell

Jennings, H 1987 *Pandaemonium.* London: Pan Books

Joad, C E M (ed) 1957 *The English Counties*. London: Odhams Press

Johnson, J 1834 *The Recess or Autumnal Relaxation in the Highlands and Lowlands; a serio-comic tour to the Hebrides*. London, 1834

Johnson, P c 1986 *Trams in Blackpool*. Leicester: A B Publishing

Jones, I 1971 *Stone-Heng*. Farnborough: Gregg International Publishers

Jones, J 1572a *The bathes of Bathes ayde ...* London: William Jones

Jones, J 1572b *The Benefit of the Auncient Bathes of Buckstones*, etc. London

Jones, S 1718 *Whitby, a Poem. Occasioned by Mr Andrew Long's recovery from the jaundice, by drinking of Whitby spaw-waters*. York: Tho Hammond

Jordan, A and Jordan, E 1991 *Away for the Day: The Railway Excursion in Britain, 1830 to the Present Day*. Kettering: Silver Link

Kane, J 2007 '"A whirl of wonder!" British amusement parks and the architecture of pleasure 1900–1939'. Unpublished PhD thesis, The Bartlett, University College London

Kane, J 2013 *The Architecture of Pleasure: British Amusement Parks and the Architecture of Pleasure 1900–1939*. Farnham: Ashgate

Keate, G 1779 *Sketches from Nature; taken, and coloured, in a journey to Margate*. London: J Dodsley

Keay, A and Watkins, J 2013 *The Elizabethan Garden at Kenilworth Castle*. Swindon: English Heritage

Kellett, J R 1969 *The Impact of Railways on Victorian Cities*. London: Routledge & Kegan Paul

Kelly 1846 *Post Office London Directory, 1846* (facsimile edn. King's Lynn: Michael Winton, 1994)

Kelly 1855 *Kelly's Directory of Kent*. London

Kelly 1883 *Kelly's Directory of Cambridge, Norfolk and Suffolk: with coloured maps, 1883*. London: Kelly & Co

Kelly 1887 *Kelly's Directory of Sussex, 1887*. London: Kelly & Co

Kelly 1889, *Kelly's Directory of Devonshire, 1889*. London: Kelly & Co

Kelly 1906 *Kelly's Directory of Essex, 1906*. London: Kelly's Directories Ltd

Kidd, W 1831 *The Picturesque Pocket Companion to Margate, Ramsgate, Broadstairs & the parts adjacent*. London: William Kidd

Kilvert, F 1977 *Kilvert's Diary 1870–1879: Selections from the Diary of the Rev Francis Kilvert*. Harmondsworth: Penguin

Kime, W 2005 *The Lincolnshire Seaside*. Stroud: Sutton

King, J 1737 *An Essay on Hot and Cold Bathing*. London: John King

Kisling, V N (ed) 2000 *Zoo and Aquarium History: Ancient Animal Collections to Zoological Gardens*. Boca Raton and London: CRC Press

Kniveton, G et al 1996 *Centenary of the Borough of Douglas 1896–1996: A Celebration*. Douglas: Manx Experience

Kuin, R J P 1983 *Robert Langham: A Letter*. Leiden: Brill

Lackington, J 1974 *Memoirs of the First Forty-Five Years of James Lackington*. New York and London: Garland

Lavery, P (ed) 1974 *Recreational Geography*. Newton Abbot: David & Charles

Layton-Jones, K and Lee, R 2008 *Places of Health and Amusement: Liverpool's Historic Parks and Gardens*. Swindon: English Heritage

Lee, E 1848 *The Baths and Watering-Places of England, considered with reference to their curative efficacy, with observations on mineral waters, bathing, etc*. London

Lee, W 1795 *Ancient and Modern History of Lewes and Brighthelmston*. Lewes

Lewis, C 1980 *Great Yarmouth: History, Herrings and Holidays*. Cromer: Poppyland

Lewis, J 1736 *The History and Antiquities, Ecclesiastical and Civil, of the Isle of Tenet*. London: John Lewis and Joseph Ames

Lewis, S 1840 *A Topographical Dictionary of England ... and the Islands of Guernsey, Jersey and Man ... with maps ... and a plan of London, etc*. London

Lewkenor, J 1693 *Metellus his Dialogues the First Part, containing a relation of a journey to Tunbridge-Wells*. London: printed by Tho Warren, for N Rolls

Leyden, J 1903 *Journal of a Tour in the Highlands and Western Islands of Scotland in 1800*. Edinburgh and London: Blackwood & Sons

Linane, F 2003 *London: The Wicked City*. London: Robson

Little, B 1952 *Cheltenham*. London: Batsford

Liveing, E 1954 *Adventure in Publishing: The House of Ward Lock 1854–1954*. London: Ward Lock

Longmore, J 1989 'Liverpool Corporation as landowners and dock builders, 1709–1835', *in* Chalklin, C W and Wordie, J R (eds) *Town and Countryside: The English Landowner in the National Economy, 1660–1860*. London: Unwin Hyman

Love, C 2007 'An overview of the development of swimming in England, c 1750–1918'. *The International Journal of the History of Sport*. **24**/5, May 2007, 568–585

Loveday, J 1890 *Diary of a Tour in 1732 through parts of England, Wales Ireland and Scotland*. Edinburgh: Roxburghe Club

Lowerson, J 1995 *Sport and the English Middle Classes 1870–1914*. Manchester: Manchester University Press

Luke, T D 1903 *Anæsthesia in Dental Surgery, etc*. London: Rebman Limited

Luke, T D 1908 *A Manual of Natural Therapy*. Bristol: John Wright and Sons Ltd

Luke, T D 1913 *Text-Book of Massage and Swedish Gymnastics and Other Exercises*. London: Scientific Press

Luke, T D 1919 *Spas and Health Resorts of the British Isles*. London: A & C Black

Luke, T D 1922 *Manual of Physio-Therapeutics*. London: William Heinemann

Lybbe Powys, Mrs P 1899 *Passages from the Diaries*. London: Longmans and Co

Lyell, C 1830–3 *Principles of Geology: being an attempt to explain the former changes of the earth's surface, by reference to causes now in operation*. London: John Murray

Lyon, J 1813–14 *The History of the Town and Port of Dover, and of Dover Castle; with a short account of the Cinque Ports*. 2 vols, Dover and London

Lyons, J A 1763 *A Description of the Isle of Thanet, and particularly of the Town of Margate*. London

Macky, J 1714 *A Journey through England*, 2 vols. London: T Caldecott

Macky, J 1722 *A Journey through England*, 2 vols. London: J Hooke, J Pemberton

Macky, J 1723 *A Journey through Scotland*. London: J Hooke, J Pemberton

Macky, J 1725 *A Journey through the Austrian Netherlands*. London: J Hooke, J Pemberton

Mahomed, D 1822 *Shampooing; or, benefits resulting from the use of the Indian medicated vapour bath, as introduced into this country*. Brighton: E H Creasy

Mahomed, H 1843 *The Bath; a concise history of bathing, as practised by nations of the ancient and modern world, with remarks on the moral and sanative influence of bathing*. London

Mahomet, S D 1997 *The Travels of Dean Mahomet: An Eighteenth-Century Journey Through India*. Berkeley, CA; London: University of California Press

Maitland, P 1936 'The architect'. *The Architectural Review* **LXXX** July 1936, 18–28

Manco, J 1992 'Bath and "The Great Rebuilding"'. *Bath History* **IV**, 25–51

Manship, H 1854 *The History of Great Yarmouth*. Great Yarmouth: L A Meall

Margary, I D 1973 *Roman Roads in Britain*. London: John Baker

Markham, G 1610 *Markhams Maister-Peece, or, What doth a Horse-man lacke. Containing all possible knowledge whatsoeur … touching the curing of all maner of diseases or sorrances in horses, etc*. London: Nicholas Okes

Mavor, W F 1798–1800 *The British Tourists; or, Traveller's Pocket Companion through England, Wales, Scotland, and Ireland. Comprehending the most celebrated tours in the British Islands*. London

Mawman, J 1805 *An Excursion to the Highlands of Scotland and the English Lakes*. London: Poultrey

McConville, S 1981 *A History of English Prison Administration*. London: Routledge & Kegan Paul

McIntyre, S 1981 'Bath: The rise of a resort town, 1660–1800', *in* Clark, P (ed) *Country Towns in Pre-Industrial England*. Leicester: Leicester University Press, 197–249

McLellan, H B 1834 *Journal of a Residence in Scotland, and Tour through England, France, Germany, Switzerland and Italy*. Boston [Mass]

Middleton, V T C 2005 *British Tourism: The remarkable Story of Growth*. Oxford: Elsevier Butterworth-Heinemann

Miele, C 1998 'The first architect in the world in Brighton'. *Sussex Archaeological Collections* **136**, 149–75

Miller, J W 1926 'History of heliotherapy in tuberculosis'. *Medical Life* **XXXIII**, 143–6

Miller, W 1888 *Our English Shores*. Edinburgh: Oliphant, Anderson and Ferrier

Mills, D R (ed) 1989 *Twentieth-Century Lincolnshire*. Lincoln: History of Lincolnshire Committee for Lincolnshire History and Archaeology

Millward, R 2003 'Railways and the evolution of Welsh holiday resorts', *in* Evans, A K B and Gough, J V (eds) *The Impact of the Railway on Society in Britain*. Aldershot: Ashgate, 211–23

Minnis, J 2014, *England's Motoring Heritage from the Air*. Swindon: English Heritage

Miskell, L 2011 'A town divided? Sea-bathing, dock-building and oyster-fishing in nineteenth-century Swansea', *in* Borsay, P and Walton, J (eds) *Resorts and Ports: European Seaside Towns since 1700*. Bristol: Channel View Publications, 113–25

Mitchell, B R 1962 *Abstract of British Historical Statistics*. Cambridge: Cambridge University Press

Mitchell, B and Penrose, H 1983 *Letters from Bath 1766–1767 by the Rev John Penrose*. Stroud: Sutton

Mitchell, B 1986 'English Spas'. *Bath History* **1**, 189–204

Moir, E 1964 *The Discovery of Britain: The English Tourists 1540–1840*. London: Routledge & Kegan Paul

Moore-Colyer, R 2007 *Roads and Trackways of Wales*. Ashbourne: Landmark Publishing Ltd

Morgan, K (ed) 1992 *An American Quaker in the British Isles: The Travels Journals of Jabez Maud Fisher, 1775–1779*. Oxford: Oxford University Press

Morgan, N J and Pritchard, A 1999 *Power and Politics at the Seaside: The Development of Devon's Resorts in the Twentieth Century*. Exeter: University of Exeter Press

Moritz, C P 1965 *Journeys of a German in England in 1782*. London: Jonathan Cape

Morley, J 1984 *The Making of the Royal Pavilion Brighton: Designs and Drawings*. London: Published for Sotheby Publications by Philip Wilson

Morley, M 1966 *Margate and its Theatres, 1730–1965*. London: Museum Press

Morrice, R 2001 'Palestrina in Hastings'. *The Georgian Group Journal* **XI**, 93–116

Morris, C (ed) 1984 *The Illustrated Journeys of Celia Fiennes*. London: MacDonald and Co

Morrison, K A and Minnis, J 2012 *Carscapes*. New Haven and London: Yale University Press

Morriss, R 1993 *The Buildings of Bath*. Stroud: Sutton

Morton, H V 1927 *In Search of England*. London: Methuen & Co

Moryson, F 1617 *An Itenerary written by Fynes Moryson, Gent*. London: J Beale

Moss, W G 1824 *The History and Antiquities of the Town and Port of Hastings, illustrated by a series of engravings, etc*. London: W G Moss

Moss, W 2007 *The First Liverpool Guidebook by W Moss 1797*. Lancaster: Palatine Books

Moule, H J 1883 *Descriptive Catalogue of the Charters, Minute Books and Other Documents of the Borough of Weymouth and Melcombe Regis*. Weymouth: Sherren & Son

Mulcaster, R 1581 *Positions wherein those primitive circumstances be examined, which are necessarie for the training up of children, either for skill in their booke, or health in their bodie, etc*. London: T Vautrollier

Murphy, P 2009 *The English Coast: A History and a Prospect*. London: Continuum

Nall, J G 1867 *Great Yarmouth and Lowestoft*. London

Nathaniels, E 2012 'James and Decimus Burton's Regency New Town, 1827–37'. *The Georgian Group Journal* **XX**, 151–70

Nattes, J C 1806 *Bath: Illustrated by a Series of Views*. London: William Sheppard, William Miller

Neale, R S 1981 *Bath 1680–1850: A Social History*. London: Routledge & Kegan Paul

Neild, B 1972 *Farewell to the Assizes*. London: Garnstone Press

Neller, R M 2000 *The Growth of Mablethorpe as a Seaside Resort 1800–1939*. Mablethorpe: S B K Books

NGRC and Genders, R 1990 *The NGRC Book of Greyhound Racing*. London: Pelham Books

NHLE - The National Heritage List for England https://historicengland.org.uk/listing/the-list/ [accessed 9 December 2017]

Nicholls, R J *et al* 2011 'Sea-level rise and its possible impacts given a "beyond 4°C world" in the twenty-first century'. *Philosophical Transactions of the Royal Society of London A* **369**, January 2011, 161–81

North, C 1991 'Miss Portman's Cornish diary, 1820'. *Journal of the Royal Institution of Cornwall* New Series **II**, I, 269–76, 272

Norton, C and Park, D 1986 *Cistercian Art and Architecture in the British Isles*. Cambridge: Cambridge University Press

O'Byrne, A F 2003 'Walking, Rambling and Promenading in Eighteenth-Century London: A Literary and Cultural History'. PhD thesis, University of York

Osborne, B and Weaver, C 1996 *Acqua Britannia*. Malvern: Cora Weaver

Osborne, C 1860 *Charlotte Osborne's Stranger's Guide to Hastings and St Leonards*. Hastings

Osborne, J 1989 *Entertaining Elizabeth 1: The Progresses and Great Houses of Her Time*. London: Bishopgate Press

Ousby, I 1990 *The Englishman's England*. Cambridge: Cambridge University Press

Oxford Dictionary of National Biography (ODNB), http://www.oxforddnb.com

Palmer, M G 1943 'A diarist in Devon'. *Report and Transactions of the Devonshire Association* **LXXV**, 211–43

Palmer, M G 1944 'A diarist in Devon'. *Report and Transactions of the Devonshire Association* **LXXVI**, 215–47

Park, S nd *A Brief History of the Vine Hotel*. Typescript

Parkin, C 1776 *The History and Antiquities of Yarmouth*. Lynn

Parry, K 1983 *Resorts of the Lancashire Coast*. Newton Abbot: David & Charles

Pawson, E 1977 *Transport and Economy: The Turnpike Roads of Eighteenth Century Britain*. London: Academic Press

Pearson, L F 1991 *The People's Palaces: The Story of the Seaside Pleasure Buildings of 1870–1914*. Buckingham: Barracuda

Pearson, R E 1968 'Railways in relation to resort development in east Lincolnshire'. *East Midland Geographer* **4**/29, 281–94

Peet, H (ed) 1908 *Liverpool in the Reign of Queen Anne 1705 and 1708*. Liverpool: Henry Young & Sons

Perkin, H J 1976 'The "social tone" of Victorian seaside resorts in the north-west'. *Northern History* **XI**, 180–94

Pevsner, N and Lloyd, D 1967 *Hampshire and the Isle of Wight*. Harmondsworth: Penguin

Pevsner, N *et al* 1989 *Lincolnshire*. Harmondsworth: Penguin

Phillips, J 1970 *Phillips' Inland Navigation*. Newton Abbot: David & Charles

Pickering, M 2008 *Blackface Minstrelsy in Britain*. Aldershot: Ashgate

Pigot, J 1976 *Pigot & Co's Commercial Directory for Derbyshire 1835*. Matlock: Derbyshire County Council

Pimlott, J A R 1947 *The Englishman's Holiday*. London: Faber

Pimlott, J A R 1976 *The Englishman's Holiday*. Hassocks: The Harvester Press Limited

Pococke, R 1887 *Tours in Scotland 1747, 1750 and 1760*. Scottish Historical Society

Polley, M 2011 *The British Olympics: Britain's Olympic Heritage 1612–2012*. Swindon: English Heritage

Poole, A L 1955 *From Domesday Book to Magna Carta 1087–1216*. Oxford: Clarendon Press

Poole, R 1983 'Oldham Wakes', *in* Walton, J K and Walvin, J (eds) *Leisure in Britain 1780–1939*. Manchester: Manchester University Press, 71–98

Porter, R 1982 *English Society in the Eighteenth Century*. Harmondsworth: Penguin

Porter, R 1997 *The Greatest Benefit to Mankind: A Medical History of Humanity from Antiquity to the Present*. London: Harper Collins

Porter, S 2015 *The Tower of London: The Biography*. Stroud: Amberley Publishing

Pottle, F A (ed) 1950 *Boswell's London Journal 1762–3*. London: William Heinemann

Powicke, M 1962 *The Thirteenth Century 1216–1307*. Oxford: Clarendon Press

Poynter, F N L 1953 'A seventeenth-century medical controversy: Robert Witty versus William Simpson', *in* Underwood, E A (ed) *Science, Medicine and History*, 2 vols. London: Oxford University Press, 2, 72–81

Prebble, J 1973 *The Lion in the North*. Harmondsworth: Penguin

Preedy, R E 1992 *Roller Coasters – Their Amazing History*. Leeds: Robert E Preedy

Pritchard, T W 2009 *St Winefride, Her Holy Well and the Jesuit Mission c 660–1930*. Wrexham: Bridge Books

Pulling, J 1983 *Volk's Railway Brighton, 1883–1983 Centenary*. Brighton: Brighton Borough Council

Quincey, T 1775 *A Short Tour in the Midland Counties of England: performed in the summer of 1772, together with an account of a similar excursion undertaken September 1774*. London: Thomas Quincey

Quinn, P 1999 *The Holy Wells of Bath and Bristol Region*. Little Logaston: Logaston Press

Ramsay, M 1977 'John Howard and the discovery of the prison'. *The Howard Journal of Penology and Crime Prevention*. **16**/2, 1–16

Ransom, P J G 1984 *The Archaeology of the Transport Revolution 1750–1850*. Tadworth: World's Worth

Read, S 1986 *Hello Campers!: Celebrating 50 Years of Butlins*. New York and London: Bantam Press

Reid, D A 2000 'Playing and praying', *in* Daunton, M (ed) *The Cambridge Urban History of Britain III, 1840–1950*. Cambridge: Cambridge University Press, 745–807

Reid, T 1795 *Directions for Warm and Cold Seabathing; with observations on their application and effects in different diseases*. London: T Cadel & W Davies; Ramsgate: P Burgess

Relhan, A 1761 *A Short History of Brighthelmston, with remarks on its air, and an analysis of its waters, particularly of an uncommon mineral one, etc*. London: W Johnston

Richardson, H 1998 *English Hospitals 1660–1948*. Swindon: RCHME

Ringler, W A (ed) 1962 *The Poems of Sir Philip Sidney*. Oxford: Clarendon Press

Roberts, P and Taylor, I 2013 *Racecourse Architecture*. New York: Acanthus Press

Roberts, R 1976 *A Ragged Schooling: Growing Up in the Classic Slum*. Manchester: Manchester University Press

Robinson, D 1981 *The Book of the Lincolnshire Seaside: The Story of the Coastline from the Humber to the Wash*. Buckingham: Barracuda

Robinson, D 1998 *The Cistercian Abbeys of Britain*. London: Batsford

Robinson, F 1848 *A Descriptive History of Southport, … on the western coast of Lancashire*. London: Hall & Co

Rolf, V 2011 *Bathing Houses and Plunge Pools*. Oxford: Shire

Rollier, H A 1927 *Heliotherapy*. London: Humphrey Milford

Rosen, A 1981 'Winchester in transition, 1580–1700', *in* Peter Clark (ed) *Country Towns in Pre-Industrial England*. Leicester: Leicester University Press, 143–95

Rowntree, A 1931 *The History of Scarborough*. London: J M Dent

Rowzee, L 1632 *The Queenes Welles, that is, a treatise of the nature and vertues of Tunbridge water, etc*. London: J Dawson

Rubenhold, H 2005 *Harris's List of Covent Garden Ladies*. Stroud: Tempus

Rubin, G 2011 *Crap Days Out*. London: John Blake Publishing

Russell, R 1752 *A Dissertation on the Use of Sea-Water in the Diseases of the Glands*. London

Rutherford, S 2004 *The American Roller Coaster*. St Paul MN: Motorbooks International

Rutherford, S 2010 'Claife Station and the picturesque in the Lakes', *in* Walton, J K and Wood, J *The Making of a Cultural Landscape: The English Lake District as Tourist Destination 1750–2010*. Farnham: Ashgate, 201–18

Ryall, I 1800 *Ryall's New Weymouth Guide, containing a description of Weymouth the mineral spring at Nottington, and whatever is worthy of notice at … Portland, Abbotsbury, Bridport; the distances from Weymouth to the principal*. Weymouth

Rymer, J 1777 *A Sketch of Great Yarmouth, in the County of Norfolk; with some reflections on Cold Bathing*. London

Saleeby, C W 1928 *Sunlight and Health*, 4 edn. London: Nisbet & Co Ltd

Salter, M 2015 *Medieval Bridges*. Malveen: Folly Publications

Sands, M 1987 *The Eighteenth-Century Pleasure Gardens of Marylebone*. London: Society for Theatre Research

Sargent, A 2001 'RCHME 1908–1998: A history of the Royal Commission on the Historical Monuments of England'. *Transactions of the Ancient Monuments Society* 45, 57–80

Saunders, P (ed) 2012 *Salisbury and South Wiltshire Museum Medieval Catalogue*. Salisbury: Salisbury and South Wiltshire Museum

Schopenhauer, J, with Michaelis-Jena, R and Merson, W (transl and eds) 1988 *A Lady Travels: Journeys in England and Scotland*. London: Routledge

Scott, W 1894 *St Ronan's Well*, https://www.gutenberg.org/files/20749/20749-h/20749-h.htm [accessed 9 December 2017]

Scurrell, D 1982 *The Book of Margate*. Buckingham: Barracuda

Searle, M V 1982 *Lost Lines: An Anthology of Britain's Lost Railways*. Andover: New Cavendish Books

Sellar, W C and Yeatman, R J 1999 *1066 and All That*. London: Methuen

Sewell, R C 1846 *Gesta Stephani: Regis Anglorum, et Ducis Normannorum*. London: Sumptibus Societatis

Sharples, J and Stonard, J 2008 *Built on Commerce: Liverpool's Central Business District*. Swindon: English Heritage

Shaw, G T 1987 *Liverpool's First Directory*. Liverpool: Scouse Press

Shaw, P 1734 *An Enquiry into the Contents, Virtues and Uses of the Scarborough Spaw-Waters*. London: Peter Shaw

Shaw, P 1735 *A Dissertation on the Contents, Virtues and Uses, of Cold and Hot Mineral Springs; particularly, those of Scarborough: in a letter to Robert Robinson. Esq, recorder of that corporation*. London: Ward and Chandler

Shepherd, T H and Britton, J 1829 *Bath and Bristol with the counties of Somerset and Gloucester displayed in a series of views including the modern improvements, picturesque scenery, antiquities, etc.* London: Jones & Co

Sherry, D 1972 'Bournemouth – a study of a holiday town'. *The Local Historian* 10/3 126–34

Short, T 1734 *The Natural, Experimental, and Medicinal History of the Mineral Waters of Derbyshire, Lincolnshire, and Yorkshire, particularly those of Scarborough*. London: Thomas Short

Simmons, J 1986 *The Railway in Town and Country, 1830–1914*. Newton Abbot: David & Charles

Simmons, J and Biddle, G (eds) 1999 *The Oxford Companion to British Railway History, from 1603 to the 1990s*. Oxford: Oxford University Press

Simond, L 1968 *An American in Regency England: The Journal of a Tour in 1810–1811*. London: The History Club

Simpson, C H 1896 *The London Pleasure Gardens of the 18th Century*. London: MacMillan

Simpson, E 1997 *Going on Holiday*. Edinburgh: National Museum of Scotland

Simpson, E 2013 *Wish You Were Still Here: The Scottish Seaside Holiday*. Stroud: Amberley Publishing

Simpson, W 1669 *Hydrologia Chymica*. London

Simpson, W 1679 *History of Scarborough Spaw*. London

Smee, W R 1871 *National Holidays, and in reference to Sir J Lubbock's Bank Holiday Bill*. London

Smith, J 2005 *Liquid Assets: The Lidos and Open Air Swimming Pools of Britain*. Swindon: English Heritage

Smith, J R 1991 *The Origins and Failure of New South-End*. Chelmsford: Essex Record Office

Smith, T P 1982 'The geographical pattern of coaching services in Kent in 1836'. *Archaeological Cantiana* XCVIII, 191–213

Smollett, T 1995 *The Expedition of Humphry Clinker*. Ware: Wordsworth Classics

Somerset, A 2012 *Queen Anne*. London: HarperPress

Spencer, B 1990 *Pilgrim Souvenirs and Secular Badges – Salisbury Museum Medieval Catalogue Part 2*. Salisbury: Salisbury and South Wiltshire Museum

Spencer, B 2010 *Pilgrim Souvenirs and Secular Badges – Medieval Finds from Excavations in London: 7*. Woodbridge: The Boydell Press

Staelens, Y 1989 *Weymouth through Old Photographs*. Exeter: Dorset Books

Stafford, F and Yates, N 1985 *The Later Kentish Seaside (1870–1974)*. Gloucester: Sutton

Starsmore, I 1975 *English Fairs*. London: Thames and Hudson

Steers, J et al 1979 'The storm surge of 11 January 1978 on the east coast of England'. *The Geographical Journal* July 1979, 145/2 192–205

Steinke, W A 1974 'The influence of English decorated style of the Continent: Saint James in Toruń and Lincoln Cathedral'. *The Art Bulletin* 56/4, December 1974, 506–16

Stenton, F M 1936 'The road system of medieval England'. *The Economic History Review* 7/1 (Nov 1936), 1–21

Stewart-Brown, R 1911 'Maps and plans of Liverpool and district by the Eyes family of surveyors'. *Transactions of the Historic Society of Lancashire and Cheshire* 62, 143–74

Stockdale, F W L 1817 *A Concise Historical & Topographical Sketch of Hastings, Winchelsea, & Rye, including also several other places in the vicinity …* London: P M Powell

Stoye, J 1989 *English Travellers Abroad 1604–1667*. New Haven and London: Yale University Press

Strange, J-M and Carnevali, F 2007 *Twentieth-Century Britain: Economic, Cultural and Social Change*. Harlow: Pearson/Longman

Stroud, G 2002 *Derbyshire Extensive Urban Survey: Buxton: archaeological assessment report*. Derby: Derbyshire County Council

Summers, D 1978 *The East Coast Floods*. Newton Abbot: David & Charles

Sympson, W 1679 *The History of Scarborough-Spaw*. London

Taylor, C 1979 *Roads and Tracks of the Britain*. London: J M Dent & Sons

Taylor, H 1997 *A Claim on the Countryside: A History of the British Outdoor Movement*. Edinburgh: Keele University Press

Taylor, K S 2012 *Dry Shod to Chippenham*. Bradford on Avon: Ex Libris Press

Temple Patterson, A 1966 *A History of Southampton 1700–1914*, 2 vols. Southampton: Southampton University Press

Thomas, J 1971 *Scotland: The Lowlands and the Borders*. Newton Abbot: David & Charles

Thomas, R H G 1980 *The Liverpool and Manchester Railway*. London: Batsford

Thomson, G S (ed) 1943 *Letters of a Grandmother 1732–1735*. London: Jonathan Cape

Thomson, J R 1893 *Pelton's Illustrated Guide to Tunbridge Wells*. Tunbridge Wells: Richard Pelton; London: Simpkin, Marshall & Co

Thornes, R and Leach, J 1991 'Buxton Old Hall: the Earl of Shrewsbury's tower house re-discovered'. *Archaeological Journal* **148**, 256–68

Thornes, R and Leach, J 1994 'Buxton Hall'. *Derbyshire Archaeological Journal* **114**, 29–53

Thorold, P 2003 *The Motoring Age*. London: Profile

Tinniswood, A 1998 *The Polite Tourist*. London: National Trust

Toulmin Smith, L 1964 *The Itinerary of John Leland in or about the years 1535–1543*. Carbondale: Southern Illinois University Press

Toulmin, V 2011 *Blackpool Pleasure Beach*. Blackpool: Boco Publishing

Touzeau, J 1910 *The Rise and Progress of Liverpool from 1551–1835*. Liverpool: Liverpool Booksellers Co

Tower, E 1871–4 'Richard Fowke's journey to Freeston Shore'. *Leicestershire Archaeological and Historical Society Transactions*, **III**, 364–70

Towner, J 1996 *An Historical Geography of Recreation and Tourism in the Western World 1540–1940*. Chichester: John Wiley & Sons

Townshend, C H 1840 *A Descriptive Tour in Scotland*. Brussels: Hauman & Co

Trease, G 1967 *The Grand Tour*. London: Heinemann

Trench, R 1990 *Travellers in Britain: Three Centuries of Discovery*. London: Aurum Press

Trigg, H R 1892 *A Guide to Hayling Island*. London

Tunstall, G 1670 *Scarborough Spaw Spagyrically Anatomised*. London

Turnbull, G L 1977 'Provincial road carrying in England in the eighteenth century'. *The Journal of Transport History*. New Series **IV**/1, 17–39

Turner, W 1562 *A Booke of the Natures and Properties, as well of the Bathes in England as of other Bathes in Germany and Italy*. London

Turnock, D 1998 *An Historical Geography of Railways in Great Britain and Ireland*. Aldershot: Ashgate

Tyrer, F 1968–72 *The Great Diurnal of Nicholas Blundell of Little Crosby, Lancashire*, 3 vols. Manchester: Record Society of Lancashire & Cheshire

Urry, J 2003 *The Tourist Gaze*. London: Sage Publications

Vaughan, J 1974 *The English Guide Book c 1780–1870*. Newton Abbot: David & Charles

Verne, J 1992 *Backwards to Britain*. Edinburgh: Chambers

Vicary, T 1587 *The Englishemans Treasure: With the true Anatomie Of Mans Bodie*. London: John Perin

Vicary, T 1613 *The English Mans Treasure …* London: Thomas Creede

Victoria County History, 1935 *Rutland II*. London: St Catherine Press

Wallace, J 1797 *A General and Descriptive History of the Ancient and Present State of the Town of Liverpool …* Liverpool

Walsham, A 2011 *The Reformation of the Landscape*. Oxford: Oxford University Press

Walton, J K 1974 *The Social Development of Blackpool, 1788–1914*. PhD thesis, University of Lancaster

Walton, J K 1979 'Railways and resort development in Victorian England: the case of Silloth'. *Northern History* **XV**, 191–209

Walton, J K 1980 'Railways and resort development in north-west England, 1830–1914', in Sigsworth, E M (ed) *Ports and Resorts in the Regions*. Hull: College of Higher Education, 120–37

Walton, J K 1983 *The English Seaside Resort: A Social History, 1750–1914*. Leicester: Leicester University Press

Walton, J K 1998 *Blackpool*. Edinburgh: Edinburgh University Press; Lancaster: Carnegie Publishing

Walton, J K 2000 *The British Seaside: Holidays and Resorts in the Twentieth Century*. Manchester: Manchester University Press

Walton, J K 2007 *Riding on Rainbows*. St Albans: Skelter Publishing

Walton, J K 2010a 'Setting the scene', in Walton, J K and Wood, J *The Making of a Cultural Landscape: The English Lake District as Tourist Destination 1750–2010*. Farnham: Ashgate, 31–48

Walton, J K 2010b 'Landscape and society: the industrial revolution and beyond', in Walton, J K and Wood, J *The Making of a Cultural Landscape: The English Lake District as Tourist Destination 1750–2010*. Farnham: Ashgate, 69–86

Walvin, J 1978 *Leisure and Society, 1830–1950*. London: Longman

Warner, R 1801 *The History of Bath*. Bath: R Cruttwell

Warren, G 1978 *Vanishing Street Furniture*. Newton Abbot: David & Charles

Warren, W L 1961 *King John*. London: Eyre and Spottiswoode

Watkin, D 2000 'The architectural context of the grand tour: the british as honorary Italians', in Hornsby, C *The Impact of Italy: The Grand Tour and Beyond*. London: British School at Rome, 50–62

Watson, R and Gray, M 1978 *The Penguin Book of the Bicycle*. Harmondsworth: Penguin Books

Watts, R B 1820 *The Margate Steam Yachts' Guide*. London

Webb, D 2001 *Pilgrims and Pilgrimage in the Medieval West*. London: I B Taurus

Wells, D 2014 *Tiny Stations*. Basingstoke: AA Publishing

Whereat, J c 1855 *Whereat's New Hand-book to Weston-super-Mare and its Neighbourhood*. Weston-super-Mare

Whishaw F 1969 *Whishaw's Railways of Great Britain and Ireland (1842)*. Newton Abbot: David & Charles

White, A 1998 'The Victorian development of Whitby as a seaside resort'. *The Local Historian*, May 1998, **28**/2, 78–93

White, W 1836 *White's History Gazetteer and Directory of Norfolk*. Sheffield: William White

Whiteman, W M 1973 *The History of the Caravan*. London: Blandford Press

Whiting, R 1986 *Cheltenham, in Old Photographs*. Gloucester: Sutton

Whittaker, M 1984 *The Book of Scarborough Spaw*. Buckingham: Barracuda

Whyman, J 1980 'A three-week holiday in Ramsgate during July and August 1829'. *Archaeologia Cantiana* **96**, 1980, 185–225

Whyman, J 1981 *Aspects of Holidaymaking and Resort Development within the Isles of Thanet, with particular reference to Margate, c 1736 to c 1840*. New York: Arno Press

Whyman, J 1983 'The Kentish portion of an anonymous tour of 1809', in Detsicas, A and Yates, N (ed) *Studies in Modern Kentish History*. Maidstone: Kent Archaeological Society, 139–86

Whyman, J 1985 *Kentish sources. 8, The early Kentish Seaside: 1736–1840: Selected Documents*. Gloucester: Sutton for Kent Archives Office

Whyman, J 1993 'The significance of the hoy to Margate's early growth as a seaside resort'. *Archaeological Cantiana* **111**, 17–41

Wilkes, P 1989 *Fairground Heritage*. Burton-upon-Trent: Trent Valley Publications

Wilkinson, J 1994 *The Letters of Thomas Langton, Flax Merchant of Kirkham, 1771–1788*. Manchester: Carnegie Publishing

Wilkinson, W R 2002 *Salford by the Sea: 75 Years a City and its Children*. Salford: W R Wilkinson

Williams, B 1964 *The Whig Supremacy 1714–1760*. London: Oxford University Press

Williams, D 1788 *Royal Recollections on a Tour to Cheltenham, Gloucester, Worcester and Places Adjacent, in the year 1788*. London

Williams, J and Salvage, A nd *A History of Margate's Winter Gardens*. Fifth

Williamson, R W 1973 *Popular Recreations in English Society 1700–1850*. Cambridge: Cambridge University Press

Wills, A and Phillips, T 2014 *British Seaside Piers*. Swindon: English Heritage

Willsher, P 2002 *Fred Pontin: The Man and his Business: The Authorised Biography of Sir Fred Pontin*. Cardiff: St David's Press

Withey, L 1998 *Grand Tours and Cook's Tours: A History of Leisure Travel, 1750–1915*. London: Aurum Press

Wittie, R 1660 *Scarborough Spaw*. London

Wittie, R 1667 *Scarborough Spaw*. York

Wood, J 1742 *An Essay towards a Description of the City of Bath*. Bath

Wood, J 1969 *A Description of Bath 1765*. Bath: Kingsmead Reprints

Wood, N 1912 *Health Resorts of the British Isles*. London: Hodder and Stoughton

Woods, M and Warren, A S 1990 *Glass Houses: A History of Greenhouses, Orangeries and Conservatories*. London: Aurum Press

Woolgar, C M 1999 *The Great Household in Late Medieval England*. New Haven, CT: Yale University Press

Woolrich, A P 1973 'An American in Gloucestershire and Bristol: the diary of Joshua Gilpin 1796–7'. *Transactions of the Bristol and Gloucestershire Archaeological Society* **XCII**, 183–9

Worsley, G 2007 *Inigo Jones and the European Classicist Tradition*. New Haven and London: Yale University Press

Wright, G N 1988 *Roads and Trackways of Wessex*. Ashbourne: Moorland Publishing Ltd

Wright, G N 2008 *Turnpike Roads*. Oxford: Shire

Wroughton, J 2004 *Stuart Bath: Life in the Forgotten City, 1603–1714*. Bath: The Lansdown Press

Wroughton, J 2006 *Tudor Bath: Life and Strife in the Little City, 1485–1603*. Bath: The Lansdown Press

Wyatt, M 1996 *White Knuckle Ride*. London: Salamander

Young, G 1983 *A History of Bognor Regis*. Chichester: Phillimore

Zuelow, E G E 2016 *A History of Modern Tourism*. London: Palgrave

Index